de Gruyter Studies in Organization 64
Asian Business Networks

de Gruyter Studies in Organization

International Management, Organization and Policy Analysis

An international and interdisciplinary book series from de Gruyter presenting comprehensive research on aspects of international management, organization studies and comparative public-policy.
It covers cross-cultural and cross-national studies of topics such as:
- management; organizations; public policy, and/or their inter-relation
- industry and regulatory policies
- business-government relations
- international organizations
- comparative institutional frameworks.

While each book in the series ideally has a comparative empirical focus, specific national studies of a general theoretical, substantive or regional interest which relate to the development of cross-cultural and comparative theory are also encouraged.

The series is designed to stimulate and encourage the exchange of ideas across linguistic, national and cultural tradition of analysis, between academic researchers, practitioners and policy makers, and between disciplinary specialisms.
The volumes present theoretical work, empirical studies, translations and 'state-of-the art' surveys. The *international* aspects of the series are uppermost: there is a strong commitment to work which crosses and opens boundaries.

Editor:

Prof. Stewart R. Clegg, Faculty of Business and Technology, University of Western Sydney, Macarthur, Campbelltown, Australia

Advisory Board:

Prof. Nancy J. Adler, McGill University, Dept. of Management, Montreal, Quebec, Canada
Prof. Richard Hall, State University of New York at Albany, Dept. of Sociology, Albany, New York, USA
Prof. Gary Hamilton, University of Washington, Seattle, Washington, USA
Prof. Geert Hofstede, University of Limburg, Maastricht, The Netherlands
Prof. Pradip N. Khandwalla, Indian Institute of Management, Vastrapur, Ahmedabad, India
Prof. Surenda Munshi, Sociology Group, Indian Institute of Management, Calcutta, India
Prof. Gordon Redding, University of Hong Kong, Dept. of Management Studies, Hong Kong

Asian Business Networks

Editor
Gary G. Hamilton

Walter de Gruyter · Berlin · New York 1996

Gary G. Hamilton, Professor of Sociology, Department of Sociology,
University of Washington, Seattle, Washington, USA

With 33 tables and 14 figures

♾ Printed on acid-free paper which falls within the guidelines of the
ANSI to ensure permanence and durability.

Library of Congress Cataloging-in-Publication Data

Asian business networks / edited by Gary G. Hamilton.
      p.   cm. − (De Gruyter studies in organization ; 64)
    Includes bibliographical references and index.
    ISBN 3-11-013159-5 (alk. paper)
    1. Strategic alliances (Business) − Asia. Southeastern.
2. Business enterprises − Asia. Southeastern − Communication systems.   3. Social networks − Asia. Southeastern.
4. Communication in management − Social aspects − Asia.
Southeastern.   5. Interorganizational relations − Asia.
Southeastern. I. Hamilton, Gary G. II. Series.
HD69.S8A85 1995
658′044′0959−dc20   95-44302
                                                     CIP

Die Deutsche Bibliothek − Cataloging-in-Publication Data

Asian business networks : [with 33 tables] / ed. by Gary G.
Hamilton. − Berlin ; New York : de Gruyter, 1996
  (De Gruyter studies in organization ; 64 : International man-
agement, organization and policy analysis)
  ISBN 3-11-013159-5
NE: Hamilton, Gary G. [Hrsg.]; GT

Typesetting: Converted by Knipp Medien und Kommunikation oHG, Dortmund. −
Printing: Gerike GmbH, Berlin. − Binding: D. Mikolai, Berlin. − Cover Design:
Johannes Rother, Berlin.

Preface

A decade ago, in 1984, when I taught for a year in the Graduate Institute of Sociology at Tunghai University in Taiwan, Asian business networks was a topic ignored by nearly everyone. A few scholars of Japanese society were beginning to examine the Japanese mode of production and were discovering the vast intermarket networks and vertical *keiretsu* that structure the Japanese economy. At that time, little was known about the *chaebol*, the business groups in South Korea, and even less about the business networks in the Chinese-dominated economies of Taiwan, Hong Kong, and Southeast Asia. It was in 1984 that Kao Cheng-shu, a Professor of Sociology at Tunghai University and a contributor to this book, and I began to study the organization of the Taiwan economy, and in the course of that study, we discovered for ourselves the ubiquitousness and significance of business networks in Taiwan.

In the past decade, at the same time that Professor Kao and I began to investigate the business networks in Taiwan, many others were also discovering the importance of business networks in other Asian countries as well. Most of the initial attention was directed at uncovering the structure of business networks in Japan and, somewhat less so, the business networks in South Korea. Even less attention was devoted to understanding the business networks in Chinese-dominated economies, and even today, these networks are still relatively unstudied, although this situation seems to be changing with the increasing interest in business connections among the Chinese in Southeast Asia.

In light of the increasing interest in Asian economic organization, I am very pleased that the Studies in Organization Series sponsored by Walter de Gruyter has supported the publication of this book. With the exception of the conclusion, all the chapters in this book were originally published in a limited edition in 1991 by the Centre of Asian Studies, at the University of Hong Kong, under the title of "Business Networks and Economic Development in East and Southeast Asia." As explained in the following introduction, these chapters report on original research undertaken between 1986 and 1989, and were presented at a workshop held at the University of Hong Kong in the Fall of 1989. To date, the studies in this volume represent one of the only comparative analyses of Asian business networks available and one of the very few to feature an analysis of business networks in the Chinese economies of East and Southeast Asia. It is, therefore, a privilege to make these studies more widely available outside of Asia.

In preparing this volume for publication, I have added brief introductions for each major section and a concluding chapter that discusses the theoretical significance of Asian business groups in light of recent publications. I have also shortened the book by dropping two of the four original chapters on Taiwan, and I made minor typological corrections in the texts of the remaining chapters.

For the de Gruyter edition, I want to acknowledge the encouragement of Stewart Clegg, the series editor, and the considerable patience of de Gruyter's editor, Dr. Bianka Ralle. I particularly want to thank Professor Edward Chen, Director of the Centre of Asian Studies at the University of Hong Kong, for approving this reissue and to thank Coonoor Kripalani-Thadani, Assistant to the Director, Centre of Asian Studies, for her work on the first edition and for her encouragement of the second.

Acknowledgments

Many people need to be thanked for their assistance in making this book possible. The individual chapters in this book were first presented in a conference held at the University of Hong Kong. The conference was initially arranged by the East Asian Business and Development (EABAD) Research Program and the Institute of Governmental Affairs at the University of California, Davis. Special thanks go to Jean Stratford and Florence Nelson in IGA for their work in processing grant applications and in their ongoing efforts to keep things going smoothly in the early stages of planning, to Sasha Bessom for her work in preparing the manuscript for its initial publication, and to Chung Wai-keung for assisting in preparing the manuscript for the de Gruyter edition.

Personnel at the Centre of Asian Studies at the University of Hong Kong handled all the local arrangements. Our sincere appreciation go to them for their highly professional work, which allowed the conference to go smoothly throughout the entire proceedings. In particular, we want to thank Coonoor Kripalani-Thadani for coordinating the local arrangements; Carol Chan for her assistance in providing support services during the conference as well as after the conference, when the book was being prepared for publication; and Cathy Wong for preparing the manuscript for publication.

The conference was funded by a conference grant from the National Science Foundation. Some additional funding came from a Pacific Rim Grant awarded to the EABAD research projects from the President's Office of the University of California. Gary Hamilton also wishes to acknowledge that the funding used in the preparation of this book came from a grant from the National Science Foundation (SES-8606582) and from the Guggenheim Foundation.

A special word of acknowledgment goes to all those who attended the conference and who participated in sharpening the research focus, thus improving everyone's contribution. In particular, we wish to thank Tu I-ching, Lin Pao-an, Nicole Biggart, and Patricia Woelk; they all made excellent presentations at the conference, but are otherwise not represented in this volume.

Contents

The Industrial Organization and Growth of the Korean Chaebol: Integrating
Eun Mee Kim

Industrial Policy and Organizational Efficiency: The Korean *Chaebol*
William Zeile

Part Three

Gary G. Hamilton

Introduction: Business Groups and Economic Development

Edward Chen and Gary G. Hamilton

In the past forty years the economies of East and Southeast Asia have been transformed. The economic growth in the region began with Japan's recovery after World War Two. In the 1950s and part of the 1960s, the Japanese economy grew at an annual rate of over 10 percent. Then, beginning in the 1960s, the economies of Hong Kong, Singapore, Taiwan, and South Korea took off, growing at even faster rates than the Japanese economy had grown in the previous decade. Over the last thirty years, these four economies increased at an annual rate of about 10 percent, making them among the fastest growing economies in the world during the century. In the middle 1970s and then accelerating in the 1980s, Thailand and Malaysia in Southeast Asian and the People's Republic of China, particularly in South China, began to show signs of hyper-growth. Between 1977, when the PRC began its economic reforms, and 1989, when the economy entered a recessionary period, the mainland economy expanded at around 10 percent per annum, and in the same period the Thai and Malaysian economies grew even faster. In the 1990s it appears that Indonesia, Vietnam, and perhaps the Philippines may enter a period of rapid development. Clearly, East and Southeast Asian economic growth has been rapid, sustained, and extensive, so much so that even during recessionary intervals in the global economy, all of these Asian economies have fared far better than their counterparts in Europe and the Americas.

The economic miracle of the East and Southeast Asian economies has naturally aroused tremendous interest in explanations for their success. It does not take long to realize that the fast growing economies share one commonality – export-oriented industrialization based on labor-intensive manufactured products at first, and more sophisticated products at a later stage. In the 1950s and 1960s, export-oriented industrialization was a path-breaking development strategy when import-substitution industrialization was very much in vogue. Export-oriented industrialization was first undertaken by the East Asian economies of Hong Kong, Taiwan, Singapore, and South Korea and later by Southeast Asian economies. Discovering that export-oriented industrialization explains rapid economic growth is not quite sufficient for us to understand why some countries have been doing better than others. What is also important is to understand the contributing factors that make export-oriented industrialization workable and successful. In this regard, most analysts resort to the policy and institutional variables at the macro level. Specifically, most writers stress government policy or laissez faire market forces, cultural factors such as Confucianism, and political institutions such as developmental autocratic states, and they debate about which of these factors is the most important cause for Asian capitalism: government, economy, or culture. What most analysts do not discuss is how economic activities are organized and conducted at the micro level.

In contrast to the conventional approach of explaining Asian economic growth, the chapters in this book address one of the most important, but least understood aspects of Asia's economic transformation: the development and spread of Asian business networks, and how Asians actually organize their own economic activities. The ideas for the research upon which this book is based, in fact, grew out of our collective observation that, despite a lot of writing on Asian economies, very few people had actually studied how Asians create and expand their businesses. Such studies should be complementary to those at the macro level and would contribute to a better understanding of Asian economic growth under export-oriented industrialization.

This book represents the product of a collective research project on the organization of Asian capitalist economies. It also represents one of the first serious attempts to examine Asian business networks from a comparative Asian perspective. The idea for the research project began in 1985, when a number of us realized that the East and Southeast Asian economies, despite many differences among them, had some distinctive organizational features. Moreover, we also realized that very little research had been done on the organization of any of these economies except for Japan, and even that research at the time was not well known among Western writers. Based upon this recognition, we decided we would begin an international multidisciplinary research project examining the organizational and institutional foundations of Asian capitalism.

Our initial planning meeting for the project was held in 1986 at the University of California at Davis. At that meeting, we laid the groundwork for forming research teams at the University of Hong Kong, National University of Singapore, Tunghai University in Taiwan, and the University of California, Davis. Then, in the following year, several more colleagues from Japan and the United States joined the research project.

The object of our collective research was defined broadly as the organizational features of Asian capitalism, but in practical terms researchers began to focus on relationships among firms. There are two reasons that the focus narrowed to inter-firm relationships. First, we quickly recognized that the most important organizational feature of Asian capitalist economies is that they are organized through networks of firms. Whereas companies in many Western economies are more or less autonomous from and competitive with other companies, firms in East and Southeast Asia are interlinked, are connected to one another and so create vast, cooperative networks of independent firms. Our investigations showed that the largest networks in each society dominated the economic landscape. The top six business groups in Japan, the top ten in South Korea, the top five in Hong Kong – all control a very large portion of key sectors in these economies. Although firms in Western societies may have a monopolistic hold on some product lines, the network structure of Asian economies and the relative economic power of these networks make the patterns in Asian economies quite different from the patterns of competitive inter-firm relations that exist in Western economies.

Second, we also recognized that these networks of firms differ dramatically among the different societies in East and Southeast Asia. Specifically, we found that Chinese inter-firm networks are similar in Taiwan, Hong Kong, and Singapore, but that these differ from Japanese and South Korean networks, which in turn differ from each other. Recognizing the differences in business networks among these countries, we decided to try to capture the institutional features and organizational dynamics of the business networks in each location.

Starting the research process with this common frame of reference, the researchers represented here have produced one of the first books to analyze the network structure of Asian economies in theoretical, empirical, and comparative terms. The chapters grew out of papers that were first presented in a conference held between June 20-22, 1989. The Centre of Asian Studies at the University of Hong Kong hosted the conference, and the conference was sponsored by the East Asian Business and Development Research Program at the University of California with a grant from the National Science Foundation in the United States. Each paper was discussed at length in the conference and suggestions for revisions were made. The authors then, in full knowledge of the other papers, rewrote their own papers so as to emphasize the significant and distinctive features of their own cases. Therefore, although only a few of the papers draw out the differences among societies in a systematic way, all of the papers are implicitly comparative because the author themselves, through their participation in the collective research process, became sensitized to the distinctive features of their own cases.

The papers have been arranged so that it is easy for readers to make their own comparisons among countries. Part One concentrates on Chinese business networks generally and specifically in the three Chinese dominated economies: Taiwan, Hong Kong, and Singapore. Part Two groups papers analyzing business networks in the Japanese and South Korean economies. A conclusion that has been added to this edition of the book compares business networks more fully within and among these economies.

The first set of papers on Chinese business provide general frameworks by which the similarities among Chinese business networks, regardless of their location, may be analyzed. In his paper, Wong Siu-lun looks at the dynamics of Chinese entrepreneurship and argues that the underlying foundation for this entrepreneurship is personal trust. Wong then proceeds to describe the nature of personal trust and how trust in people differs from what he calls system trust, such as trust in law. Gordon Redding addresses the same thesis, showing its consequences for the development of business organizations. He suggests that the reliance up-on personal trust narrows the organizational possibilities that Chinese can use to create firms; accordingly, Chinese firms tend to be weak – in that they come and go and tend to be quite small relative to firms in other societies – but they also are embedded in strong inter-firm networks. Gary Hamilton develops the same thesis through making historical comparisons between Western and Chinese societies. He argues that the network characteristics of the Chinese economy are rooted in such local institutions as kinship and regionality, whereas firm autonomy in the West rests upon strong states and legal institutions. Collectively, these three pa-pers provide a general theoretical context for the case studies of business networks in the different Chinese societies.

The case studies in the three Chinese economies of Taiwan, Hong Kong, and Singapore follow in next section. The first two papers deal with business rela-tions in Taiwan. Drawing on his research team's interviews with many prominent businessmen in Taiwan, Kao Cheng-shu explains that personal trust is the cor-nerstone of capitalism in Taiwan. He outlines the characteristics of personal trust and shows how it is institutionalized in Taiwan. Ichiro Numazaki elaborates the same theme in his case studies of several business conglomerates in Taiwan; he shows in a concrete way how interpersonal linkages lay the groundwork for in-terfirm linkages and how the resulting interfirm relations change over time. In the next paper, on network dynamics in the organization of the Hong Kong economy, Gilbert Wong documents the shifting business alliances at the top of the Hong Kong economy. He shows that Chinese-owned conglomerates have been replac-ing the British-owned groups that only two decades ago controlled the Hong Kong economy.

The last three papers in this section deal with aspects of Chinese business in Southeast Asia. In the first of these, Tong Chee Kiong describes several very large family-owned business networks that are centered in Singapore but that stretch throughout East and Southeast Asia. Tong shows even with such extensive hold-ings, family-owned networks retain many of the features of small family firms, namely centralized control (or what he calls "centripetal" authority), highly per-sonalized management, and network diversification. In contrast to networks of large business networks in Hong Kong and Singapore, the next paper documents the operation of a geographically extensive network of small and medium sized Chinese firms in Southeast Asia. This is Eddie C.Y. Kuo's case study of an inci-dent in which the Malaysian government tried to restrict an area of commerce – the trade in mandarin oranges – that was controlled by Chinese traders in Singa-pore. Kuo's paper provides a vivid illustration of the extension, flexibility, and strength of personal networks among Chinese. In the last paper in this section, Tan Hock explains a peculiarity of the Singapore economy. Unlike Chinese busi-nesses in Taiwan and Hong Kong, Chinese entrepreneurs in Singapore tend to be located in only a few sectors of the economy, and are particularly absent from Singapore's manufacturing sector. Tan's detailed analysis shows the significance of government policy in channelizing Chinese entrepreneurship.

Part Two of the book consists of three papers on Japanese business networks and two papers on South Korean business networks. Drawing on his many previous studies on Japanese business groups, Okumura Hiroshi summarizes the most important organizational features of the Japanese economy. Okumura shows that in Japan, as in the Chinese areas, relationships are very important, but unlike in Chinese societies, these relationships tend to be intercorporate and are not based upon family and regional ties. He also shows that these relationships are not economically defined, but rather that they are stable, long term linkages that precede any economic negotiation. Ueda Yoshiaki looks more closely at these intercorporate relationships, particularly at the patterns of interlocking directorates found in Japan. His analysis not only shows the centrality of business groups in Japan, but also suggests the complexity of the linkages among firms. In his paper, Marco Orrù presents an original framework within which to analyze the macro-structure of the Japanese economy. Based on his empirical analysis of Japanese group networks, he shows that business groups represent clusters of firms linked to each other in varying degrees of strength, as if in a gravitational field. Expanding this gravitational metaphor, he examines a variety of cluster configurations that exist in Japan.

The two papers on business networks in South Korea present equally detailed empirical examinations of economic organization in that country. Eun Mee Kim provides a theoretical framework to analyze Korean business groups, called *chaebol*, that combine organizational and political economy perspectives. Framing her topic theoretically, she then gives a detailed historical analysis of the growth of the *chaebol* to a position of dominance within the Korean economy. Drawing on an extensive database on the Korean *chaebol*, William Zeile subjects the same themes to an economic analysis of productivity. He documents the *chaebol*'s proportional role in the South Korean economy and shows the relationship between the *chaebol*'s rate of growth, their economic efficiency, and their ability to obtain government loans.

In the concluding chapter, Gary Hamilton outlines the theoretical and economic importance of Asian business networks. He argues that business networks provide an "institutional medium" by which Asian economies are socially organized. This institutional medium – the orientation toward relationships – is historically and socially constructed and varies significantly among Asian societies. Understanding this orientation is therefore important for understanding not only how to operate in these societies, but also how to interpret them and how to explain differences in their economic performance.

Taken together, the chapters in this book give a rich analysis of the complexity of East and Southeast Asian business networks. They all document the role of business networks in Asian economies, but after reading these chapters, one can only conclude that the differences among Chinese, Japanese and South Korean

business networks are as important to economic performance as are their similarities. The Chinese business networks are largely personal networks and are organized primarily through kinship circles and ties of common origins. Japanese
business networks are predominantly intercorporate ties that cement together a
vast community of firms. The South Korean business networks are dominated by
elite business families that have been privileged by a strong state.

Although resting on different institutional foundations, the business networks
in all these societies have structured the rapid economic development that has occurred throughout the region. As a group, we believe that it would be inaccurate
to argue that the reason these economies have industrialized is due strictly to these
business networks. Many societies have industrialized, but they have done so in
very different organizational and institutional environments. We do believe, however, that it would be accurate to argue that business networks in Asia provide the
medium for economic development. The East and Southeast Asian economies are
organized by means of these networks, and how these economies actually develop depends largely on the organizational dynamics and potential of these inter-
firm networks. What Gordon Redding argues in Chapter Three for Chinese businesses appears to be true for the entire region: In every country of the region the
business networks are more significant – that is, stronger – than the individual
firms that make up the networks. Networks are the main units of analysis for all of
the economies. Therefore, if one would understand Asian economic development,
one must first understand Asian business networks.

Part One

Chinese Business Networks: A Comparative View

Introduction

Wherever Chinese live and work – in Southeast Asia, in Canada, in Hong Kong, in the People's Republic of China – the social networks that they create are similar in structure and in mode of operation. One of the primary questions of the chapters in this section concern whether these similarities are superficial and, therefore, have very little impact on the way Chinese businesses are organized in different locations, or whether these similarities are consequential and have significant impacts on Chinese businesses wherever they occur. Such "either/or" questions are difficult to answer because reality does not conform to the neat categories imagined by social scientists. Nonetheless, as the authors of these chapters did their research in widely diverse settings, it became apparent to them, through discussing this research with each other, that Chinese social organization shapes the way Chinese do business in all settings. The economic consequences of this social organization are so pronounced that, analytically, the major organizational divide of this book had to be the contrast between Chinese and non-Chinese systems of economic organization.

This contrast is significant on many levels. In terms of industrial structure, Chinese-dominated economies are segmented, whereas Japanese and South Korean economies are internally more integrated. In this connection, the role of big business conglomerates illuminates the contrast. As the chapters in Part Two show, in Japan and South Korean economies, large business groups form vertically integrated networks of firms that produce final products for export and local consumption. These large conglomerates provide the integrating structure for both economies and dominate the technologically most advanced sectors. In Chinese economies, by contrast, large business groups typically do not produce final products and are not the leaders in manufacturing technology. In Taiwan and Hong Kong, the small and medium-sized firms control the final goods and export sectors; in Singapore large multi-national firms, often from the United States and Japan, play this role. In all these locations, the largest Chinese-owned business networks are upstream suppliers of intermediate products, such as plastics or cloth, that other unconnected firms use to produce final goods, or they provide services, such as shipping or banking, or they own and manage property. Accord-

Introduction

ingly, these large networks do not coordinate the economy in the same way that the large business groups do in Japan and South Korea.

The configuration of the networks differ, too. In the Japanese case, shared corporate ownership of member firms in a network is the rule. In South Korea, prominent families own the controlling shares of network firms. Despite differences in ownership, however, in both the Japanese and Korean cases, the business networks are large, vertically integrated, and highly capitalized, and they require considerable "work-process" coordination. Managerial controls, therefore, are very important. Chinese networks, however, are not as vertically integrated, and the owners do not concentrate as much on integrated management, as do the other two cases. Like South Korea, large and small Chinese business networks are family owned, but in contrast to the Korean networks, Chinese family holdings, when they become substantial, tend to be segmented into unrelated businesses, each of which has separate management. The Chinese family owners want to control assets, more than the work process, and thus the larger the group becomes, the more the family focuses on portfolio management. Chapters by Numazaki and Tong show this pattern very well.

Finally, the political economy in these countries also differ, although often in subtle ways. The network integrated economies of Japan and South Korea require considerable support by the state. State policies and state officials play important roles in managing labor and capital, and in facilitating continued economic expansion. In Taiwan and Hong Kong, however, the governments are somewhat less intrusive and less directly involved in the coordination and promotion of large business interests. The state and private sectors normally occupy different spheres of economic activity, with the state playing the essential role in building infrastructure but a much smaller role in the export manufacturing. When Chinese businesses and the government come into close contact, they often find themselves in conflict. In Singapore, as Tan Hock's chapter shows, the government plays a predominate role, so much so that government policies have marginalized Chinese entrepreneurs, pushing them out of manufacturing and most small and medium-sized firm sectors.

If the organization of networks in Chinese society is an important contributing factor to the development of a distinctively Chinese mode of economic activity, then what are characteristics of these networks, how do they arise, and what are their effects upon economic activity? In the following Section A, the answers to these questions are general and theoretical; in Section B, the answers are framed more empirically in the context of specific economies.

A. General Perspectives

Chinese Entrepreneurs and Business Trust

Wong Siu-lun

The ethic of trust is central to the business success of Chinese entrepreneurs in Hong Kong and in overseas communities.[1] The importance of this value has been underlined by numerous empirical studies. In an investigation on a vegetable wholesale market in Hong Kong, Robert H. Silin (1972, p. 337) found that "*xin-yong,* or trust, was the crucial factor in upholding the complex network of trading relations." In my own study of the Hong Kong textile industrialists and small factory owners, the virtue of trustworthiness was extoled with one voice when entrepreneurs were asked to describe the qualities of a successful businessman (Wong 1988a, pp. 166-167; Sit and Wong 1989, p. 116).

The emphasis on trust existed not only among the industrialists in Hong Kong. It prevailed in the overseas Chinese business communities as well. In a study of the Chinese living in a small trading town in Java, Edward Ryan highlighted the "focal" value of wealth in the community. In the pursuit of wealth, it was deemed essential by the Chinese there to have *kepertjajaan,* or trust. Ryan observed that "[the] possession of capital is considered of much less importance than the possession of *kepertjajaan*" (1961, p. 25). In another study of the Chinese merchants in South Vietnam prior to the communist takeover in 1975, Clifton A. Barton argued that the economic success of the Chinese was based on their greater degree of credit-worthiness. He noted that "Chinese merchants were successful in direct proportion to the amount of *sun yung* they possessed" (Barton 1983, p. 49).

Types of Trust

Yet what exactly is meant by "trust"? It is a term much used, but seldom defined. In trying to unravel the various levels of meaning, I shall rely on the insights of three sociologists who have contributed to the clarification of the concept. The American sociologist Bernard Barber defines trust in terms of the content of the expectations that social actors have of one another. He identifies three kinds of expectations. The most general is the expectation of the continuity of the natural and moral order. Second is the technical competence of actors in roles. Third is the expectation on the fiduciary responsibilities of social actors, that is, "their duties in certain situations to place others' interest before their own" (Barber 1983, p. 9). Thus, for Barber, there is general trust, technical trust, and fiduciary trust.

Niklas Luhmann, a German sociologist, tackles the problem of trust in terms of its function and the social mechanisms which sustain it. He distinguishes between confidence and trust. In his view, confidence relates to the existence of danger which is an external condition. Trust, on the other hand, assumes a situation of risk which is created by the internal decisions made by an actor (Luhmann 1988, p. 97).

On the basis of such a distinction, Luhmann proceeds to differentiate between what he calls "personal trust" and "system trust." Both are attempts to reduce social complexity so that human beings can act. Personal trust is dependent on familiarity and is thus limited in scope. As social life becomes more complex, system trust is required which is built on impersonal and generalized "media of communication" such as money, power, and truth. According to Luhmann (1979, p. 50):

Anyone who trusts in the stability of the value of money... basically assumes that a system is functioning and places his trust in that function, not in people. Such system trust is automatically built up through continual, affirmative experience in utilizing money. It needs constant 'feedback' but does not require specific built-in guarantees and is therefore incomparably easier to acquire than personal trust in new and different people all the time.

System trust, therefore, is independent of individual motivations. "While, in personal trust, one must penetrate [self-presentation], anticipate deception and arm oneself against it, the case of system trust relieves one of these requirements for trust." By relieving such burdens and absorbing certain functions of familiarity, system trust stands beyond personal trust. In Luhmann's view, the transition from a reliance on personal trust to system trust is part of the "great civilizing processes" of modern life (Luhmann 1979, pp. 57-58).

Before Luhmann, another German sociologist, Max Weber, explored the problem of trust in his comparative study of world religions. His major concern was with the basis on which trust was given, whether it was built on particularistic or on universalistic grounds. The former, particularistic trust, was rooted in the "community of blood" and rested upon purely personal, familial, or semi-familial relationships (Weber 1951, p. 237). The latter, universalistic trust, was built on the "superior community of faith" such as the Puritan sects in the West. In their business dealings, the Puritan entrepreneurs acted "without regard to the person in question... without hate and without love, without personal predilection and therefore without grace, but sheerly in accordance with the factual, material responsibility imposed by his calling, and not as a result of any concrete personal relationship" (Weber 1966, p. 235).

It was this orientation which laid the firm foundation for capitalistic enterprises to emerge in Western Europe. While in China, Weber argued, because of the dependence on particularistic trust, "there failed to originate on the economic plane those great and methodical business conceptions which are rational in nature and are presupposed by modern capitalism" (Weber 1951, p. 242).

Max Weber's analysis of the economic ethos of traditional China reminds us of the necessity to reconcile the industrial inertia as found in late imperial and modern China with the vigorous entrepreneurship as shown in contemporary Hong Kong and overseas Chinese communities. Part of the explanation of this paradox lies in the distinction made by Weber himself between the problem of origin and the problem of diffusion of capitalism. There were inherent obstacles preventing capitalism from emerging on its own in traditional China. But Weber believed that the Chinese would be quick to adopt the capitalistic form of business once it had been invented in the West.

I have pursued this line of explanation before by examining the interaction between traditional Chinese values and the local institutional structure in generating the momentum for the modernization of Hong Kong (Wong 1986). I would like to take another step in that direction in this paper by using the notion of trust. With the conceptual clarifications made by Barber, Luhmann, and Weber in mind, it can be argued that business trust as found in late traditional China was personal and particularistic in nature. Through contacts with the West, system trust and universalistic trust have been established in Hong Kong and in overseas Chinese communities, thus providing a congenial environment for entrepreneurship to grow. I shall examine this hypothesis in the following sections.

System Trust

Is there a high level of system trust in Hong Kong? There are grounds to believe that there is, particularly in connection with the institutions of justice, power, and opportunity. Let me first consider the question of trust in the legal system. In the social indicators survey conducted in 1988 jointly by the Social Sciences Research Centre of the University of Hong Kong, the Centre for Hong Kong Studies of the Chinese University of Hong Kong, and the Department of Applied Social Studies of the Hong Kong Polytechnic, popular faith in the local judicial system was gauged.

Among 1,662 respondents interviewed, 66 percent thought that the Hong Kong legal system in general was fair. Specific questions on legal culture were posed to a sub-sample of 396 respondents. It was found that 67 percent of them expressed trust in Hong Kong judges and 63 percent in lawyers. The majority of the respondents also perceived the effectiveness of legal action in conflict resolution. When asked the question, "Do you think that taking legal action is an effective way to solve your dispute with other people?", 67 percent of the respondents gave positive answers (Kuan et al. 1991, pp. 209, 216-217). Similar findings are reported in Lau and Kuan (1988). Such a favorable attitude towards litigation has been confirmed by the rising rate of court cases. In 1971, Hong Kong recorded 5.7 civil cases per 1,000 inhabitants. This rate surpassed those of Japan (1.2 cases), the United Kingdom (3.6 cases), and Australia (5.3 cases). The rate rose in Hong Kong to 6.8 cases in 1976 and 15 in 1981, and it levelled off to 11.7 in 1986 (Lau and Kuan 1988, pp. 141-142).

However, the strong measure of trust in the legal system as shown in the 1988 survey should be treated with suitable caution. It might have been strengthened by apprehension about 1997. Popular appreciation of the value of the judiciary could have been heightened after the Sino-British negotiation about the future of Hong Kong. People may come to treasure what they think they are about to lose. But the magnitude of such an effect is difficult to determine in retrospect. The situation is further compounded by the existence of some apparent contradictions in the findings. In the same survey, it was discovered that the majority of the sub-sample had doubts about their ability to comprehend the judicial system. About half of them thought that "the law and the courts are too complicated to understand." It is also striking that over three-quarters of the respondents (76 percent) believed that court proceedings were biased against the poor (Kuan et al. 1991, pp. 208, 210; see also Lau and Kuan 1988, p. 125). In the minds of most respondents, fairness of the legal system obviously did not mean equality in treatment and outcome.

How important is system trust in law for the Hong Kong Chinese entrepreneurs in conducting their business? Little is known on the subject which calls for detailed research. Nonetheless, it is worth noting that even in the United States where people are supposedly fond of going to court, it has been found that businessmen seldom resort to legal sanctions to settle disputes. As an American entrepreneur has been quoted as saying, "One doesn't run to lawyers if he wants to stay in business because one must behave decently" (S. Macaulay 1963, p. 61). Similarly, in South Vietnam, a Vietnamese manager has reportedly stated, "We have never taken a customer to court... Even if a customer refuses to pay, court action would not be initiated because if this happened Chinese businessmen would become afraid of the company and would take their business elsewhere" (Barton 1983, p. 52). Yet the reluctance to take legal action should not be taken to imply automatically that system trust in law is of little significance in business. Just as the threat of violence is essential in buttressing political authority, the availability of legal justice as a last resort is needed in upholding business contracts.

Popular trust in the judiciary is matched by strong faith in the political system in Hong Kong. In the previously cited social indicators survey, nearly half of the respondents (48 percent) expressed a high level of trust in the Hong Kong government in spite of its colonial nature. Only 18 percent said that they had no faith in it. In contrast, they had far less faith in the British and Chinese governments. A quarter of them showed a lack of confidence in the former, and more than 40 percent indicated distrust of the latter (Lau et al. 1991, p. 199).

Political trust in the Hong Kong government is apparently built on faith in the civil service bureaucracy and not in any particular political leader. When respondents were asked to indicate their level of trust in various leadership bodies, it was the government officials as a group that emerged on top (Lau et al. 1991, p. 202). The civil service bureaucracy had obviously proved its worth through its performance, so much so that 70 percent of the respondents agreed with the statement that "though Hong Kong's political system is not perfect, it is already the best under the present circumstances" (Lau et al. 1991, p. 182). Its success in gaining legitimacy was due, at least in part, to what Ambrose King (1975) has called "the administrative absorption of politics" through the co-optation of local elites and grass-root leaders into the colonial administration. The government initiated wide-spread consultation for decision-making and adopted a non-ideological and non-interventionist position in dealing with the economy.

The *laissez faire* policy, as a general principle, was supported by the majority of the respondents in the 1988 indicators survey. About 57 percent agreed with the policy. However, their opinions on specific issues showed that most of them would favor a more interventionist government in economic matters. There was overwhelming support for the government to control unscrupulous business activities (87 percent), to set up long-term economic policies (86 percent), to help actively in the development of some industries and commercial undertakings (85 percent), and to protect Hong Kong industries from outside competition (76 percent) (Lau et al. 1991, pp. 192-193).

The entrepreneurs in Hong Kong held similar attitudes. Among the cotton spinners, I have found that the majority of them subscribed to the *laissez faire* position and were far less enthusiastic about the doctrine of social responsibility which was prevalent among industrialists in Britain. Yet most of them clamored for government support. They obviously wished the government to provide the infrastructure such as controlling inflation and regulating finance and prices, while leaving them a free hand to run their businesses (Wong 1988a, pp. 87-89).

The bedrock of support for *laissez faire* was actually located in the small and medium industrial sector. In our survey of the small factory owners, Victor Sit and I found that they simply wanted to be left alone. Most of them felt that the government's attitude towards them was either permissive (37 percent) or neutral (33 percent), but not encouraging. On the other hand, they did not express any strong desire for government support or assistance in the services needed for running their factories (Sit and Wong 1989, pp. 208-211). Therefore, the entrepreneurs in particular and the Hong Kong people in general appeared to trust the government to exercise restraint and not meddle in the economy. If anything, they were inclined to urge the government to adopt a more active role in the economic sphere.

Besides faith in the legal system and the civil service bureaucracy, trust in the opportunity structure for self-advancement in Hong Kong is also powerful. In the 1987 survey of small factory owners, we asked them to indicate their standing in life on a hypothetical ladder five years ago, at present, and five years from now. The bottom of the ladder represented the worst possible life situation, and the top represented the best. About half of the entrepreneurs ranked themselves as low in standing five years ago. As for their standing at the time of interview, the majority placed themselves in the middle category. When they were asked to predict their future standing, about 46 percent thought they would reach the top rung of the ladder in five years' time. The substantial upward shift reflected a general anticipation among the entrepreneurs of continuing improvements in their life situation and the perception of availability of opportunities for advancement in the small industrial sector (Sit and Wong 1989, pp. 125-129; see also Sit et al. 1979, pp. 311-317).

In the 1988 indicators survey, it was found that the majority of respondents perceived the society as open with ample room for advancement. About 83 percent believed that employees could have the chance to become bosses; 84 percent believed that in the past ten years Hong Kong had provided more opportunities for upward mobility; and 94 percent believed in the efficacy of self-endeavor. With respect to the best route for mobility, most of them chose the channels of 'starting one's own business' (49 percent) or 'acquiring professional qualification' (37 percent), with the former option more preferred. Their optimism about opportunities for advancement was strong enough to sustain a belief that the socioeconomic status of their children would be better than their own both before and after 1997. However, when it came to the direct impact of 1997, the majority of them, regardless of their self-assigned class position, believed that the capitalists would be the group to be hardest hit while the middle classes would come out relatively unscathed after the transfer of sovereignty (Thomas W.P. Wong 1991, pp. 159, 165, 168-169).

Personal Trust

Through the above examination of the legal, political and mobility structure of Hong Kong, it is clear that system trust has been solidly established. Yet this has not diminished the vigor of personal trust in business life. Particularistic ties still prevail, with little sign of being superseded by universalistic orientations. In a study on the inculcation of economic values in business families in Taiwan, Stephen M. Olsen discovered unexpectedly that universalism or an impersonal business code was not upheld by the school boys he surveyed. He concluded that "[the] rejection of competition and the relative emphasis on particularism as opposed to universalism in a business code... are probably an integral part of the pattern of business values in urban Taiwan" (Olsen 1972, p. 276).

More specifically, a study on the characteristics of the Chinese style of management in Hong Kong indicated that both Chinese entrepreneurs and business executives tended to highlight four features, namely the importance attached to dedication and diligence; the significance of friendship in establishing business networks; the sensitivity to interpersonal relations; and the non-exclusive nature of business cooperation which was not confined to small groups (Tuan et al. 1986, p. 34).

In seeking bank loans to start their operations in the 1950s, Shanghainese cotton spinners in Hong Kong relied on personal ties to gain access to local British banks. They enlisted the help of a fellow Shanghainese who used to work for the Bank of China in industrial lending to act as a go-between. This Shanghainese banker told me how he made new financial arrangements for his friends in cotton spinning after he arrived in Hong Kong (Wong 1988a, p. 118):

I knew these spinners personally, so I approached the Hong Kong and Shanghai Bank on their behalf. We had to persuade the colonial officials and the Bank that textiles were good for Hong Kong. It was not too difficult when they saw the financial side of it. This was the period just after the war, and there was a big demand for textiles. Because of the demand, textiles were very profitable... When the Bank saw the profit, they said, 'Here's the money. Lend it to them.' So I functioned as an informal adviser for the Bank. I held a dinner on its behalf every week. Later I became very busy. But the Bank said, 'We need you.' So I stayed, first for three years, then six years, until now. There has never been any contract.

At the other end of the industrial scale, the small factory owners in Hong Kong also depended heavily on particularistic relations to get business orders. Highly personalized methods were used, such as introductions and recommendations by former employers or employees, friends and relatives. Impersonal channels such as advertising and sales promotion were seldom used. In the elaborate subcontracting system underlaying much of production and sales arrangements in the small industrial sector, agreements were mostly made verbally on an informal basis. Only about one-third of the small industrialists interviewed in 1987 reported that their subcontracts were formalized in written documents (Sit and Wong 1989, pp. 154-155, 188).

In the range of personal relations used by Chinese entrepreneurs to maintain business trust, family and regional ties are particularly important. On the whole, family ties play a critical role in cementing the internal organization of Chinese firms in Hong Kong, while regional ties are prominent in regulating inter-firm transactions.

In an attempt to account for the political stability in Hong Kong, Lau Siu-kai has proposed the concept of "utilitarianistic familism." As an explanation for Hong Kong's economic dynamism, I have used the term "entrepreneurial familism." By "utilitarianistic familism," Lau (1982, p. 72) means "the normative and behavioral tendency of an individual to place his familial interests above the interests of society and other individuals and groups... Moreover, among familial interests, material interests take priority over non-material interests."

When I use the term "entrepreneurial familism," I am referring to an ethos which involves the family as the basic unit of economic competition. The family provides the impetus for innovation and the support for risk-taking. Entrepreneurial familism is not confined to the rich among the population in the form of family firms. It permeates the whole society. Where there is little physical capital to be deployed, heads of less well-off families still marshal their limited resources and try to cultivate human capital for collective advancement (Wong 1988b, p. 142).

The ideas of utilitarianistic and entrepreneurial familism carry several implications. First of all, they indicate that money is being used as a medium of emotional expression as well as a medium of economic exchange among the Hong Kong Chinese. This phenomenon is shown, for example, in the tendency for filial piety to be expressed in terms of financial support for one's parents. Consequently, the norm of economic reciprocity is observed and strengthened in the interaction among family members. Instrumental and expressive considerations are intermingled and undifferentiated.

Second, familism as a general motivating force will not be able to fully account for the economic vitality found in Hong Kong. It is rather a special type of familism operating in the context of precariousness. One of the striking features of Hong Kong society is the large component of refugees in its population. I think it is here that we can find the parallel with Max Weber's theory of the Protestant ethic and the spirit of capitalism. The refugee mentality prevailing in Hong Kong and other newly developing economies in Asia has instilled in their inhabitants an inner psychological tension not unlike that experienced by the Puritans as described by Weber. In their struggle to obtain this-worldly "salvation" and some assurance of security for themselves and their families, they also seem to have unleashed a transformative social force (Wong 1988c, pp. 553-554).

Third, personal trust among family members can facilitate quick decisions and secrecy, making the family unit adaptable to rapidly changing situations. But will this create distrust outside the family and inhibit wider economic cooperation? In the case of traditional China, Maurice Freedman (1971, pp. 158-159) has pointed out that "competition and conflict are inherent at all levels of the social system; brother contends with brother, segment with segment, lineage with lineage, the lineage with the state. But there is also harmony because each contender must be united against its opponent... Harmony and conflict are not mutually exclusive; on the contrary, they imply each other."

Similarly, trust and distrust are not mutually exclusive. It is a matter of gradation, not dichotomy. Trust can extend beyond the family to sustain economic order because the boundary of the family group is not a sharp one marking off insiders and outsiders. Arthur Smith, who lived among the Chinese in the late Qing dynasty, pinpointed mutual suspicion and absence of sincerity as two major characteristics of the Chinese people. His observations were acute: "There are said to be two reasons why people do not trust one another: first, because they do not know one another, and second, because they do. The Chinese think that they have each of these reasons for mistrust, and they act accordingly" (A.H. Smith 1894/1986, p. 246). Smith was correct but partial with such a description. He did not recognize that trust and distrust among the Chinese are two sides of the same coin. For them, trust is neither absolute nor unconditionally given.

The last implication of the special brand of familism found in Hong Kong is its impermanence. Since sons are equal heirs in a Chinese family, there is an inherent tendency towards segmentation in the life cycle of the family. A centrifugal force exists, making Chinese family firms strong in entrepreneurship but weak in management. As the family is not a permanent entity, family reputation is likewise short-lived. The Chinese family does not furnish a secure basis for long-term business trust to be maintained. Therefore entrepreneurs, in their business dealings, are fully aware that trustworthiness is essentially tentative and transient, and personal trust has to be continually renewed.

In inter-firm transactions, regional ties based on common territorial origins are more important than familism. One of the characteristics of the Hong Kong economy is the proliferation of small firms. This phenomenon represents a triumph of markets over hierarchies (Williamson and Ouchi 1981). Why do Chinese entrepreneurs tend to create small business units and rely on subcontracting relations rather than setting up big corporations through vertical integration? The sociologist Mark Granovetter (1985, p. 503) has provided a clue: "Other things being equal, we should expect pressures toward vertical integration in a market where transacting firms lack a network of personal relations that connects them... On the other hand, where a stable network of relations mediates complex transactions and generates standards of behavior between firms, such pressures should be absent."

In Hong Kong, regional ties play an important role in the establishment of a stable network of personal relations mediating economic transactions for several reasons. First of all, an individual's place of origin has long been emphasized by the Chinese state as a mechanism of social control, thus affirming it as a basic social identity. Second, because of the tradition of regional specialization in occupational activities in China, people from the same locality usually have common economic skills and outlook. Third, regional identity is flexible. For instance, I can trace my origin to my home county of Pan Yu, and widen it to metropolitan Guangzhou, the province of Guangdong, and southern China. The regional scope can contract or expand to suit the situation. Fourth and last, an important condition exists in Hong Kong which keeps most Chinese entrepreneurs within the effective reach of their regional networks. It is the credential barrier imposed by educational qualifications which reduces their possibilities for occupational and geographical mobility. In the 1987 survey of small entrepreneurs (Sit and Wong 1989, pp. 97-100), it was found that the majority of industrialists had a Chinese type of education which was either not recognized or not valued in Hong Kong. As immigrants, most of them were not proficient in English, which was the key to stable administrative or commercial careers. Thus they turned to small scale industry for advancement and had to mobilize regional ties for their business activities.

The essence of entrepreneurship, according to the economist Joseph Schumpeter (1934, p. 66), is the ability to innovate. However, under perfect competition, innovation is not an economically rewarding pursuit. The profits generated by the innovator will be quickly diluted by imitators. In order to protect his profits, an entrepreneur can be expected to try to achieve closure or the monopolization of specific business opportunities by erecting economic or social barriers to entry. In the Chinese case, entrepreneurs tend to dominate the market by activating particularistic ties such as regional networks rather than by building large, impersonal corporations.

Particularistic ties are used to fulfill two crucial functions. One is that they provide a firmer basis for trust within the network. Members can have more information with which to evaluate one another's credit-worthiness. They can also exert greater control over those who do not conform by invoking communal sanctions. The other is that they furnish a justification for discrimination. It can be claimed that people with common ties belong to a moral community with shared rights and obligations, so that it is legitimate to keep economic benefits within the network. But since particularistic ties are flexible in nature, the boundary between insider and outsider is rarely clear-cut and the monopoly seldom absolute. Personal networks are constantly breaking up and being regrouped. Thus economic order has to be achieved through the multiple overlaps of shifting personal networks.

This special mode of establishing economic order is a continuation from the past. In traditional China, as the sociologist Gary Hamilton points out, regional associations [*tongxiang hui*] performed the function of stabilizing the marketplace and laying the foundation for trustworthiness. These associations regulated the commercial conduct of their members by establishing reliable economic standards and by building regionalized reputations such as the dependability of the Shanxi bankers or the excellence of Fujianese paper products. In Europe, honesty had a legal and religious meaning, enforced by the courts. In China, it rested on the cohesiveness and identity of regional groups which reinforced personal honor. Gary Hamilton says (1985, pp. 203-204), "In this sense, to be trustworthy and hence commercially reliable was to be clannish... Clannishness was to business success in China what religious affiliation was to business success in frontier America."

Confucianism and Modernization

Chinese and Western cultures differed, particularly in religious beliefs. Max Weber observed that "[the] Confucian ethic intentionally left people in their personal relations as naturally grown... Puritan ethic, however, rather suspected these purely personal relationships as pertaining to the creatural... Trust in men, and precisely in those closest to one by nature, would endanger the soul" (Weber 1951, pp. 240-241).

In view of such a difference in religious ethic, when we ask the question, "Why are economic relations personalized among Chinese entrepreneurs?", we should pose at the same time the query, "Why should economic relations be impersonal in the first place?". The sociologist Talcott Parsons has proposed the notion of "pattern variables" which have been widely used to assess traditional and modern orientations. These are the distinctions between particularism and universalism, affectivity and affective neutrality, collectivity-orientation and self-orientation, ascription and achievement, and diffuseness and specificity (Parsons 1951, p. 67). From Max Weber's analysis, it is clear that the popular usage of pattern variables, such as the tendency to equate modernism with universalism and impersonality, has distinctive religious underpinnings. Moreover, Talcott Parsons himself recognizes that the paired variables are often mutually dependent rather than exclusive in the sense that over-emphasis on one end of the continuum will generate tension which calls for compensation at the other end. For example, the dominance of instrumental considerations and impersonality in the work place will heighten the expressive function of the family to stabilize adult personalities in modern Western societies. His analysis assumes the separation of different spheres of activity -the economic from the social, the work place from the family. Strong boundaries exist between different spheres.

Yet the pattern of social arrangement among the Chinese is different. Spheres are apparently not clear-cut; boundaries seem weak. As Liang Shu-ming (1949/1987, pp. 77-94) and Fei Xiao-tong (1947/1985, pp. 21-28) have argued, Chinese society was constructed with an emphasis on social bonds, not on individuals. It was built on networks and differentiation, not on groups and uniformity. Thus personal and impersonal attitudes, expressive and instrumental acts were not sharply distinguished. Without strong boundaries marking off various spheres of activity, the mediating function was diffused rather than institutionalized. Therefore, there were few specialized and respectable "middleman" roles in Chinese society. Every entrepreneur must take on mediating activity on an amateur basis from time to time.

Chinese entrepreneurs thus have to invest considerable time and resources in order to personalize economic relations and to undertake diffused mediating functions. However, the personal trust created through these means are not totally secure, because family ties are impermanent and regional ties are elastic and not strictly binding. There are limits to the usefulness of personal ties in maintaining trust. To complement personal trust, system trust is required. In Hong Kong, system trust is created mainly through the stable sociopolitical and economic framework afforded by British colonialism. Without such system trust, social investment in personal trust will become excessive and too costly for business.

On the other hand, system trust cannot operate in a void. It is not self-sufficient. In the absence of an omnipotent God to back it up in the Chinese case, it needs to be embedded in the dense network of particularistic ties. System trust and personal trust are mutually reinforcing, not mutually antagonistic. When attempts are made to institute system trust at the expense of personal trust, such as the case in the People's Republic of China where comradeship as a universalistic ethic was extoled as a substitute for friendship (E. Vogel 1965), the unintended result was widespread suspicion and inter-personal strain.

Personal trust and system trust, universalism and particularism, tradition and modernity are not dichotomous concepts. In traditional China, particularism as embodied in the Confucian School and universalism as espoused by the Legalist School were once locked in intense conflict. But when the law as formulated by the Legalists was actually adopted by the imperial government, the Confucianists stopped spending their energies on vain arguments and fought for practical accommodation instead. They tried to introduce into the legal code the principle and spirit of *li*. This led to what Ch'u T'ung-tsu (1961, pp. 267-279) has called "the Confucianization of law." Subsequent generations of Confucianists effectively reconciled the two apparently opposing principles of law and propriety.

A central tenet of Confucianism is the Doctrine of the Mean. The ideal is to attain balance. Expressed in sociological language, it is to achieve a dynamic equilibrium. Without deliberate design, almost by accident, such an equilibrium has been attained in Hong Kong between personal trust and system trust, between Chinese tradition and Western modernism. As a result, entrepreneurship flourishes. But the balance is delicate. It needs to be maintained. It needs to be renewed. It needs understanding and creative care for it to remain dynamic.

Notes

[1] A draft outline of this paper was presented as "The Social Foundations of Inter-firm Networks Among Chinese Businesses in Hong Kong" in the International Conference on Business Groups and Economic Development in East Asia held on 20 June 1989 at the Centre of Asian Studies of the University of Hong Kong. A revised version was delivered as an Inaugural Lecture entitled "Chinese Entrepreneurs and Business Trust" at the University of Hong Kong on 30 March 1990. I wish to thank Professor Gary Hamilton, Dr. Veronica Pearson, and my wife, Linda, for their comments on various drafts.

References

Barber, Bernard. 1983. *The Logic and Limits of Trust.* New Brunswick: Rutgers University Press.

Barton, Clifton A. 1983. "Trust and Credit: Some Observations Regarding Business Strategies of Overseas Chinese Traders in South Vietnam." Pp. 46-63 in *The Chinese in Southeast Asia,* eds. Linda Y. C. Lim and L.A.P. Gosling. Singapore: Maruzen Asia.

Ch'u, T'ung-tsu. 1961. *Law and Society in Traditional China*. Sorbonne: École Pratique des Hautes Études.

Endacott, George. 1962. "The Beginnings." Pp. 23-37 in *University of Hong Kong: The First 50 Years 1911-1961*, ed. Brian Harrison. Hong Kong: Hong Kong University Press.

Fei Xiao-tong. 1947/1985. *Xiangtu Zhongguo* [Rural China]. Shanghai: Guancha She. Rpt. in Beijing: Joint Publishing Co.

Freedman, Maurice. 1957. *Chinese Family and Marriage in Singapore*. London: Her Majesty's Stationary Office.

Freedman, Maurice. 1971. *Chinese Lineage and Society: Fukien and Kwangtung*. London: The Athlone Press.

Granovetter, Mark. 1985. "Economic Action and Social Structure: The Problem of Embeddedness." *American Journal of Sociology* 91: 481-510.

Hamilton, Gary G. 1985. "Why no Capitalism in China? Negative Questions in Historical, Comparative Research." *Journal of Developing Societies* 1: 187-211.

King, Ambrose Yeo-chi. 1975. "Administrative Absorption of Politics in Hong Kong: Emphasis on the Grass Roots Level." *Asian Survey* 15: 422-439.

Kuan, Hsin-chi, Lau Siu-kai, and Wan Po-san. 1991. "Legal Attitudes." Pp. 207-223 in *Indicators of Social Development: Hong Kong 1988*, eds. Lau Siu-kai, Lee Ming-kwan, Wan Po-san and Wong Siu-lun. Hong Kong: Hong Kong Institute of Asia-Pacific Studies, The Chinese University of Hong Kong.

Lau, Siu-kai. 1982. *Society and Politics in Hong Kong*. Hong Kong: The Chinese University Press.

Lau, Siu-kai and Kuan Hsin-chi. 1988. *The Ethos of the Hong Kong Chinese*. Hong Kong: The Chinese University Press.

Lau, Siu-kai, Kuan Hsin-chi, and Wan Po-san. 1991. "Political Attitudes." Pp. 173-206 in *Indicators of Social Development: Hong Kong 1988*, eds. Lau, Siu-kai, Lee Ming-kwan, Wan Po-san and Wong Siu-lun. Hong Kong: Hong Kong Institute of Asia-Pacific Studies, The Chinese University of Hong Kong.

Liang, Shu-ming. 1949/1987. *Zhongguo Wenhua* [The Essence of Chinese Culture]. Chengdu: Luming Shudian. Rpt. in Hong Kong: Joint Publishing.

Luhmann, Niklas. 1979. *Trust and Power*. Chichester: John Wiley & Sons.

Luhmann, Niklas. 1988. "Familiarity, Confidence, Trust: Problems and Alternatives." Pp. 94-107 in *Trust: Making and Breaking Cooperative Relations*, ed. Diego Gambetta. Oxford: Basil Blackwell.

Macaulay, Stewart. 1963. "Non-contractual Relations in Business: A Preliminary Study." *American Sociological Review* 28: 55-67.

Mellor, Bernard. 1962. "The American Foundations." Pp. 159-170 in *University of Hong Kong: The First 50 Years 1911-1961*, ed. Brian Harrison. Hong Kong: Hong Kong University Press.

Olsen, Stephen M. 1972. "The Inculcation of Economic Values in Taipei Business Families." Pp. 261-295 in *Economic Organization in Chinese Society*, ed. William E. Willmott. Stanford: Stanford University Press.

Parsons, Talcott. 1951. *The Social System*. New York: The Free Press.

Ryan, Edward Joseph. 1961. "The Value System of a Chinese Community in Java." Ph.D. thesis. Cambridge, Mass.: Harvard University.

Schumpeter, Joseph A. 1934. *The Theory of Economic Development: An Inquiry into Prof- its, Capital, Credit, Interest, and the Business Cycle.* Cambridge, Mass.: Harvard Uni- versity Press.

Silin, Robert H. 1972. "Marketing and Credit in a Hong Kong Wholesale Market." Pp. 327- 352 in *Economic Organization in Chinese Society*, ed. W.E. Willmott. Stanford: Stanford University Press.

Sit, Victor Fung-shuen, and Siu-lun Wong. 1989. *Small and Medium Industries in an Export-Oriented Economy: The Case of Hong Kong.* Hong Kong: Centre of Asian Stud- ies, University of Hong Kong.

Sit, Victor Fung-shuen, Siu-lun Wong, and Tsin-sing Kiang. 1979. *Small Scale Industry in a Laissez-Faire Economy.* Hong Kong: Centre of Asian Studies, University of Hong Kong.

Smith, Arthur H. 1894/1986. *Chinese Characteristics.* New York: Fleming H. Revell. Rpt. in Singapore: Graham Brash.

Tuan, Chyau, Danny S. N. Wong, and Chun-sheng Ye. 1986.*Guoren chongyezhe yanjiu: Xianggang yu Guangzhou diqu de gean fenxi* [Chinese Entrepreneurship under Capital- ism and Socialism – Hong Kong and Guangzhou Cases]. Hong Kong: Centre of Asian Studies, University of Hong Kong.

Vogel, Ezra. 1965. "From Friendship to Comradeship: The Change in Personal Relations in Communist China." *The China Quarterly* 21: 46-60.

Weber, Max. 1951. *The Religion of China.* New York: The Free Press.

Weber, Max. 1966. *The Sociology of Religion.* London: Social Science Paperbacks.

Williamson, Oliver E., and William G. Ouchi. 1981. "The Markets and Hierarchies Program of Research: Origins, Implications, Prospects." Pp. 347-370 in *Perspectives on Organi- zation Design and Behavior*, eds. Andrew H. Van De Van and William F. Joyce. New York: John Wiley & Sons.

Wong, Siu-lun. 1986. "Modernization and Chinese Culture in Hong Kong." *The China Quarterly* 106: 306-325.

Wong, Siu-lun. 1988a. *Emigrant Entrepreneurs: Shanghai Industrialists in Hong Kong.* Hong Kong: Oxford University Press.

Wong, Siu-lun. 1988b. "The Applicability of Asian Family Values to Other Sociocultur- al Settings." Pp. 134-152 in *In Search of An East Asian Development Model*, eds. Peter L. Berger and Hsin-Huang Michael Hsiao. New Brunswick: Transaction Books.

Wong, Siu-lun. 1988c. "Prosperity and Anxiety in Hong Kong." Pp. 549-554 in *Conference on Successful Economic Development Strategies of the Pacific Rim Nations*, ed. Chung- Hua Institution for Economic Research. Taipei: Chung-Hua Institution for Economic Re- search.

Wong, Thomas W.P. 1991. "Inequality, Stratification and Mobility." Pp. 145-171 in *Indica- tors of Social Development*, eds. Lau, Siu-kai, Lee Ming-kwan, Wan Po-san, and Wong Siu-lun. Hong Kong: Hong Kong Institute of Asia-Pacific Studies, The Chinese Univer- sity of Hong Kong.

Yang, Lien-sheng. 1987. *Zhongguo Wenhou Zhongboo, Bao, Bao Zhi Yiyi* [The Meaning of Reciprocity, Guarantee, and Undertaking in Chinese Culture]. Hong Kong: The Chinese University Press.

Weak Organizations and Strong Linkages: Managerial Ideology and Chinese Family Business Networks

S. Gordon Redding

This paper is designed to explore the idea that the fundamental source of strategic effectiveness in Overseas Chinese family businesses is the strength of network ties.[1] The firms themselves tend to be either small, and thus limited in capacity, or large and relatively unstable. Nonetheless, the economic systems in which they are dominant, notably those of Hong Kong and Taiwan, but also the Chinese networks of ASEAN, are vibrant and successful. A dilemma thus presents itself: How can organizations that are themselves so constrained produce economies that are so dramatically efficient? A significant portion of the explanation may lie in the linkage mechanisms that allow such organizations to transcend their inherent limitations. The proposition is thus one of weak organizations and strong linkages.

Reference to "strength" in linkages is worthy of some clarification in that the meaning is not necessarily that of permanence of bonding. The strength implied is that of strategic adaptability, and this will rest upon the flexibility, low cost, and breadth of choice of such linkages. Their strength lies in their strategic effectiveness, not in their long-standing cohesion, although this latter factor is still an underlying and relevant force.

Cultural Influences

The study of the influence of culture on patterns of business behavior and on the relative success or failure of businesses is still in an early and relatively primitive stage of development. Progress is now visible on two fronts: first, an increasing amount of empirical data is becoming available; and second, a number of theoretical advances are fostering the necessary collaboration between disciplines. Without the latter, the required cross-fertilization of ideas will not be realized and the true complexity of interacting forces involved will not be acknowledged.

It has been perhaps natural for attention to be paid increasingly to East Asia in this intellectual and eventually practical endeavor. It is there that the most dramatic examples have emerged, and it is there also that the most intriguing contrasts may be seen. Empirical advances are visible in the now voluminous literature on

Japanese management, although large gaps in the database, and a tendency for repetition of received wisdom have been remarked upon (Wilkinson 1980, Dunphy and Stening 1986). More recently, the previously sparse literature on other success stories such as that of South Korea and the Overseas Chinese is now growing quickly and provides a more solid basis for analysis (e.g. Jacobs 1985, Jones and Sakong 1980, Jesudason 1989, Limlingan 1986, Wong 1988, Yoshihara 1988, Redding 1990).

The construction of more complete frameworks for analysis typifies recent theoretical advances, and the acceptance of these frameworks by such core disciplines as economics, sociology, and organization studies demonstrates that the search for monocausal explanations is now at an end. Although they invariably start with a particular perspective, the new multi-disciplinary approaches are attempting to merge the insights of many disciplines. Recent examples of programs for this purpose are those coordinated at the American Academy of Arts and Sciences,[2] the East-West Center,[3] and the University of Hong Kong (Redding and Whitley 1990). Work expressing the ideal of inter-disciplinary co-operation is represented in, for instance, Lavoie (1990) and Whitley (1990).

This paper is located theoretically in the "Beyond Bureaucracy" framework explained most completely so far in Whitley (1990) and in Redding and Whitley (1990). This approach emerged from a search for a sociology of firm behavior, and takes as its main premise the notion that different societies will produce different "recipes" for economic coordination and control. In world market terms, the resulting economic behavior, such as selling things to people in other countries, may be equally successful, but achieved by different combinations of elements. More particularly, the Western bureaucracy form of large organization is no longer the standard to be followed, as it is no longer exclusively the most effective economic instrument for world business.

The empirical base for this paper is a study of the strategies of 95 companies in Hong Kong and 415 companies in Taiwan, all of which are owned and directed by Overseas Chinese.[4] Other data are incorporated from a separate, parallel study of Overseas Chinese managerial ideology (Redding 1990).

The intention is to outline connections between (a) cultural norms in the areas of authority relations and trust, and (b) business strategies, especially in terms of decisions to specialize or diversify, and to show the subsequent relationship to networking. This is done in the context of Whitley's (1987, 1990) larger model of business practices, which is a framework addressing how distinct recipes working effectively in different societies come to institutionalize ways of handling the following three concerns:

1) How are resources and activities authoritatively coordinated, integrated with other necessary resources, changed, and developed? For example, how do some recipes display typically large scale complexity (e.g. Korea) and others typically restricted complexity (Overseas Chinese).

2) How are authority relations within each enterprise structure organized, loyalties mobilized, and work allocated?
3) How are enterprises related to each other and integrated with major social institutions?

An outline answer to such questions, and thus a framework for more empirical probing, is given in Table 1. This table illustrates the main "ingredients" used in the recipes for the four main types illustrated. The variation in the degree of business specialization is striking in the Far East. Clark (1979) has pointed out, in describing "clubs" of industry in Japan, how firms tend to focus quite narrowly on one field of activity. Similarly, the specialization normally displayed by the typical Chinese family business has been remarked upon (Redding 1990). In Korea, by contrast, the *chaebol*, now the dominant actor in that economy, displays a monolithic capacity for large-scale coordination and control across a wide spectrum of technologies, industries and markets, a trait it also shares with Western divisionalized bureaucracies.

The workings of the economy still require that transactions between economic units be coordinated. It is inevitable that firm specialization will always be accompanied by connections among firms. These may take the form of contracting relationships which commonly go beyond the purely rational to become both stable and long-lasting.

The Effect of Managerial Ideology

One of the influences on the business strategies of Overseas Chinese entrepreneurs is the set of norms and values that this distinct business culture has inherited from its historical experience. Although they may be subdivided into regional sub-groups, the Overseas Chinese of Hong Kong, Singapore, Taiwan, Indonesia, Malaysia, Thailand, and the Philippines, nevertheless, share a great deal of common heritage such as the following:

1) An upbringing within a powerful system of Chinese socialization that instills such Confucian virtues as familism, filial piety, respect for authority, and diligence;
2) an experience as refugees, either directly in the present generation, or indirectly via family tradition;
3) an experience of oppression, directly in Taiwan, indirectly in Hong Kong due to the continuing threat from a totalitarian China, and covertly in ASEAN (with the exception of Singapore) as a repressed, economically successful minority.

Table 1:   East Asian Enterprise Structures

	Large Japanese Enterprises	Korean *Chaebol*	Chinese Family Businesses	U.S. Diversified Corporation
Enterprise Specialization and Development				
Business Specialization	High	Low	High	Low
Relational Contracting	High	Low	Medium	Low
Evolutionary Strategies	High	Medium	Medium	Low
Authority, Loyalty and the Division of Labor				
Personal Authority	Low	High	High	Low
Enterprise Loyalty	High	Medium	Medium	Low
Role Individuation	Low	Low	Low	High
Enterprise Co-ordination				
Horizontal Co-ordination	High	Low	Medium	Low
Vertical Co-ordination	High	High	Low	Low

Source: Whitley (1990, p. 68).

The combination of the original cultural basis of Chinese civilization, powerful and clear as it is, and varying degrees of oppression throughout the region, leads to a relatively homogeneous set of beliefs about the conduct of economic activity. These have been studied in a sample of 72 chief executives in Hong Kong, Singapore, Taiwan and Indonesia, and reveal the pattern of beliefs illustrated in Figure 1. The origins of such beliefs and their present disposition is discussed in detail in Redding (1990) but may be outlined briefly here.

Three themes serve to summarize the impact of Chinese social history on its people, and although these data come from a sample of Overseas Chinese, it would

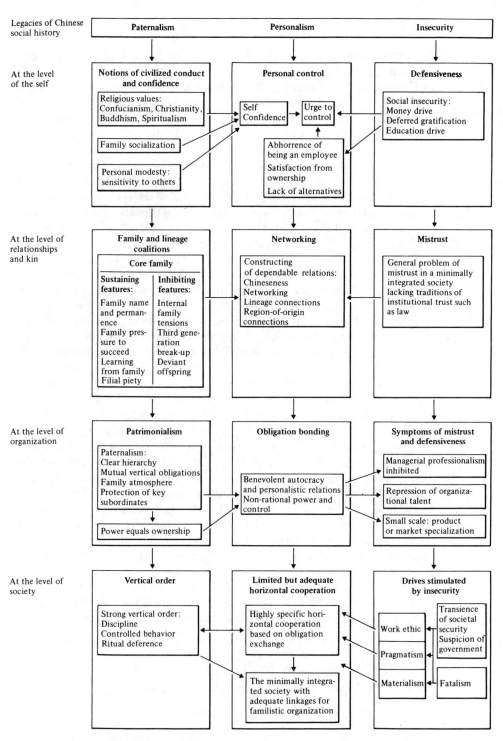

Legacies of Chinese social history

Paternalism | **Personalism** | **Insecurity**

At the level of the self

Notions of civilized conduct and confidence

Religious values: Confucianism, Christianity, Buddhism, Spiritualism

Family socialization

Personal modesty: sensitivity to others

Personal control

Self Confidence → Urge to control

Abhorrence of being an employee

Satisfaction from ownership

Lack of alternatives

Defensiveness

Social insecurity: Money drive Deferred gratification Education drive

At the level of relationships and kin

Family and lineage coalitions

Core family

Sustaining features: | **Inhibiting features:**
Family name and permanence | Internal family tensions
Family pressure to succeed | Third generation break-up
Learning from family | Deviant offspring
Filial piety |

Networking

Constructing of dependable relations: Chineseness Networking Lineage connections Region-of-origin connections

Mistrust

General problem of mistrust in a minimally integrated society lacking traditions of institutional trust such as law

At the level of organization

Patrimonialism

Paternalism: Clear hierarchy Mutual vertical obligations Family atmosphere Protection of key subordinates

Power equals ownership

Obligation bonding

Benevolent autocracy and personalistic relations Non-rational power and control

Symptoms of mistrust and defensiveness

Managerial professionalism inhibited

Repression of organizational talent

Small scale: product or market specialization

At the level of society

Vertical order

Strong vertical order: Discipline Controlled behavior Ritual deference

Limited but adequate horizontal cooperation

Highly specific horizontal cooperation based on obligation exchange

The minimally integrated society with adequate linkages for familistic organization

Drives stimulated by insecurity

Work ethic

Pragmatism

Materialism

Transience of societal security Suspicion of government

Fatalism

Source: Redding (1990, p. 83).

Figure 1: The Spirit of Chinese Capitalism

be easy to make a case for their relevance for China as well. The themes are paternalism, personalism, and insecurity.

Paternalism, and all the ethics of familism that surround it, is the main principle undergirding social structure in Chinese societies. It provides support for stable hierarchical relations, and defines authority for contexts outside the family as well as inside, allowing the society in general to be described as essentially patriarchal (Hamilton 1984).

Personalism is a response to the problem of establishing reliable horizontal relationships across social interactions in a context where trust cannot be assumed (in fact is likely to be denied) and where institutionalized law is inadequate for underpinning transactions with any sense of reliability. Transactions come to be guaranteed by bonds of interpersonal trust, and thus personal relationships become especially crucial in the workings of society and the economy.

Insecurity is partly a reflection of the general problem of mistrust in a familistic social setting under conditions of scarce resources. Families are essentially competing with each other for survival. Insecurity is exacerbated by a long standing inability of Chinese governments to provide for more than the most primitive needs of the majority of the population, a "tradition" emerging from many factors including totalitarian decadence, the inefficiency of productive systems (Elvin 1973), and population pressures (Fairbank 1987). The experience of the average Chinese person, and the folklore of the family, have commonly led to a perception of life being a matter of survival by one's wit and energy under threatening conditions, and with no help from the state.

These forces may be seen at work in the espoused beliefs of modern-day entrepreneurs. The self-confidence which can be generated in a role-based social system (see Hamilton 1984) when a person is fully socialized into a role, turns into an obsession with personal control when faced with the insecurity prevalent in the society at large. At a different level of analysis, family coalitions handle the problem of mistrust by extensive networking to cement crucial specific relationships. In such a context, organizations deal with the problem of trust by making use of a family model, which in turn displays paternalism and the patrimonial relations of a benevolent autocracy. Society stabilizes around the strong vertical ties of an essentially Confucian order, and generates limited but adequate horizontal cooperation.

Given this background, it is possible to speculate that an Overseas Chinese chief executive's view of an appropriate strategy for his firm will be colored by the following definitions of corporate circumstances:

1) It is essential to retain control of the firm in the interests of long-term family prosperity.
2) Risks should be hedged to protect family assets.
3) Key decisions should remain within an inner circle.

4) Dependence on non-belongers, for such essentials as managerial, technical, or marketing skills should be carefully limited.

In such circumstances, one would anticipate that firms would operate within the confines of a set of constraints that reduce the influence of any professional managerial elite.

A further feature is that the handling of inter-firm connections would likely make use of networks of interpersonal obligation. Personalizing trust-bonds substitutes for a system of legal contracts so normal in Western contexts (Landa 1981).

Strategic Patterns

Two studies have attempted to specify the strategic patterns found in the Chinese family business. Limlingan (1986) has proposed a four-stage model, the final outcome of which will depend on a specific country environment. This is illustrated in Figure 2 and relates especially to the operations of Chinese businesses in the Asean countries.

Based on data from Hong Kong, Wong (in this volume) has proposed a three stage model in which firms proceed through the following phases of change:

1) Acquisition of start-up capital from export industry (or shipping), i.e. money from abroad;
2) achieving growth via property development by acquisition of companies with substantial land holding, or buying newly formed sites;
3) further expansion or diversification by acquisition of major business establishments.

Yoshihara (1988) has also indicated the tendency of Chinese entrepreneurs, in the uncertainties of the *ersatz* economies of ASEAN, to gravitate towards a position of "rentier capitalists" as the ideal strategy for survival.

The question of business expansion begs a further question. What is the business that is being expanded? Before considering the determinants of strategy, one needs to acknowledge the difficulty in defining the appropriate unit of analysis.

If we take the legal firm as the prime unit of economic action, then one set of conclusions is possible: that the firm normally stays within a narrow field of specialization normally associated with the knowledge and inclinations of the paterfamilias. On the other hand, networking can provide an expansion of activities without necessarily requiring a more complex integrative structure. The principal economic actor thus becomes an informal coalition, a linked network of units, each node being a legally defined firm.

Overseas Chinese
The Sequence of Strategies

Entry (Trading)
- Low margin/high volume to achieve market share
- Use of Chinese community as resource base
- Low margin reduces local ill-will
- Force out competition (who have no access to network)
- High profit from high volume is not obvious

Growth (Distribution)
- Having achieved market share (+ capital accumulation) search for economies of scope via
  (a) *Additional products* for same market (e.g. buying or selling 2 commodities instead of 1)
  (b) *Additional services* for same market (e.g. milling rice, as well as buying it
  (c) *Reduce investment* in present market (e.g. paying for rice with fertilizer)
  (d) *Reduce costs* of serving present market (e.g. trucks take rice to city, return with farm supplies)

Risk (Entrepreneurship)
- Pursuit of business deals using
  – Cost-free information resulting from trading
  – Chinese community infrastructure
  – Access to credit

Ascendancy (Industrialist)
Develop larger scale strategy depending on national economic policy

Stages in the Strategic Process
for Overseas Chinese

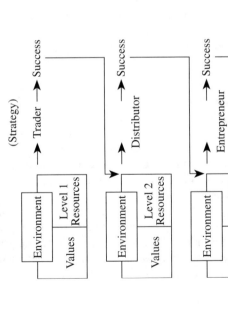

Source: Limlingan (1986).

Figure 2: Overseas Chinese Strategies

Hong Kong and Taiwan Business Strategies

As a means of studying strategy by its results rather than as a set of intentions (see Mintzberg and Waters 1982), companies in Hong Kong and Taiwan under ethnic Chinese ownership were analyzed in terms of their principal activities. This approach inevitably means that the collected data relate to legally defined firms rather than the networks in which they are located. Further interpretation of the data is thus required.

Two simple issues will be considered now: How specialized do such firms remain? Secondly, what activities do they gravitate towards?

Because of the nature of the data bases it is necessary to consider the Hong Kong sample and the Taiwan sample separately. The Hong Kong sample of 93 companies is the entire population of publicly listed companies in Hong Kong that are Chinese majority owned and managed. These publicly listed companies represent the most successful Hong Kong examples of Chinese creating large enterprises.

The Taiwan sample of 415 companies contains many which are not listed on a stock exchange. The sample was taken from a compendium of major Far Eastern companies (Carr 1987) and companies were selected "on the grounds of their sales volume or balance sheet or their importance to the business environment of the country in which they are based." Because the sample is not restricted to publicly listed firms, the Taiwan sample is likely to penetrate more deeply into the economy and to contain companies of a more closely owned and controlled character.

Table 2 presents data on the connections between the main fields of activity in the companies and thus gives some indication of the linkage between strategy and structure.

Table 2: Types of Connectedness within Companies in Hong Kong and Taiwan

	Hong Kong		Taiwan	
	No. of Companies	%	No. of Companies	%
Related	37	40	65	16
Horizontal	23	25	306	74
Vertical	13	14	32	7
Unrelated	20	21	12	3
Total	93	100	415	100

Companies whose component businesses are related have all their components basically in the same field, such as financial services or hotels. Horizontal businesses have closer connections between their sub-units such as "property investment" and "property agency," so that a flow of transactions horizontally between them is likely. Vertical businesses have similarly close connections, but this time as links in a commodity chain, such as "manufacturing jewelry" and "retailing jewelry."[5]

The key conclusion here is that companies tend to stick with one product market. Only 21 percent of companies in the Hong Kong sample and only 2.9 percent of those in the Taiwan sample cover a range of unrelated businesses. The conglomerate form is thus unusual. In the Hong Kong case, 93 companies report 611 main activities, or 6.36 each on average. But of these, 40 percent report businesses that are related, or, in other words, in basically the same field. A further 25 percent are characterized by horizontal connections that also provide some unity. In the Taiwan case, the 415 companies report only 1024 activities or only 2.47 each on average. The vast majority (74 percent) are horizontally connected.

The activities towards which Hong Kong firms gravitate are clear testimony to the seductive power of the rentier role. Out of the total of 611 areas of activity recorded, only 101 are related to manufacturing. Another 124 are related to property, 121 to financial investment, and the remainder to tertiary activities. It is clear that making money work in ways other than manufacturing is preferred, but that in achieving this intention, a high degree of focus is retained.

In the Taiwan case, this feature is almost entirely absent with less than 1 percent of companies reporting property or finance as fields. One must conclude either that there has been serious bias in compiling the list of "Major Companies of the Far East" or that the structure of the economy in Taiwan is radically different from that in Hong Kong. State control of the financial sector is, for instance, clearly an important determinant of the skewed distribution of activities in Taiwan.

The overall conclusion drawn from the data is that Chinese owned and managed companies typically respond by concentrating their effort in one main field, and then growing through replicating the same formula or through horizontally spreading into connected fields.

One might conclude that the growth of the firm, seen through Western eyes, is constrained by this structural and strategic limitation, and yet, paradoxically, the growth of the economy is demonstrably not suffering. A prima facie conclusion is that the larger structures of cooperation needed for an economy to flourish and to manage economic exchanges are reliant on a peculiarly effective mechanism for interfirm linkages.

Explaining the Network Strength

It was proposed earlier that the strength of Chinese economies derived from a system of economic exchange and cooperation that obtains its value less from its power of bonding than from its flexibility and capacity to re-align relations. The bonds referred to are thus not necessarily permanent. In fact their maintenance is dependent on questions of expedience. This is, at one level, a pragmatic and utilitarian set of relations, a system of what is occasionally and cynically seen as mutual exploitation. In practice, however, a complement of emotional connections and felt obligations, underpinned by a protoreligious ethic of mutual supportiveness, serves to inject a degree of morality into economic activity, a kind of morality that Weber would have recognized as being conducive to economic endeavors.

This moral connectedness, selective though it may be, lies at the heart of Chinese business success and illustrates the critical contribution of a value system to the building of a successful economy. As Poggi (1983, p. 83), attempting to boil the Weberian argument down to its essentials, has noted: "No capitalist development without an entrepreneurial class; no entrepreneurial class without a moral charter; no moral charter without religious premises."

The study of the managerial ideology of 72 Overseas Chinese chief executives (Redding 1990) has provided some insight into the way in which a secular form of Confucianism pervades and structures the consciousness of the key actors in the sense we are observing. The head of the Chinese family business lives out values of paternalism, the disciplined exchange of vertical obligations, and the cultivation of specific horizontal bonds of obligation and friendship, all of which appear as selections from the wider Confucian ethic. State Confucianism, with its theories of government and its practices of aloof and obscure superiority via scholarship, is abandoned or at least put on one side as of only marginal interest. Instead certain key lessons, bound up with the perpetuation of social order via family discipline and family coherence, are selected out and retained. This secular Confucianism remains morally powerful and highly relevant in the world of business relationships, as well as in society in a wider sense. The ideology of Chinese chief executives is an elaboration around the theme of control in the face of limited trust. This is a strong prima facie explanation of why firms stay in one field. It provides a terrain for business decisions that can still be dominated by a very small elite group of owners, and often by a single individual. The allocation of roles in such firms has been depicted by Limlingan (Figure 3). His analysis suggests that professional management is restricted to basic managerial decisions, as opposed to the strategic decisions that remain the monopoly of the family coalition.

If we just consider the networking processes, there are two forces that especially foster it and contribute to its strength. These are (a) the ethic of trust, and (b) the relatively greater power of the key actors. The significance of trustworthiness has been noted commonly as a key component of economic exchange for the Overseas Chinese (Silin 1976, Barton 1983). In practice the breaking of trust

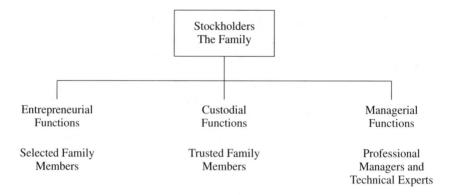

Source: Limlingan (1986).

Figure 3:   Organizational Structure of the Chinese Managerial System

has widespread social ramifications; the individual concerned is likely to be os-
tracized and to find it difficult to re-establish connections. With such penalties, on
the one hand, and, on the other hand, with encouragement from the ethical system,
the trustworthiness of interpersonal bonds serves to reduce dramatically the cost
of economic transactions within a limited sphere. Eventually, of course, with very
complex relations, interpersonal trust is so difficult to extend beyond a narrow circle that it turns into a constraint, but that constraint is seemingly acknowledged in
strategic limitations that appear self-imposed.

The second force is that of individual power. If you are negotiating with another
person and if the exchange is to be maximally efficient, he or she needs to have
the power to speak on behalf of a whole organization without going back to seek
approval for any decisions reached. The virtual domination of both strategy and
operations by key individuals in the Chinese family business serves this need. The
person making the agreement is in a position to "deliver." The extent to which
this works, i.e. the proportion of companies and interactions to which it applies,
is uniquely high in the economic cultures of the Overseas Chinese because they
are almost totally reliant on the family business form of enterprise.

The Larger Context of Efficiency

It was argued at the outset of this paper that explaining the efficiency of economic
systems requires complex and multi-disciplinary models. To concentrate on networking is not then to suggest that networking alone is the prime determinant of
growth. It is clearly very important in the Chinese case, but it lies in the context
of a wider system.

Some notion of the sources of efficiency in the wider system is available from a recent study by Tam (1990) aimed at contrasting Chinese and Japanese business systems. His argument is that the Chinese case presents what, at first glance, appears to be a series of anomalies, which include the following:

1) Significant industrial power released by atomistic firms;
2) excellent performance by formally untrained managers;
3) constant renewal by conservative firms;
4) high work-rates in an uncommitted workforce;
5) innovation efficiency in preference to scale efficiency.

Three of these apparent anomalies, namely (1), (3), and (5) are connected to the issue of networking, and an analysis of these three will serve to amplify the understanding of network efficiency.

Explanations of how industrial power is released by atomistic firms rest on the idea that the functional equivalent of a large Western corporation in, for instance, Hong Kong is a constellation of firms. The functional equivalent of a section supervisor in the West is an entrepreneur in Hong Kong. Coordination is not achieved by hierarchy, but by voluntary networking. Hong Kong and Taiwan enterprises normally sell to distributors in other economies in which they have limited influence. Without a stable market base, shifts in product-market requirements are met by shifting constellations in production units. The 280,000 establishments that exist in Hong Kong allow almost unlimited combinations and permutations. An example is offered by Tam (1990) of a trading firm employing 17 people which in a year had contracted with 60 establishments and directly formed 5 new ones.

The collective strength which can be mobilized via the permutations is set in a business context of changing demand, and thus of uncertainty and insecurity. Strategically, the competitive advantage that the system produces is its capacity to cope with environmental turbulence, a challenge that more hierarchical structures commonly fail to meet. The efficiency of Chinese business systems needs to be understood in this comparative sense, before its international significance can be fully appreciated.

The paradox of constant renewal in conservative structures is explicable in terms of a stream of new entrepreneurs splitting off from established firms and setting up new firms. The system, however, does not simply exhibit fission of this nature. It also exhibits a re-fusion process, in which networking plays a key part. In order to develop a network of dependable connected firms, a firm attempting to deal with uncertainty may actively promote the formation of new firms. Employees will be helped to become employers, with their original loyalty being perpetuated by mutual self-interest.

The pursuit of innovation efficiency in preference to scale efficiency is an outcome of a situation in which industry dominance by key players is difficult. If nobody dominates the industry, then anyone can move in. The constant fission of small units also contributes by denying the possibility of keeping new business formulae secret. Each company is surrounded by an army of entrepreneurs watching for opportunities, and each company contains within it another cohort of potential entrepreneurs ready to spring out and start on their own. In a particular year, a single company will begin the manufacture of wigs, plastic flowers, watches, or telephones; a year later there will be hundreds of companies doing the same, each locking onto and expanding the complexity of the core network.

Conclusion

The study of organizations is incomplete if the unit of analysis remains the legally-bounded firm. The embeddedness of organizations in a societal context leads to certain formulae or recipes becoming dominant on the grounds of their special appropriateness for that context. Such recipes can work equally well to produce goods competitively in world markets.

An important component of any recipe is the way economic exchange in a society is coordinated and made to run smoothly. In many Western economies, the main efficiencies in coordination derive from large-scale organization. In the case of the Overseas Chinese, the equivalent efficiencies derive from networking.

The Chinese networks derive their legitimacy and attraction from certain cultural predispositions, most of which are traceable to Confucian values. The very success of these networks encourages other cultural predispositions, such as patrimonial authority patterns, which give high organizational influence to key individuals, and an ethic of trustworthiness, which provides discipline and moral justifications to the system. This reciprocation releases other forms of efficiency, which can be explained technically in terms of low transaction costs, strategic flexibility, and a capacity for innovation, all of which facilitate a continuation of the successful recipe in the future.

Notes

[1] The support of the Institute for the Study of Economic Culture, Boston University, is gratefully acknowledged for the research reported here.
[2] This program, coordinated by Tu Wei-ming, incorporates the work of a range of disciplines, and includes sub-units headed by E.F. Vogel, R. MacFarquhar, and W. Rosofsky, among others.
[3] This program, also multi-disciplinary, is coordinated by R. Dernberger.
[4] I am indebted to Mr. K.K. Wong for his collation of data for this part of the study.
[5] These characterizations are generalizations only and represent the overall "feel" of a company's operations. Sub-components may still deviate in some cases from the pattern.

References

Barton, C.A. 1983. "Trust and Credit: Some Observations Regarding Business Strategies of Overseas Chinese Traders in Vietnam." Pp. 46-64 in *The Chinese in Southeast Asia: Vol 1 Ethnicity and Economic Activity,* eds. L.Y.C. Lim and L.A.P. Gosling. Singapore: Maruzen Asia.

Carr, J.L., ed. 1987. *Major Companies of The Far East: Vol 2: East Asia.* London: Graham and Trotman.

Clark, R. 1979. *The Japanese Company.* New Haven: Yale University Press.

Dunphy, D. and B. Stening. 1986. *Annotated Bibliography of the Japanese Management Literature.* Hong Kong: Asian Research Service.

Elvin, M. 1973. *The Pattern of the Chinese Past.* Stanford: Stanford University Press.

Fairbank, J.K. 1987. *The Great Chinese Revolution: 1800-1985.* New York: Harper and Row.

Hamilton, G.G. 1984. "Patriarchalism in Imperial China and Western Europe: A Revision of Weber's Sociology of Domination." *Theory and Society* 13: 393-425.

Jacobs, N. 1985. *The Korean Road to Modernization and Development.* Urbana, Ill.: University of Illinois Press.

Jesudason, J.V. 1989. *Ethnicity and the Economy: The State, Chinese Business, and Multinationals in Malaysia.* Singapore: Oxford University Press.

Jones, L.P. and Il Sakong. 1980. *Government, Business and Entrepreneurship in Economic Development: The Korean Case.* Cambridge MA: Harvard University Press.

Landa, J.T. 1981. "A Theory of the Ethnically Homogeneous Middleman Group: An Institutional Alternative to Contract Law." *The Journal of Legal Studies* X: 349-362.

Lavoie, D. 1990. "The Discovery and Interpretation of Profit Opportunities." Paper given at the Conference on The Culture of Entrepreneurship. Boston: The Institute for The Study of Economic Culture, Boston University.

Limlingan, V.S. 1986. *The Overseas Chinese in ASEAN: Business Strategies and Management Practices.* Manila: Vita Development Corporation.

Mintzberg, H. and J.A. Waters. 1982. "Tracking Strategy in an Entrepreneurial Firm." *Academy of Management Journal* 25 (3): 465-499.

Poggi, G. 1983. *Calvinism and The Capitalist Spirit: Max Weber's Protestant Ethic.* London: Macmillan.

Redding, S.G. 1990. *The Spirit of Chinese Capitalism.* Berlin, New York: de Gruyter.

Redding, S.G. and R.D. Whitley. 1990. "Beyond Bureaucracy: Towards a Comparative Analysis of Forms of Economic Resource Co-ordination and Control." Pp. 79-104 in *Capitalism in Contrasting Cultures,* eds. S.R. Clegg and S.G. Redding. Berlin, New York: de Gruyter.

Silin, R.H. 1976. *Leadership and Values: The Organization of Large-scale Taiwanese Enterprises.* Cambridge MA.: Harvard University Press.

Tam, S. 1990. "Centrifugal versus Centripetal Growth Processes: Contrasting Ideal Types for Conceptualizing the Development Patterns of Chinese and Japanese Firms." *Capitalism in Contrasting Cultures,* eds. S.R. Clegg and S.G. Redding. Berlin, New York: de Gruyter.

Whitley, R.D. 1987. "Taking Firms Seriously as Economic Actors: Towards a Sociology of Firm Behaviour." *Organization Studies* 8: 125-147.

Whitley, R.D. 1990. "Eastern Asian Enterprise Structures and the Comparative Analysis of
  Forms of Business Organizations." *Organization Studies* 11: 47-74.
Wilkinson, E. 1980. *Misunderstanding: Europe vs Japan.* Tokyo: Chuokoron-sha.
Wong, Siu-lun. 1988. *Emigrant Entrepreneurs: Shanghai Capitalists in Hong Kong.* Hong
  Kong: Oxford University Press.
Yoshihara, K. 1988. *The Rise of Ersatz Capitalism in South-East Asia.* Singapore: Oxford
  University Press.

The Organizational Foundations of Western and Chinese Commerce: A Historical and Comparative Analysis

Gary G. Hamilton

This essay examines regional relationships (*tongxiang guanxi*) and family firms in the conduct of Chinese business. Other writers for this volume have examined this topic theoretically and in the context of various modern economies in East and Southeast Asia. My attempt here will be to add to this already substantial analysis a comparative and historical perspective. The goal of my particular effort is to understand the peculiar network structure of the modern Chinese economies through systematic contrasts with Western economic organization.

With this goal and perspective in mind, let me state my conclusion first: The organizational matrix of commerce among commoners in late imperial and modern China rested upon ties of kinship and of native place origins. Those readers who know about Chinese society might think this conclusion is entirely unremarkable, but I want to assure them from the outset that the conclusion is not as commonplace as it might appear at first glance.

I divide my discussion into two parts, both of which will be overly brief. The first part will consist of a historical, comparative analysis of commercial organizations. In this section, I argue that Western commerce rested on a completely different organizational matrix from China's. In the West, commercial organizations in the private sphere rested upon legal institutions and upon individualism, neither of which had central importance in China. When the differences between China and the West are examined closely, truly substantial contrasts emerge, contrasts that are unexplained by simple references to the importance in China of family and friends.

In the second part, I argue that kinship and native place collegiality constitute an "institutional medium" out of which people create organized networks. In this regard, kinship and collegiality in China play roles analogous to those played by law and individuality in the West, but with very different developmental trajectories and outcomes. Therefore, to understand commerce in China as an organized activity is to understand how buying and selling is embedded in this institutional medium and is represented organizationally by structured networks.

Changes in Western Commercial Organization

To describe Western commercial organization in just a few pages is, of course, to oversimplify the topic a lot. But all I want to do here is to give a sense of the development and change over time in the institutional context of Western commercial organization.

One can trace the change in commercial organizations in Western Europe from the fall of the Roman Empire to modern times through four basic periods. First, until the twelfth century, commerce was largely embedded in the patrimonial structure of Medieval Europe. To be more precise, economic organization was institutionally fixed in manorial, or what Weber (1988, pp. 92-93) referred to as *oikos* (i.e., household) economies. The Mediterranean economies of antiquity as well as the European feudal economies rested upon the patrimonial preferences of the landed nobility, which included kings and church prelates as well. Heads of households claimed full authority over the livelihood of those falling within their patriarchal jurisdiction, which included a full range of slaves, servants, and serfs, in addition to those related by blood and marriage. Rulers of kingdoms and empires and heads of religious groups modeled themselves as patriarchs, often in competition with the landed aristocracy.

When commercial activity was embedded in patrimonial institutions, it was, in a sense, all private. This included inter-regional trade as well. Just like local economic activity, non-local (i.e., inter-household) trade was subsumed within the households of powerful individuals, particularly the royal families. For instance, the rulers and their personal (i.e., patrimonial) staffs favored internationally mobile dependent merchants, primarily foreign and Jewish groups, as the means to organize those spheres of economic activity under their household control.

The second period of change occurred roughly from the twelfth until the sixteenth century. During this period we see a shift away from commercial organizations embedded in patrimonial household economies to those based upon commercial organizations set in independent urban enclaves. In part, the competition among contenders for power in the Middle Ages allowed for the development of chartered cities that became institutional arenas falling outside the normal control of patrimonial authorities.[1] The growth of independent cities was sufficiently widespread and was of such importance that, by the fourteenth century, there began to be decisive shifts in the institutional arenas of Western commerce. The main shift was from an institutional arena where all economic activity was dominated by great households, which included the royal households, to a reemergence of a public sphere, in which the king's household moved from a private concern to represent the body politic (Kantorowicz 1957; Poggi 1978; Strayer 1970). The king's administration, as well as chartered cities, became public domains, and insofar as commerce was regulated through guild organizations, the legitimacy of those controls was mediated through public collectivities as certified by a royal charter.

The best indication of this shift in the high Middle Ages occurred when rulers in Western Europe began to favor native merchants, to support local guild structures, and to ban foreign merchants (Beardwood 1931). The reasons for this shift are complex and do not have to do entirely with the quickening tempo of commerce or with urban growth. Of course, the shift in royal patronage from foreign to local merchants resulted not only because of the contentiousness of local merchants, but also because rulers in the long run gained greater revenues from local than from foreign merchants. Foreign merchants paid license fees and were vulnerable to bribes, whereas native merchants paid sales taxes.[2] But the shift also reflected a more comprehensive trend that resulted from state building efforts that transformed the royal households, moving them from strictly patrimonial holdings to public spheres. As Kantorowicz (1957) shows so aptly, kings during this period came to represent the public body. The legal system based on this reconceptualization and adapted from Roman legal codes in part followed from, and in part promoted this trend (Anderson 1978, 1979). Similarly, chartered cities became caught up in this reconceptualization; in effect everything that was not private and manorial became public and incorporated into a national order.

The third major shift occurred gradually between the sixteenth and the eighteenth centuries with the development and spread of state sponsored companies (Braudel 1982; Cole 1971). This shift coincided with the rise of absolute monarchies and their mercantilistic policies. On the domestic scene, the local economy became privatized. Cities lost their independence from state control and became absorbed into the legal framework of the state. In this context, urban guilds, too, lost their independent authority to regulate trade and industry. They became organizations of private interests that collapsed as the collectivities ceased to legitimate public interests. Moreover, the collapse of guilds altered the relations between urban centers and rural hinterlands. Without guild restrictions, urban merchants began to nurture rural connections, setting off the proto-industrialization that occurred throughout northwestern Europe during this period.

The major shift of the period, however, occurred on the international scene. The state fostered the international economy as a large public realm over which kings, as the representatives of the public, claimed the right to organize. The states granted trading licenses and land charters to groups of local adventurers in order to create greater national wealth from colonial gains. States served as the organizational site for public companies, such as the East India Company. These companies actively sought mercantilistic advantages for each nation. Internationally, it was a period of adventure capitalism in which large scale sporadic commercial activity was embedded in state institutions and, just like the military, became a part of "public" policy (Curtin 1984; Jones 1987, pp. 104-149; Hobsbawn 1968, p. 42).

In the fourth period of change, between the eighteenth and the twentieth centuries, domestic and international economic activities were privatized and became inexorably intertwined.[3] The key economic actors were private citizens and individual firms. State legal institutions, put in place to guarantee the political rights of citizens also guaranteed their economic rights to own property and to enter contracts. During this period, all the market institutions with which we are now familiar came into being. Large multi-divisional corporations, banks, stock markets, insurance companies all became institutionalized fixtures of a private economy.[4]

The market economy as we know it today is a social and political invention of the last three centuries. It is neither an evolutionary outcome of market forces, nor a "natural" result, as Adam Smith put it, of the propensity to truck and barter. Moreover, the economic conception of a self-interested rational economic actor is not universal fiction; it is a European fiction, entirely a product of Western enlightenment thought that was enacted through political legislation and embodied in economic institutions.[5] Western politicians and economic actors constructed in reality the idea of a free market economy, and with this construction in mind they reinterpreted the public and private spheres and reassigned the private sphere – within the institutional arena of individual rights guaranteed through public laws – the prerogative to organize the economy.

The dramatic changes in commercial organizations through Western history – from their embeddedness in patrimonial prerogative to their embeddedness in laws regulating free individuals – mark the changes in the institutional character of Western society, and each change necessitated a reconfiguration in commercial organizations. One should, however, not overstate the ideological content of these shifts as much as the organizational consequences. Many analysts celebrate the rise of freedom and of legality without recognizing that these same general principles that once applied only to patriarchal lords now expanded, in ever more generalized forms, to individuals under all forms of economic and political conditions. What occurred was not so much an absolute change in the principles of organization, as in the institutional arenas in which those principles were enacted. At least since the rise of urban commercial centers in the high middle ages, the two main cornerstones of Western economies were the ability of individuals to exercise of their individual will, apart from all others (e.g., rights to and over private property and rights to make contracts), and the existence of commercial institutions built on and protected by the state's legal institutions.

For all its complexity and dynamism, the Chinese economy during the imperial period, from 221 BC to 1911 AD, was characterized by neither of these two cornerstones.

Changes in Chinese Economic Organization

By late imperial times, Chinese society had developed a complex market economy: Commodities were traded in marketplaces and prices of commodities (including the prices of land, labor, and capital) were not officially set, but rather were established through processes of buying and selling. The organizing principles of, as well as actual institutions supporting China's vast market economy, however, differed greatly from those found in the West.

The difference in the organizing principles is crucial for understanding the Chinese economy in the imperial era. In the West, economic organization always cohered around those who controlled access to economic sectors and who had jurisdiction over economic institutions. This was always a question of domination, of who had the political power to regulate and to profit from the economy. It is significant that only in the period of constitutional governments did citizens emerge with more or less exclusive rights to unfettered access to the economy, where they could profit as much as they could profit, where they could control as much as they could control within the law.

In China, however, domination and control, on the one hand, and individualism bound only by laws, on the other, are foreign. In China the emphasis was always upon harmony, upon a relational order which solicits obedience to those relationships. Joseph Needham (1956, p. 582) makes the following point:

The Chinese notion of Order positively excluded the [Western] notion of Law... The Chinese world-view depended upon a totally different line of thought [from the law-based world-view developed in the West]. The harmonious cooperation of all beings arose, not from the orders of a superior authority external to themselves, but from the fact that [the Chinese] were all parts in a hierarchy of wholes forming a cosmic pattern, and what they obeyed were the internal dictates of their own natures.

This point cannot be emphasized enough. Chinese organizational principles rest upon inviolate social relationships; people must obey the "internal dictates" of those relationships.[6] In Chinese, the obligation to obey is called *xiao*, loosely translated as filial piety. The important point here is that within Chinese cosmology, there is no theoretical or practical way to separate "humanness" – that is, the essential character of humanity – from relationships. In contrast, in the West, humanness was always connected with the divine, with individual eternal salvation, and hence, in theory, the individual was always set apart from earthly relationships.

The Chinese emphasis on a hierarchy of ordered relationships and on harmony among those relationships formed a powerful world view for creating social and political institutions. The Chinese imperial economy had always been embedded in institutions of order. The crucial issue in the Chinese setting is not the Western question of who had control over the economy or over economic institutions. Instead, the crucial issue for China was how should the world, including the economy, be harmoniously arranged, and how could people's livelihood be guaranteed, for people's livelihood is the basis for world order. For the Chinese, in principle, everyone always has a part to play in creating and maintaining economic harmony.

Now we can turn to the institutional enactments of these briefly outlined organizational principles. As with the West, the development of a Chinese market economy was not a product of an evolutionary process, but rather its formation was marked by a series of rather sharp institutional shifts and, between these shifts, by long periods of incremental change. If we just consider the imperial period, we can identify three major shifts in the institutionalized arrangements designed to achieve economic harmony in the empire.

In each of these shifts, approximately the same set of actors were involved. The responsibilities for the economy were divided among the three social strata that created the hierarchy of relationships for order in imperial China: the emperor and his imperial household, the official governing apparatus, and the commoners. Early in the imperial period, contending groups settled on a roughly defined division of labor designed to establish and maintain economic order.[7] The emperor was responsible for coordinating the relations between China, the "middle kingdom" (*zhongguo*), and the rest of the world (*tianxia*). Accordingly, the imperial household organized all "international" economic exchanges and set up "markets" run by imperial household personnel to facilitate imports and exports. The imperial household also established official monopolies in a few essential commodities, such as salt and copper trade, that were widely distributed but centrally controlled.[8]

The second group having economic responsibilities were the scholars/officials. By long tradition, outer court officials who governed China through an administrative apparatus had the duty to maintain economic order within their areas of responsibility. Their primary responsibility concerned the collection and redistribution of the empire's basic foodstuffs, particularly rice. They collected taxes in kind, and they established a national granary systems to regulate the price of rice and to provide insurance against natural disasters (Wong 1982). They did not have the duty to intervene directly in the economy, but rather had the duty to correct those situations likely to lead to disorder.

The third status group, the commoners, had the primary responsibility for all basic economic activities. The commoner status group was divided into functional categories ranked according to their centrality for maintaining economic order. The normative order prescribed the following hierarchy: Scholars ranked first, because they taught people social responsibility, without which no order was possible at all; peasants ranked second, because they grew the staples of life; artisans ranked third, because they manufactured the material goods needed to live decently and to be productive; and merchants ranked last, because they only moved and sold things abundant in one area to other areas where they were less abundant. In practice, of course, there was in all periods much diversity in how people actually ranked, and in the last dynasties, with the ruralization of China's market economy, there was so much mobility across categories that the merchant status group lost whatever stigma it had in earlier times.

As in the West, the fundamental changes that occurred during long historical periods were not so much changes in the principles of organization as they were changes in the institutional arenas in which the principles themselves were enacted. In the first period, roughly from the Han to the beginning of the Song dynasties (202 BC-960 AD), the strategy to maintain economic harmony was embedded in a society organized largely around heredity. This was the period in which Chinese state and society consisted of a political division between great families and the imperial household. The great families were large land controlling lineages whose members had exclusive access to education, to public office, to much of the society's wealth, and to upper class marriage partners, thus being able to perpetuate themselves. The imperial strategy to maintain order and continuity in a society largely hereditary was to forbid commoners from changing the economic categories of their birth and to regulate closely the economic activities of people in those categories. To this end, as Denis Twitchett (1968, p. 69) states, "the most important form of government control [upon merchants and artisans] was the system of official markets."[9] A geographical area was set aside in all major cities for merchants and artisans, who were required to live and work in such an area and to dress according to their social status. In the international and capital markets, special government officials – usually inner court officials – had the duty to supervise all aspects of manufacture and business, including sumptuary regulations.

The second period of change began in the late Tang and continued through the Song dynasties, roughly from the eighth to the thirteenth centuries. During this period, the hereditary privileges of the great families gradually declined, and with that decline came the end of formal constraints of social mobility for commoners. The official market system of the Tang period disappeared and in its place arose an urban-centered economy resting largely on urban oriented institutions, and regulated by outer court officials and by an extensive system of brokers. Officials supported the development of strong urban merchant associations (*hang*), and through them they supervised all aspects of trade and manufacture. In addition, through the *hang* head men, officials collected revenues that consisted primarily of transit and sales taxes. By the time of the Southern Sung dynasty, the government had established one or more tax stations in 1,431 major cities throughout China, and collected a large percentage of all taxes from commerce (Ma 1971, p. 66).

The third period of change began in the Ming and continued through the Qing dynasties, roughly from the fourteenth through the nineteenth centuries. The Song economic institutions were largely destroyed during the Mongol conquest, which not only wiped out many urban centers and the trading patterns within them, but also systematically elevated non-Chinese merchant groups to commercial prominence (Endicott-West 1989). With the founding of the Ming dynasty, the institutional focus turned away from an urban centered economy, as it was in the Song, toward a rural centered economy. In the beginning, peasant self-sufficiency was the goal of the first Ming emperor, who limited the presence of officials in the

countryside and who reduced their role in land and commercial taxation.[10] Moreover, he began to eliminate systematically the large land owning elites, killing
some and disbursing many.

This shift in institutional focus strengthened non-elitist local rural associations,
especially lineage organizations. There is now considerable evidence to show that
the patrilineal, patrilocal structure of Chinese society stems largely from Ming
times, rather than from earlier periods.[11] As a complex marketing system developed in the late Ming and Qing periods, its economic organizations were, accordingly, extensions or adaptations of the institutions of rural society, particularly in
the form of networks spawned by ties of kinship and of common regional origin.

The strategy of maintaining economic harmony in the Ming and Qing periods
did not rest upon regulating commoner mobility, as it did from the Han to the
Tang; nor did it rest upon the government creating and maintaining urban market institutions, as it did during the Song period. Instead, in the last two dynasties, the government strategy was to create and supervise self-regulating (what
Susan Mann calls liturgical) associations designed to strengthen orthodoxy in social relationships.[12] As Kwang-Ching Liu (1990) put it, the government's strategy
in this period was to rule through culture.

Regional Relationships and Family Firms in the Conduct of Modern Chinese Business

This has been a long introduction to my explanation of the roles of regional and
kinship relations in Chinese business, but I have framed my topic in this way to
emphasize the similarities and differences between China and the West. In both locations vast economic changes have occurred, but the changes result more from
shifting institutional focuses than from alterations in the basic principles of social organization. Moreover, in both locations the institutional focus has shifted
from state centered institutions to commoner – or citizen – centered institutions.
In modern times, the private sphere in both locations has become the focal point
of economic action and of independent economic decision-making. But the similarities between the two locations stop here. The way commoners in China and
citizens in the West expanded their economic potential could not have been more
different. In this final section, I want briefly to describe these differences, by looking at the organization of markets in both locations.

Over the course of the nineteenth century, Western market economies developed distinctive market institutions that rested upon the legal rights of individuals
and that coordinated the exercise of individual wills. The direction of changes in
market institutions standardized the rules of economic competition and regulated
the relations among individual players. With the rules of fair play legalistically es-

tablished by the state, market players could compete to the end, with the winners taking everything and the losers going bankrupt.

The crucial point of contrast with the Chinese case is the role of the Western state. Following a long tradition, the Western state, through its legal framework, took charge of the standardization process and guaranteed the institutional structure of fair play. Moreover, the entire logic, and indeed the actual direction, of lawmaking for the economy, as in other institutional spheres, has been to consider individualized players and to make the rules apply equally to all.

In China, over the course of the Ming and Qing dynasties, the Chinese market economy also developed distinctive sets of market institutions. These institutions, however, rested upon regional and kinship relations. The institutions themselves, some of which I will describe below, were individually created and guaranteed through state sponsored groups, that is, through various kinds of self-regulating kinship and commercial associations. The state did not intervene in this process and did not attempt to standardize or otherwise systematize the results. The state's interest in market institutions was primarily to preserve order in society, and it did this by upholding the ethical demands of social relationships, which in turn strengthened the manner in which liturgical groups defined the same social relationships.

These points are admittedly abstract, so let me now specify them. One should think of Chinese market institutions as resting on two types of social relationships, those of collegiality and those of kinship.[13] The ordering principles of these were suggested by the *wulun*, the five relationships specified in Confucian writings, but in actual practice the meanings of these relationships were worked out in practicing groups, and differed somewhat throughout China. The crucial point for this discussion is that the relationships of collegiality and kinship spawned two types of economic networks, both of which played important roles in China's market economy. To oversimplify the case a bit, one can say that collegiality in China plays a role analogous to law in the West, whereas kinship plays a role analogous to individualism. A further explanation is in order.

Like law, collegiality served as the force to guarantee creditable market behavior. The state in China did not standardize weights and measures, did not back its own currency, did not enforce *a priori* the validity of contracts, and did not support credit institutions. In fact the state supplied none of the institutional supports that form the bedrock of Western market economies. Instead, in China, it was merchant associations that made the market predictable and continuous.[14]

The character of Chinese merchant associations differed from the guilds of medieval Europe. European guilds were organizations of local merchants that set the conditions of trade in their hometowns. Chinese commercial associations, however, were organizations of non-local merchants and artisans. In the Ming/Qing period they were often associations of non-local people coming from the same regional area. These associations were called *huiguan*, and as many have shown, this type of regional association became a dominant force in commerce only in the late Ming and Qing dynasties (Ho 1966; Liu 1988). They are urban manifestations of a fundamentally rural society. As shown elsewhere (Hamilton 1979), such regional associations are commonplace organizational devices used throughout the modern Third World by temporary rural-to-urban migrants. There were also many commercial associations in China that were not called *huiguan*, but even these typically had regional underpinnings, because regional collegiality was among the most binding of all social relationships other than kinship and, as Fei Xiaotong (1992) argues, making alliances based upon one's regional origins is, in fact, an extension of kin relationships.

Of particular importance in China, however, was the role that these regional associations played in urban areas. As Susan Mann (1987) shows, such merchant groups paid taxes through their association. But more important than this, the groups also had the liturgical function to stabilize the marketplace for continuous buying and selling. Each group established its own weights and measures, fixed its own prices, and otherwise established an entire set of rules governing the economic behavior of its members. Should violations of these rules occur, the groups had the capacity to sanction individual members.

In the late imperial period, then, regional collegiality was an established type of social relationship that people could draw upon (*la guanxi*) for their personal interests. As such, it represented an institutionalized medium, on the basis of which all types of people could organize groups. Unlike Western groups, in which you are either a member or you are not, Chinese groups resemble networks of people linked together through social relationships and are without formal boundaries. Regional collegiality, in fact, was a type of social relationship that had no exact meaning assigned to it, and in fact its definition varied wherever groups formed. Sometimes a home town, sometimes a home district, sometimes a home province, and other times an entire region served as the definition of regionality (Hamilton 1985). Whatever the definition, however, belongingness was always a function of actual social relationships among people. The actual networks defined the groups, and actual social relationships defined the extent and the content of a morality founded upon the regional bond.

Now let us turn to the second type of social relationship underpinning Chinese market institutions. Collegial relations formed the foundations for merchant and artisan associations; kinship relations formed the foundations for family firms. The network spawned by regional collegiality built trust and predictability in the marketplace, but the network spawned by kinship created reciprocal economic advantages. On the surface, this second relationship, the ties of kinship, would seem to be similar to that found in the West. After all, as Alfred D. Chandler (1977) shows, the "traditional" business organization in the West was the family firm. But the closer we look at Western and Chinese family firms, the more we realize that they are products of very different family structures which are embedded in very different institutional environments.

For the West, the traditional family firm is, in truth, the personal property of one individual, the head of the household, the patriarch. The family firm was the individual unit of competition in the marketplace, and the owner could exercise his right over the firm as if it were an extension of his household. The development of corporate law, of course, separated business property from personal property, but this separation rested on the notion that the corporation itself acted as an individual, and that the owners of the corporation, regardless of their numbers, represented that singular individual.

In China, however, families rest on social relationships and not on the patriarchal structure of authority and ownership that occurs in the West. As Fei Xiaotong (1992, p. 14) has so nicely described it, "families in the West are organizations with distinct boundaries," but in China families (*jia*) are ambiguous, without exact boundaries, because the scope of who is included within any one family "can be expanded or contracted according to the specific time and place." In reality, families in China represent networks of people joined together by specific sets of familial relationships. The closer the kinship tie, the more binding the obligation to obey the requirements of hierarchical relationships within the family. Hugh Baker (1979, pp. 15-16) describes the kinship "pecking-order" as resting on three types of superiority/inferiority relationships: "generation, age, and sex." "Theoretically," he says, "any one person should know precisely where he stands in the family by referring to this order: there is a water tight chain of relationships which makes clear to whom each owes respect and obedience." In China, no one person controls the family, but all are obligated within its networks.

In China, the organization of the family and the organization of the family firm overlap (Hamilton and Kao 1990). The Chinese family firm is represented by a series of relationships that can be expanded or contracted depending upon time and place. The boundaries of what should be included in the firm are often ambiguous because they are not defined explicitly by property, ownership, or control. Instead, the boundaries are defined by networks of people linked together by social relationships. Not all the people so linked would be related through some kinship tie, but they might be. For instance, in a small firm all workers might be part of the same extended family: grandparents, parents and children. If, however, the firm were prosperous, some more distant members of the family, as well as unrelated people, might be added.

Chinese family firms, however, typically do not grow large, but rather remain small.[15] There are two general reasons for this. First, Chinese practice partible inheritance, with each son receiving an equal portion of his father's estate. Because of this practice, it is difficult to maintain a large firm over several generations. Large firms would eventually be split into smaller firms. Second, given the first reason, a common strategy for prosperous families was to start multiple businesses. It seems likely that these multiple business would draw upon kinship ties in an effort to create a network of mutually supporting firms, each of which would be run by individuals linked through a kinship network.

These networks of personal advantage enable people to invest in a range of businesses and to establish areas of economic concentration. But it does not allow for single individuals to own it all. The logic of network building at both the kinship and regional level prevents economic monopolization in a Western sense. On the one hand, in China, the network-based market economy rested on reciprocal relationships. The ethics of these relationships formed the rules of the economic game, so to violate the relationships, and hence to seek unfair advantage, was to jeopardize one's credibility in the marketplace, which was tantamount to financial ruin. On the other hand, in the West, the firm-based market economy rested on impersonal laws and individual competition. Even among friends, it was a winner-take-all environment. Seeking morally unfair advantage in the West has always been legally okay.

Unlike in the West, individual family firms are not the basic unit of the Chinese imperial and modern economies. Rather the basic units are the networks spawned by regional collegiality and by kinship. These networks formed the organizational structure of the Chinese imperial economy, and as the opportunities for economic gain grew over time, the networks expanded and carried ever increasing levels of commercial activities. By the nineteenth century, the opportunities greatly enlarged with the contacts with Western economies. Following these opportunities, the Chinese expanded their economic networks throughout China, into Southeast Asia, and in large urban enclaves through much of the world. Because these networks build on trust and on reciprocal economic advantage, they largely bypass Western market institutions that lodge trust in laws and seek economic advantage only in economies of scale and in individual entrepreneurship.

Notes

[1] This is substantially Weber's conclusion (1968, pp. 1212-1374) in his analysis of the European city, which he terms a case of "non-legitimate domination." Also see Henri Pirenne (1952) and Paul M. Hohenberg and Lynn Hollen Lees (1985: Part One, pp. 1-98).

[2] For a nice comparison along these lines, see Koebner (1964).

[3] This privatization occurred in Western Europe, and coincided with the development of the opposite response in the form of communism and socialist solutions to a privatized economy.

[4] For a recent descriptions, see Charles A. Jones (1987).

[5] For insight into the creation of market institutions, see Hirschman (1977).

[6] This is spelled out in more detail in Hamilton (1984, 1990).

[7] These debates, which occurred in the Han Dynasty (206 BC-220 AD) are recorded in the *Discourses on Salt and Iron* (Gale 1973).

[8] Emperors also set aside imperial household estates and established imperial household factories to care for household requirements, which also included revenues for

the privy purse. For all imperial household ventures, the dominant principle of organization stressed dependency between the emperor and persons in charge of the activities. Equally, ties of kinship and of collegiality based upon regional origin, while by no means absent, were unacceptable principles for organizing activities. A few examples will suffice. Throughout most of the Ming dynasty, eunuchs, literally cut off from family and regional ties, were the primary persons who ran and sometimes staffed the core household activities, including the imperial monopolies. The Qing emperors used eunuchs less extensively than did the Ming emperors, but still relied on them, as well as other types of personal dependents such as bondservants and their fellow Manchus, to run the entire spectrum of household activities. Qing emperors placed such dependents in charge of the imperial factories and estates.

[9] Peasants were controlled through a complex tax and residency system. See Denis Twitchett (1963, pp. 63-95).

[10] For a good account of the Ming tax system, see Huang (1974).

[11] For a survey of the literature, see Watson (1982).

[12] I use the term "liturgical" following Weber's meaning: "For the ruler liturgical methods mean that he secures the fulfillment of obligations through the creation of heteronomous and often heterocephalous associations held accountable for them" (1968, p. 1022). The *lichia* and *baochia* systems of control are only two examples of a broad range of liturgical associations supported during the Ming/Qing period, including lineage councils and various kinds of merchant associations. Also see Susan Mann's (1987) use of the concept.

[13] The ordering principles were those of *sangang* and *wulun,* the three bonds and the five relationships. Cemented by strictures of *xiao* (filial piety), these relationships were inviolate, as sacred as a person's relationship to God was in the West. All persons were enjoined to define themselves entirely in terms of their permanent social relationships and to fulfill the obligations of those relationships. There was no transcendental route of escape from these relationships, as there was in the West, so that the only sources of superior fitness became defined as complete selflessness in *situ.* The virtuous widow, the filial son, the upright official – all could achieve sagehood, but only in place. For a fuller description of the relationship between ancestor worship, lineage organization, and egalitarian religion, see Schwartz (1985, pp. 26-29).

[14] For a more complete analysis of this point, see Hamilton (1985).

[15] For a fine analysis of the dynamics of Chinese firms, see Wong Siu-lun (1985).

References

Anderson, Perry. 1978. *Passages from Antiquity to Feudalism.* London: Verso.

Anderson, Perry. 1979. *Lineages of the Absolutist State.* London: Verso.

Baker, Hugh. 1979. *Chinese Family and Kinship.* New York: Columbia University Press.

Beardwood, Alice. 1931. *Alien Merchants in England, 1350-1377, Their Legal and Economic Position.* Cambridge, Mass.: The Mediaeval Academy of America.

Braudel, Fernand. 1982. *The Wheels of Commerce.* New York: Harper and Row.

Chandler, Alfred D. 1977. *The Visible Hand.* Cambridge, Mass.: Harvard University Press.

Cole, Charles Woolsey. 1971. *French Mercantilism, 1683-1700*. New York: Octagon Books.

Curtin, Philip D. 1984. *Cross-Cultural Trade in World History*. Cambridge, UK: Cambridge University Press.

Endicott-West, Elizabeth. 1989. "Merchant Associations in Yuan China." *Asia Major* (Third Series) 2 (2): 127-154.

Fei, Xiaotong. 1992. *From the Soil: The Foundations of Chinese Society*. Berkeley: University of California Press.

Gale, Esson M. 1973. *Discourses on Salt and Iron: A Debate on State Control of Commerce and Industry in Ancient China*. Taipei: Ch'eng-wen Publishing.

Hamilton, Gary G. 1979. "Regional Associations and the Chinese City." *Comparative Studies in Society and History* 21 (3): 338-353.

Hamilton, Gary G. 1984. "Patriarchalism in Imperial China and Western Europe: A Revision of Weber's Sociology of Domination." *Theory and Society* 13 (3): 393-426.

Hamilton, Gary G. 1985. "Why No Capitalism in China." Andreas E. Buss (ed.), *Max Weber in Asian Studies*. Leiden: E.J. Brill.

Hamilton, Gary G. 1990. "Patriarchy, Patrimonialism and Filial Piety: A Comparison of China and Western Europe." *British Journal of Sociology* 41 (1): 77-104.

Hamilton, Gary G. and Cheng-shu Kao. 1990. "The Institutional Foundations of Chinese Business: The Family Firm in Taiwan." *Comparative Social Research* 12: 95-112.

Hirschman, Albert. 1977. *Passion and the Interests*. Princeton: Princeton University Press.

Ho, Ping-ti. 1966. *Zhongguo Huiguan Shihlun*. Taipei: Taiwan hsueh sheng shu chu.

Hobsbawm, Eric J. 1968. *Industry and Empire*. New York: Penguin.

Hohenberg, Paul M. and Lynn Hollen Lees. 1985. *The Making of Urban Europe, 1008-1950*. Cambridge, Mass.: Harvard University Press.

Huang, Ray. 1974. *Taxation and Governmental Finance in Sixteenth-Century Ming China*. Cambridge, UK: Cambridge University Press.

Jones, Charles A. 1987. *International Business in the Nineteenth Century*. New York: New York University Press.

Jones, Eric J. 1987. *The European Miracle: Environments, Economies, and Geopolitics in the History of Europe and Asia*. Cambridge, UK: Cambridge University Press.

Kantorowicz, Ernst H. 1957. *The King's Two Bodies: A Study of Mediaeval Political Theology*. Princeton: Princeton University Press.

Koebner, Richard. 1964. "German Towns and Slave Markets." *Change in Medieval Society*, ed. Sylvia L. Thrupp. New York: Appleton-Century-Crofts.

Kriedte, Peter, Hans Medick, and Jürgen Schlumbohm. 1981. *Industrialization Before Industrialization*. Cambridge, UK: Cambridge University Press.

Kriedte, Peter. 1983. *Peasants, Landlords, and Merchants Capitalists: Europe and the World Economy, 1500-1800*. Cambridge, UK: Cambridge University Press.

Liu, Kwang-Ching. 1988. "Chinese Merchants Guilds: An Historical Inquiry." *Pacific Historical Review* 57 (1): 1-23.

Liu, Kwang-Ching. 1990. *Orthodoxy in Imperial China*. Berkeley: University of California Press.

Ma, Laurence J.C. 1971. *Commercial Development and Urban Change in Sung China (960-1279)*. Ann Arbor: University of Michigan, Michigan Geographical Publication No. 6.

Mann, Susan. 1987. *Local Merchants and the Chinese Bureaucracy, 1750-1950*. Stanford: Stanford University Press.

Needham, Joseph. 1956. *Science and Civilisation in China.* Vol. 2. Cambridge, UK: Cambridge University Press.

Pirenne, Henri. 1952. *Medieval Cities: Their Origins and the Revival of Trade.* Princeton: Princeton University Press.

Poggi, Gianfranco. 1978. *The Development of the Modern State.* Stanford: Stanford University Press.

Schwartz, Benjamin I. 1985. *The World of Thought in Ancient China.* Cambridge, Mass: Harvard University Press.

Strayer, Joseph R. 1970. *On the Medieval Origins of the Modern State.* Princeton: Princeton University Press.

Twitchett, Denis. 1963. *Financial Administration under the T'ang Dynasty.* Cambridge, UK: Cambridge University Press.

Twitchett, Denis. 1968. "Merchants, Trade, and Government in Late T'ang." *Asia Major* 14 (1): 63-95.

Watson, James L. 1982. "Chinese Kinship Reconsidered: Anthropological Perspectives on Historical Research." *China Quarterly* 92: 589-622.

Weber, Max. 1968. *Economy and Society.* New York: Bedminster Press.

Weber, Max. 1988. *The Agrarian Sociology of Ancient Civilizations.* London: Verso.

Wong, R. Bin. 1982. "Food Riots in the Qing Dynasty." *Journal of Asian Studies* 41 (4): 767-788.

Wong, Siu-lun. 1985. "The Chinese Family Firm: A Model." *British Journal of Sociology* 36 (1): 58-72.

B. Chinese Business Networks in Taiwan,
   Hong Kong, and Singapore

"Personal Trust" in the Large Businesses in Taiwan: A Traditional Foundation for Contemporary Economic Activities[1]

Kao Cheng-shu

Introduction

In this paper I am trying to offer an analysis of the role that "personal trust" plays in Taiwan's large businesses. Hopefully, this analysis will enhance better understanding of Taiwan's socio-economic structure. In the past few years, there have been many studies that have tried to explain Taiwan's dramatic economic success. Most of these studies examine Taiwan's experience from various perspectives, including Confucian ethics, macro-economies, world-system analysis, political economy, social class analysis, and dependency theory.[2] These works have provided some explanations; nevertheless, what they gain in breadth, they lose in depth. What the research team at Tunghai University is trying to do is to obtain an in-depth understanding of the way the economy actually works in Taiwan. Most micro-economic and micro-social details of Taiwan's businesses remain unclear.

Recently, however, a few scholars have begun to pay attention to these aspects (Greenhalgh 1988; Hamilton and Kao 1987, 1990; Lam 1989; Numazaki 1987; Peng 1989). These writers point out the important roles which families and interpersonal networks play in Taiwan's economic development. Although many of these writers correctly recognize families and networks as the basic social institutions of Taiwan's businesses, they seem to suggest that this explanation merely holds for small and medium sized businesses. Some argue when firms grow beyond a certain size, it is necessary to adopt a new set of organizational and institutional principles (Huang 1988; Li and Cheng 1987). From their point of view, familial institutions are "modernizing" rapidly, and their significance in the economy will diminish very soon (Galenson 1979). These arguments, however, tend not to be supported by detailed research and tend to underestimate the importance of social and cultural legacies.

Beginning in February 1987, the Institute of East Asian Social Development at Tunghai University has conducted a research project on "The Institutional Foundations of Chinese Business." Since that period, we have gathered extensive interview data on 55 large businesses in Taiwan (including such enterprise groups such as Tatung, Far Eastern, Acer, Hsin Kwang, Rebar, Pacific, Tainan Textiles, and President).[3] In the interviews, our research team discovered that familial re-

lationships and networks still prevail and are critically important to the operation
of large businesses.

Recently, Gary Hamilton (1989) called the Chinese type of capitalism in Taiwan, "*guanxi* capitalism." It is crucial to point out that *guanxi* is extremely important in business ownership and management (Peng 1989). The businesses in
Taiwan are primarily based on personal connections among businessmen and families. In his study of enterprise groups in Taiwan, Ichiro Numazaki (1987) insists
that enterprise groups are not independent actors, rather they are "embedded" in a
web of partnerships. I agree with these writers. However, if we want to understand
the networks (*guanxi*) and partnerships, as well as *how and why* they work as they
do, then we must also understand the underlying mechanism that allows the economy to work this way. In our studies, we have found that "personal trust" is one of
the key mechanisms upon which *guanxi* and partnerships are based. Without understanding these values and the processes associated with them that have come
out of Chinese tradition, an adequate analysis of Chinese businesses is impossible.

Personal Trust in Business Organization

When we interviewed the board directors and the general managers of the large
businesses, we asked them to tell us the major criteria for recruiting people and for
selecting business partners. Almost without exception, they said "personal trust"
is the first principle. When they select the managerial personnel for the firm, professional competence and experience are certainly important, but "personal trust"
is the necessary condition. It seems not to be feasible for an employer to hire a top
manager with whom he is not familiar. In other words, this person must be either
personally known by the boss (*laoban*) or be introduced by a person whom the
boss trusts. It is exceptional for someone to obtain a high position by virtue of his
professional competence alone. In some cases, he might be put into a middle level
position at the beginning; after a period of time, if he is able to demonstrate his
loyalty, then he becomes "trustworthy," and he has a chance to be promoted.

Interestingly enough, we observed that even sons and relatives of the boss have
to undergo this same process. Usually, for example, the apparent successor is put
into a medium-high position for the first two or three years. Then when he becomes familiar with the operation of the business and with the key personnel, he
will rise to a higher position. The reason for this process is that in order to become
the leader of the organization, the successor-to-be needs not only the *laoban*'s
trust, but also the trust of other key people. Without this support, his leadership
will be ineffective. In our cases, many successors took years to rise to the top position.

Externally, when a firm or enterprise group seeks a partnership with other people or businesses, the same principle applies. Usually, there will be no cooperation

without intimate *guanxi*. If they want to make a linkage, it is necessary to find the "right" person first. The cooperative inter-business relationship is primarily based upon the personal trust between the two major *laoban*. If this kind of trust exists, the deal is rather easy to make. The lack of inter-business relationships is one of the major reasons that there are so many medium-small size businesses in Taiwan; often they cannot find a trustworthy person with whom to cooperate, so they would rather work by themselves. Even in those large business groups, the core group is usually constituted by family members, good friends, or old colleagues. According to Peng Huei-jen's recent study of the top ninety-seven large business groups, practically speaking and without exception, the core group is formed by people having close personal ties with one another (Peng 1989). From this perspective, it is "personal trust" which makes the network of partnerships actually work.

We do not want to overstate the role of "personal trust," but our analysis clearly shows that it is a necessary condition for doing business. Both within and between business organizations, "personal trust" is a basic organizational principle.

Having stressed the importance of "personal trust," we will now analyze its basic characteristics. This type of "trust" is certainly particularistic, but it is not based upon ascribed relationships alone. Rather, we should stress that it is an achieved relationship. Persons with ascribed relationships have certain advantages in obtaining "personal trust," because they have more opportunities to develop a trusting relationship. However, there is no guarantee that they will be automatically trusted. It depends upon their achievements, upon demonstrating that they can be trusted. Therefore, in Chinese society "trust" is inseparable from "personal intimacy." Although intimacy is not equivalent to "trust," it is a prerequisite.

From this perspective, in contrast to stereotyped impressions, "personal trust" is not purely subjective, affective, and "irrational." In order to obtain "trust," persons have to demonstrate certain qualities according to intersubjective rules. These rules are not objectified, but are usually well recognized by the people involved. Because such informal, rather than formal, rules are used predominantly to regulate business activities, Western contractual relationships do not prevail. Obviously, I am not suggesting that there are no contractual relationships within or between business organizations. The crucial point is that formal contractual rules are not the basic rules making up the structure of the everyday life-world of Taiwan's businesses. Interestingly enough, even for computer firms, unless they are doing business with Westerners, most transactions rest upon "personal trust" instead of formally defined rights and obligations. In other words, businessmen would not sign a contract without "personal trust." A contract without the preexistence of "trust" is merely a piece of paper. Put differently, if "personal trust" exists, the formal contract is not all that necessary, or just serves as a supplementary reminder. One well-known entrepreneur in southern Taiwan told us, "Chinese people simply do not have the habit of observing contracts" (*Society and Economy*, March 1989). Another successful young businessman points out, "It is still quite common to make a deal worth several million dollars just by a telephone call" (*Society and Economy*, June 1989). Because they are so complex, large businesses tend to adopt certain formal rules; nevertheless, "personal trust" in a traditional manner still is the basis for business transactions.

"Personal trust" as a basic rule for interaction has a normative dimension as well. Normally, when one does business with persons whom he trusts, formally defined contracts and rules tend to be considered as insults. People interpret the demand for a formal contract as a sign of "distrust." Formalities are applicable only to unfamiliar people.

From this perspective, we can clearly observe that there is a hierarchical differentiation among personal relationships. Usually, when we talk about personal relationships, we do not differentiate them. But in reality, we notice that successful business relationships are only those that are based on intimate and trustworthy *guanxi*. If we do not make this distinction, *guanxi* would be too general to explain the business world. In this way, having *guanxi* is merely the first step. It is also necessary to develop a kind of reciprocal trust; only then does the personal relationship become functional. Accordingly, we may say that "personal trust" is a fundamental mechanism which makes personal relationships work.

Personal Trust in its Institutional Context

After discussing the role of "personal trust" in its organizational context, we have to put it in a wider institutional framework to understand how and why it works in this manner. As has been pointed out, "firms... are 'embedded' in an institutionalized social order" (Hamilton, Orrù, Biggart 1987). Businesses do not operate in a vacuum. Institutional structure shapes the basic patterns of business, and insofar as personal trust is an organizational principle, it is also supported by the institutional environment. To demonstrate this, I will discuss the role of personal trust in three institutional contexts.

First of all, I will discuss the political structure, which has tremendous impact upon the way businesses operate. Basically, this political system is still a kind of "personal rule." Certainly, there is a parliament, a bureaucracy, and so forth. However, policy making is primarily controlled by a few top officials. From our interviews, businessmen constantly complain that our policy making is rather unpredictable and inconsistent. When the top governmental officials change, policies change, and rules also change. Under the circumstances, businessmen have already learned that they cannot calculate their business future based upon an objective industrial policy. Those having some good connections with important government officials may be able to learn the information in advance and to adapt themselves to future conditions. But for those having no *guanxi*, the way to survive and minimize possible problems is to do business with people whom they can trust. Quite a few studies suggest that personal connections with top government officials are important (Liu 1975). However, according to our interviews, this is not completely true. Although *guanxi* is helpful in some ways, it cannot guarantee success. On the one hand, not all large businessmen have access to those officials who are responsible for making decisions. On the other hand, even if they establish some personal relationships with officials, others may have similar connections. Under these circumstances, *guanxi* becomes neutralized. Given this situation, we should not overemphasize the importance of personal connections between politicians and businessmen. Most of the businessmen say that the most reliable sources of information come from close relationships within and among business organizations. This type of relationship is more predictable, consistent, and controllable.

Secondly, I will discuss the structure of financial institutions. Except for a few local financial establishments, practically speaking, all banks in Taiwan are under the control of the central and provincial governments. Although, the government has recently adopted a policy of liberalization and is considering setting up private banks, the banking system is still part of the administration. Under these circumstances, banks play a controlling, rather than a supporting role. They maintain stability, rather than foster development. According to our interviews, it is a unanimous opinion that banks do not provide prompt support for businesses. Businessmen complain that banks are too conservative and bureaucratic. At best, banks provide some mortgage loans. Credit loans do not exist, because bank managers simply do not want to take the high risk. Taking high risks could jeopardize their careers: because they are civil servants, if they make any mistake, they could be penalized according to civil service law (*Society and Economy*, May 1989).

Certainly, because large businesses have large assets, comparatively speaking, they tend to receive loans easier than do medium or small size enterprises. Nevertheless, large businesses still have to draw financial resources from different places when they need money (Lin 1991). In this context, in order to guarantee the sources of capital investment, businessmen rely heavily upon the private sector, which includes family members, friends, and business partners.

The private sector, therefore, is the most important source of funds for businesses. Under the circumstances, either in capital formation or in investment, businessmen always have to build a back-up system that can support them at the right time and in the right place. In this institutional context, a personal network based upon "personal trust" is the foundation of this back-up system. Since Chinese businessmen are not used to the concept of "credit" in the Western sense, they work, instead, with "personal trust." They certainly like to obtain loans from banks, but in reality, they often need to work things out differently.

I want to point out, however, that the reason for the underdevelopment of credit system is not the responsibility of the banking system alone. Both sides, banks and businesses, constitute and reinforce the existing structure. According to our interviews with the bank managers, banks have their difficulties too (*Society and*

Economy, May 1989). As we have mentioned earlier, Chinese businessmen have
different sets of normative standards. There is a hierarchical differentiation. There
is one set of standards for the "outsider" and another set for those whom they trust.
It is a common practice for most businesses, large or small, to have two or three
accounting books. This practice may not be legally correct, but it is socially and
culturally acceptable. It has been a common habit in the business world for a long
time, long before the Western banking system was introduced. In this perspective, we understand that it is really difficult for clerks to evaluate objectively a
loan project and for the managers to make the right decision unless they personally are well-acquainted with the person. Otherwise, the transaction is risky indeed. Therefore, even when dealing with mortgage loans, a personal relationship
based upon trust is even more important than an "objective" assessment. Relying
upon personal relationships is not merely a matter of emotionality but of rational
calculations.

Finally, I shall discuss the legal system. Almost without exception, businessmen told us that most elements of the existing legal system are either out-of-
date or inapplicable to the operation of businesses (*Society and Economy*, March
1989). Due to the traditional lack of commercial laws and the rapid economic development in Taiwan, there is a tremendous gap between the legal system and
the business world. One typical example is the development of "underground investment companies" that have recently attracted more than sixty billion dollars
(about U.S. $2,400 million) "illegally." The reason why we call them "illegal" is
because there is no applicable rule to regulate them yet. In the past five years, it
has been a booming business. Officially, these investment companies registered
themselves as ordinary companies instead of as financing or banking agencies.
However, in reality, they function as banks. They receive money deposits from
their customers and pay them a very high rate of interest. These companies then
invest their money mostly in the stock market and in real estate. Usually, as long
as the stock and real estate markets are sound, they are able to gain sizable profits
and promptly pay the interests owed to their investors. Through the personal networks of the investors, these companies attract more people and more money. It
is the snow-balling effect that keeps the whole business going.

By 1989, the government had noticed this rather risky development and tried
to curb it. However, since the investors put their money in these companies vol-
untarily and privately, and since these companies pay the investors money in a
so-called bonus, rather than "interest," government officials find it difficult to de-
tect and then prosecute these "illegal" activities. In the spring of 1989, the second
largest investment company, Yong-An business group, ran into financial difficulties and stopped paying investors their monthly "bonus." The whole case quickly
became chaotic and difficult to resolve, because there is no legal protection for
the several thousand investors. The court can help little, since the whole matter
has not been arranged formally and legally, but rather privately and personally.
Until the existing laws regulating banks are updated, the Ministry of Finance and

the law enforcement agencies lack sufficient legal grounds to effectively regulate these new rising underground businesses.

The backwardness and vagueness of Taiwan's laws have certainly created barriers and inconveniences for business. Nevertheless, on the other side of the same coin, the backwardness and vagueness unintentionally provides flexibility. As the general manager of the largest PC board company in Taiwan points out, "Since the government does not intervene, we have enough space to grow" (*Society and Economy*, May 1989). From the businessman's point of view, it would be helpful if the legal system were rational, calculable, and updated; but since changing the system is something beyond their control, they simply have to find ways to minimize their risks and maximize their profits. Again, due to practical needs, businessmen fall back on their trusted personal networks. Since the existing legal system cannot provide protection for the rights of their businesses, "personal trust" is a necessary mechanism to make the world less risky. As quite a few managers suggest, to hire somebody you already know and trust is much safer than to employ someone with whom you are not familiar. Since to develop reciprocal trust takes time and effort, it is a big investment (*Society and Economy*, May 1989). Besides, if something unexpected happens, the existing legal system usually is not able to solve the problem promptly and adequately anyway. Therefore, the best way for executives to manage their businesses is to select a "trustworthy" person at the very beginning. In case anything develops in the wrong way, it is better to find the "right" person to negotiate and settle the problem. This approach is very traditional but also very functional.

Interestingly enough, most of the large businesses do not have legal departments within their organizations. They seldom go to court to settle their disputes. Some of them have advisors for legal affairs, but only for special cases. The largest automobile company in Taiwan, Yue Loong Motor group, was established in 1956, but they only established their legal department three years ago (*Society and Economy*, March 1989). When we asked the general manager of a large computer company about the matter of copyright, he told us, "Going to court not only cannot solve the problems, but also jeopardizes the relationships with other companies, since everybody knows each other" (*Society and Economy*, January 1989). From their perspectives, it is more useful and reliable to manage their businesses through personal relationship based on trust.

Of course, we are not saying that the existing legal system is not functioning at all. As a matter of fact, businessmen also complain that there are too many laws. However, what we stress here is that the ordinary business operation is not based upon following legal rules. Instead, "personal trust" is a major foundation. In this institutional context, businessmen believe that managing things by legal rules costs too much and provides too few benefits. At best, it is one of the last resources.

Concluding Remarks

In conclusion, I want to make several points. First of all, I want to suggest that enterprises, both large and small ones, work within the same social institutional framework. Since the principle of "personal trust" is still prevailing in most of the spheres of our everyday life, businesses are embedded in this order too. Certainly, businesses can always adapt themselves to new rules, but the new pattern is inevitably a fusion or mixture that includes previous ways of doing things. In other words, there will be no quick and total transformation. The prominent role of "personal trust" in contemporary large businesses in Taiwan clearly reveals the inertia of tradition. Any fusion or mixture grows out of such tradition. From our point of view, it is a matter of necessity, not of choice, for businessmen to hold on to the traditional patterns of doing business. Only by investigating the phenomena from an institutional perspective are we able to discover the structure of everyday life and the mechanisms underlying it. The more we understand our daily life, the better we can delimit the structural necessities and our possible choices based upon those necessities. This paper is merely a small step toward this long-term goal.

Secondly, by interpreting Taiwan's business organizations from this perspective, we are able to see how traditional factors, whether they are part of the Confucian culture or not, actually shape the ways businesses work. Now, we are in a better position to go beyond the so-called "Confucian ethic" thesis. Furthermore, analysts suggest that the Chinese way of managing businesses is much too "person-centered." Such people argue that if Taiwan is to modernize its businesses, businessmen should adopt Western legal rules; personal rules are simply too arbitrary, irrational, and emotional. Obviously, this understanding is very naive and stereotyped. These analysts tend to use Western standards to evaluate Chinese businesses, when in fact these standards have grown out of a very different institutional context than that found in Asia. The understanding gained from our research shows that the reality is rather different from what Westerners might imagine. As a matter of fact, "personal trust" is not merely a kind of sentimental tie. Instead, as we have suggested, it is quite instrumentally rational. If we take the existing institutional structure into consideration, then we realize that personal trust can provide businessmen with security, because it is used to reduce risks. Personal trust also provides businesses with flexibility, because it helps to mobilize resources promptly. Lastly it provides predictability, because personal trust has normative rules, which, although they are not formalized, people are still obliged to follow. In this sense, *guanxi* relationships may be "irrational" in a formal sense, but formal rationality has never been the only rationality that makes capitalism work. In reality, modernity everywhere contains simultaneously both the continuity and the transformation of tradition.

Notes

[1] I want to thank Professor Lennet Daigle for his helpful suggestions. In this paper, I share the basic ideas with my assistants in the Institute of East Asian Social Development. I am thankful to Edward Kao for his prompt help too.

[2] For some recent work on linking Confucianism to Taiwan's economic development, see the proceedings of the International Conference on Confucianism and Economic Development in East Asia on May 29-31, 1989, sponsored by Chung-Hua Institution for Economic Research in Taipei. There were more than ten papers including: Ramon Myers, "Ideas, Orientations and Economic Behavior: Confucianism and Chinese Economic Development"; Chung-ying Cheng, "Totality and Mutuality: Confucian Ethics and Economic Development"; Thomas Metzger, "Confucian Culture and Economic Modernization: An Overview of the Issues"; M. J. Levy, Jr., "Confucianism and Modernization"; and John Fei, "Chinese Cultural Values and Industries Capitalism."

[3] These interviews, as well as other relevant material, can be found in Society and Economy, which is a journal published by The Institute of East Asian Social Development at Tunghai University.

References

Galenson, Walter, ed. 1979. *Economic Growth and Structural Change in Taiwan.* Ithaca: Cornell University Press.

Greenhalgh, Susan. 1988. "Families and Networks in Taiwan's Economic Development." *Contending Approaches to the Political Economy of Taiwan,* eds. Edwin Winckler and Susan Greenhalgh. New York: M.E. Sharpe.

Hamilton, Gary G. 1989. "Patterns of Asian Capitalism: The Cases of Taiwan and South Korea." Program in East Asian Culture and Development Research Working Paper Series, No. 28. Davis: Institute of Governmental Affairs, University of California.

Hamilton, Gary G. and Cheng-shu Kao. 1987. "Max Weber and the Analysis of East Asian Industrialization." *International Sociology* 2 (3): 289-300.

Hamilton, Gary G. and Cheng-shu Kao. 1990. "The Institutional Foundations of Chinese Business: The Family Firm in Taiwan." *Comparative Social Research* 12: 95-112.

Hamilton, Gary, Marco Orrù, and Nicole Biggart. 1987. "Enterprise Groups in East Asia: An Organizational Analysis. *Shoken Keizai* 161: 78-106.

Huang, Kwang-kuo. 1988. "The Modernization of Chinese Family Enterprise." *The Chinese Power Game,* ed. Huang Kwang-kuo. Taipei: Chu-li Publishing.

Lam, Danny Kin-kon. 1989. "Guerrilla Capitalism: Export Oriented Firms and the Economic Miracle in Taiwan (1973-1987)." *Journal of Sunology: A Social Science Quarterly* 4 (1).

Li, Kou-ting and Cheng, Mou-tsai. 1987. *The Strategy of Our Country's Economic Development.* Taipei, Taiwan: Lien Ching Publishing Co.

Lin, Pao-an. 1991. "The Social Sources of Capital and Investment in Taiwan's Industrialization." *Business Networks and Economic Development in East and Southeast Asia,* ed. Gary G. Hamilton. Hong Kong: Centre of Asian Studies, University of Hong Kong.

Liu, Ging-ching. 1975. *An Analysis of Postwar Taiwan's Economy: 1945-1965*. Tokyo: Tokyo University Press.

Numazaki, Ichiro. 1987. "Comments on Enterprise Groups in East Asia." *Shoken Keizai* (162): 10-29.

Peng, Huei-jen. 1989. "The Guanxi of Entrepreneurs in Taiwan and its Transformation: A Sociological Perspective." Ph.D diss.: Tunghai University, Taichung.

The Role of Personal Networks in the Making of Taiwan's *Guanxiqiye* (Related Enterprises)[1]

Ichiro Numazaki

Introduction

This paper describes a few examples of intricate human relationships that link large corporations in Taiwan, and thereby examines the role played by personal networks in the making of the so-called *guanxiqiye* or "related enterprises," a Chinese version of business groups that emerged and developed in Taiwan.

The term *guanxiqiye* is not an analytical concept developed and used by academics. It is an expression used very loosely by corporate actors themselves; hence it lacks any precise definition. However, the phrase – which is the combination of two ordinary words *guanxi*, i.e., "relationship," and *qiye*, i.e., "enterprise" – does have a peculiar flavor, for the former component *guanxi* has very special meaning in Chinese. The word indicates a personal relationship loaded with affection and mutual obligations. In sociological terms, *guanxi* can be defined as "personalistic, particularistic, non-ideological ties between persons – based on a commonality of shared identification" (Jacobs 1976, pp. 80-81). The "shared identification" may be kinship, place of origin, year of birth, education and so forth.

In local parlance, then, *guanxiqiye* implies a group of companies that share "something" in common. That something usually is a small circle of owner-managers who are closely tied together by kinship, marriage and other social bonds. *Guanxiqiye*, therefore, means a cluster of enterprises owned and controlled by a group of persons tied by a network of various *guanxi*.

The originator of the term is not known, but in the 1970s the concept of *guanxiqiye* gained wide currency in both business and academic circles, thanks in large part to the publication of "Business Groups in Taiwan," a bi-annual study of some 100 largest *guanxiqiye*, by a private market research firm, China Credit Information Service (hereafter CCIS).[2] CCIS's research was the first such attempt to apply a certain set of criteria and to identify Taiwan's large conglomerates in a systematic manner.[3]

Today, some corporate groups themselves refer to their organizations as *guanxiqiye* and openly acknowledge their member corporations by attaching the designation "so-and-so *guanxiqiye*" to each member's name and/or by using a common corporate logo.[4] For instance, Cathay Life Insurance Co., Ltd. not only calls itself *Linyen Guanxiqiye Guotai Renshou* (Cathay Life Insurance, a Linden Related Enterprise) but also uses a large green tree as the basic design of its logotype along with other Linden Group companies. In my observation, increasing numbers of corporate groups – including relatively small, unknown ones – have started to use the term *guanxiqiye* in referring to themselves. Others do not make explicit their group membership, but the presence of the same persons or their relatives and other close associates on the board of directors of two or more companies easily reveals their relatedness. As a result, these unacknowledged groups too are regarded by many as *guanxiqiye*.

What kind of human relationship, then, is involved in the making of *guanxiqiye*? What sort of personal networks are mobilized to raise capital? How are political connections cultivated and used? Along which lines is the ownership of corporations inherited? These are the questions to which this paper seeks answers.

Networks of Joint Investments: The Case of the Tainanbang

One of the most basic intercorporate relations is the capital linkage between two corporations. It may be established when the same person owns stocks in two separate companies (CCIS calls it the "brother [sister] type" relationship [Zhonghua Zhengxinsuo 1987, p. 32]) or when one corporation holds some shares of another corporation (the "parent-subsidiary [mother-child] type" relation according to CCIS [Zhonghua Zhengxinsuo 1987, p. 32]).

If X (person or corporation) holds shares of companies A and B, while Y (person or corporation) holds shares of companies B and C, then there exists a somewhat more complex network of investment ties connecting companies A, B and C; A and C are linked by virtue of the fact that both X (owner of A) and Y (owner of C) hold shares of company B. This third arrangement – the "marriage type" relationship in CCIS's terminology (Zhonghua Zhengxinsuo 1987, p. 33) – often results from the formation of new partnerships; if previously independent entrepreneurs X and Y decide to invest jointly in a new venture, then the new enterprise becomes a bridge between other firms owned separately by X and Y. Such partnerships were, and still are, an effective way of pooling limited financial resources for new businesses in Taiwan, where capital is scarce and government credit tight. The "marriage type" relationship, therefore, is the most important type of linkage that allows Taiwan's entrepreneurs to expand their business activities.

The question I would like to address in this section is this: Who "gets married" with whom? In other words, does any kind of social relationship exist between those entrepreneurs who jointly invest in the same company? If so, what kind of relationship is it? In order to illuminate this issue I shall focus on the making of personal networks in and around one particular *guanxiqiye*, the so-called *Tainanbang* or "Tainan Clique."[5] The history of this group reveals much about the role of personal networks in the making of *guanxiqiye* and in Taiwan's business circle at large.

The Beginning: Xinhexinghang

The origin of *Tainanbang* dates back to the late 1920s when Taiwan was still under Japanese colonial rule. In 1927, Wu Kedu found a post as an accountant at a store named Xinfuxinghang owned and run by Hou Yuli. A year later, Wu Kedu's eldest son, Wu Xiuqi was hired as an apprentice at the same shop. Reportedly, the father and son obtained their jobs through networks of *tongxiang* or common place of origin and of *tongzong* or common surname; Hou Yuli's wife, Wu Wuxiang and the Wu Kedu family came not only from the same village but also from the same surname group within it (Lin 1985, pp. 12-13). In 1930, through his brother Wu Xiuqi's introduction, Wu Zunxian found a job as an apprentice at another clothier shop, Xinfufahang, operated by Hou Yuli's paternal uncle Hou Ji. Later, Wu Zunxian's younger brother, Wu Junjie also served as an apprentice at yet another clothier shop in Tainan. The Wu Kedu family thus began their business careers; their association with the Hou family first started through an employee-employer relationship. Young Wu Xiuqi, in particular, quickly gained the confidence of Hou Yuli and was promoted to accountant at the age of eighteen when his father Wu Kedu left the store due to illness. This suggests that a relationship of "personal trust" was formed between Wu Xiuqi and Hou Yuli.[6]

In 1934, Wu Kedu and his sons quit their jobs and started their own clothier shop, Xinhexinghang, in Tainan city. The firm was organized as a Chinese-style partnership, *hegu*, which literally means "combined shares." The initial capital of 4,500 *yuan* was divided into nine shares, and according to Wu Xiuqi's recollection (n.d., pp. 115-17), the shares were provided by the following people: Wu Kedu and Wu Xiuqi along with Wu Xiuqi's four paternal cousins, three shares or 1,500 *yuan*; Wu Zunxian and Wu Kezhang, Wu Kedu's younger brother and adopted father of Wu Zunxian, two shares or 1,000 *yuan*; Wu Zhangxing, another younger brother of Wu Kedu, one share or 500 *yuan*; Wu Xiuqi's father-in-law, Lai Hua, one share; Wu Xiuqi's wife, Lai Lianqiao, one share; and Wu Xiuqi's paternal cousin's husband, Wang Jinchang, one share. The initial management staff of Xinhexinghang consisted of Wu Kedu (firm representative and accountant), Wu Xiuqi (manager), Wu Zunxian (purchase and bill collection) and Wu Junjie (sales and general affairs).

It needs to be emphasized here that not only Wu Kedu's immediate family members, but also not so close consanguineous kin as well as affinal relatives are mobilized to raise capital. In short, investors are recruited from Wu Kedu and his sons' *guanxi* network. Another interesting point here is that not all partners are engaged in actual management; some remained pure investors or "silent partners" who only earn profits on their shareholdings. As Hamilton (1989, p. 22) points out, these silent partners – or "*guanxi* owners" in Hamilton's terms – are rather distant relatives of the core owner-managers. This suggests, first, that partners are not equal in terms of either the amount of investment or the degree of management responsibilities and, second, that management and ownership are separated to some extent in Chinese-style partnerships.

Although Wu Kedu and his sons left their posts at Hou Yuli's and Hou Ji's stores, that did not end the relationship between the Wus and the Hous. On the contrary, close association continued. For instance, when the Wu family started their new shop, it was the Hous who stood surety for the Wus to open a checking account at a local bank. Hou Yuli, in particular, later became an important partner and financial supporter of the Wus.

Soon after Xinhexinghang started its operation, World War II erupted and the Japanese government control over commercial activities was tightened. In 1944, severe shortages of materials forced the firm to shut down. It was only after Taiwan's "Restoration" to Chinese Nationalist rule in 1945 that the Wu family were able to resume their business. Xinhexinghang, though reorganized, still exists today and functions as a sort of holding and investing company for the Wus and their associates.

The Big Step: Tainan Spinning Co., Ltd.

The real foundation of *Tainanbang* was laid down with the establishment of Tainan Spinning Co., Ltd. in 1955. In 1953, the Nationalist government announced a plan for permitting two new 10,000 spindle spinning factories. Having heard of this, the Wus of Xinhexinghang started preparation for applying for one.

On the one hand, they called on Hou Yuli to invest in this new business. At that time, the two families already had one partnership, a weaving factory founded in 1951. This venture was terminated in 1959, but the new spinning factory was to become the core corporation for *Tainanbang*.

On the other hand, the Wus invited Wu Sanlian, a prominent Taiwanese politician and then the first popularly elected mayor of Taipei city, to participate in the preparation committee. Not coincidentally, Wu Sanlian came from the Wu Kedu family's home village. Moreover, they are both surnamed Wu and believed to have descended from the same ancestor several generations back. In short, they were *tongzong* as well as *tongxiang*. The reason for inviting Wu Sanlian as a partner was purely political. To secure government approval over other competitors, the Wus and the Hous needed someone for lobbying activities, and they found one in the person of Wu Sanlian. Although Wu Sanlian is reported to have said that he argued only for reason and not for special favor (Yang 1983, p. 18), Wu Xiuqi acknowledged once that Wu Sanlian's contribution was the greatest in securing

government approval (Lin 1985, p. 16). In light of the fact that the other factory approved by the state was the one in which the Nationalist Party had substantial investment, it appears that Wu Sanlian's political connections were helpful for
the *Tainanbang*, to say the least. When the company was finally established and
he was elected chairmen of the board, Wu Sanlian was short of cash and had to
borrow money to pay for the minimum shares required of chairmen by law (Wu
1987, pp. 225-26). This also suggests that what Wu Sanlian had was nothing but
political assets.

In addition to Wu Sanlian, whose position as chairman of the board was rather
symbolic, the initial management of Tainan Spinning Co., Ltd. included Wu Xiuqi
as president and Hou Yuli as one of the managing directors. It is reported, however, that Hou Yuli remained a pure investor and entrusted management responsibility to Wu Xiuqi (Gao 1985, p. 21); Hou Yuli became an important "silent partner"
of Wu Xiuqi. This also meant that the capital linkage of the "marriage type" was
created between the Wu Kedu family's Xinhexinghang and Hou Yuli's Xinfuxinghang; the two firms "got married" via newly founded Tainan Spinning. Here, the
alliance of the three families, Wu Kedu and his sons, the Hous and Wu Sanlian,
was formed. The backbone of *Tainanbang* was thus created.

Expansion: President Enterprise Corp.

Combining their capital in varying degrees, the same group of key investors, the
Wu brothers and the Hou family, have established a series of corporations that
are today regarded as members of *Tainanbang*. CCIS lists some 27 companies as
the members of Tainan Spinning Group (Zhonghua Zhengxinsuo 1987, p. 258).
In some cases, however, new entrepreneurs were invited to join the group. Here,
I shall discuss one such instance, Gao Qingyuan.

In 1946, sixteen year old Gao Qingyuan joined the then reopened Xinhexin-
hang as an apprentice, relying on his kinship ties to the Wu Kedu family; Gao
Qingyuan was a maternal cousin of Wu Xiuqi's wife (Wu 1987, p. 39). In 1949,
Gao Qingyuan left the firm and with his former colleagues and friends started a
clothier store of his own, Dexingbuhang – just as the Wu family once did with
the Hou family's shops. In 1953, Dexingbuhang was reorganized into a new dyeing factory, Dexing gongsi, which later evolved into Tak Hsing Enterprise Co.,
Ltd., an apparel maker. These developments involved other leaders of *Tainanbang*
as well. Gao Qingyuan apparently maintained close relationships with his former
employers, although he was becoming increasingly independent.

When Tainan Spinning was established in 1955, Wu Xiuqi invited Gao
Qingyuan to work for the new company as a manager. Gao Qingyuan agreed. He
was once more an employee of his former boss. It is reported that Gao Qingyuan
wanted to try management of a large-scale enterprise (Zhenglun Chuban Gongsi
1983, p. 456). Thus, Gao Qingyuan left the top management of Dexing gongsi –

though presumably he retained his shares – and became a middle-ranking manager at Tainan Spinning, where he worked for twelve years. Then, in 1967, financially backed by the Wus and the Hous, Gao Qingyuan took initiative in creating a new food company, President Enterprise Corp. From the beginning till today, he has been the president of this firm and in fact the chief executive officer, although Wu Xiuqi has been the chairman of the board. Moreover, Gao Qingyuan is chairman of the fifteen subsidiaries of President Enterprise Corp. which together with the mother company constitute a self-acknowledged *guanxiqiye* of its own, *Tongyi Guanxiqiye* or President Group. In short, Gao Qingyuan became an important owner-manager with his own sphere of influence within the network of *Tainanbang* leaders.[7]

The pattern of building the President Enterprise Corp. is quite similar to that of Tainan Spinning Co., Ltd., in that the former boss provides capital and lets the trusted former employee manage the new firm; Hou Yuli is to Wu Xiuqi what Wu Xiuqi is to Gao Qingyuan. In other words, based on the bond of "personal trust," the relationship between employer and employee is transformed to that of senior and junior partners, with the latter being an active manager and the former remaining a "silent partner."[8]

Reaching Out: Ties to Other Guanxiqiye

One important characteristic of Taiwan's *guanxiqiye* is that it is not a closed group. Various capital and personal relationships exist between different *guanxiqiye*. Here I shall discuss one example of such cross-group networks.

In his memoir (Wu 1987, pp. 70-71), Wu Zunxian mentions his association with Gu Zhenfu, chairman of Taiwan Cement and China Trust. Gu Zhenfu belongs to the higher circle of Taiwan's business and political elites; he not only heads Taiwan Cement Group and China Trust Group but also serves as president of the Chinese National Association of Industry and Commerce, and is a member of the Standing Committee of the Nationalist Party's Central Committee. How did their association begin?

Wu Zunxian recalls that he and Gu Zhenfu are *tongnian*, i.e., born in the same lunar calendar year, and that, along with some other *tongnian* friends, they used to meet and dine once a month "to discuss anything but politics" (Wu 1987, p. 71). According to one account, this meeting of the same-aged entrepreneurs and officials was started more than twenty years ago by twelve members. Besides Wu Zunxian and Gu Zhenfu, the members included several financial bureaucrats and well-known businessmen like Wang Yongqing of Formosa Plastics Group and Cai Wanchun of Cathay Group (Sima 1988, p. 24). Such an informal circle across *guanxiqiye* and government institutions must have served as an important channel of communication and cooperation between the state and business and between different *guanxiqiye*.

A case in point is the establishment of trust companies by members of this age-based network in 1971 when the government for the first time permitted the entrance of private entrepreneurs into the trust business. Wu Zunxian tells that he was first approached by Cai Wanchun to invest in his planned Cathay Trust, but he opted for another plan by Gu Zhenfu to reorganize China Securities and Investment Co. – in which both Wu Zunxian and Gu Zhenfu already had stakes -into a trust company (Wu 1987, pp. 70-71). Here, we can see how informal networks function in working out new partnerships or reorganizing existing ones across the boundaries of *guanxiqiye*.

Political Connections

As the role of Wu Sanlian in the *Tainanbang* indicates, links to the political circle are an important aspect of personal networks around *guanxiqiye*. In Wu Sanlian's case, it was his *tongxiang* or native place fellows who approached him for access to government officials. It seems that leaders of the *Tainanbang* were eager to cultivate such ties, for they supported Wu Sanlian in several elections prior to the establishment of Tainan Spinning Co., Ltd. Being a native Taiwanese and a well known anti-Japanese activist, Wu Sanlian was an ideal candidate for political office in the early years of the Nationalist rule. In Wu Sanlian, the fledgling *Tainanbang* found a channel of communication and connection with political decision makers. As the group grew, other links were formed with the state bureaucracy and the Nationalist Party. The above mentioned *tongnian* group to which Wu Zunxian belonged included some financial bureaucrats and such people as Gu Zhenfu, who was entrenched in both business and political circles. Recently, Gao Qingyuan has risen within the party hierarchy.

On the one hand, these developments suggest that political connections are actively cultivated by entrepreneurs in a similar way in which business ties are formed, that is, through very personal *guanxi* networks based on a certain "sameness" (*tong*), such as the same place of origin, *tongxiang*, or the same age, *tongnian*. Especially in the early days of Taiwan's industrialization, political ties were crucial in launching large-scale manufacturing firms, for government approval was necessary for both opening a new factory and obtaining needed raw materials. On the other hand, the government and the party sometimes sought partners in private business; the outsider elites who dominated the state apparatus needed both supporters and clients in the business circle.

In sum, ambitious entrepreneurs who aspired to expand their business attempted "networking from below" in order to hook up with the political elite, while some politicians did "networking from above" to find associates in the private sector.[9] In the following, I shall present examples of such networking.

Networking from Below: Formosa Plastics Group

Formosa Plastics Group is probably the most famous *guanxiqiye* in and outside Taiwan, and the rise of its owner, Wang Yongqing, from an unknown lumber merchant to the internationally renowned "plastics king," is a legendary success story. But how did he get there?

The plan for a new plastics factory was devised by the government in the early 1950s, when Taiwan was struggling to industrialize its economy. Initially, the government choice for undertaking the plan was He Yi of Yuen Foong Industrial Co., a brother and partner of He Chuan of the Yuen Foong Yu Paper Mfg.; at the time, the Hes were the only entrepreneurs experienced in the chemical industry. When the plastics factory was built, the He family owned some 80 percent of the shares. The remaining 20 percent was in the hands of Wang Yongqing and his associate, Zhao Tingzhen, who applied to participate in the project (Zhenglun Chuban Gongsi 1983, p. 11).

Prior to this plastics venture, Wang Yongqing and Zhao Tingzhen were already business partners. According to Wang Yongqing's own account, he came to know Zhao Tingzhen when Zhao, who owned a construction company, began purchasing lumber from Wang's store (Lu 1986, p. 42). It is also reported that Wang helped Zhao financially when he was in need, and that Zhao repaid Wang's favor by ordering most of the materials he needed from Wang (Guo 1985, p. 20-21). The relationship between Wang Yongqing and Zhao Tingzhen, therefore, was built over time through repeated transactions; their *guanxi* is of an achieved, rather than of an ascriptive, nature.[10]

When the nationalist state started to promote private industries with the financial backing of American aid, Zhao Tingzhen invited Wang Yongqing to apply jointly for such projects as a cement plant and a rubber tire factory, neither of which the Wang-Zhao partnership was able to obtain (Lu 1986, p. 43). But, finally, they were able to participate in the plastics venture.

Although Wang Yongqing, a local Taiwanese, did not have any tie to the Nationalists, Zhao Tingzhen, a native of Jiangsu Province and a graduate of Shanghai University, had such a connection, and an important one at that: first of all, Zhao himself once worked in the government, and thus was familiar with the bureaucracy; second and more significantly, his maternal cousin, also a Jiangsu man, was a prominent financial bureaucrat who eventually served as minister of finance; finally, Zhao Tingzhen was reportedly an old friend of the organizer of the Subcommittee on Chemical Industry – a subsection of the Committee on Industrialization -which took initiative in introducing petrochemical industries into Taiwan (Lu 1986, p. 43). Though it is impossible to prove exactly what happened, it is easy to imagine that such connections were crucial for Wang and Zhao to obtain needed information and to secure favorable review of their application. It is difficult to believe, to say the least, that an unknown lumber merchant like Wang

Yongqing was able to plug into any government sponsored project without such political linkages.

Soon after the plastics factory was built, He Yi, the senior partner of the venture, toured Japan, Europe, and the U.S. to inspect the plastics industries in those locations. Based on his observations abroad, He Yi realized that his Taiwan plant did not have a promising future and decided to pull out of the project, selling most of his stocks to Wang Yongqing who was willing to take it over despite He Yi's pessimistic assessment (Zhenglun Chuban Gongsi 1983, pp. 11-12). Thus, Wang Yongqing became the major owner of Formosa Plastics which, contrary to He Ye's prediction, grew into one of the world's largest plastics producers.

Incidentally, He Yi and his family did not pull out completely from Formosa Plastics. Members of the He family today still own minority shares in the company and occupy several seats on the board of directors. In fact, according to one businessman I interviewed, it is believed that He Chuan helped Wang Yongqing financially when the new factory was struggling to survive. Wang Yongqing himself is reported as saying that he received the greatest support and care from He Chuan (Liao 1987, p. 81).

Wang Yongqing's case vividly illuminates how a small-scale merchant used networks of *guanxi* to penetrate into the top echelon of government officials.

Networking from Above: Chien Tai Cement Co.

It is well known that in Taiwan the state and the ruling Nationalist party own and run an array of corporations. It is also known that the Nationalist Party through a few holding companies invests in many ostensively private corporations (Liang 1988, pp. 125-33). Put differently, the party has reached out to some private entrepreneurs and engaged in partnerships with them. How did such relationships develop?

One example of such partnerships between the Party and private business is Chien Tai Cement Co., now owned jointly by the Nationalist Party and private Tuntex Group. In a recently published interview (Liu 1989), the present leader of the Tuntex Group, Chen Youhao said that the cooperative relationship was first started between his father Chen Qingxiao and Li Chonglian, who was a "good friend" of Chen Qingxiao and then the chairman of Chien Tai and also a member of the Party's Finance Committee. Chen Youhao also stated that, according to his father, it was Li Chonglian who approached Chen Qingxiao for advice because the party's cement plant was too small, was in the red, and hence needed an infusion of capital. Chen Qingxiao, on the other hand, had earned some profits from his textile business and was just looking for a good investment opportunity. Regrettably, it is not clear as to the nature of the "friendship" between Chen Qingxiao and Li Chonglian, but it is evident that such a personal link helped bring a private entrepreneur in cooperation with the Nationalist Party's financial officer. In addition, the Chen's invested in another party's firm, a textile mill, also run by Li Chonglian; their good relations with the party seems to have continued until the present time.

Networks of Inheritance

So far in this paper, I have emphasized the broadly based and highly pragmatic nature of personal networks involved in the making of *guanxiqiye*. Finally in this section, I would like to discuss the rather closed side of human relationships concerning *guanxiqiye*, that is, the inheritance of family ownership and the division of *guanxiqiye*.

The rule of inheritance in Chinese society is, in principle, equal partition among brothers born by the same father. In the case of family business, if assets are owned jointly by brothers, "[s]hares in the enterprises are clearly assigned at the beginning and each son inherits shares from his father only" (Mark 1972, p. 70). This practice has two consequences for *guanxiqiye*.

First, most companies are held by a few founding fathers, and therefore, when they pass away, their sons become leading share holders, often overnight. This brings about many problems. For example, prepared or not, sons suddenly have to make strategic business decisions; they may not have good relationships with their father's partners and may cause disarray in the management. A case in point is San Yang Industry Co., Ltd., the flagship of San Yang Industry Group, which produces Honda autos and motorcycles in Taiwan. When its founder, Huang Jijun, died in 1979, his eldest son, Huang Shihui, was summoned back from abroad to inherit the group and succeed to his father's position, despite the fact that Huang Shihui had no management experience – he was a physician and had practiced medicine in the U.S. and Japan for more than twenty years. To make matters more complicated, Huang Jijun was not the sole owner of San Yang Industry Co., Ltd.; he had a close junior partner Zhang Guoan, and it was Zhang Guoan, a skillful manager, who actually ran the company as its president. But the Huang-Zhang partnership could not be maintained over the generational change. Soon after Huang Shihui succeeded to the chairmanship of the firm, he stripped Zhang Guoan of the presidency and made him an honorable but powerless "advisor." As a result, Zhang Guoan left the company and parted with San Yang Industry Group. He now heads a *guanxiqiye* of his own.[11]

Secondly, partition of family holdings could induce division of large *guanxiqiye* into smaller groups. The most famous of such cases is the Cathay Group, which was founded by Cai Wanchun along with his family, relatives and friends. The group was headed by Cai Wanchun until 1979 when he had a stroke and became incapable of running his business. Subsequently, the group was divided into four units, each headed by his sons and his brothers: Cathay Trust Group led by

Cai Chennan, Cai Wanchun's eldest son; Cathay Plastics Group led by Cai Chenzhou, the second eldest son of Cai Wanchun; Cathay Life Insurance Group – now called Linden Group – led by Cai Wanlin, Cai Wanchun's younger brother; and Cathay Insurance Group – now called Foremost Group – led by Cai Wancai, another younger brother of Cai Wanchun (Zhonghua Zhengxinsuo 1980, pp. 545-75). Later, still another subgroup, Sun Lai Group led by Cai Chenyang and Cai Chenwei, two younger brothers of Cai Chenzhou, split off from Cai Chenzhou's Cathay Plastics Group (Zhonghua Zhengxinsuo 1985, pp. 839-46).[12]

Thus, the original group was divided along patrilineal lines. However, an interesting point is that Cai Chennan alone was born of Cai Wanchun's first wife, and his brothers, Cai Chenzhou, Cai Chenyang, and Cai Chenwei, were born of Cai Wanchun's second wife (Gu 1985, p. 10-11). It, therefore, seems that when the group was first divided, Cai Wanchun's sons were split into two groups along their mothers' line and inherited separate groups of corporations.

The Cai family's case indicates that matrilineal ties also are important in family division. In fact, it is reported that within the Cai family, the relations are more intimate among brothers who have the same mother (Gu 1985, pp. 167-68). The bond of intimacy and affection seems to have influenced the pattern of regrouping among brothers after family division.

Concluding Remarks

By way of conclusion, I shall summarize some general characteristics of personal networks around Taiwan's *guanxiqiye* and propose an agenda for future research.

First, I would like to reiterate the very pragmatic nature of network utilization in making joint investments or cultivating political connections; almost any kind of network is used if it is useful. In particular, patrilineal *guanxi* plays an important role, and partnerships between paternal brothers and cousins are the most conspicuous form of making joint investments. Also salient in partnerships are affinal relationships. Lastly, circles of people who share a certain "commonality," such as *tongxiang* or *tongnian*, are of great importance. These are the *guanxi* that presupposes some "sameness," that is, social relationships of an ascriptive nature. But, as in the case of Wang Yongqing and Zhao Tingzhen, *guanxi* between business partners may be an achieved one; it can be established through series of exchange. What these diverse *guanxi* share, however, is that all are horizontal networks which allow individuals to expand their contacts beyond the narrow confines of immediate family. This type of personal network enables entrepreneurs to mobilize a wide range of people for investment and political purposes.

Second, in contrast with the above cases, the networks involved in inheritance are vertical ones. Father-son relationship stands out as the basic principle of inheritance, but mother-son link also seems to play a role in deciding which brother groups with whom. In the case of inheritance at least, these vertical networks function as a mechanism for drawing group boundaries. In passing, I would like to note that not a few prominent entrepreneurs in Taiwan have more than one wife, and, therefore, matrilineal bonds may be as important a factor as patrilineal ties in determining how the ownership of business groups is transferred from one generation to another. This is an interesting topic for future research.

Finally, I would like to point out that personal networks of business group leaders extend well beyond the boundaries of *guanxiqiye*, as the case of *Tainanbang*'s Wu Zunxian's network suggests. In fact, my dissertation (Numazaki 1992) shows that capital links among leading entrepreneurs are so intertwined that they are woven into the large web of interfirm relations. In light of this, I have a hypothesis that Taiwan's *guanxiqiye* is less a "business group" than a relatively dense cluster of corporations in the much larger network of cross-investments and interlocking directorship, what I prefer to call "the web of partnerships." In my opinion, it is this wide network of entrepreneurs that is the social foundation of what Hamilton (1989) calls Taiwan's "*guanxi* capitalism." Furthermore, it is my contention that the existence of such broad inter-group linkages distinguishes Taiwan's *guanxiqiye* sharply from its East Asian cousins, namely, South Korean *chaebol* and Japanese *kigyoshudan,* both of which have rather clear boundaries between groups and a more institutionalized command structure within each group.[13]

These items definitely call for further empirical investigation. As a social network analyst with a structuralist bent, however, I strongly suspect that the configuration of larger networks in which business groups are "embedded" – to borrow the expression of Mark Granovetter (1985) – has at least as much determining effect on the structure and behavior of business groups as cultural norms and values (e.g., Confucianism). I am proposing, then, that researchers of East Asian business groups ought to pay as much attention to the structure of relationships "between" business groups as to the organization "within" them.[14]

Notes

[1]   The research on which this paper is based was conducted in Taiwan from October 1986 through August 1989 with the financial support of the following institutions: The Joint Committee on Chinese Studies of The American Council of Learned Societies and The Social Science Research Council; Wenner-Gren Foundation For Anthropological Research; United States National Science Foundation; Urban Affairs Program of Michigan State University; and Sigma Xi, The Scientific Research Society. I am grateful to all of them. I am also indebted to the Institute of Ethnology, Academia Sinica for sponsoring me as visiting research associate and providing me with invaluable assistance.

[2]   The publication began in 1972. Since then, eight issues have been published so far. In this paper, names of corporations are translated into English according to CCIS's ren-

dering. Otherwise, Chinese firm names are romanized in Mandarin using the *pinyin* system. All personal names of business people are romanized also in Mandarin, although in reality they may be pronounced more frequently in Minnan dialect (Taiwanese).

[3] CCIS uses its own set of criteria to identify membership of each *guanxiqiye*. As I have argued elsewhere (Lee et al. 1987, pp. 15-17), however, CCIS's criteria are somewhat arbitrary. In fact, CCIS's grouping of corporations sometimes diverges from the self-acknowledged group membership. For example, President Enterprise Corp. lists 15 companies as its *guanxiqiye* in its latest pamphlet (*Tongyi Qiye Gongsi* n.d.). But, CCIS does not list them as a separate group and includes only five of the 15 affiliates along with the President Enterprise Corporation in Tainan Spinning Group instead (Zhonghua Zhengxinsuo 1987, pp. 255-71). Hence, it is inappropriate that most previous studies of Taiwan's business groups – including my own – have relied uncritically on CCIS for identification of business groups (e.g., Numazaki 1986; Hamilton et al. 1987; Chou 1988). This paper therefore focuses more on actual linkages between individuals and firms regardless of their apparent group identity.

[4] Not all business groups call themselves *guanxiqiye*. Some use the term *jigou* or "organization," others *jituan* "group." However, in my observation, the most popular term is *guanxiqiye*, hence its choice as the generic term for such groups.

[5] The Chinese word *bang* generally means "clique" or "faction." In commerce, however, it specifically indicates a group of merchants who originated from a common locality. In the case of the *Tainanbang*, the group leaders all come from Tainan prefecture. The following account of the *Tainanbang* is based on the memoirs of Wu Xiuqi (n.d.) and Wu Zunxian (1987), the key brothers who built the group.

[6] The importance of "personal trust" in Chinese business is discussed more fully by Cheng-shu Kao in his chapter in this book.

[7] According to a manager I interviewed, managers of key corporations affiliated with the *Tainanbang*, including President Enterprise Corp., hold monthly meetings to facilitate communication within the group.

[8] Such a development seems not uncommon in Taiwan. For instance, Zhang Guoan started as an employee of Huang Jijun, but as their business grew into one of the largest motorcycle builders in Taiwan, Zhang Guoan became an important junior partner of Hou Jijun in terms of both ownership and management of their company, San Yang Industry Co., Ltd. For more details, see Zhang (1987).

[9] The contrast of networking from below and from above was first suggested to me by Mr. Liao Kuo-wei of Kyoto University at a seminar held by Japan Securities Research Institute in Osaka, May 30, 1988. I am grateful to Mr. Liao for his suggestion.

[10] In fact, even when individuals share such commonalities as a similar place of origin or the same surname, the commonality alone is not sufficient for creating trustworthy *guanxi*; "personal trust" must be earned through deeds. Cheng-Shu Kao's chapter in this volume also discusses this point.

[11] For the details of this whole event, see Zhang Guoan's autobiography (Zhang 1987, pp. 247-58).

[12] This does not mean that ownership is completely re-aligned so as to make each new group independent. Despite the division, cross-holding of shares still exist across these five groups.

[13] The similarities and differences between business groups in Japan, South Korea, and Taiwan are discussed extensively in Hamilton et al. (1987).
[14] Some chapters in this volume have moved already towards this direction: both Marco Orrù and Yoshiaki Ueda explore networks across large enterprise groups in Japan, and Gilbert Wong examines the patterns of interlocking directorships between business groups in Hong Kong.

References

Chou, Tein-Chen. 1988. "Aggregate Concentration Ratios and Business Groups: A Case Study of Taiwan." *Jingji Lunwen Congkan* 16 (1): 79-94.
Gao, Zongzhi. 1985. "Genshen Yemao de *Tainanbang* [Deeply Rooted and Thickly Growing Tainan Clique]." Pp. 7-55 in *Weijizhong de Caituan Bangpai* [Financial Cliques in Crisis], ed. Jiaodian Chubanshe Bianji Weiyuanhui. Taipei: Jiaodian Chubanshe.
Granovetter, Mark. 1985. "Economic Action and Social Structure: The Problem of Embeddedness." *American Journal of Sociology* 91: 481-510.
Gu, Zu. 1985. *Guotai hongloumeng* [Cathay's "Dream of the Red Chamber"]. Taipei: Ershiyi Shiji Chubanshe.
Guo, Tai. 1985. *Wang Yongqing Fendoushi* [A History of Wang Yongqing's Struggle]. Taipei: Yuanliu Chubanshe.
Hamilton, Gary G. 1989. "Patterns of Asian Capitalism: The Cases of Taiwan and South Korea." Program in East Asian Business Culture and Development, Working Paper Series, No. 28. Davis: Institute of Governmental Affairs, University of California.
Hamilton, Gary G., Marco Orrù, and Nicole Woolsey Biggart. 1987. "Enterprise Groups in East Asia: An Organizational Analysis." *Shoken Keizai* 161: 78-106.
Jacobs, Bruce J. 1976. "The Cultural Bases of Factional Alignment and Division in a Rural Taiwanese Township." *Journal of Asian Studies* 36: 79-97.
Lee, Hahn-Koo, Ichiro Numazaki, and Yoshiaki Ueda. 1987. "Comments on 'Enterprise Groups in East Asia' by Hamilton, Orrù and Biggart." *Shoken Keizai* 162: 10-29.
Liang, Yonghuang. 1988. "Pouxi Quanguo Zuida de Konggu Gongsi [Dissecting the Largest Holding Companies in the Nation]." *Caixun* 74: 125-33.
Liao, Qingzhou. 1987. *Dangdai Qiyejia Chenggong de Gushi* [Success Stories of Today's Entrepreneurs]. Taipei: Jingji Ribao.
Lin, Shurong. 1985. "Zouchu Gubao de Tainanbang [Tainan Clique, Group Out of an Old Village]." *Gongshang Shidai* 41: 4-36.
Liu, Chuanyu. 1989. "Dongdishi Jituan Yijun Tuqi [Tuntex Group Suddenly Rises]." *Caixun* 84: 326-31.
Lu, Qingyuan. 1986. "Wang Yongqing, Zhao Tingzhen Heli Kaichuang Taiwan Shihua Wangguo [Wang Yongqing, Zhao Tingzhen Jointly Built Taiwan's Petrochemical Kingdom]." *Caixun* 49: 42-47.
Mark, Lindi Li. 1972. "Taiwanese Lineage Enterprises: A Study of Familial Entrepreneurship." Ph.D. diss. Berkeley: University of California.
Numazaki, Ichiro. 1992. "Networks and Partnerships: The Social Organization of the Chinese Business Elite in Taiwan." Ph. D. diss. Ann Arbor: Michigan State University.

Numazaki, Ichiro. 1986. "Networks of Taiwanese Big Business: A Preliminary Analysis."
    Modern China 12: 487-534.

Sima, Xiaoqing. 1988. *Qiye Julong* [Dragons of Business]. Taipei: Wenjing Chubanshe.

Tongyi Qiye Gongsi. n.d. *Tongyi Qiye* [President Enterprise Corporation]. n.p.: Tongyi Qiye
    Gongsi (pamphlet).

Wu, Xiuqi. n.d. *Qishi Huiyi* [Recollections of My Seventy Years of Life]. n.p.: Xiuqui Wu.

Wu, Zunxian. 1987. *Rensheng Qishi – Wu Zunxian Zizhuan Huiyilu* [Seventy Years of My
    Life: Recollections of Wu Zunxian]. Taipei: Caituanfaren Wu Zunxian Wenjiao Gongyi
    Jijinhui.

Yang, Aili. 1983. *"Tainanbang* [Tainan Clique]." *Tianxia Zazhi* 20: 15-26.

Zhang Guoan. 1987. *Lilian – Zhang Guoan Zizhuan* [Experience: Autobiography of Zhang
    Guoan]. Taipei: Xi'nianlai Chubanshe.

Zhenglun Chuban Gongsi. 1983. *Taiwan Daqiyejia Fendoushi* [A History of Taiwan En-
    trepreneurs' Struggles]. 2 vols. Taipei: Xinianlai Chubanshe.

Zhonghua Zhengxinsuo. 1987. *Minguo Qishiqi Nian / Qishiba Nian Ban Taiwan Diqu Jitu-
    an Qiye Yanjiu* [Business Groups in Taiwan 1988/1989]. Taipei: Zhonghua Zhengxinsuo.

Zhonghua Zhengxinsuo. 1985. *Minguo Qishisi Nian / Qishiwu Nian Ban Taiwan Diqu Jitu-
    an Qiye Yanjiu* [Business Groups in Taiwan 1985/1986]. Taipei: Zhonghua Zhengxinsuo.

Zhonghua Zhengxinsuo. 1980. *Minguo Liushijiu Nian Ban Taiwan Diqu Jituan Qiye Yanjiu*
    [Business Groups in Taiwan 1980]. Taipei: Zhonghua Zhengxinsuo.

Business Groups in a Dynamic Environment: Hong Kong 1976-1986

Gilbert Wong

In this paper I wish make a contribution to the study of business groups in Hong Kong through an analysis of the changing patterns of interlocking directorates among the largest public companies and banks in Hong Kong in the period 1976 to 1986.

Theoretical Framework

Business Groups in General

There are two main approaches to the study of business groups: a bottom up approach rooted in economic theories focusing on resource dependence and market imperfections, and a top down approach rooted in political science theories and emphasizing the distribution of power among the dominant groups in a society (Hamilton et al. 1988).

The resource dependence perspective postulates that organizations generally cannot generate all the resources they need internally and are dependent to varying degrees on resources supplied from the environment. Very often there are great uncertainties in the supply of those resources (e.g., financial capital, raw materials) which are critical for the survival of the company. One of the main focuses of study from this perspective is, therefore, on the strategies used by organizations to secure and to manage the uncertainties arising from the unpredictable supply of these resources.

While this perspective recognizes the importance of the actions of other organizations in the environment, its focus of attention and its unit of analysis is the individual organization; hence the business group per se is not of interest. A related theoretical framework, that of "market failure" (Williamson and Ouchi 1981) considers the origins and aggregated effects of relationships between individual firms and their environment, and hence puts the business group into the picture. This theoretical framework takes into account that under certain circumstances, markets do not function "perfectly" in the allocation of resources. The main reason for this imperfection is the imperfect and/or incomplete exchange of information among business transactors when the number of actors who are knowledgeable in a particular kind of transaction is relatively small. This leads to uncertainty in the exchange relationship and the uncertainty is further aggravated by the "opportunistic behavior" of some transactors who want to exploit the situation to their advantage. In this respect, the concern of resource dependence theory and market failure theory is the same, i.e., how do organizations deal with uncertainty. The market failure framework deals with the issue at a system level and suggests that, with market failure, firms extend itself outward and try to replace the market by authoritative and qusai-authoritative means. The former of these would include mergers and joint ventures, while the latter would include interlocking directorates, and industry agreements to regulate the business. In this framework, business groups formed by interlocking directorates, cross share holdings, family ties, or other means is a kind of semi-organization serving a resource allocative function somewhere in between the perfect market and the self-contained organization.

In both the resource dependence and market failure perspectives, the environment is perceived as "structured" and the structure is mainly described in terms of industry characteristics such as the level of concentration within each industry and the transactional relationships across industries. These parameters have been shown to be significant in determining the uncertainty coping strategies used by organizations. It was found that for mergers across industries, merger activities between two industries positively correlates with the level of transactional activities between the same two industries (Pfeffer and Salancik 1978).

However, applying this kind of industry based analysis in the business environment of the export-oriented economies of the Newly Industrialized Countries (NICs) in Asia such as Hong Kong is problematic.

First, the United States, where most of these studies were conducted, is a more self-contained economy than the export oriented economy of Hong Kong. The various stages of production, as well as the final consumers of the products, are located within the same economy. In Hong Kong, the industrial production is largely confined to one or a few stage(s) of the production process, and the consumers of the final output are located outside the territory. Thus the pattern of resource exchange between industries within the economy could not be used to describe the resource interdependence of Hong Kong industries.

Second, in the industrialized countries, there tend to be significant barriers of entry to some industries. These barriers are caused by the higher level of technology used in some production processes, the high level of professionalization of the work force, and the strength of trade unionism. In Hong Kong, these conditions exist only at a much lower level, with the result that barriers of entry to most industries are also low.

Third, as the source of environmental uncertainties facing business in Hong Kong largely emanates from the political economies of its major trading partners –

the industrialized nations -businesses in Hong Kong are more concerned with external, international issues such as protectionism, level of consumer expenditure, and price of raw materials rather than the resource interdependence relationship within the territory.

These differences in the industrial structure of Hong Kong suggest that the strategies used to manage uncertainties are also different. Utilizing horizontal mergers and vertical integration to reduce uncertainty management were the principal means of risk management described by Chandler (1977) in his study of the growth of American big corporations, but these cannot be used as the main strategies in Hong Kong businesses. From the viewpoint of the Hong Kong businesses, the target companies concerned are numerous and scattered all around the industrialized countries. Many of them will be too big for Hong Kong companies to take over (although there are exceptions), and the legal and financial process of takeover would be unfamiliar to most Hong Kong businessmen, not to mention that there may well be legal or social obstacles to such foreign takeover bids.

The upshot of this limitation is that businesses are more inclined to use other strategies for coping with uncertainties. For example, they would enhance their adaptive ability by using labor intensive technology, subcontracting and by keeping down the size of their establishments. This situation is found in the manufacturing industries in Hong Kong (Redding and Tam 1985).

Another important strategy for business organization themselves is to act collectively or in concert with the government. A good example of this strategy is the action to lobby for the government's support in the negotiation of textile export quotas from Hong Kong to Europe and North America. This is done largely through the government's Textile Advisory Committee, which is closely involved in the negotiating process and in which are represented most of the major textile and garment businessmen in Hong Kong.

Business groups in this context becomes a significant vehicle through which collective actions, including national development strategies, are being carried out. Studies of business groups in some Asian countries have shown that they have indeed fulfilled such a function (Jones and Sakong 1980; Johnson 1982; Hamilton et al. 1987). However, these studies also found that the structure of the business groups, as well as their relationship with their national government, are different in each country. In Korea, large businesses are grouped into *chaebols*, where the member firms are closely controlled by the central holding companies which are owned by an individual or a family. In turn, the central holding companies are directly managed by the South Korean state through planning agencies and fiscal controls (Hamilton and Biggart 1988). In Japan, the state does not intervene directly but is rather more concerned with creating and promoting strong intermediate powers, acting as coordinator of activities and mediator of conflicting interests (Johnson 1982). Thus, while the business groups in Japan are comparable in size to those of Korea, they have fewer direct connections with the state and are much less obedient to the state's directives (Abegglen and Stalk 1985; Eads and Yamamura 1987). In Taiwan, the government is much more selective and uses more restraint in its intervention, which gives rise to an economy with a much more decentralized pattern of industrialization, a low level of concentration, and a predominance of small and medium-sized firms (Myers 1986).

These national variations suggest that business groups are also a result of the authority system and social institutions in these societies. That bring us to the political economy and institutional perspectives on the study of business groups.

The political economy perspective views the firm as a vehicle by which corporate leaders, as members of a dominant class, exercise power over the society in general. The two dominant themes in this perspective are (1) how different units in the dominant groups become united to pursue their common interests, and (2) the relationship between the government and the business elites. Business groups in this perspective are a means by which ties are formed between corporations and their owners/senior managers who shared similar interests. They both delineate the spheres of influence and act as vehicles of exploitation.

While the political economy perspective is concerned with describing the system of alliances between powerful groups in the society, it does not attempt to explain the basis of the alliances. In order to explain the difference, we need to turn to the institutional environments of the societies in which the business groups are found.

Whitley has identified four features of the institutional environment which have significant impact for the formation of a distinctive "business recipe" (1990). They are the system of authority relationships, the system for establishing trust and mutual support, the primacy of the family, the states' policies of economic development, and the characteristics of the financial systems.

These institutional features also lead to differences in the characteristics of business groups found in Asian countries. Thus the primacy of family relationships means that commitment to one's family overrides all other loyalties. Translated to business relationships, this means that in a Chinese society, the ties between firms owned by the same family are stronger than those between firms owned by different families. In contrast, because of their feudalistic history, the Japanese have developed a stronger commitment to broader collectivities. Relationships among firms in a business group are built on mutual obligations to the group per se. Membership in the Japanese business groups could thus be more widespread than would be the case in Chinese business groups, which are "naturally" limited to a smaller size defined by family relationships.

This difference is reinforced by the difference in the mechanisms for establishing trust between the Chinese and Japanese societies. The "*guanxi* networks of mutual support in Chinese society are usually tied to common background characteristics, whereas Japanese obligation networks are formed across such categories and demonstrate an ability to form strong bonds between people with different backgrounds" (Whitley 1990, p. 60). Thus, the firm-owners in a Chinese business group, if they are not related by family ties, are likely to come from the same region in China, such as Shanghai, or Teochow.

The role of financial institutions in providing finance for business development also accounts for the centrality of financial institutions in the business groups. In Japan, the banks that finance the business activities of the member firms of a *keiretsu* usually occupy a central position in the group. In Taiwan where much of the capital comes from the "kerb market," financial institutions in business groups are less prominent.

Besides inter-firm relationships, the relationships between the business and government also vary in accordance with the institutional context. Those relationships may, in turn, impact interfirm relationships themselves. In each society, the government has a choice of what form of relationship they should have with the businesses. Historically, many factors are important in determining the choice; "but it seems likely that the most important [factors] were not economic factors at all. Rather the key decisions about state/business relations should be seen in a much larger context, as flowing from the attempt on the part of political leaders to legitimize a system of rule. Each regime [Japan, South Korea, and Taiwan] was at a crucial point in its own survival after wars and occupations, and needed to establish a rationale for its own existence. In fashioning such a rationale, each regime in the end resorted to time-tested, institutionally acceptable ways to fashion a system of political power" (Hamilton and Biggart 1988, p. 81). The institutional environment, therefore, gives the final configuration to the business groups found in a country given a "world" economic relation and a historically determined political system.

Interlocking Directorates

The study of business groups as defined by interlocking directorates is dominated by the same "top down" resource dependence approach and the "bottom up" political approach described earlier. The institutional context of the societies in which the interlocking directorates are found tends to be ignored in most studies.

From the resource dependence perspective, the most frequently studied relationship is the one between capital dependence and financial interlocking (Dooley 1969, Pfeffer 1972, Allen 1974, Pennings 1980). It is hypothesized that the greater a firm's dependence on an external source of finance, the more likely it is for the firm to establish a directorate tie with a financial institution, either by appointing a representative from a financial institution to its board, or by "sending" one of the firm's directors into the board of a financial institution. Results of studies testing this hypothesis have been mixed (Pfeffer 1972, Pennings 1980).

From the political science perspective, the most frequently studied issue is the power and position of banks and financial institutions within the interlocking directorate network. Because of their control over financial capital, it has been argued that the banks and financial institutions are able to exercise control over major corporations in the society. A related theory suggested that the financial and non-financial corporations are inter-connected to form a cohesive network that serves to consolidate the class interest of the elites in a society.

These two perspectives give rise to the current debate on whether interlocking directorates serve as mechanisms of cooptation or control (from a resource dependence perspective) or as a means of consolidating class (elite) interest. We feel that these two functions in practice overlap with each other. Financial institutions occupy a central and influential position in the business network exactly because they have control over a critical resource, i.e., the financial resources needed by many organizations. Once the institutions acquire influence, they would take steps to consolidate their power by forging links with important actors in the environments, such as large industrial companies and the government.

What is more interesting to us, therefore, is how organizations are able to obtain control over critical resource in the first place, how other organizations respond and relate to them after they have obtained control over the resources, and how the resulting inter-organizational relations give rise to the different patterns of business groups found in the Asian economies. This is what we attempt to do with respect to the changing pattern of interlocking directorates in Hong Kong in the period 1976-1986.

An Integrated Model

An attempt is made to integrate all the three approaches to the study of interlocking directorates in Hong Kong. This attempt is made because it is felt that the three approaches do not contradict each other and all have their merits. For example, in studying the business strategies of major corporations in Asia, the resource dependence approach would indicate to us the conditions under which the resource dependent relationships becomes critical for the corporations' survival. The political economy and the institutional approaches would help us understand the specific strategies the corporations would take in a society. A model that integrates the three perspective is given in Figure 1.

The two elements in the models that are the main concerns of the resource dependency theories are the economic environment and the inter-organizational relations. Issues of ownership are also indirectly involved when these theories postulate that mergers and joint ventures are being used as mechanisms to cope with environmental uncertainty. The four elements that are the main concerns of the political economy perspective are ownership structure, political environment, power and class cohesion, and inter-organizational relations. The institutional environment in this model acts as a background factor that shapes the relationships of the elements mentioned above.

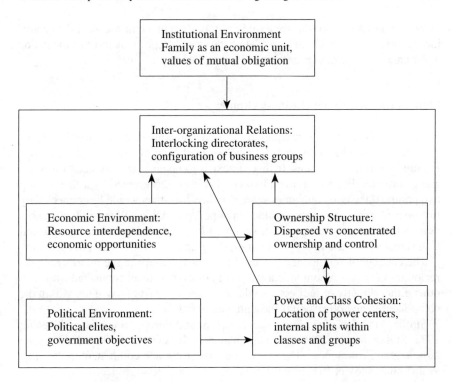

Figure 1:   An Integrative Model to Explain the Formation and Functioning of Business
Groups

We shall now apply the integrated model to the development of business groups
in Hong Kong in the ten-year period 1976 to 1986. This period is chosen because
during this time, we see the decline of the once dominant British commercial interests and the rise of powerful Chinese business groups in Hong Kong. It would
be interesting to see how well our integrated model could account for this significant change in the economy.

Research Sample

The sample which we used to identify the business groups are the top 100 largest
publicly listed non-financial companies ranked by annual turnover and the top
25 largest local banks (and deposit-taking companies which are equivalent to the
merchant banks in United Kingdom) ranked by their assets in the 1976, 1981, and
1986. The market capitalization of the 100 non-financial corporations accounts for
about 80 percent of total market capitalization and the total assets of the 25 banks

in the sample again accounts for a similar proportion of all the assets of the locally incorporated banks in Hong Kong. Thus the sample represents most of the major non-financial corporations and banks in Hong Kong.

Method for Identifying Business Groups

In this study the graph theory technique is used to examine the pattern of interlocking directorates. Graph theory is a branch of mathematics which studies the configuration of links and points. In this context, a company is represented by a point, and a common director between two companies is represented by a line joining two points. If the two companies share two directors, they would be connected by two lines. A graph is simply a collection of points and lines. When all the connections between points consist of one or more lines, the graph is called 1-graph, and if the connections are two or more lines, the graph is called a 2-graph, and so on.

The concept of "component" is used to identify groups in the interlocking directorates network. A component is a set of points that are all connected with each other either directly or indirectly so that one can move from any point within the component to any other points through a number of steps.

Similar to results of studies done in the U.S. and Europe (Sonquist and Koenig 1975; Stokman et al. 1985), most companies in the sample are included within a large 1-graph component. The size of the largest 1-graph component in the three years under study is 104, 108, 99 in 1976, 1981, and 1986 respectively.

Thus, in order to identify meaningful business groups within the interlocking directorate network, more stringent conditions are needed. Sonquist and Koenig (1975) and Lim (1981) used the criteria of 2-graphs to break the network up into smaller components. Similar techniques were use in a 10-countries study of interlocking directorates in Europe (Stokman et al. 1985). The decision on what order of graph to use depends on whether it could help identify groups which are meaningful in a particular context. In this study, meaningful groups do not appear until 3-graphs and 4-graphs are used. Business groups in this study are defined as those components with a minimum of three companies linked together with each other directly or indirectly by 3-graphs or 4-graphs.

Hong Kong Business Groups

The Political Economy of Hong Kong in 1976

In a review of the political structure in Hong Kong, Rear (1971, p. 66) suggested that "power is exercised in the Colony through a tacit alliance between business interest and the bureaucracy." Davies in his study of the overlapping membership between political bodies, boards of directors, and government advisory boards in 1976 came to a similar conclusion. "In general it can be concluded that there is in Hong Kong a relatively small elite which controls the policy process. It is in the main non-Chinese and with a large proportion of expatriates. However, the interconnections between the Chinese and the non-Chinese are such as to make it plausible to claim that there is a basic similarity of attitude. This similarity is produced, it seems, by a community of interest in a small number of major financial and business concerns at the board level; by pattern of common membership in a small number of clubs; by a level of income... and by a shared involvement in numerous charitable organizations and their public functioning" (Davies 1977, p. 77).

The business interests referred to by these authors were mainly the trading houses (hongs) started by British entrepreneurs in the late nineteenth and early twentieth century. The four major hongs are Jardine and Matheson, Swire, Hutchison and Wheelock Marden. To this list must be added the business interests of the Kadoorie family and the Hong Kong and Shanghai Banking Corporation (now renamed the Hongkong Bank, or simply, the Bank) which serves as the de facto central bank in Hong Kong. In 1976, the same four hongs control one of the two English newspaper in Hong Kong, the two power companies, two of the three container ports, the only Hong Kong airline and aircraft maintenance companies, the telephone company, most of the properties in the central financial district, Peak tram, Hong Kong tramway, and a host of other businesses such as dockyards, wharfs, hotels, and supermarkets. Traditionally, the chief executives of all the hongs would be represented on the board of the Hongkong Bank. These "taipans" would also be members of the Royal Hong Kong Jockey Club, whose chief administrator would also be represented on the board of the Bank. The Chairman of the Bank in turn would always be the chief steward of the Jockey Club. This network was so tight and the power of the elite group of businessman was so great that it has been said that "power in Hong Kong resides in the Jockey Club, Jardine and Matheson, the Hong Kong and Shanghai Bank, and the Governor – in that order" (Hughes, 1976, p. 15).

The configuration of the interlocking directorate network components and their inter-connections largely reflects the dominant position of the hongs and are shown in Figures 2.

As further detailed in Table 1, according to our criteria, we have identified seven tightly knit business groups. One of these group consist of seventeen companies and is further broken down into three sub-groups using 4-graph components. Some indication of the "size" and importance of these groups are measured by the number of companies in the group and the group's proportion of total stock market capitalization. The centrality of a business group is measured by the number of companies that is linked to the group as a whole through common directorships. Appendix One gives a brief description of the main business and companies of these groups.

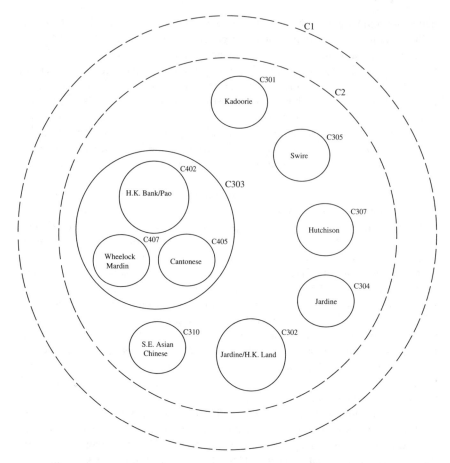

C1 and C2: loosely connected components of 1-graph and 2-graph.
C3xx and C4xx: tightly knit components of 3-graph and 4-graph.

Figure 2:   Business Groups in 1976 as Identified by the Network of Interlocking Directorates

In the 1976 network, except for two small groups, the major business groups
are made up of and controlled by non-Chinese business families or organizations.
Most of the groups are controlled by a single business family. This is true for the
Kadoorie, Swire, Jardine, Hutchison, and Wheelock Marden groups. Most of the
companies in these groups are also companies with a long history (more than forty
years) in Hong Kong. However there were also joint ventures between the groups.
For example, many of the support services provided at the airport were owned by
Jardine and Swire.

Table 1:   Profiles of Business Groups in 1976

Group Name	Control by Chinese?	No. of Companies	% Market Capitalization	Group Centrality-no. of Companies connected with the group
S.E. Asian Asian (310)	yes	4	0.24	17
Kadoorie (301)	no	3	4.92	33
Swire (305)	no	3	7.07	25
Hutchison (307)	no	6	7.73	32
Jardine (1) (304)	no	3	7.27	18
Jardine/ H.K.Land (302)	no	5	10.14	42
Mixed (303)	mixed	17	30.80	41*

Sub-divisions within the mixed group

HK Bank/ Y.K. Pao (402)	mixed	5	20.51	40
Cantonese (405)	yes	5	7.02	40
Wheelock Marden (407)	no	5	3.18	13

* This is not equal to the sum of the centralities of the sub-divisions as companies in the sub-divisions may be linked to the same companies.

   Most of the companies within the business groups were in the hotel, property, and public utilities industries. In proportion to their representation in the sample, very few are from the manufacturing or the banking industries.
   The business of Chinese families tend to be less diversified and concentrated in the property sector. A few of them were in the hotel and shipping business. Their business establishments also have a shorter history in Hong Kong. (The exception is Bank of East Asia.) This is a surprising fact, given that Hong Kong is a Chinese city.
   The network is clearly dominated by the Jardine groups of companies. The two Jardine groups together accounted for 17.41 percent of the total market capitalization.

The two Jardine groups were connected to 60 companies while the large mixed group was connected to 41 companies. However, the size of the later groups is clearly due to the presence of the Hongkong Bank. The Bank *alone* was connected to forty companies. It *alone* accounted for 14.16 percent of the stock market capitalization. If the share of the Hang Seng Bank is added, the proportion would go up to 17.7 percent. The Bank and Jardine groups constituted the two centers in the network.

The configuration of the business groups thus reflects the dominant position of the British business in Hong Kong. An analysis of political representation in Hong Kong in 1975 shows that the expatriates (mostly British) took up more than 50 percent of the seats in the legislative and executive councils in the Colony (Davies 1989). (These two councils are analogous to the legislature and cabinet of a nation state.) Business representation in these two councils were 30 percent and 40 percent respectively. This overlap of political and economic power lends support to a "class" theory of business groups, which postulates that the business groups are a manifestation and vehicle of domination.

The Seeds of Change

Given the dominant position of the British business groups in Hong Kong in 1976, it was difficult for other business groups to compete directly with the business groups and to grow within the economy of Hong Kong. The industrial and urban development of Hong Kong in the 1970s, however, opened up two avenues where Chinese entrepreneurs could escape the domination of the established groups. One avenue was the manufacturing industry which was mainly oriented for export. As the markets were located overseas, they were outside the sphere of influence of the established hongs. Even so, the hongs are still able to exert considerable influence because they controlled the economic infrastructure, such as port and air-transport facilities.

The other avenue was the property development industry. In order to understand the opportunities provided by the property development industry, we need to sketch a brief history of the industry and its relation to the banking and finance industry.

The early 1950s was one of the most traumatic period in the history of Hong Kong. The communist takeover of the mainland and the United Nation embargo on trade with China had destroyed the entrepot trade which was the foundation of the economy. Hong Kong then turned to industrialization for its livelihood. As it was still at the early stage, few resources were devoted to property development, despite the large influx of refugees from China. A second factor which hindered property development was the building regulations which imposed a low plot ratio for building sites, making it almost impossible for developers to construct high density buildings of the type commonly found in Hong Kong today. Development projects were usually small in size and mainly financed from the developer's own resource, bank loans, and proceeds from the pre-sale of the property under construction.

By the early 1960s Hong Kong had nicely recovered from the post-war trauma. Its export industry was so successful that there was abundant cash to finance property development. This change, occurring jointly with a relaxation of the building ordinance, fueled a property boom. High density building projects were developed during this time. The pioneer in this field was the Goodyear Property Development Company, which was one of the companies within the Southeast Asian Chinese Group identified in the 1976 network. Developers were quick to realize that there was a great demand for accommodations resulting from population pressure and from the increasing size of the well-to-do middle class. Under such conditions, and further fueled by rampant speculations, property and land prices went up dramatically. Among the speculators were bank managers who jumped on the bandwagon to become financier-cum-developers. The lack of regulation in the banking industry allowed the banks to overextend themselves, which finally led to the banking crisis in 1964-1965. It was under this circumstances that the largest Chinese Bank, the Hang Seng Bank was taken over by the Hongkong Bank, and a moratorium was imposed by the government on issuing new banking licenses. The crisis was then closely followed by the "Star Ferry" riots of 1966 and the civil disturbance of 1967 caused by a spillover of the Cultural Revolution from China. The economy dipped sharply but picked up quickly again towards the end of the decade.

In the 1970s, the Hong Kong property development industry came of age. This was made possible by a massive public housing program and a parallel development in the security and banking industry that revolutionized the conventional method of property financing in Hong Kong. Under the leadership of Sir Maclehose, the new Governor of Hong Kong who arrived in 1971, the government launched one of the largest projects in public housing and urban development in Asia. In 10 to 15 years time, more than half of the Hong Kong's population was living in public housing estates, which are mainly located in the New Territories. Side by side with the public building program was the development of equally large private estates. Together, the two developments turn sleepy villages, such as Shatin and Tuen Mun, with populations of several thousands, into urban centers with populations of over several hundreds thousands each.

Such massive developments needed equally massive financing. This was made possible by new development in the security and banking industry. Hitherto, the Hong Kong Stock Exchange was the only stock exchange in Hong Kong; the shares traded were mainly those of British firms and the utilities. It was not an active market and hardly fulfilled its function as a medium for raising equity capital. In the early part of the 1970s, three new exchanges were formed and a spate of companies were floated in the market. While many of these flotations were speculative, and indeed the share market bubble burst in 1973, the stock market became more mature in the mid to late 1970s and served as an important source of capital for fast growing property development companies. The flagship companies of the major Chinese business groups, which we shall describe in greater details in a later section, went public mostly in this period or in the early part of the 1980s.

Another source of finance was opened by the 1976 "Deposit-taking Company Ordinance." This ordinance enabled deposit-taking companies to conduct most of the business hitherto conducted by licensed banks. This meant that international banks could now participate in the financial market despite the moratorium on the issue of banking licenses. Their participation brought to the property developers in Hong Kong contacts and access to the vast resources of international financial market to the property developers in Hong Kong.

The Power Broker – Hongkong Bank as King-maker

Two major takeover battles where Chinese were successful in wresting control of major companies from the hongs precipitated the changes in the structure of interlocking directorate network that we observed in 1976. These were the takeover of Hutchison by K.S. Li and the Hong Kong and Kowloon Wharf by Y.K. Pao. In both cases Hong Kong Bank was either the seller of the major block of shares or the provider of the major source of finance for the takeover. It is somewhat surprising that the institution that helped Chinese entrepreneurs to take on established British interest was the Hongkong Bank. The Bank was and continues to be run by British executives who have close associations with the hongs. One possible reason could be that the Bank was one of the few, if not the only company, which was not controlled by family interest and hence their managers could act more "professionally" supporting whomever they saw as having the greatest potential as the future captains of Hong Kong business. It was also possible that, because of the active role the Bank played in supporting the growing industries of Hong Kong (Yao 1983), it had a much better appreciation of the potentials of the businesses run by the Chinese companies.

Two Case Studies

The stories of the rise of K.S. Li's and Y.K. Pao's groups of businesses illustrate how the new Chinese business groups arose under the circumstances described above.

K.S. Li group: K.S. Li came from an ordinary family. He first went into the plastic industry in the 1950s and by early 1960s he was reputed to have accumulated 50-60 million Hong Kong dollars from the business. From the mid 1960s to early 1970s, he bought a lot of properties when the prices were relatively low. In the 1970s, he shifted his main business to the property development. His flagship company, Cheung Kong, went public in 1972. In 1974, he set up Canadian Eastern Finance, a deposit-taking company as a joint venture with the Canadian Imperial Bank of Commerce. K.S. Li was made a director of the Hongkong Bank in 1978. Previous to this, in 1975, Hongkong Bank acquired a large chunk of Hutchison's shares in a rescue operation. Then, in 1979, the Bank sold the shares to Cheung Kong giving it the control over the Hutchison group. In the following week, K.S. Li was made a director of the China International Trust and Investment Corporation (CITIC) which is one of the first major investment vehicles set up by the State Council of China. After the acquisition of Hutchison together with its myriad of businesses, Li's group of companies made further acquisitions of British interests such as Green Island Cement and Hong Kong Electric in Hong Kong and overseas businesses such as Husky Oil of Canada in the early 1980s.

Y.K. Pao group: Y.K. Pao had a better head start than K.S. Li. His family was in the banking industry in Shanghai. He came to Hong Kong in 1949 with a reasonable amount of cash in hand to start business afresh. He spotted the potential growth of the shipping industry at that time, especially after the close of the Suez Canal, and devised a new way of financing his shipping operations. The growth of his companies, however, was strongly supported by the Hongkong Bank. Accordingly, Hongkong Bank took up to 45 percent of the shares of World Maritime Bahamas Ltd, which was the main shipping company of Y.K. Pao in 1964, and later on, together with the Industrial Bank of Japan, acquired 37 percent shares of World Finance International, which was another major company under Y.K. Pao's control. The Bank also had a 10 percent stake in Eastern Navigation, which was the publicly listed company in Y.K. Pao's group.

In 1978 Cheung Kong was seeking to acquire enough shareholding in Hongkong and Kowloon Wharf to gain control of the company's valuable land assets, which were located primarily at Tsimshatsui at the tip of the rapidly developing Kowloon peninsula. Under the influence of the Hongkong Bank, Cheung Kong sold their accumulated shares to Y.K. Pao at a substantial profit. With his substantial shareholding, and in response to an attempt by Hong Kong Land to gain absolute control over Wharf, Y.K. Pao managed to take over the company in 1980. At that time Y.K. Pao was the deputy chairman of the Hongkong Bank, and it was widely believed that the takeover was financed by Hongkong Bank or its subsidiary.

The acquisition of Hongkong and Kowloon Wharf firmly established the Y.K. Pao group in the property development and hotel industries. In 1984, the group acquired the Wheelock Marden group of companies, thus diversifying further into property and retail businesses. Diversification continued with the acquisition of the U.S. based Omni group of hotels and the British Standard Chartered Bank in 1988.

Three Stages of Growth

The growth pattern of K.S. Li's and Y.K. Pao's group of companies suggest a model of growth of big Chinese business groups in three stages. First is the acquisition of start-up capital from businesses outside Hong Kong, such as the export industry or shipping. The second stage is achieving growth to substantial size through property development. This is usually achieved by the acquisition of companies with substantial holdings of land, such as the utilities or wharfs and godowns companies, or by acquiring newly formed sites. The third stage is further expansion and diversification by acquisition of major business establishments. It was when the companies moved into property in a big way that they offered their shares to the public and hence came into view in the interlocking directorate network. It should be noted that, because of the loose regulations, the founding entrepreneur of a company usually does not lose control of the company when he offers the company's shares to the public.

Other Chinese business groups that seem to be getting into the second stage in this period are the T.S. Kwok group, which acquired Kowloon Motor Bus, and the S.K. Lee group, which acquired control of Hong Kong and China Gas and Hong Kong and Yaumati Ferry in 1980 and 1981 respectively. The former of these groups appears in the 1981 network and the latter appears in the 1986 network.

Interlocking Directorate Network in 1981

The changes in the late 1970s had produced a very different configuration in the 1981 interlocking directorate network which are shown in Figure 3.

According to our criteria we have identified three tightly knit business groups as shown in Table 2. One of these groups consists of 31 companies and is further broken down into seven sub-groups using 4-graph components. A description of the business groups is given in Appendix Two.

There are both integration and differentiation in the 1981 network. Besides two small groups, most companies are connected in one big tightly knit group labeled as the Mixed Group in Table 2. Within this group, there are differentiations between the sub-groups in terms of nationality, size, and centrality.

In terms of size, the network is still dominated by the Bank and Jardine. The Bank accounted for 9.8 percent while the small Jardine group of two companies – Jardine Matheson and Hong Kong Land – accounted for 11.54 percent of the stock market capitalization. In both cases the proportion had decreased when compared with similar figures in 1976. Moreover there were dramatic changes in the relative sizes of the companies within the Jardine group of companies. Whereas Jardine's share of the market capitalization had dropped dramatically from 7.05 percent to 2.95 percent; that of Hong Kong Land had risen from 6.2 percent to 8.59 percent.

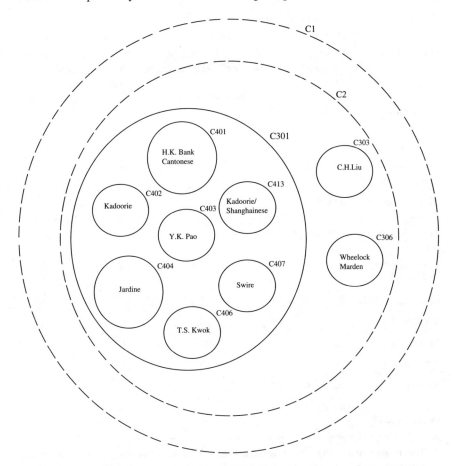

C1 and C2: loosely connected components of 1-graph and 2-graph.
C3xx and C4xx: tightly knit components of 3-graph and 4-graph.

Figure 3:   Business Groups in 1981 as Identified by the Network of Interlocking Direc-
           torates

In terms of centrality, Hong Kong Bank was still dominant. It alone was connected to thirty-six other companies. The Bank together with the Cantonese group
constituted the center of the network in 1981. The 1976 network center based on
the Jardine group had disappeared.

Two business groups based on traditional hongs, the Hutchison group and
Wharf group, had disappeared. These were the results of the two major takeovers
of the hong companies by local Chinese entrepreneurs described in a previous section. The result on the network is that Y.K. Pao's group of companies had become
a separate group. The Hutchison group of companies, now under the umbrella

Table 2:   Profiles of Business Groups in 1981

Group Name	Control by Chinese?	No. of Companies	% Market Capitalization	Group Centrality-no. of Companies connected with the group
Major Groups				
C.H. Liu (303)	yes	3	0.95	18
Wheelock Marden (306)	no	6	2.53	8
Mixed (305)	mixed	31	61.21	56*
Sub-divisions within the mixed group				
Cantonese/HK Bank (401)	yes	13	33.06	56
Kadoorie 1 (402)	no	3	5.27	35
Y.K. Pao (403)	yes	3	5.15	28
Jardine (404)	no	2	11.54	16
T.S. Kwok (406)	yes	2	2.39	26
Swire (407)	no	3	3.40	30
Kadoorie/ Shanghai (413)	mixed	3	0.17	17

*   This is not equal to the sum of the centralities of the sub-divisions as companies in the sub-divisions may be linked to the same companies.

of K.S. Li's group of companies, was included within the Cantonese/Hongkong Bank group.

A new feature in the network is the rise of new multi-company Chinese business groups. Unlike the Cantonese businessmen from the 1976 Cantonese/Hongkong Bank groups which were well established businesses before the Second World War, these new Chinese businesses became well established only in the 1960s.

The Hongs Lose Out

A question could be raised as to why the hongs were not able to profit from the property boom as much as the Chinese businesses. There are four reasons that this might have been the case. The first reason could be that because of the speculative nature of the property market, the conservative hongs wanted to avoid the risk. Indeed many Chinese businesses had gone bankrupt because of the property market. The Goodyear Property Development Co. was a good example of how a very successful company went bankrupt in a very short period of time. Second, the property developments in the 1970s and 1980s were mainly high density building developments in the New Territories. The senior executives of the hongs, mainly expatriates, tended to live and work in different areas in Hong Kong that are more luxurious and less crowded. Hence, they did not have the intimate knowledge of these areas, which made it difficult for them to undertake very large financial commitments to these development projects. Thirdly, it could be that they lacked faith in the future of Hong Kong. Being British, they have the option of moving out more easily than their Chinese counterparts. Investing in landed property would neutralize this advantage because it further committed their investment to remain in the colony. Finally, property ownership has always been a means to build up family prestige and wealth in traditional Chinese villages. Chinese businessmen, therefore, value property foremost as a form of investment, and they readily accept a speculative nature of industry as a sine qua non of business.

The changing economic conditions of the colony thus provided the opportunities for the rise of powerful Chinese entrepreneurs. But how that opportunity was being exploited was determined by the political and institutional conditions of society found at the time. Political factors again triggered off major changes in the network in the following period.

The Effect of the Sino-British Negotiation 1982-1984

The confidence crisis arising out of the Sino-British negotiation over the fate of Hong Kong's sovereignty in 1997 precipitated a crash in the property market. The early 1980s was accordingly a shake-out period when many companies went bankrupt. It was also a period when the Chinese business groups consolidated their control over their constituent companies. There were also those who lost heart and left the territory. The most prominent of these was the major Chinese shareholder of the Wheelock Marden group. He decided to sell out his shareholding, and Y.K. Pao was successful in taking control of the group.

The Jardine group had suffered a severe blow in this period, partly as a result of their response to takeover threats from Chinese entrepreneurs. After the takeover of Hongkong and Kowloon Wharf, Jardine and Hong Kong Land bought a substantial volume of each others shares so that a potential predator would have to take the two companies together, an effort considered to be impossible. Unfortunately this mutual reinforcement became a mutual burden as Hong Kong Land incurred major losses during the property market crash. The result was a further shrinkage in the size and centrality of the Jardine group of companies.

The Network in 1986

The configuration of the interlocking directorate network in 1986 is shown in Figure 4. According to our criteria we have identified nine tightly knit business groups as shown in Table 3. A brief description of the business groups is found in Appendix Three.

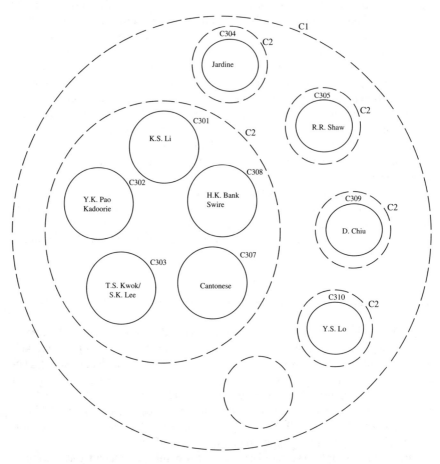

C1 and C2: loosely connected components of 1-graph and 2-graph.
C3xx and C4xx: tightly knit components of 3-graph and 4-graph.

Figure 4: Business Groups in 1986 as Identified by the Network of Interlocking Directorates

The network in 1986 is much more differentiated into separate business groups. Unlike the previous years there is not a large tightly knit group that encompassed a large number of companies and that linked up the Chinese and non-Chinese business groups.

Table 3:   Profiles of Business Groups in 1986

Group Name	Control by Chinese?	No. of Companies	% Market Capitalization	Group Centrality-no. of Companies Connected with the Group
K.S. Li (301)	yes	4	12.78	37
Y.K. Pao/ Kadoorie (302)	mixed	11	13.31	24
T.S. Kwok/ S.K. Lee (303)	yes	8	7.56	38
Jardine (304)	no	2	6.00	10
R.R. Shaw (305)	yes	3	1.43	20
Cantonese (302)	yes	5	7.07	32
H.K. Bank/ Swire (309)	no	4	15.58	32
D. Chiu (309)	yes	3	0.19	13
Y.S. Lo	yes	3	0.55	0

   The rise of separate multi-company Chinese business groups has become much more prominent. This was coupled with a corresponding decrease in the number of non-Chinese business groups. The importance of the Jardine group further declined. It now accounted for only 6 percent of the total stock market capitalization and was connected to only ten other companies.

   Hongkong Bank continued its dominance in terms of size. It alone accounted for 8.33 percent of the stock market capitalization. However, its centrality in the network has decreased significantly. It alone was connected to only sixteen companies, and the Hong Kong Bank/Swire group as a whole was connected to only thirty-two companies, making it rank third in centrality among the business groups.

   Taking into account the number of companies in a group, and acknowledging the significance of the Hongkong Bank as an independent institution, the K.S. Li group had become the most important business group in terms of both market capitalization and centrality. This group accounted for 12.78 percent of market capitalization and was connected to thirty-seven other companies. The dominance of the K.S. Li group, however, was not overwhelming. There were four other groups that were also significant in terms of size and centrality (i.e., those which account-ed for more than 6 percent market capitalization and with group centrality greater than twenty).

Compared with the relatively high group centralities of the 1976 and 1981 busi-ness groups, the inter-connections among the business groups had decreased. As a whole, we can describe the network as loosely connected and multi-centered. Furthermore, within the Chinese groups, ownership tended to be more concentrat-ed and there were more directors holding multiple executive positions in several companies. These characteristics are similar to those found in Taiwan Business groups (Hamilton et al. 1987) and can be attributed to the Chinese businessmen's personalized style of management and their obsession with maintaining control over their investments (Redding 1990).

Conclusion

This story of the changing patterns of the interlocking directorate network in Hong Kong in the period 1976 to 1986 thus illustrates the interaction of economic, polit-ical and institutional factors in shaping the characteristics of the business groups in Hong Kong. The resource dependence perspective is certainty correct in the proposition that organizations seek to connect or take over other organizations that control the supply of a critical resource. One of the main objectives of the major takeover bids in the period under consideration was indeed for the precious landholdings of the target companies.

This line of reasoning is less helpful if we want to explain why certain resources become critical. The resource dependence perspective would explain changes in terms of typical production processes or the industrial structure of the industry in which the organizations are located. However, in our case, the explanation lies in the entrepreneurs' decision to exploit the opportunities created by social and political changes. It has little to do with the characteristics of the industries them-selves. The importance of a resource is, therefore, determined by the strategies of the entrepreneurs. The characteristics of these strategies, or in Whitley's term, the "business recipes" are determined by the institutional context found in the soci-ety concerned. Some of the institutional factors we found important in shaping the business groups are the relationship between the dominant economic actors, the relationship between the financial institutions and the businesses, and the role of the government as a developmental agent.

Inevitably, political and economic factors influence each other. But there are periods when certain factors come to dominate the situation. In 1976, the struc-ture of the business groups is largely a reflection of the political domination of the British. In 1981, the Chinese businesses made a triumphant entry to the scene largely because of their economic power. Finally in 1986, the political factor again provided a major stimulant for change leading to an apparent replacement of the British interests with those of the Chinese. The resulting network, therefore, takes on a shape which reflects the "Chinese mode" of business relations.

Appendix One: A Brief Description of Business Groups in 1976

The Southeast Asian Chinese Group – This consists of two property development companies and two banks. They were all controlled by Malaysian and Singaporean Chinese interest. All of these companies had financial trouble in the early 1980s and all went bankrupt as a result.

The Kadoorie Group – This group consists of three companies controlled by the Kadoorie family. The most important one is China Light and Power, which is one of the two franchised companies to supply electricity in Hong Kong. One of the companies, the Hong Kong and Shanghai Hotel, is in the hotel industry and runs the Peninsula Hotel, one of the most prestigious hotels in the world. It was the object of a major take-over battle in the mid 1980s. The third company in the group is a property development company.

The Swire Group – Containing one of the traditional hongs, the Swire Pacific, the group runs a diversified business with interests mostly in trading, property, transportation (airline and shipping), and industries. There were three companies in the group, all directly or indirectly controlled by John Swire & Sons, a private company in Britain.

The Hutchison Group – Also containing one of the traditional hongs, the Hutchison International, the group consists of four associated companies of the Hutchison group and runs a well diversified business. The group was taken over by K.S. Li in the late 1970s. The group also includes a Chinese property development company (Tai Cheung Properties Ltd.) with whom Hutchison ran another joint-venture company within the group (City and Urban Properties Ltd.).

The Jardine and Matheson Group – The group consists of three companies, one of which is the famous 'Princely Hong' – Jardine and Matheson of Hong Kong. It runs a well diversified business and is closely associated with Hong Kong Land, the property giant company which owns most of the property in the Central District, the financial center of Hong Kong. The article of association of Hong Kong Land require that its chairman always be the chairman of Jardine Matheson.

The Jardine/Hong Kong Land Group – Jardine Matheson had substantial but not majority share holdings in four of the five companies in the group. Executives from Jardine were well represented in the boards of these companies. The four companies include Hong Kong Land, which has been described previously, City Hotel, and Harbor Center Development, both of which were involved in the hotel industry, and Hong Kong and Kowloon Wharf (Wharf) which also has a diversified business. Wharf was taken over by Y.K. Pao in the late 1970s. The fifth company in the group is Bank of East Asia, which is one of the largest Chinese banks in Hong Kong.

The Wheelock Marden Group – The group also includes one of the traditional hongs, Wheelock Marden. The group runs a diversified business. It was also taken over by Y.K. Pao in the early 1980s.

The Cantonese Group – The group consists of five companies. Except for the Hang Seng Bank, each of these companies was under the management of an independent owner. All of the companies were founded before World War II. The original founders were in their sixties or seventies, and their children or second generation relative are beginning to take up responsible positions in the company. The most important company within the group is the Hang Seng Bank, which was the largest Chinese bank in Hong Kong until the mid 1960s, when it was taken over by the Hongkong Bank during a banking crisis. The business of other companies in the group are mainly property development, hotel, and shipping.

The Hongkong Bank and Y.K. Pao Group – This is a rather mixed group of five companies. The most important one is the Hongkong Bank, which is the largest bank in Hong Kong and one of the largest in the world, ranking in the top twenty. The ownership of the bank is very diffuse; no one is allowed to own more than 1 percent of the Bank's share, and the top management is made up of all British executives. Two companies in the group, mainly in shipping, are controlled by Y.K. Pao. The fourth company, South China Morning Post, publishes one of the two English newspapers in Hong Kong and its view is commonly taken to represent that of the business establishment. Both the Bank and Hutchison had substantial holdings of the company's shares. The fifth company in the group is Hong Kong Electric, a franchised utility company. It appears that the Bank, Jardine, Hong Kong Land, and Wheelock Marden were all substantial share-holders of the company.

Appendix Two: A Brief Description of Business Groups in 1981

C.H. Liu Group – This small group consists of China Motor Bus, one of the two franchised bus companies in Hong Kong, a Bank, and an investment company of the Liu family.

Wheelock Marden Group – This group remained largely unchanged from their 1976 position.

Cantonese Bank Group – This group becomes a combination of the Cantonese group and the Hongkong Bank/Y.K. Pao group of companies. Two sets of companies associated with these groups in 1976, those of the Pao family and Chao family, had left this group by 1981. The Pao family formed a separate group, and the

Chao family's shipping company had financial trouble, so that only the family's property company remained in our list of the top 100 companies. The newcomers in the Cantonese Bank Group were four companies under the control of K.S. Li's family.

Kadoorie Group – This group remained largely unchanged from its 1976 position.

Y.K. Pao Group – This group consists of Wharf and Harbour Centre Development acquired from the Jardine/Hong Kong Land group in 1976 and Pao's flagship company.

Jardine Matheson Group – This group consists of just Jardine Matheson and Hong Kong Land, the flagship companies of the two Jardine groups in 1976.

T.S. Kwok Group – This is a new group consisting of two property development companies. The family was one of the rising stars among the Chinese businesses, as we have mentioned in a previous section.

Swire Group – This group remained largely unchanged from their 1976 position.

Kadoorie/Shanghainese Group – This is a small group of manufacturing companies. One is directly under the control of the Kadoorie family, and the other two are joint ventures between the Kadoorie family and the Shanghainese families. This is expected as the Kadoorie family has a long history of business involvement in Shanghai.

Appendix Three: A Brief Description of Business Groups in 1986

K.S. Li Group – This group consists of four companies under the control of the K.S. Li family. It split off from the 1981 Hongkong Bank/Cantonese group together with Hong Kong Electric, which K.S. Li had acquired in the period. One of the L.S. Li group companies, International City Holdings, was privatized.

Y.K. Pao/Kadoorie – This is a combination of four groups from 1981. The Wheelock Marden group was taken over by Y.K. Pao and was absorbed into Pao's network. This 1981 Kadoorie group's network was now integrated with the Kadoorie/Shanghainese group, which in turn was connected with Y.K. Pao's network.

T.K. Kwok/S.K. Lee – T.S. Kwok, S.K. Lee and K.H. Fung started together as business partners. They later divided their businesses, with Fung mainly involved in the financial businesses and the other two in property development. Both T.S. Kwok and S.K. Lee appeared to follow similar strategies in acquiring utility companies for the land that these companies possessed. T.S. Kwok acquired Kowloon Motor Bus and then subsequently spun off the property development side of the business to form Manor House Holding Ltd. S.K. Lee acquired both Hong Kong and China Gas and Yaumati Ferry in the late 1970s and the early 1980s.

Jardine Matheson Group – The group consists of the same two companies as in 1981. Efforts were being made to spin off the non-property elements from Hong Kong Land.

R.R. Shaw Group – This group consists of three companies, two of which are controlled by R.R. Shaw. Shaw is the king of Chinese movies. He has substantial shareholdings in HK-TVB which was one of the two television stations in Hong Kong. He is well connected in the Shanghainese business community.

Cantonese Group – This group was separated from the 1981 Hongkong Bank/Cantonese group, whose members are similar to the 1976 Cantonese group. The difference was that instead of the Chao family, the group now included the Fu family, which owned the Furama Hotel. It is interesting to note that similar to other members in the group, Furama is run by second generation Chinese business entrepreneurs.

Hongkong Bank/Swire – This group consists of four companies, two from the 1981 Swire group (the third company in the Swire group was privatized), Hongkong Bank, the South China Morning Post.

D. Chiu Group – This group consists of three companies, all under control of the Chiu family. They were in a wide variety of businesses such as entertainment, banking, and property.

Y.S. Lo – The group consisted of three companies, all under the control of the Lo family. They were all property development companies.

References

Abegglen, James C. and George Stalk. 1985. *Kaisha, The Japanese Corporation*. New York: Basic Books.

Allen, Michael P. 1974. "The Structure of Interorganizational Elite Cooptation." *American Sociological Review* 39: 393-406.

Chandler, Alfred, Jr. 1977. *The Visible Hand: The Managerial Revolution in American Business*. Cambridge, Mass.: Harvard University Press.

Davies, Stephen N.G. 1989. "The Changing Nature of Representation in Hong Kong Politics." *Hong Kong: The Challenge of Transformation*, eds. K. Check-Milby and M.Mushkat. Hong Kong: Centre of Asian Studies, University of Hong Kong.

Davies, Stephen N.G. 1977. "One Brand of Politics Rekindled." *Hong Kong Law Journal* 39: 44-80.

Dooley, Peter C. 1969. "The Interlocking Directorate." *American Economic Review* 59: 314-23.

Eads, George C. and Kozo Yamamura. 1987. "The Future of Industrial Policy." *The Polit-ical Economy of Japan, I: The Domestic Transformation,* eds. K. Yamamura and Y. Ya-suba. Stanford, Cal.: Stanford University Press.
Hamilton, Gary G. and Nicole Wooley Biggart. 1988. "Market, Culture, and Authority: A Comparative Analysis of Management and Organization in the Far East." *American Journal of Sociology* 94 (supplement): 52-94.
Hamilton, Gary G., Marco Orrù and Nicole Biggart. 1987. "Enterprise Groups in East Asia: An Organizational Analysis." *Shoken Keizai* (Financial Economic Review) 161: 78-106.
Hamilton, Gary G., W.J. Kim, and William Zeile. 1988. "The Network Structures of East Asian Economies." Paper presented at the Apros Conference, 6-8 April, 1988, Firms, Management, the State and Economic Cultures, Hong Kong.
Hughes, Richard. 1976. *Borrowed Place, Borrowed Time: Hong Kong and Its Many Faces.* Hong Kong: André Deutsch.
Johnson, Chalmers. 1982. *MITI and the Japanese Miracle.* Stanford, Cal.: Stanford Univer-sity Press. Jones, Leory and Il Sakong. 1980. *Government, Business and Entrepreneur-ship in Economic Development: the Korean Case.* Cambridge, Mass.: Harvard Univer-sity.
Lim, Mah-hui. 1981. *Ownership and Control of the One Hundred Largest Corporations in Malaysia.* Kuala Lumpur: Oxford University Press.
Orrù, Marco, Nicloe Woolsey Biggart, and Gary G. Hamilton. 1991. "Organizational Iso-morphism in East Asia: Broadening the New Institutionalism." *The New Institutionalism in Organizational Analysis,* eds. W.W. Powell and P. DiMaggio. Chicago: University of Chicago Press.
Pennings, Johannes M. 1980. *Interlocking Directorates.* San Francisco: Jossey-Bass.
Pfeffer, Jeffrey. 1972. "Size and Composition of Corporate Boards of Directors." *Adminis-trative Science Quarterly* 17: 218-228.
Pfeffer, Jeffrey and G.R. Salancik. 1978. *The External Control of Organizations.* New York: Harper and Row.
Rear, John. 1971. "One Brand of Politics." *Hong Kong, The Industrial Colony*, ed. Keith Hopkins. Hong Kong: Oxford University Press.
Redding, S.Gordon 1990. *The Spirit of Chinese Capitalism.* Berlin, New York: de Gruyter.
Redding, S.Gordon and Simon Tam. 1985. "Networks and Molecular Organizations: An Exploratory View of Chinese Firms in Hong Kong." *Perspectives in International Busi-ness,* eds. K.C. Mun and T.S. Chan. Hong Kong: Chinese University Press.
Sonquist, John and Thomas Koenig. 1975. "Interlocking Directorates in Top U.S. Corpo-rations: A Graph Theory Approach." *The Insurgent Sociologist* 5 (3): 196-230.
Stokman, Frans, N. Rolf Ziegler, and John Scott, eds. 1985. *Networks of Corporate Power: A Comparative Analysis of Ten Countries.* London: Polity Press.
Whitley, Richard D. 1990. "Eastern Asian Enterprise Structures and the Comparative Anal-ysis of Forms of Business Organizations." *Organization Studies* 11 (1): 47-74.
Williamson, Oliver E. and W.G. Ouchi. 1981. "The Market and Hierarchies and Visible Hand." *Perspective on Organization Design an Behavior,* eds. Andrew Van de Van and William Joyce. New York: John Wiley.
Yao, Y.C. 1983. "Financing Hong Kong's Early Post War Industrialization." *Eastern Bank-ing: Essays in the History of the Hong Kong and Shanghai Banking Corporation,* ed. Frank H.H. King. London: The Athlone Press.

Ethnicity, Polity, and Economy: A Case Study of the Mandarin Trade and the Chinese Connection[1]

Eddie C.Y. Kuo

Introduction

A study of the cultural foundations of Chinese businesses in Southeast Asia must look not only at the internal organization of such businesses, but also at the external connections among them. Typically, business connections among Chinese firms are ethnically based and often oriented towards a dialect group. The extension of such inter-connectedness forms a Chinese trading network, involving multiple linkages among Chinese businessmen located in different cities or countries who play key roles at different junctions in the business transactions for the manufacture or trade of commodities. Such business networks and connections have often been established over years of continuous business relations. They are particularistic in nature, characterized by mutual trust and confidence. As such, they are strong and resistant to external interference from government or business competitors.

The present case study analyzes the network of the mandarin orange trade, which connects producers and exporters in China, middlemen in Singapore, and wholesalers, retailers, and finally consumers in Malaysia. This is a truly Chinese network as mandarin oranges, a product of Chinese origin, are distributed through various ethnic Chinese traders until they reach Malaysian consumers who are mostly Chinese by ethnic origin. In addition, this network is distinctively Chinese in the sense that its business transactions follow certain patterns that are also typically Chinese. The paper presents and analyzes events surrounding an attempt made by a national government to intervene in this network, and discusses the way the network reacted to such an attempt. As such, the case study illustrates an intriguing interplay between elements of ethnicity, polity and economy.

Mandarin Oranges and Mandarin Trade

Among the Chinese in Southeast Asia, mandarin oranges carry special symbolic significance in the celebration of the Chinese New Year, the most important of all festivals for the Chinese. During the festive season, mandarins are displayed at the family altar as offerings to household gods and ancestors. They are also offered together with sweets and cakes to welcome New Year visitors. Visitors similarly will bring some mandarin oranges, usually an even number, as presents when paying the traditional New Year's visit. In return, the host may also offer some mandarin oranges to the visitors when they go home. It is not unusual that the same oranges may pass on from hand to hand when visitors move from family to family on New Year goodwill visits.

Why are mandarin oranges given such symbolic significance in the Chinese New Year festival? Not only is the seasonal fruit the color of gold, but its Cantonese pronunciation, *gum*, is also a homophone for "gold." To give mandarin oranges, therefore, suggests an offering of gold, hence wealth and prosperity. One would never decline them as presents, as it would mean one would be declining wealth and prosperity in the new year. While this custom has a distinctive Cantonese origin, the symbolic significance of mandarin oranges during the Chinese New Year has been adopted by other ethnic Chinese in Southeast Asia over many generations of contact among the dialect groups. The Cantonese origin of the custom also explains the reason that it has to be the mandarin orange, pronounced *gum* (gold) in Cantonese, and not just any other kind of oranges, which are called *chan* in Cantonese and which connotes no auspicious significance.[2] The customary use of mandarin oranges for ceremonial and social purposes makes the mandarin trade a lucrative business in Southeast Asia during the Chinese New Year Festival.

Traditionally, this seasonal fruit is exported from the port of Shantou (Swatow), in Guangdong province, China, near its producing area, and shipped to Singapore (often via Hong Kong) for local consumption and redistribution to Malaysia which has a large Chinese population. According to statistics from the Trade Development Board of Singapore, in 1983, for instance, Singapore imported a total of 14,853 tons of mandarins valued in Singapore dollars at 23,591,000 CIF, of which 9,775 tons, or 65.8 percent, were imported from China, almost all from Shantou, valued at S$14,517,000. On the other hand, Singapore re-exported 5,092 tons of mandarins, or 52.1 percent of its imports, valued at S$7,989,000 FOB; of these re-exports 84.8 percent (4,317 tons valued at S$6,257,000 FOB) went to West Malaysia.[3]

The network of the mandarin orange trade, through the various stages from production to distribution and consumption, is dominated by Chinese businessmen. The strong Chinese connection in this and other trade goods from China, however, is considered by the Malaysian government to be monopolistic, and hence incompatible with its overall national economic goals. Malaysia has taken measures and implemented import constraints to discourage indirect trade with China via Singapore and to break the monopoly of the Chinese network. Many of such policies and measures are not based on purely rational economic considerations, but may also be due to ethnic and political reasons. In Malaysia, trading with China has become an issue that involves an intricate and complex interplay between polity, ethnicity, and economy, all within Malaysia's national boundaries and beyond.

These intricate relations are revealed in an incident involving the import of mandarin oranges to Malaysia which took place just a few weeks before the Chinese New Year in 1985. The present study focuses on this 1985 incident to analyze the changing trading relations between China, Singapore, and Malaysia, at a time when all parties involved responded variously to changing social, political and economic environments, both domestic and international. The 1985 mandarin incident has to be understood within the politico-economic context of Malaysia. A brief discussion of Malaysia's New Economic Policy (NEP) and related policies of direct trade with China is therefore in order.

The NEP and Chinese Businessmen in Malaysia

For more than ten years, since its independence in 1957, Malaysia maintained a *laissez faire* economic framework. Economic development during this period brought benefits to the foreign sector and Chinese businesses in Malaysia. The majority of the Malays, who concentrated on cottage industries, however, had not been able to share the benefit from economic advancement. The discrepancy in the economic status between the Chinese and the Malays continued to widen. Tension mounted, and dissatisfaction over this discrepancy among the Malays, who considered themselves *bumiputras* (sons of soil), led to ugly racial riots in 1969.

In 1970, the younger Malay leaders pressured the government into adopting an interventionist role in the economy. They sought to lessen dependence on the Malaysian Chinese for the nation's economic development and to increase the economic power of the Malays through a greater control of the nation's economic resources. A new economic strategy, called the New Economic Policy (NEP), was implemented in 1971. This was an ambitious 20-year plan, aiming (1) to accelerate the process of restructuring Malaysian society to correct the economic imbalance, and (2) to eradicate poverty by raising income levels and increasing employment opportunities for all Malaysians, irrespective of race (Mid-Term Review of the Second Malaysia Plan, 1973, p.1; quoted in Jesudason 1989, p. 71).

The most prominent feature of the policy was the expansion of the role of the state in an attempt to counterbalance Chinese and foreign economic dominance. The Malays were targeted to own and control at least 30 percent of the share capital of the corporate sector by 1990, from a base of less than 2 percent in 1970. State enterprises such as the Perbadanan Nasional (PERNAS) were established "to acquire assets to be held in trust for the Malays and other indigenous groups until such time as they [were] in a position to acquire these shares on their own" ("Mid-Term Review of the Second Malaysia Plan," 1973, p. 14; quoted in Jesudason 1989, p.72). Under the NEP, these state enterprises enjoyed special privileges from governmental bodies to counterbalance the economic dominance of the Chinese businesses. Accordingly, state controls increased in the early 1970s.

The small and medium scale Chinese businesses, which were mainly in the retail and wholesale trades, transport, and in the lower end of the construction and manufacturing sector, subsequently faced problems of increased competition. They found it difficult to compete with new Malay firms for government contracts. Nevertheless, as Jesudason (1989, p. 148) puts it, the Chinese businessmen had the advantage of a buyer-seller-retail network, where the transactions are influenced by ethnic ties and loyalties. As a result, Chinese retailers were able to depend on the large urban Chinese population for a secure business. This is a significant factor in accounting for the Chinese responses to the 1985 mandarin orange incident which forms the focus of the present case study. Chinese small businesses have also managed to evade state regulation through the use of a Malay front to act as a shield for the Chinese entrepreneur. Malay individuals were paid a monthly sum to obtain permits from the respective ministries. This practice, referred to as "Ali-Baba" partnerships,[4] was prevalent in sectors where Chinese were denied licenses in favor of Malays (Nonini 1983).

The larger Chinese businesses were less concerned about being displaced than about looking for new frontiers for expansion. Although they were required to offer at least 30 percent Malay ownership at special discounts when issuing shares, this posed no major problem because, being large, these corporations had the financial resources to absorb the costs incurred (Jesudason 1989, p. 150). In the meantime, under these constraints, large Chinese companies began to venture into property development instead of manufacturing because it promised fewer hazards and quicker returns. These conglomerates also increasingly relied on mergers and takeovers as a development strategy, spreading their assets and business activities beyond the national borders (Jesudason 1989, p. 150).

According to a study conducted by Gerakan (*Sunday Times*, 26 March 1989), the NEP, an opposition party whose members are predominantly Chinese, had achieved its major objective by the mid-1980s, as the ownership rights of *bumiputras* in the entrepreneurial sector had exceeded the 30 percent target. The report, however, pointed out that, while the NEP had succeeded in creating major Malay financial groups, it had failed to produce small Malay businessmen. In other words, wealth had been distributed to a small class of Malays only. The party also criticized the government for restricting the participation of other Malaysians (in all probability referring to the Chinese) in some economic areas through licensing, employment, housing, land resettlement, and education policies, while *bumiputras* were given shares at special rates. Although the Gerakan study highlights the success of the NEP in reaching its 30 percent *bumiputra* ownership target, it implies that such preferential policies are no longer justified. The report itself represents the continuing economic struggle of the Chinese against the political dominance of the Malays.

Encouraging Direct Trade with China

When the Malaysian government shifted to the interventionist approach in 1970, it also embarked upon a program of establishing direct trade with socialist nations. The most important direct trade link that Malaysia wanted to establish was that with China. This was intended not only to capture the lucrative China trade, but also to promote *bumiputra* retail enterprises in competition with local Chinese businessmen (Gale 1981, p. 110).

Traditionally, goods from China to Malaysia were imported via Hong Kong and Singapore. Dealers in these third countries charged Malaysian importers a 4-5 percent commission. PERNAS, the state enterprise, wanted to gain monopoly of this trade and to do away with the need for third countries. The monopoly was to be fashioned such that PERNAS, appointed in 1971 as the sole agent to deal with trading with socialist countries, would be given exclusive regulatory authority to approve import licenses for goods from China. Malaysian importers would then obtain their goods direct from China after paying a half percent commission to PERNAS. It was expected that the lower commission should attract the Malaysian importers to do away with the middlemen in Hong Kong and Singapore. Furthermore, the new policy should make licensed Malay traders highly competitive with traditional Chinese traders. This was intended to serve as an initial step to PERNAS's control of Chinese imports by denying import licenses to Chinese businessmen in favor of *bumiputra* enterprises.

The Chinese businessmen realized PERNAS's enormous potential influence on the structure of the Malaysian economy. Through political and commercial channels, they urged the government to continue to allow businessmen to import goods through Hong Kong and Singapore, even though this meant paying higher commissions and hence higher costs to them. They anticipated problems arising from direct import of perishables from China and the possibility of a breakdown in the flow of trade which would lead to higher prices, thus threatening their livelihood (Gale 1981, p. 113).

In the meantime, China responded coolly to the gesture of PERNAS which neglected to negotiate with the Chinese authorities before announcing the plan to take over Malaysia's China trade. Apparently, the Malaysian government presumed, wrongly it turned out, that state corporations in China would prefer to deal with their counterparts, rather than through Chinese traders in third countries. At the Guangzhou Spring Fair in April 1972, PERNAS officials were faced with Chinese exporters who refused to sell them certain goods that China had been exporting to their traditional importers. Instead, the Malaysian delegates were referred to the very dealers whom they had wanted to bypass (Gale 1981, p. 114). Blood turned out to be thicker than water; the Chinese connection remained strong.

Because the Chinese authorities were reluctant to abandon their ties with the traditional middlemen, PERNAS gradually had to relinquish its aims to promote direct *bumiputra* participation in the China trade. The decline in *bumiputra* representation was prominent in subsequent Malaysian trade missions. The 90-strong delegation which left for China in April 1973 included only 15 Malay traders, a contrast to the previous year's racially "balanced" group. In April 1979, only 9 *bumiputras* were included in the 239-strong delegation (Gale 1981, p. 115). The Chinese authorities thus had in actuality frustrated PERNAS's plan to monopolize the China trade in order to promote *bumiputra* enterprises. According to Gale, "PERNAS had become little more than an agency through which the traditional non-Malay dominated trade was conducted" (1981, p. 115).

By 1981, PERNAS had already organized 19 trade missions to China. Negotiations with China was slow and tedious. Malaysian initiatives to establish direct trade links on a government-to-government basis persisted throughout the 1980s. Each year, talks centered on direct trading and the need for the Chinese to open their markets to bumiputras, and not just deal with businessmen of Chinese origins. In 1985, a top-level inter-ministerial committee comprising officials from the Ministries of Foreign Affairs, Trade and Finance, and Home Affairs and the Malaysian Industrial Development Authority (MIDA) was set up to look into ways to expand direct trade with China (*Straits Times*, 29 April 1985).

Although Malaysia's trade with China had been growing steadily – from M$704 million in 1974 to more than M$1.1 billion in 1984 (*Straits Times*, 29 April 1985) – until that time the Malaysian government still could not attain its goal of bypassing third countries and conducting trade with China through PERNAS, which represented *bumiputra* interests. The mandarin orange incident in 1985 represented an unsuccessful attempt of PERNAS (and the Malaysian government behind it) to achieve their goal of bypassing the middlemen in third countries, Singapore in particular, and to establish *bumiputra* monopoly to replace traditional Chinese traders.

The 1985 Mandarin Orange Incident

On 14 and 15 January 1985, under the scorching tropical sun, 13 lorries of mandarin oranges entering Johor Bahru from Singapore through the Causeway were seized at the Malaysian customs. A total of 20,000 crates (100 each) of mandarin oranges worth M$700,000 were involved. Four days later, the Malaysian importer paid M$280,000 in duties and taxes to claim the perishable fruit. The Malaysian government later explained that the importer had violated its approved permit (AP) which allowed him to buy and import direct from China, but not via third countries. Although the Chinese importer had technically violated the direct trade rule, this was the first time the government took action to detain shipments of Chinese fruits imported through Singapore.

The government action confirmed earlier newspaper reports that PERNAS had attempted to monopolize the mandarin trade by bypassing traditional importers. According to one report, PERNAS had in early January approached Kuala Lumpur Fruits Wholesalers' Association and offered to supply 80,000 crates of mandarins for the Chinese New Year. The offer was rejected by the wholesalers because PERNAS demanded 50 percent deposit and full payment at the time of delivery. This was considered unfavorable when compared with the practice among Singapore traders, who would provide the goods to Malaysian wholesalers on credit for 30-45 days. Moreover, the latter were also not sure of the quality or the source of the supply. They also indicated that they were not ready to abandon their traditional trading partners in Singapore because they had established mutual trust and confidence, "following Chinese ways of business management" for years and even generations (*Kin Kwok Daily News*, 7 January 1985).

The incident at the Causeway confirmed the fear of traditional Chinese traders that PERNAS, backed by the government, was taking actions to break up the Chinese trading network in mandarin oranges and to replace it with a *bumiputra* monopoly. Indeed, on 18 January 1985, the Ministry of Trade and Industry (MTI), under increasing pressure, confirmed that 2 APs (approved permits) had been given to 2 *bumiputra* companies in December 1984 to import 450,000 crates of mandarins from China. Another 20 applications, presumably from traditional traders, were being considered (*Sin Chew Jit Poh*, 19 January 1985). As the market demand for mandarins in the 1985 Chinese New Year season was estimated to be about 500,000 to 600,000 crates, the approved import granted to the two *bumiputra* companies would have constituted up to 80-90 percent of the total demand. This constituted a *de facto* monopoly in supply.

Disrupting a long-practiced trading pattern, the Malaysian government triggered a series of chain reactions from parties involved, both within and outside of Malaysia. First, Chinese fruit importers/wholesalers in Malaysia were naturally concerned and were the first to respond. In addition to making strong protests, they were quick to suggest a thinly veiled threat of boycott. After an urgent meeting on 18 January, Kuala Lumpur Fruits Wholesalers' Association declared that, although the Association as a group would not boycott the purchase of Chinese mandarins from Satria Utara (a *bumiputra* company licensed to import mandarins), it had no control if individual traders were to take such actions (*Sin Chew Jit Poh*, 19 January 1985). Three days later, it was again reported that the wholesalers had decided not to apply for APs to import Chinese mandarins from Singapore. Instead, as an attempt to break up the monopoly plot, many were turning to Taiwan and Pakistan for supplies (which did not require APs). They again stressed that, although they would not encourage traders or customers to take such actions, they would however not exclude "the possibility of a boycott" (*Sin Chew Jit Poh*, 22 January 1985). The sentiments were shared by the Chinese fruit traders from other cities in Malaysia.

Politicians, especially those claiming to be champions of Chinese causes, were quick to manipulate the incident to court the favor of the Chinese community. The opposition Democratic Action Party (DAP), which is predominantly Chinese-based, made a public statement on 17 January condemning the government's attempt to monopolize the mandarin trade. On 18 January, DAP Secretary-General announced that: "Unless the government withdraws its attempt to monopolize, I suggest that people should seriously consider boycotting all imported Chinese mandarins to protest such unending interferences to our traditional life style" (*Sin Chew Jit Poh*, 19 January 1985). The ethnic and cultural sentiments of the Chinese were aroused.

Not to be left behind, the Youth Movement of the Malaysian Chinese Association (MCA), which is a constituent member of the ruling Barisan Nasional (National Front Coalition), also made a strong statement to protest the move by MTI and warned against the possibility of a boycott. The mainstream MCA leaders, however, were in a difficult position as many of them were in the Cabinet and had apparently failed to prevent the MTI from taking the action in the first place. They were criticized by the opposition as "traitors" who had "sold out" Chinese interests to the Malays.

Chinese fruit hawkers who formed the retail network appeared to be willing participants in the mandarin boycott. In the first place, they had to rely on traditional wholesalers for the supply of mandarins and hence had little choice but to support the cause of their traditional suppliers. Second, they shared the long-term interest with traditional wholesalers in retaining the mandarin trade within the Chinese network, because this would mean the same generous credit terms and guarantee of supplies and low costs. Third, they obviously shared the same anti-*bumiputra* (if not anti- government) sentiments against this latest attempt to interfere with what they perceived to be *Chinese* business and a *Chinese* way of life.

On several occasions, government ministers and officials made public appeals to retailers to terminate the boycott of the sales of mandarins. According to some hawkers, however, it was the customers who were boycotting Chinese mandarin oranges. Incidents of verbal abuses and even violence were reported by some retailers who did not "cooperate" in the boycott and displayed Chinese mandarins for sale. It could not be determined whether secret society members were also involved in the boycott. Considering the nature of Chinese secret societies in Malaysia, their involvement would not be unexpected.

At the end of the commodity chain, Chinese consumers apparently also supported the boycott despite the symbolic significance of the fruit. The issue and the cause involved were apparently serious enough for them to be prepared to make a sacrifice. A customer who supported the boycott suggested that Chinese consumers "can simply buy at most two kilograms of mandarins for *bai-shen* (worship) purposes." As for gifts and personal consumption, "we can buy ordinary oranges from other countries" (*Kin Kwok Daily News*, 17 January 1989). It is interesting to note that the religious significance of Chinese mandarins was still upheld. Many customers readily accepted mandarins from Taiwan and Pakistan as substitutes. According to an informant, some of the old folks actually justified the use of "ordinary oranges" as substitutes in the New Year Festival by quoting a precedent in the 1942 Chinese New Year shortly after Japanese invasion. The message was, it seems, the Chinese mandarin was important, but not indispensable and unsubstitutable. While deeply tradition-bound, the Chinese were also practical and pragmatic. Traditional practices could be compromised to meet exigencies.

In the meantime, the government had to give in to the pressure from the Chinese community. On 29 and 30 January, the MTI approved a total of 33 APs to import 295,000 crates of Chinese mandarins from third countries. On 4 February, just about 2 weeks before the Chinese New Year (which fell on 20 February) the MTI declared that it had approved more than 100 APs to import Chinese mandarins from third countries. According to an MTI spokesman, the supply of mandarins was disrupted by a "trade dispute," and the Ministry "could do nothing about the reluctance of retailers to sell mandarin oranges to the public" (*Straits Times*, 12 February 1985).

The *bumiputra* company Satria Utara, which had been given an AP to import 430,000 crates of mandarin oranges, had its share of problems. Not only was it having great difficulty obtaining orders from traditional wholesalers, it also had problems in getting supplies from China. Accordingly to the *Straits Times* (5 March 1985), Satria Utara was unable to get enough cash to place the orders for the fruits worth S$14.5 million from the Guangdong Province Shantou Special Economic Zone Import and Export Association. The firm thus had to approach local fruit wholesalers for full advance cash payments, which were later trimmed to 50 percent. The offer was rejected. As a result, the company had to cancel 270,000 crates and pay M$917,500 to exporters in China as compensation for the cancellation. By late January, Singapore traders, facing an uncertain market, had already canceled 2 shipments of 120,000 crates from China. (The original order was 6 shipments.) The imported mandarins earlier intended for the Malaysian market were dumped on Singapore customers through supermarket promotions or were re-exported to other countries, including Brunei and Indonesia. In China, the canceled orders (both from Singapore traders and Satria Utara) were being redirected to Beijing and other Chinese cities for local consumption (*Lianhe Zaobao*, 2 February 1989). By the time the MTI granted APs to traditional Malaysian wholesalers, it was too late for the latter to re-order new shipments through Singapore to be in time for the New Year, even if sales could be guaranteed.

The 1985 Chinese New Year passed with many losers and few winners among those involved in the mandarin incident. Traditional Chinese wholesalers in Malaysia (and exporters in Singapore) lost their M$2 million mandarin business.[5] Traditional retailers suffered a loss in fruit sales in this major festive season. The *bumiputra* companies, which expected to take a major cut in the mandarin trade through shrewd maneuvering, suffered a great loss as a result of the boycott. The Chinese community ended up with a Chinese New Year without the blessing of "gold" (*gum*) symbolized by the Chinese mandarin. And the Malaysian government endured a political loss both in credibility and in Chinese popular support.

These were the costs all involved parties had to pay when a closed network was disrupted by an external element, in this case through an act of state intervention. The case attests to both the strength and the vulnerability of the Chinese network in the trading of Chinese products in Southeast Asia.

Ethnic Connection and State Intervention

The network of the Chinese mandarin trade, as illuminated in the 1985 incident, involves a series of close connections between Chinese businessmen located in different cities and countries. The Chinese-dominated trading network consists of producers and exporters in China, represented by state corporations, importers/exporters in Singapore, wholesalers in Malaysia (and other parts of Southeast Asia), retailers in cities and towns with concentrations of Chinese population, and finally, ethnic Chinese consumers. The strong network and business connections have been established over years of continuous business relations.

The distribution of mandarin oranges from Shantou (Swatow) and Chaozhou (Teochew) is handled exclusively by the state-run Shantou Special Zone Import and Export Association. As the quantity of the fruit produced by farmers, unlike manufactured goods, cannot be readily controlled, the officials at the Association play an important role in determining the amount of mandarins to be distributed to different contending wholesalers in a particular year. Through many years of business exchanges accompanied with personal contacts, importers/wholesalers from Singapore have cultivated and established long-term personal relations (*guanxi*), which go beyond purely business contracts to entail obligations of reciprocity, with staff of the Shantou group. The relationship has no doubt been reinforced by the Teochew-dialect based regional ties between the exporters in China and fruit-vegetable traders in Singapore (as well as wholesalers in Malaysia) who are mostly of Teochew origin.

At the Guangzhou Autumn Fair, major mandarin traders from Singapore have been successful in securing purchase orders to import mandarins from Shantou and Chaozhou for distribution to Singapore, Malaysia, Brunei, and until 1984, Indonesia. Such *guanxi* relations are ethnic-based to the extent that Malay business representatives from Malaysia find it difficult to establish direct trading contracts with China. Moreover, they are also tradition-bound and based on personal ties, as even Malaysian Chinese businessmen have difficulty breaking into this "preferred trader" status cultivated by Singaporean traders over the years. A sense of mutual trust and reciprocal obligation has been deeply entrenched. In obligation to such long-term *guanxi,* Chinese exporters are reluctant to break up the traditional practice to bypass their "old customers and old friends" in Singapore.

Traditional importers/exporters in Singapore thus enjoy a competitive advantage in their ability to secure supplies of mandarins from China for re-distribution to other cities in Southeast Asia. This advantage occurred in the first place because Singapore is supported by well-developed port and warehouse facilities, making it historically the entrepot between China and Southeast Asia. As such, traditional wholesalers in Malaysia became dependent on Singapore for supplies of mandarins, as well as other goods. They order from Singapore at the price set by Singapore fruit traders, and are given credit terms of up to 30 to 45 days. Over years of business contact, they have also established long-term *guanxi* with the Singapore traders, and hence enjoy near exclusive rights to import mandarins through Singapore. They find this pattern of economic exchange manageable, less risky, and mutually profitable. Moreover, bound by the existing *guanxi*, it would be tantamount to a breach of trust if the traditional Malaysian wholesalers tried to bypass their Singapore "partners" and establish direct trading relations with China.

The same pattern of business cum social relations also extends to the next level of transactions between traditional wholesalers and retailers who form the distribution network in Malaysia. Both sides are relying on an established pattern of mutual support based on obligations of reciprocity. Retailers in particular are dependent upon larger dealers for supplies of goods and for credit to finance their business with minimum capital. The retail network comprises a group of loyal hawkers who in turn give wholesalers better control of the market.

Finally, at the end of the trading network are consumers who are predominantly Chinese. Due to the symbolic significance attached to Chinese mandarins during the Chinese New Year season, the demand has been strong and sustained. It is this sustained demand that helps maintain the network of trade in mandarin oranges described above. The demand for and consumption of mandarins among Southeast Asian Chinese are thus more than purely economical; they also connote cultural significance. This is the reason why the response of the Malaysian Chinese to the 1985 incident was colored with strong ethnic sentiments. The boycott might have been less effective had the product involved been less "Chinese" than the mandarins were. At the same time, the act of boycott was intended to prevent the government from intervening in the import of not just mandarins, but all products from China. The feeling was "This year, mandarins; next year, what else?". Chinese consumers did not seem to mind celebrating the festival without mandarins; they were in fact celebrating in part for the success of still another collective move which defeated a *bumiputra* takeover.

From the above discussion, it is clear that the network of mandarin trade is exclusively Chinese; it does not allow easy entry by "alien" elements. The competitive advantage of the Chinese network has been recognized by Dr. Mahathir, the present Prime Minister of Malaysia, in his controversial 1970 book, *The Malay Dilemma* (1970, pp. 32-33):

Chinese business methods and the extent of their control of the economy is such that competition between their community and other communities is quite impossible. Their close-knit communal business tie-ups and connections, their extensive hold over the wholesale and retail business, their control of transportation, their powerful banks and their own wealth are such as to constitute an impregnable barrier against any substantial encroachment by other communities in their economic preserves in a free enterprise society.

As such, the strength of the Chinese trading network lies in its monopoly. As observed by Linda Lim (1983, p. 8; italics added), "Once established, monopolies tend to perpetuate themselves, particularly if *personalistic business and social networks* exist as barriers to the entry of newcomers." Referring to Chinese economic monopolies in Southeast Asia, Lim (1983, p. 8) further observed that "Successful economic monopolies can only be broken by state intervention, and then rarely without substantial economic costs and inefficiencies."

The situation and the risk involved could not have been overlooked by PERNAS and policy makers at the MTI. There was apparently a miscalculation. In reviewing the unsuccessful attempt of PERNAS to bypass the Singapore middleman and to control the mandarin trade, it is important to explore the basis of PERNAS's decision to intervene the way it did, and to analyze how and why it failed.

One strategy to enter a closed network is to use the political strength of the state to intervene. In its attempt to accomplish the dual objectives of developing direct China trade and building up bumiputra entrepreneurship, PERNAS initially tried to establish state-to-state trading relations between state-run corporations. This was not successful due to reluctance on the Chinese side to bypass its traditional middlemen in Singapore and Hong Kong, no doubt in part due to ethnic and political considerations. The Malaysian government also tried to put pressures on the Chinese network by imposing a 5 percent surtax on goods imported through third countries. The measure again seemed to have only limited effects as the additional cost was readily absorbed by the traders and subsequently the consumers. Importers apparently still considered the existing trade pattern economical and profitable.

The last resort, then, was to control the approval of APs to import mandarins from China. Considering the importance of Chinese mandarins among the Chinese in the New Year season, the demand for the fruit, presumably fixed (with low elasticity) and unsubstitutable, seemed certain. A simple calculation based on an economic model of supply and demand suggests that whoever controls the supply also controls the market, provided, of course, that the demand is constant. It was logical to conclude that, as long as PERNAS and the *bumiputra* companies had the nearly exclusive right to import mandarins from China, under the pressure of the demand, traditional wholesalers would have no choice but to order at the terms and price set by the latter. The Chinese retail network would have to follow their wholesalers in order to distribute the mandarins. Even exporters from China would have little choice but to export their mandarins directly to state-sponsored *bumiputra* companies if they were to satisfy the need of the Chinese in Malaysia. It must have appeared to be a foolproof scheme.

As it turned out, there was a serious miscalculation. Despite the cultural importance attached, the demand for mandarins was highly elastic and substitutable, at
least under the circumstances when ethnic sentiments and solidarity were aroused.
The value of mandarins was, in the end, culturally and not economically defined.
The action of PERNAS was interpreted to be an attempt to allow Malay companies to monopolize the China trade.[6] Traditional wholesalers and other Chinese
interest groups were able to appeal to the Chinese community to support a boycott
of mandarins imported by *bumiputra* companies. The event was seen to be still another case of economic and political contention between the two ethnic communities. For the sake of ethnic interest and solidarity, tradition and custom could be
put aside, temporarily at least. The majority of Malaysian Chinese decided to boycott mandarins from China and to substitute them with those from Taiwan (which
could still be claimed to be "Chinese") and even Pakistan (which is certainly non-
Chinese).

The main mistake of the MTI and PERNAS was thus attempting to kill two
birds with one stone. When the interest of PERNAS contradicted with the interest of Chinese businesses and indirectly that of the Chinese community, the issue
of promoting direct China trade was transformed into an issue of ethnic hegemony. Although the authorities had insisted that the objective of the control on APs
was to promote direct China trade, the very fact that only *bumiputra* companies
were initially given APs was sufficient proof that the real objective was to put the
mandarin trade under the control of *bumiputra* companies. The entire Chinese network was thus mobilized to start a boycott and to resist such a move.

Conclusion and Discussion

The 1985 mandarin incident represents a case in which the attempted state intervention in market operations was frustrated by resistance of an existing trading
network and by the collective actions of consumers. Both the consumers and the
people within the trading network were representing the interest of an economically dominant but politically subdued ethnic group. The effects of government
policy on market operations were obviously limited, and indeed were quite unpredictable.

While the case study attests to the perseverance of the Chinese connection, it
nevertheless also exposes its vulnerability. The Chinese network is not as closed
as it appears. On the supply side, throughout the period of the dispute, mandarins
from Taiwan and Pakistan were mentioned by various parties (notably both the
Malaysian government and importers/wholesalers) as leverage in negotiation and
were actually purchased by Chinese consumers as substitutes for mandarins from
China.[7] The incident signifies an accelerating trend that the mandarin trade, as

with the trading of other products, is increasingly challenged by international competitors.

On the demand side, the incident demonstrated that the need of Chinese mandarins could be highly elastic. The crucial question is whether and to what extent were Chinese mandarin oranges indispensable and non-substitutable in the Chinese New Year Festival?

Our case study shows that it was neither. Cultural and symbolic significance of Chinese mandarin oranges could be compromised when the collective ethnic interest was threatened. As such, the demand for mandarin oranges was determined not by loyalty to the specific product, as expected by PERNAS, but rather by loyalty to the existing supply network, which resulted in an act of boycott. Under such circumstances, the supply and demand curves were no longer independent, as they "should be" in a "normal" situation. As the event unfolded, loyalty to the supply network won out over loyalty to the product, presumably in response to a collective threat. The price, and hence the supply, became irrelevant in determining or explaining the market. What is clear is that the factors affecting the demand for a product were various, and the result, highly unpredictable.

Traditional Chinese businessmen are integrated and connected to the trade network to the extent that they have established close personal relations (*guanxi*) with one another, which give them competitive advantages over "alien" intruders. We believe such connections become an important resource as it gives the participants the following competitive advantages:

1) Long-term mutual commitments based on obligations of reciprocity reduce uncertainties in business transactions.
2) Better information resources through information exchange and sharing maximize business opportunities and reduces risks.
3) Personal relations (*guanxi*) result in "efficiency, flexibility and informality of their operations" (Lim 1983, p. 16).
4) *Guanxi*-based credit-worthiness (*xinyong*) enhances ease of capital formation.
5) Having been established, this ethnic-based particularistic exchange network has the tendency to preserve itself as a closed system and to protect and perpetuate an existing monopoly.

It is clear then that the interdependence and mutual support of participants in a trading network are not based solely on ethnic solidarity, although the ethnic factor (including its concomitant language and cultural elements) does in an important way explain the formation of the network in the first place. (In this sense, enacting the network also serves to reassert ethnicity.) Neither can their mutual commitment be interpreted as an act of altruism. As suggested by Yao (1987, p. 107), Chinese businessmen "act and choose rationally" in pursuit of self-interest and profit maximization. The network remains strong to the extent that it continues to be a resource which provides its participants maximum profits comparative to other alternatives. It is a means and not a goal by itself.

Can the mandarin trading network continue to be a resource, and hence as a means, for the goal of profit-maximization, under changing conditions? To answer the above question, we need to settle two related issues: First, does the network provide more efficient ways of doing business, in comparison with business transactions not based on the network? And, second, does it serve to preserve an existing monopoly and hence to maximize profit? In reality, the mandarin trading network has been doing both. Yet, as the network is being threatened by attempts of the government to intervene and of other economic forces to open the market, the network cannot continue to operate and enjoy its monopoly privileges. In the long run, the crucial question is whether the existing network (or a modified form of it) can prove itself to be economically efficient in doing business. It appears inevitable that it will have to compete with other emerging networks in an open market.

This is where the "intermediation role" (cf. Limlingan 1986, p. 70) of Singapore traders in the trade network may be highly vulnerable. Chinese wholesalers and members of the Chinese community in Malaysia objected to the attempt of PER-NAS to intrude into a domain traditionally dominated by the Chinese. They had no objection to direct trade with China provided it could give them better quality, lower prices, and higher profits. In fact, the common complaint has been that the Malaysian government has not done enough to help them promote direct trade with China (such as by relaxing restrictions on Malaysian Chinese to visit China). In the 1985 incident, even though their ethnic sentiment and *guanxi* still bound them closely to their trading partners in Singapore, Malaysian importers did not, and indeed could not, object to the government appeal to bypass Singaporean middlemen.

As discussed before, one competitive advantage of Singapore traders is their ability to provide the goods on credit to Malaysian wholesalers, who in turn do the same to retailers who can then operate their business with minimum capital. Singapore importers enjoy this competitive advantage because of their stronger financial position and their access to bank credits in Singapore. With further developments in Malaysia's financial sector, there is no reason why Malaysian importers/ wholesalers cannot seek similar bank credits to finance their operations domestically. Even retailers may in the future be able to obtain overdrafts from banks or other financial houses so that they need not be bound to credit dependence on traditional wholesalers. New wholesalers and retailers can also make entries into the seemingly closed network. With modernization of economic institutions, the market will become open for competition. Existing networks which rely on traditional particularistic relations in economic exchanges will have to adapt to the changing environment to remain competitive.

Still another advantage enjoyed by Singapore traders is their ability to secure supplies of mandarins from Chinese exporters. Through the control of supplies, they also control the market. Yet they may soon lose this competitive advantage with the trend of economic "liberalization" in China. According to an informant in Singapore, fruit farmers in China are organizing themselves into "individu-al units," thus freeing themselves from the control of state-run collectives. They want to make direct contact with distributors and exporters to maximize their prof-its. Similarly, according to the informant, the state-run export corporation in Shan-tou has split into smaller companies, each competing with one another for both supplies and the distribution network. With such major changes on the supply side, traditional Singapore traders may no longer enjoy preferential treatments due to their *guanxi* with exclusive exporters. Again, the market is open for competition among old and new traders, Malaysians included.

This trend of liberalization as a result of policy changes in China, if it continues, would no doubt trigger repercussions throughout the traditional network. Liber-alization breaks the *status quo*, undercutting privileges enjoyed by participants in the traditional network. In the meantime, as we have discussed above, exporters from Taiwan and Pakistan are challenging the traditional network. New traders, including those representing supermarket chains, are emerging on the scene. The trend and the situation are conducive to the development of an open market econ-omy, wherein polity and ethnicity will likely continue to be significant elements in determining the outcome of economic transactions. During the process of tran-sition, old connections may be weakened and new alignments formed. This is a trying time for Chinese middlemen in Singapore, as well as in other parts of South-east Asia. They must learn to adapt to both new market forces and to the changing socio-political circumstances in order to survive.

Notes

[1] The study is supported by research grants from the Singapore Turf Club (GR05652K) and the National University of Singapore (RP880007), administered under the De-partment of Sociology and the Centre for Advanced Studies (CAS) at NUS. The as-sistance of Ms. Yong Pit Kee is gratefully acknowledged. I am also indebted to com-ments made by my former colleague, James Jesudason, on an earlier draft of the paper.

[2] Another explanation, which is less commonly accepted, is that the Mandarin pronun-ciation of mandarin oranges is *gan* which is a homophone for "sweetness" and is a part of the Chinese proverb, *ku jin gan lai,* meaning "bitterness ends and sweetness begins." Mandarin oranges are thereby used to symbolize the hope that the new year will be the beginning of a good year.

[3] It is understood that almost all mandarins imported to West Malaysia before 1985 were imported through Singapore. However, it cannot be determined how much of the total came from China.

[4] According to Nonini (1983, p. 195), "The 'Ali-Baba' arrangement is a legal conve-nience in which the 'Ali' is a Malay who, for a monthly fee or a lump sum of money, agrees to act as a front for the 'Baba,' a Chinese capitalist, vis-à-vis the national gov-

ernment in all areas where the government's ethnic policies affect the operation of the Chinese business." Detailed arrangements, of course, vary from case to case.

[5] While no reliable statistics on the amount of the mandarin orange trade are available for an accurate estimate of the effect of the incident in the 1985 Chinese New Year season, statistics from Singapore's Trade Development Board reveal that the export of mandarins from Singapore to Malaysia (including East Malaysia) declined from the height of 6,818 tons in 1984 to 2,116 tons in 1985. Correspondingly, Singapore imported only 4,925 tons of mandarins from China in 1985, which was less than half of the 10,024 tons imported a year earlier.

[6] Even while the mandarin boycott was in full session, the customs at Johor Bahru again detained 390 crates of garlic on 5 February 1985 and 1,170 crates of pears on 7 February 1985. Both shipments were imported from China via Singapore as a third country. (*Business Times*, 9 February 1985.) According to press reports, in their negotiation to import mandarin oranges directly from China, the Malaysian authorities had threatened to obtain supplies from Taiwan and Pakistan if the Chinese exporters insisted on trading through Hong Kong and Singapore. The Chinese apparently did not budge (*Straits Times*, 25 January 1985; *Asiaweek*, 8 February 1985). Ironically and significantly, back in Malaysia, it was traditional Chinese traders and customers who were turning to mandarins from Taiwan and Pakistan to counter government's move to monopolize the mandarin trade. Obviously, mandarins from sources outside of China (Taiwan and Pakistan in particular) are seen as viable alternatives to break into the seemingly closed and presumably monopolistic trading network.

[7] For discussions on concepts of *guanxi* and *xinyong,* see Nonini (1983) and Yao (1987).

References

Asiaweek. Various Issues. Hong Kong.

Business Times. Various Issues. Singapore.

Gale, Bruce. 1981. *Politics and Public Enterprise in Malaysia*. Singapore and Kuala Lumpur: Eastern Universities Press.

Jesudason, James. 1989. *Ethnicity and the Economy: The State, Chinese Business, and Multinationals in Malaysia*. Kuala Lumpur: Oxford University Press.

Kin Kwok Daily News. Various Issues. Kuala Lumpur.

Lianhe Zaobao (United Morning News). Various Issues. Singapore.

Lim, Linda Y.C. 1983. "Chinese Economic Activity in Southeast Asia: An Introductory Review." Pp. 1-29 in *The Chinese in Southeast Asia,* Vol. 1, eds. Linda Lim and L.A. Peter Gosling. Singapore: Maruzen Asia.

Limlingan, Victor Simpao. 1986. *The Overseas Chinese in ASEAN: Business Strategies and Management Practices*. Manila: Vita Development Corporation.

Mahathir bin Mohamad. 1970. *The Malay Dilemma*. Singapore: Times Books International.

Nonini, Donald M. 1983, "The Chinese Truck Transport 'Industry' of a Peninsular Malaysia Market Town." Pp. 171-206 in *The Chinese in Southeast Asia*, Vol. 1., eds. Linda Lim and L.A. Peter Gosling. Singapore: Maruzen Asia.

Sin Chew Jit Poh. Various Issues. Kuala Lumpur.

Straits Times. Various Issues. Singapore.

Yao Souchou. 1987. "The Fetish of Relationships: Chinese Business Transactions in Singapore." *Sojourn* 2 (1): 89-111.

Centripetal Authority, Differentiated Networks: The Social Organization of Chinese Firms in Singapore[1]

Tong Chee Kiong

Introduction

Recent studies have found that the family firm is the predominant form of Chinese business organization (Omohundro 1981, Wong 1985). Wong, in fact, argues that the Chinese family firm is not restricted to a particular locale or a specialized line of economic endeavor (Wong 1985, p. 60). This paper analyzes the organizational dynamics of Chinese family firms in Singapore's small export-oriented economy. It focuses on the firms' internal dynamics and organizational structure, particularly the ownership patterns, authority structures, division of labor, and the principles of inheritance.

Studies carried out on Chinese family firms have tended to concentrate on small-scale business organizations (Omohundro 1981, Lim and Gosling 1983, Ward 1972). This has led some scholars to question the general application of kinship principles in the organization of large business enterprises. These studies leave open the serious question of whether Chinese family firms can be organized on a larger scale (Hamilton and Kao 1990). In fact, some argue that Chinese family principles are only applicable in small-scale businesses: "Families may be the greatest obstacle to further, capital-intensive development, for they are insular and atomistic, and their resources are limited and subject to periodic break-up" (Greenhalgh 1984, p. 529). Others suggest that family firms are inadequate and may even retard the development of the business enterprise. Amyot (1973, p. 119), citing the case of the Chinese in the Philippines, suggests that, "the structure of the family corporation is admirably suited to small-scale enterprise... there seems to be a principle of limitation to the growth of the family enterprises beyond a certain point." Furthermore, due to the inherent limitation of Chinese inheritance patterns, and limited availability of relatives to use as personnel, the family is considered to be an ineffective organization for capital accumulation and for sustaining entrepreneurial drive (Willmott 1960, Fong 1936).

Wong, however, suggests that Chinese firms are not necessarily small, impermanent, and conservative. Instead, he provides a model to show that they tend to behave differently at various stages of a firm's developmental cycle (Wong 1985).

Though useful for further research, Wong did not provide solid empirical data to verify this model.

Based on fieldwork data collected in Singapore, this paper analyses the internal dynamics and organizational structure of large-scale Chinese family firms. Tracing the life history of Chinese family firms from their creation, development, and eventual disintegration, the paper details the processes and changes in the organizational structure of how Chinese firms grow from small family firms into large business conglomerates. It examines the mechanisms inherent in the process of building large Chinese businesses based on the family model. Blau (1970) hypothesizes that as a business expands, there is a necessary decentralization of authority and an increasing delegation of work. This paper demonstrates that as a Chinese firm grows and expands, there are necessary changes in the organizational structure. However, even in large Chinese conglomerates, the authority structure remains highly centralized, with decision-making centered on the founders or on core family members. Moreover, *guanxi* relationships continue to play a vital role in business transactions. The paper argues that, in Singapore, very large scale business can continue to be organized along the same kinship principles that characterized small-scale Chinese family firms.[2]

Singapore

Singapore is a small nation state situated at the southern tip of the Malayan Peninsula. Strategically situated on the trade route between the East and the West, and blessed with a natural, deep harbor, the potential of Singapore was quickly recognized by Stamford Raffles, who acquired it as a trading post for the British East India Company in 1819. It quickly realized its potential and by the nineteenth century, Singapore was already an important trading station for the British. Coupled with the very fast economic growth in the region, particularly in the trade of tin and rubber commodities from Malaya, Singapore, by the turn of the nineteenth century, was a major entrepot port, re-exporting goods from the region to the rest of the world. Trading, to this day, remains a major source of capital for the Singapore economy (Chew 1988).

The end of the Second World War saw the growth of Singapore's manufacturing sector. These early projects were mainly in the area of processing imported raw materials, such as rubber, tin, coconut, vegetable oils, and various consumer goods. By 1959, manufacturing activities became the third major source of employment in Singapore.

The third phase in the economic development of Singapore saw the rapid industrialization of the economy. The government felt that a dynamic manufacturing economy would turn Singapore into a prosperous country. The manufacturing sector developed very rapidly. Its contribution to the Singapore Gross Domestic Product (GDP) increased from 16 percent in 1967 to 22 percent in 1980 (Chew

1988, p. 8). Singapore's economy today relies on four major sectors: trade, manufacturing, transport and communication, and financial services.

The development of Chinese entrepreneurial activities closely parallel the growth of the Singapore economy. Early Chinese immigrants carved niches in sectors of the economy not taken by the British colonial rulers, particularly in the service and retail industries, but also in the import and export business. These were primarily small-scale businesses, requiring little capital, and, more importantly, quick liquidity, as many Chinese saw their presence in Singapore and Southeast Asia as a sojourn, here today to make a fortune and tomorrow to return to China.

Early on, Chinese entrepreneurs acted as the middlemen between British and other Western traders and the local people. This had important consequences because it led to the creation of networks of Chinese traders in various Southeast Asian countries. These networks continue today, with many Chinese firms in Singapore having trading links with their counterparts in Malaysia, Thailand, Indonesia, and Hong Kong.

The early trading economy gradually expanded into manufacturing and other primary sector industries. The success of Chinese entrepreneurs in the rubber industry, finally replacing British companies in both the production and distribution of rubber, is a good example (Coates 1987). The emergence of a number of Chinese banks in the 1950s further strengthened the competitiveness of the Chinese. Cheng (1985, p. 60), for example, noted that many of the founding members of these banks were, in fact, leading Chinese merchants with vast investments in rubber plantations and other real estate.

The rapid growth of the Singapore economy in the late 1960s and most of the 1970s benefited the Chinese entrepreneurs. Although there is a lack of data on the percentage of the economy held by Chinese businesses as compared with other ethnic groups, state corporations, and multinational companies, it is clear that the Chinese are an important component in Singapore's economy, particularly in the service and commercial sectors. For example, Chinese entrepreneurs have almost complete control of several primary sector industries, such as livestock rearing, coastal fishing, and orchid horticulture. Similarly, Chinese businessmen are involved in the manufacturing sector, particularly in food production, saw-milling, furniture, plastic, and rubber processing (Cheng 1985, p. 78-82). In the service sector, the Chinese are most visible in the restaurant and hotel industries, with most of the major hotel chains, such as Shangri-La, the Mandarin, Goodwook Park, being Chinese family-owned concerns. Similarly, in the banking industry, of the four leading banks in Singapore, three of them -Overseas Union Bank, United Overseas Bank, and OCBC Bank – are Chinese family-owned business enterprises. The fourth is the Development Bank of Singapore, which is partly owned by the government.

Definition of A Family Firm

There has been some debate as to what constitutes a family firm. Most definitions tend to center on three major concepts: the family, ownership, and control. Ward (1987) for example, defines the family firm as "a business that will be passed on for the family's next generation to manage and control." Emphasizing capital management, Miyamoto (1984, p. 306) suggests that family firms are "firms in which the majority of capital is held by a single family or a few families, but which is managed by non-family members."

Berle and Means (1968) stress the importance of control over ownership of stocks. They suggest that 10 percent stock ownership is sufficient for a family to maintain control of a corporation. For a large corporation in particular, the wider distribution of stocks makes it more difficult for the other shareholders to dislodge a controlling minority. However, although a family can achieve a level of largely passive control over a corporation with a small minority of the stock and representation on the board of directors, active control can be assured only when the chief executive is also a member of the controlling family. In addition, families with only minority ownership cannot exercise absolute control, which comes only with majority ownership.

A family firm can take on various forms. The family may own a majority of stocks and be in active control of the company; that is, ownership of stocks becomes an instrument of control. On the other hand, a family may own a majority of the stocks in the company, but exert only passive control. In other cases, the family exercises effective control even though it owns only a minority of the stock in the company.

The concept of control is complex. It cannot be determined by simply assigning as absolute percentage of stock ownership to it. Lim Mah Hui (1981) states that control is a form of social relationship and is influenced by such factors as the relationship between the largest shareholders; composition and nature of the directors and management; and the social and kinship network between large owners, directors, and officers.

What constitutes a family business cannot be surmised simply by majority ownership of a business by a group of relatives. Rather, I think it is a combination of effective control and ownership. A business may be considered a family enterprise if a family exercises effective control over it. In Singapore, however, ownership almost always comes in as one of the instruments of control. Chinese businessmen in Singapore still feel more secure with assuming control through real possession of the business. Thus it is really the interplay of ownership and effective control that defines a Chinese family firm.

Organization of a Chinese Family Firm

Although it is true that the dynamics involved in running a business varies with the age of the business, its size, and the type of economic activity in which it is engaged, my fieldwork reveals that there are several common characteristics of Chinese family firms. This section of the paper discusses the salient features of Chinese businesses in Singapore.

Centripetal Authority

When one thinks of a typical family firm, the picture that emerges is that of a head of household making all the decisions. This characteristic, termed as paternalism by many writers, is true of many small Chinese firms in Singapore. The founder of the business owns and manages the family business, and decision-making is highly centralized. One informant, the eldest son of a Chinese businessman, make the following comment:

My father made all the decisions when he was alive. He formed a board to help run the business; this board made the decisions. But this was only in name. In actuality my father made all the decisions himself still, especially in non-technical matters like investment, getting loans, negotiations with banks, finance companies, suppliers and so on. But he consulted the rest in very technical things. Anyway, he has the last say. After all, the business is his. Even when we, his children, had any suggestions, we had to go through our father's friends first, because my father felt that as head of the family he was to be obeyed at all times.

Another informant, when asked whether his sons ever question his decisions, said the following:

No, never. They wouldn't dare. Most of the time, I ask them for their opinion. I tell them roughly what to do. But honestly, my way of thinking is not wrong. I'm still alert and energetic. Though old, my way of seeing things is still sound. Most important in business is acute judgment. If I am clear about something, I tell them to go ahead, there's no need to discuss further.

There is a low degree of delegation of authority and responsibility because Chinese businessmen are reluctant to share information with subordinates. This forces the employees to go back to their superiors for instructions, even for minor decisions. This enables the Chinese manager to retain power in his hands. An employee of a building construction firm said:

My boss had his fingers in all the operations. Everything is extremely centralized. There is an absence of horizontal links. All of us are linked only through him (boss). He personally controls everything. We don't understand his spread sheets. We always say that he hides a lot of things from us this way. We don't know what to do next. We have to rely on him to tell us what the next step is. Now he wants us to compete with one another... so that we will not be united at the middle level. He's afraid that if we are united, we will not feed him with information. Then he will not know what is going on.

The authority of the Chinese father extends beyond the family unit into the business, because the business is also considered as a family activity. This linkage between the family and the business is important. The role of the founder does not end with his retirement. He continues to influence the decision-making process. For example, an informant who inherited his father's rubber business said that his father's resignation from the board was just a formality. As the business was a family activity, his father kept an eye on it. He continued to go to the office daily and his opinions on business policies were still heeded.

This continual involvement is important because of the credit standing and personal relationships built over the years with bankers and financiers. As one informant noted, "When the son made a mistake, all the old man had to do was to make a phone call to the bank chairman. It was still possible for him to plead for leniency because *ganqing* or sentiments are still involved."

Xinyong or Interpersonal Networks

Chinese businessmen believe in *xinyong,* a gentlemen's agreement (cf. Cheng 1985). Verbal contracts and the reputation of a person are vital for business transactions:

During my father's time, there was very little need for signing of contracts. Only with the government was there signing. Amongst the business associates, just a man's word was good enough. When my father said that he would do something, he would never go back on his word. It is dishonorable and shameful. If word goes round, his reputation will be ruined and no one will want to do business with him. If a man says "one" it must be "one" and not "two". An agreement is an agreement.

Since interpersonal trustworthiness is of utmost importance, Chinese businessmen usually only deal with those with whom they are familiar. As it is the reputation of the proprietor that is crucial, he has to personally deal with business associates. This increases the indispensability of the proprietor. *Ganqing* established over the years extends to the children because of previous good relations.

The value of trustworthiness also applies to recruitment. Chinese businessmen prefer to employ relatives and clansmen because they are supposedly more trustworthy. As one informant said of his father, "He prefers to hire people from his village. He trusted these people and believed all these people were hard working like him."

Another informant said that qualifications were not as important as diligence and loyalty, which could be expected from one's kinsmen and clansmen. In Chinese business transactions, there is a lack of formal rules and regulations. This lack of formal structure can become the basis of later conflicts within the company and can result in its eventual disintegration.

Positions of trust are specifically given to close relatives. Jobs which require the handling of money are assigned to close kin. One lady summarizes the attitude of Chinese businessmen: "You know, Chinese don't really trust other people. My dad feels that it's better to have our own family people to handle money. So my brother and sisters (we were still in school then) would take turns to sit at the counter to watch the cash." Coupled with trustworthiness is a moral obligation to support one's relatives. In early Singapore, being given a job also meant that one had the problems of food and lodging solved, since employers provided such necessities. The emphasis on kin relations results in relatives being appointed to positions of power. Ownership of the business is effectively passed on to family members, restricting the entry of outsiders into the inner circle.

A capable and diligent employee may rise to a top level position. Some of today's tycoons, for example, Goh Tjoei Kok, Kwek Hong Png, Lee Kong Chian, to name a few, started off this way. In most cases, however, important positions are reserved for close kin, especially members of the immediate family. It is a Chinese businessman's dream to pass on his business to his children. Thus as soon as they are able to work, they are initiated into the firm, first by helping out in simple things, such as watching the cash-counter, getting out inventory lists, serving customers and so on. One informant recalled that he would sit with his father everyday after school and listen to his comments about a wide range of business-related matters. Another informant noted:

Nobody sits down to teach you. We just learn from the staff there, learn from my father, my uncle, learn from mistakes. We don't know anything about management, so we solve problems through our own feeling. When problems are too big, we ring our father or uncle to consult them.

Before the children are ready to assume the mantle, the founder's relatives or trusted old friends occupy those positions until the next generation can ably fill them. Thus, when the Chairman of ER Bank retired, he asked a few of the directors in the company to step down and make way for his children.

Chinese Business and Kinship Networks

Chinese immigrants who came to Southeast Asia relied heavily on family and kin networks for identification and support:

The employees in our company are mostly people from the same village. When they first started work, their board, food, clothes, and even haircuts were provided for. The company is more like a household than a business place. Although our staff are being paid pittance, we can count on their being loyal to the company. Since they have been provided for in the early days, they will continue to stick around even if we are facing hard times and cannot pay them much.

The kin networking extends to the way the Chinese do business. Kin groups and associations forge networks of information, credit, and business contacts. Networks also give Chinese migrants access to market outlets. Because Chinese businessmen operate on the creditworthiness of prospective associates, and because this type of capital takes time to build, the helping hand of an established merchant is important.

When my father started out in the building construction business, Mr. Chai, the owner of one of the leading construction companies helped my father a lot. He channelled quite a lot of business to my father and helped our company to take off the ground. This was very important because my father was new to the industry.

Business networking can be in the form of ownership links, economic links of mutual cooperation, links formed through the sharing of common directors, or marital links. Business networking extends beyond national borders. Many large Chinese family firms have become transnational. For example, the Overseas Union Bank, the United Overseas Bank, Tat Lee Bank, and the OCBC Bank groups, all family-owned, have built strong bases in Malaysia. The Hong Leong group in Malaysia, an offshoot of the Singapore group, had developed into a semi-independent group, such that links between the Singapore and Malaysia group may be regarded as inter-group rather than intra-group in nature. Business ties are also forged with companies in Hong Kong, Taiwan, China, Japan, Indonesia, the Philippines, Thailand, the United Kingdom, the United States of America, Australia, and New Zealand. By and large, these other associations are created via joint ventures with foreign conglomerates.

Stages in the Development of a Chinese Family Firm

Although the majority of Chinese firms are small-scale family concerns, in Singapore it is no longer valid to study family business from the perspective of a single firm. Many Chinese family businesses have developed into large scale business groupings. This section documents the structural development and organizational style of Chinese family firms as they develop from small sole-proprietorships to large conglomerates. It will show that even when these companies become very large, many of the principles used in the running of a small Chinese family firm still apply.

Structural Development

The majority of Chinese immigrants in Singapore came as laborers to find work to support families back home in China. The story of Mr. Kwek, now a leading local tycoon, reflects the life histories of thousands who came.

In the year 1928, at the age of sixteen, I left my native country China to seek my fortune in Singapore... I had a brother-in-law in Singapore who was managing a hardware business, and I joined him as an apprentice... From apprentice, I rose to the position of clerk, then manager and eventually general manager. Although I had done well in my job, I felt I could perform better if I were on my own.

After saving enough and gaining sufficient experience, many started their own businesses. The *laissez faire* economy during colonial times made entry into petty trade easy. Small trading businesses in the form of wholesale or retail firms paved the way for higher forms of business enterprise. Sole proprietorships and partnerships characterized Chinese business in nineteenth century Singapore society. The capital of a small entrepreneur often came from personal savings or was borrowed from relatives.

As more capital came to be accumulated (through profitable businesses and through reinvesting surplus funds back into the firm), branches would be set up. The case of the Lee family is illustrative. From a single shop, Mr. Lee began setting up branches in various parts of Singapore. To raise capital for expansion, he invited his brother to form a partnership dealing in furniture and other household items. With more capital, the company began to diversify into other businesses, such as opening a jewelry shop. As the business expanded, Mr. Lee converted the business into a private limited company in order to take advantage of a corporate tax break. This change in the status of the business, however, had little effect on the way the business was run. When the business continued to expand, Mr. Lee decided that the various branches of the company should be registered as separate companies.

The expansion in the business resulted in relatives being invited to become shareholders. For example, Mr. Lee invited his brother to join his fast expanding business: "I knew that expanding the business meant expanding the staff strength. Mindful of the old Chinese proverb that when tackling a tiger, one needs the help of one's brothers, I invited my brother to join my firm." Thus, even when a Chinese firm expands, holdings of the parent company are largely personal ones. Often, the founder or founding members will hold the majority of the shares.

Chinese businesses, when they continue to grow, will expand into areas unrelated to the original line of business. According to an informant, "This is done in order to reduce risks." This process of segmentation is exemplified by the Kwek family business. The Kweks began as traders in the hardware line. They expanded into paint and cement manufacturing, shipchandling, and construction. They also bought rubber plantations and ventured into the real estate and property develop-

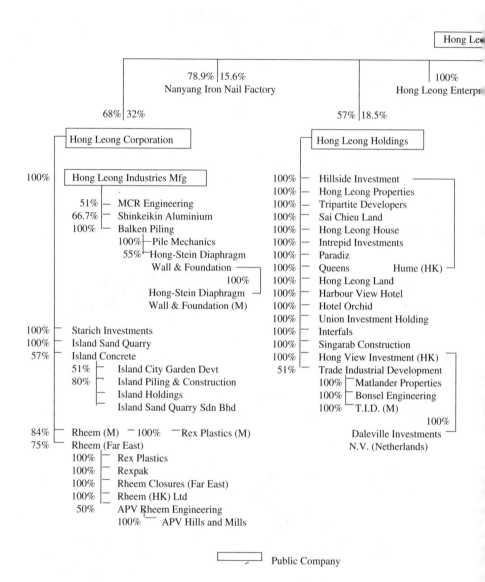

Figure 1:   Network of Hong Leong Companies in Singapore

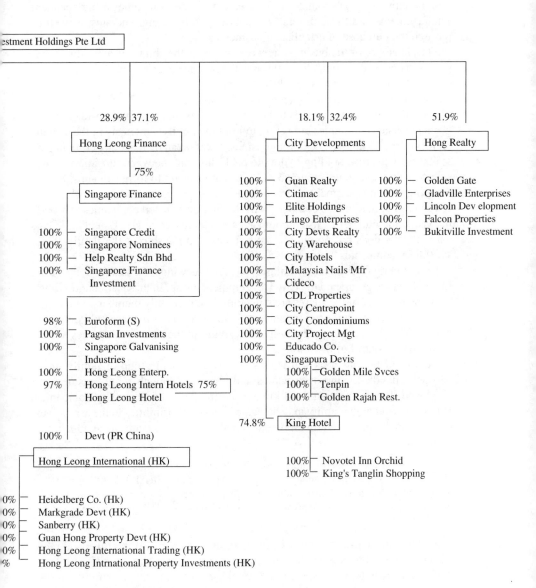

estment Holdings Pte Ltd

28.9% | 37.1%   18.1% | 32.4%   51.9%

Hong Leong Finance   City Developments   Hong Realty

75%

Singapore Finance

100% — Guan Realty   100% — Golden Gate
100% — Citimac   100% — Gladville Enterprises
100% — Elite Holdings   100% — Lincoln Dev elopment
100% — Lingo Enterprises   100% — Falcon Properties
100% — City Devts Realty   100% ⌐ Bukitville Investment
100% — City Warehouse
100% — City Hotels

100% — Singapore Credit
100% — Singapore Nominees
100% — Help Realty Sdn Bhd
100% ⌐ Singapore Finance
          Investment

100% — Malaysia Nails Mfr
100% — Cideco
100% — CDL Properties
100% — City Centrepoint
100% — City Condominiums
100% — City Project Mgt
100% — Educado Co.
100% — Singapura Devis

98% ⌐ Euroform (S)
100% — Pagsan Investments
100% — Singapore Galvanising
          Industries
100% — Hong Leong Enterp.
97% — Hong Leong Intern Hotels 75%
      — Hong Leong Hotel

          100% ⌐Golden Mile Svces
          100% ⌐Tenpin
          100% ⌐Golden Rajah Rest.

74.8% — King Hotel

100% | Devt (PR China)

100% ⌐ Novotel Inn Orchid
100% ⌐ King's Tanglin Shopping

Hong Leong International (HK)

0% ⌐ Heidelberg Co. (Hk)
0% ⌐ Markgrade Devt (HK)
0% ⌐ Sanberry (HK)
0% ⌐ Guan Hong Property Devt (HK)
0% ⌐ Hong Leong International Trading (HK)
% — Hong Leong Intrnational Property Investments (HK)

ment. In the mid-1960s, the family started Hong Leong Finance Ltd. The business group continued to grow through the creation of new companies as independent establishments and through joint ventures with other conglomerates, as well as through the purchase of established businesses.

The sheer size of the business network increases the ability of individual companies to undermine competitors through the practice of cross-subsidization. With cross-subsidization, profits are shifted from one product line to subsidize another, thus underpricing their competitors (cf. Lim and Teoh 1986, p. 346). In these huge groups, the family ceases to possess just personal holdings. Instead, nominee and trustee companies are set up to hold the family's interests in the various sectors of the business. The family business takes on an increasingly complicated structure, with cross-holdings, "double-back" holdings between subsidiaries, subsidiaries, and associated companies. Subsidiaries begin to form sub-subsidiaries, resulting in a large segmented structure, as shown in Figure 1. For example, in the Kwek family, the finance company was the first of its listed companies. Through the years, the number of listed companies has increased to six. Usually, the parent company does not go public, but remains as a flagship of the family, while subsidiary companies are publicly listed.

Hong Leong Group has several groups under its wings: for example, the Hong Leong Finance group and the City Development group. In these companies, however, the majority of the shares are still controlled by family members. In fact, the family may set up holding companies that will own shares in these publicly-listed companies. Thus, going public will raise capital for the business, but does not undermine the control of the family.

Control of the business still rests solely with a small group of family members who handle business associates and clients. Although more outsiders are employed, family members and kin are put in charge of subsidiary companies. While the head of the family may delegate some responsibilities to these relatives, decision-making, especially on financial matters, remains centralized. One informant said,

My father just says 'go there,' and we go. He will decide who to transfer, who to go where. He is the head of the family. Though I am given charge of an outlet, I still refer to my father and uncle for direction and instructions. My father and uncle visit each of the branches once or twice every week. At the end of every month, the family meets to report on sales and other matters.

When the family firm becomes a private limited company, some rules and regulations required by the Registrar of Companies, such as a Memorandum of Association and Articles of Association, annual accounts, and the declaration of dividends, must be submitted. However, the management structure remains family-centered. The Board of Directors is generally small in size, and made up of largely owner-directors, with the founder as chairman. The chairman may also take on multiple positions. For example, in one company, the Chairman was the Managing Director and Personnel Manager, as well as the Project Manager. In theory, the Board of Directors have voting rights according to the number of shares held. In practice, the Chairman makes the decision and informs the rest of the board. A company director noted:

The Board of Directors made decisions only in name. My father (owner and chairman) made most of the decisions; he only consulted the directors over technical matters. We seldom have management or other meetings. For company policies, we sometimes meet and sometimes don't. So far, there has been no crisis, so just the head of the company makes the decisions. It is slightly dictatorial; and even if he asks you, you may say something, but he will still go ahead with what he wants anyway.

Thus, even as the organizational structure becomes larger, decision-making still reflects a paternalistic-centripetal structure. For family businesses with more than one company, the general rule is for the founder or the core group (e.g. father, older sons) to be represented on all the boards. Hence, the delegation of responsibilities does not dilute the control of the chairman. When the family cannot provide sufficient manpower, the management of the family business may involve outsiders. However, strategic posts are always held by family members. The assignment of family members to sit on various boards is also a common phenomenon. The intensity of interlocking directorships determines the distribution of power.

When a Chinese family business becomes very large, the management structure becomes very formalized. In an increasingly competitive business environment, where Chinese firms have to compete with multi-national companies, efficiency and long-term planning are extremely important. Rational decision-making based on research rather than pure instinct is paramount. Large scale Chinese family businesses, such as the Hong Leong Group, Lee Kim Tah Group, United Overseas Bank Group, to cite some examples, are run very professionally. Hundreds of top and middle level staff are employed to perform operational and technical work. A key feature in large-scale Chinese firms is the rise of a professional class. In this competitive business environment, qualifications and expertise are crucial to the success of a business. In order for immediate family members to take over and run the business effectively, many Chinese businessmen make an effort to educate their children in fields relevant to the family business. Others who are already involved in the business are sent to upgrade themselves. At the same time, persons who have no relations to the family are hired at executive and managerial positions to run the company as a rational business organization. In fact, outsiders are sometimes invited to join the Board of Directors.

In the Industrial and Commercial Bank group of companies, for example, professionals like Y.K. Hwang are invited to join the Board to contribute their expertise in the development of the business. Prominent leaders such as Ong Pang Boon and Lim Kee Ming sit on the Hong Leong Finance Board. However, the emphasis on rational business and economic practices and the rise of a professional class do not alter the basic principles by which the Chinese run their companies.

A case study of a specific family business, the Hong Leong Group of companies, illustrates this principle.[3]

Mr. Kwek Hong Png came to Singapore in the late 1920s from China. He began by working as an apprentice in his brother-in-law's hardware trade. In 1941, Mr. Kwek established Hong Leong Company, which supplied equipment to rubber plantations and traded in building materials. The business began with an initial capital of $7,000, which was drawn from Mr. Kwek's personal savings. As business grew, the founder invited his three younger brothers to join the firm. Within two years, Hong Leong ventured into investments in properties and purchased many lots of vacant land. An the end of World War II, Hong Leong also started buying rubber plantations. Hong Leong Company became Hong Leong Company Private Limited in 1948, with a paid-up capital of $300,000. The Kwek brothers chose to keep their loans from banks to a minimum, relying on their own resources instead.

Anticipating growth in the property sector, Hong Realty Pte. Ltd., Garden Estates Pte. Ltd., Hong Leong Holdings Ltd., and Union Investment Holdings Pte. Ltd. were incorporated in the 1960s. These four companies jointly developed vacant land acquired in earlier years. In 1971, Hong Leong obtained a substantial interest in City Developments Ltd., which has since become one of the largest real estate and property development companies in Singapore.

The Kweks not only invested in property, they also saw the benefit of financing property developers. In 1966, Hong Leong Finance Ltd, now one of the top finance companies in Singapore, opened its doors for business. Just three years after its inception, Hong Leong Finance shares were listed in the Stock Exchange of Singapore and Malaysia. In 1979, Hong Leong Finance acquired a hundred per cent equity in Singapore Finance Ltd.

With this purchase, Hong Leong stepped into a period of vigorous acquisition of established enterprises. In previous years, expansion was accomplished through starting new businesses. In the 1970s and 1980s, the group expanded through takeovers and acquisition of companies, thus accumulating a wide range of businesses. For example, in 1981, Hong Leong Group acquired Hume (Far East) Ltd. (now known as Hillside Investments Limited), a public company which manufactured concrete pipes, beams, and steel products; Hume Gas Cylinders Pte. Ltd. (renamed Hong Leong Gas Cylinders), which turns out containers for Liquified Petroleum Gas. Hume Industries (S) Ltd. (now Hong Leong Industries) and Rheem (Far East) Pte. Ltd. were purchased in 1982 and 1985, respectively. Property development and manufacturing companies, as well as hotels were also acquired.

The philosophy behind the expansion is not to continuously enlarge one company. Rather than concentrate all the activities within one huge company, a pyramid of subsidiaries was created to handle these acquisitions. In this way, while business expands, risks are limited to the individual private companies. Economies of scale are not lost either as these companies function in mutual support.

The Kweks have not restricted their empire to Singapore. In 1946, Hong Bee Hardware Company Sendirian Berhad was formed. Hong Leong Co. Pte. Ltd. also set up a branch office in Malaysia. By 1968, a separate company, Hong Leong Co. (Malaysia) was established as an investment holding company of the family's Malaysian interests. The Malaysian Group also established similar lines of businesses as its Singapore affiliate, venturing into manufacturing and property development, as well as finance and banking. This is shown in Figure 2. Hong Leong Malaysia, under Mr. Quek Leng Chan, the nephew of Mr Kwek Hong Png, has evolved a separate identity of its own, operating quite independently of the Singapore Group. In the 1980s, Hong Leong Malaysia acquired Hume Industries (M), Carsem, Wesmalek, Far Eastern Industries, and Dao Heng.

Both Hong Leong Malaysia and Hong Kong Singapore have expanded overseas into Hong Kong, Taiwan, the Philippines, China, and the United Kingdom. Hong Leong International Ltd. and Hong Leong Company (HK) have been set up to spearhead trading, property development, and banking. The Malaysian Group is also beginning to develop business activities in the Philippines, under the umbrella of the Hong Kong Group.

The Hong Leong Group, like many other large Chinese family business groups in Singapore, shows vást diversification in their businesses, including financing, manufacturing, property development and the service industries. Despite the large number of firms and the presence of several public companies, however, control of Hong Leong is still in the hands of the Kwek family. This is done through ownership and dense interlocking of directorships across the business group (see Figures 3 & 4).[4] The public records show that the number of outsiders with a stake in the family business is large. However, the percentage of shares held by these individuals is small. For example, 10.4 percent of the shareholders in City Development hold 96.6 percent of the shareholdings. Similarly for the other public company, Hong Leong Finance, 11.7 percent of the shareholders own 94.79 percent of the stocks (Singapore Registrar of Companies).

The majority of the shareholders in the public companies are financial and non-financial institutions, and corporate firms. A number of these corporations themselves are family owned businesses or investment holding companies. The 1987 Annual Report of City Developments Ltd. for example, shows that 61.79 percent of the stocks were held by 100 percent family owned companies. Similarly, 57.66 percent of Hong Leong Finance is owned by the Kwek family. Hence, going public raises capital for the family business but does not undermine the family's control of the firms.

Most of the Kwek family's stocks in all the subsidiaries are held through Hong Leong Investment Holdings Pte. Ltd., of which all shareholders are family members. As Figure 1 shows, these holdings are held both directly and indirectly through the major subsidiaries. In 1984, three companies were registered to supplant Hong Leong Investment Holdings as the ultimate holding company for the Kwek family interests in Singapore. The apparent intention of these companies is

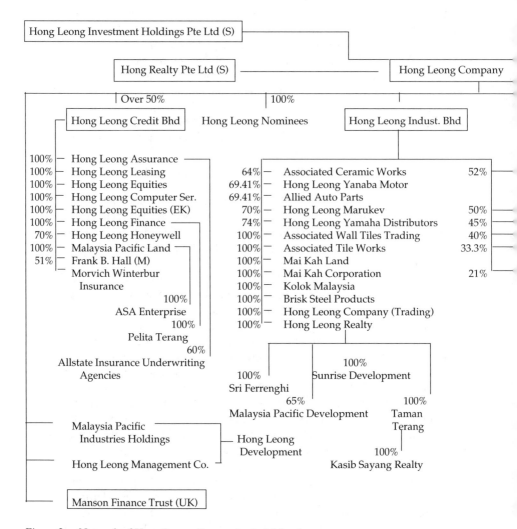

Figure 2:   Network of Hong Leong Companies in Malaysia

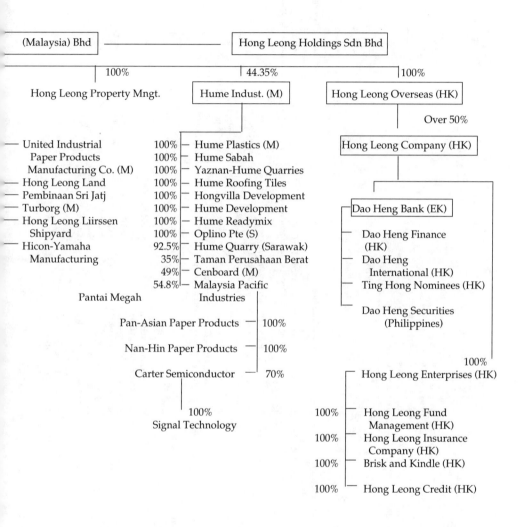

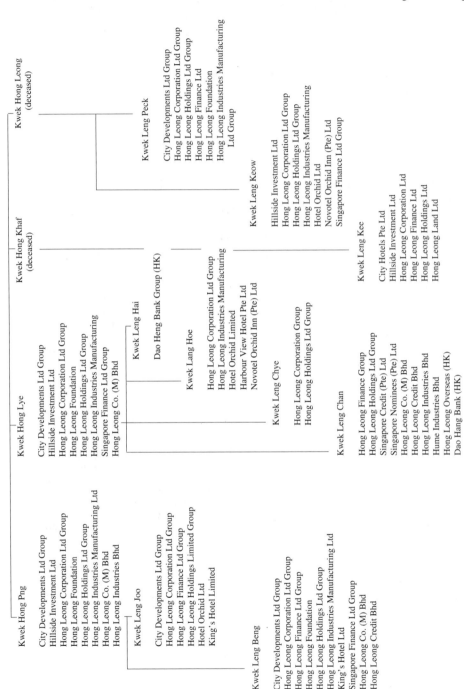

Figure 3:   Ownership Patterns and Directorship of Hong Leong Companies

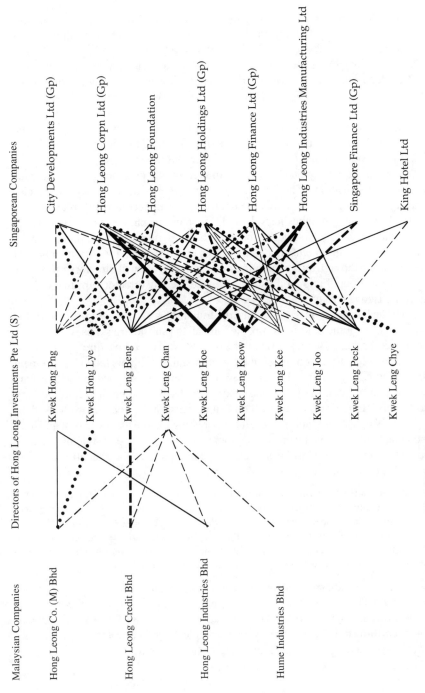

Figure 4: Interlocking Directorship of Hong Leong Companies

to consolidate ownership of the Singapore Hong Leong Group into tighter blocks controlled by immediate family members. This makes Hong Leong Investment Holdings less vulnerable to any outsiders who might attempt to buy out a family member. A provision in the articles of one of the companies states that only people "entitled or permitted" to be shareholders or directors of Hong Leong Investment Holdings may become shareholders of the new investment company. Another clause states that if, despite this provision, any non-member of Hong Leong Investment Holdings does succeed in becoming a member of the company, then the company must sell any shares which it owns in Hong Leong Investment Holdings (*Far East Economic Review*, 5 December 1985).

Control of the family business is not diluted by the presence of professionals occupying top positions. These professional managers/executives do not exercise control comparable to core family members because their control is limited to only one section of the group business. In addition, these managers are not included in the formal management structure beyond the firm(s) that they are in charge of. Only the core family members belong to this group. We can identify members of the core group through an examination of the concentration of directorships across the business group. Figure 4 illustrates the interlocking directorships that exist in the Hong Leong Group.

In a huge business concern like this, the founder Kwek Hong Png still holds the chairmanship for the holding companies and all the subsidiaries. His son and chosen successor, Leng Beng, sits on all the boards as an executive director. He is also the managing director of most of these companies. With his father's retirement from Hong Leong Finance Ltd. in 1984, Leng Beng has stepped in as chairman. His younger brother, Leng Joo, has also gradually been appointed into the various boards. Hong Png's brother used to sit on most of the boards too. Now, their sons have stepped into their places. It is interesting to note that even though Hong Leong has grown into a business conglomerate, the "hands-on" style of management of a Chinese "towkay" is still evident. For example, one executive of Hong Leong Credit commented as follows:

My Chairman sits on the 14th floor of the Hong Leong building, just one floor above the secretaries and registered offices of most of the group's companies, the busiest level where all the information is processed. He monitors day-to-day activities very closely. Take the approval of loans, for instance. Around the late 1970s and early 1980s, loans as small as $50,000 had to be personally approved by him. Now, the amount has been raised to $300,000. This is still a very small sum for a chairman to be involved.

Thus Chinese business management, even in large business groups, is based on tight personal control. The idea of an absent master and lackadaisical governance is not favored. An executive in Hong Leong said this of his Chairman: "He controls everything tightly, very tightly. For example, to prevent control from slipping through his hands, Leng Chan made sure of that when he sent his brother, Leng

Hai, to look after the company's interests in Hong Kong. Even so, Leng Chan makes regular personal visits to Hong Kong."

The basis of the chairman's power rests not only in his control of shares in the company, but also in his personal hold as the head of the family. For example, in the case of the Industrial and Commercial Bank, the Chairman, Tan Kim Chong, had retired and handed over the business to his elder son. Although he had no legal authority over the family business at all, to the day of his death, he remained in control. According to a former manager with the bank, the managers would visit him daily at his residence to give him reports of various happenings: "All the sons were afraid of him."

Thus, the centripetal authority of the patriarch is not just characteristic of small Chinese business firms, but is also applicable to large conglomerates. This authority is based on his control of the company and the family. Indeed, it is often his continuous presence that holds the family and thence the business together. The moment he relaxes his control, without the proper transfer of power, the family business inevitably divides.

Conclusion

This paper provides an indepth analysis of the internal dynamics and organizational structure of Chinese family firms in Singapore through tracing the life histories of these firms from small sole proprietorships to transnational conglomerates.

A central theme is the centripetal authority structure that characterizes Chinese firms. Decision-making processes are centered on the founder and core-family members. The informal organizational structure of Chinese firms and the importance of *guanxi* relationships in business transactions contribute to the low level of delegation of authority and responsibility. The notion of a centralized authority structure and the importance of *guanxi* relationships have also been documented in studies in Hong Kong and Taiwan. The paper also deals with the question of the applicability of kinship principles in the organization of large scale Chinese family firms. The data collected clearly demonstrate that even when a Chinese firm becomes very large, the authority structure remains highly centralized, even when there are modifications in the organizational structure of the firm. The changing economic environment in Singapore, with increasing competition from multi-national companies, has resulted in Chinese firms having to adopt more "rational" methods of management in order to remain competitive. As the Chinese firms grow larger, they take on the organizational structure of "Western" companies. The basic rules of ownership and control, however, remain essentially the same – a centralized structure with control given to a small core of family members.

Notes

[1] Research for this project was supported by grants from the National University of Singapore and the Singapore Turf Club. Special thanks to Mr Yong Pit Kee, who was the research assistant for this project. I would also like to thank Gary Hamilton, Kwok B. Chan, and Ho Kong Chong for their comments and suggestions for this paper.

[2] The fieldwork for this project was carried out from July 1987 to April 1988. Using the life-history interview method, 15 Chinese family firms, primarily in the banking and financial sectors, were surveyed and interviewed. Other businesses, including retail businesses, manufacturing, and construction firms, were also interviewed in the exploratory phase of data collection. The firms studied ranged from small sole-proprietorships with only a few workers and dealing with a single product to large scale multinationals, with thousands of workers and branch offices situated in various countries, and having a wide range of business interests.

[3] In-depth focused interviews were conducted with various personnel in each of these firms, including owners, directors, and senior management personnel as well as ordinary line workers. Interviews traced the development of each company from its inception to the present state. This allowed for data which show the dynamics of the firms and the mechanisms involved in each stage of growth and development. Interpersonal networks, conflicts and points of tensions, intra- and inter-firm relations were also gathered through these interviews. Secondary data, such as biographies, autobiographies, and materials from the archives of the Oral History Department served to supplement the interview data collected. These secondary data also allowed for the cross-verification of data.

[4] To trace the inter-firm networks and interlocking directorships, a central problem addressed in this paper, the records of the Registrar of Companies in Singapore provided an invaluable source of data. Articles of memorandum, annual reports, and press cuttings allowed for the documentation of ownership patterns, Board of Directors, and share ownerships in each of the firms studied. As the larger conglomerates, such as Hong Leong Group of Companies and United Overseas Group have business interests that extended beyond Singapore, fieldwork was also conducted in Malaysia. Two field trips were made, one to interview informants based in Kuala Lumpur and another to collect data from the Registry of Companies situated in Kuala Lumpur, Malaysia.

References

Amyot, Jacques. 1973. *The Manila Chinese: Familism in the Philippines Environment.* Quezon City: Ateneo De Manila University.

Berle, Adolf A. and Gardiner Means. 1968. *The Modern Corporation and Private Property.* New York: Harcourt, Brace, and World.

Blau, Peter. 1970. "A Formal Theory of Authority in Organizations." *American Sociological Review* 35: 201-18.

Cheng, Lim-keak. 1985. *Social Change and the Chinese in Singapore.* Singapore: Singapore University Press.

Chew, Soon-beng. 1988. *Small Firms in Singapore.* Singapore: Oxford University Press.

Coates, Austin. 1987. *The Commerce in Rubber.* Singapore: Oxford University Press.

Deyo, Fredric C. 1976. *Decision-making and Supervisory Authority in Cross-cultural Perspective: An Exploratory Study of Chinese and Western Management Practices in Singapore.* Singapore: Chopmen Enterprises.

Fong, H.D. 1936. "Industrial Capital in China." Industrial Series, Bulletin No. 9. Nankai: Institute of Economics.

Greenhalgh, Susan. 1984. "Networks and Their Nodes: Urban Society on Taiwan." *The China Quarterly* 99: 529-552.

Hamilton, Gary and Kao Cheng-shu. 1990. "The Institutional Foundations of Chinese Business: The Family Firm in Taiwan." *Comparative Social Research* 12: 95-112.

Jesudason, James. 1989. *Ethnicity and the Limits of Economic Rationality: The State, Chinese Business and Multinationals in Malaysia.* Singapore: Oxford University Press.

Lau, Hong-thye. 1974. "Social Structure of Small Chinese Business Firms in Singapore." Singapore: Academic Exercise, Department of Sociology, University of Singapore.

Lee, Poh-ping. 1978. *Chinese Society in Nineteenth Century Singapore.* Kuala Lumpur: Oxford University Press.

Lim, Linda Y.C. and L.A. Peter Gosling, eds. 1983. *The Chinese in Southeast Asia.* Singapore: Maruzen Asia.

Lim, Mah-hui. 1981. *Ownership and Control of the One Hundred Largest Corporations in Malaysia.* Kuala Lumpur: Oxford University Press.

Lim, Mah-hui and Teoh Kit-fong. 1986. "Singapore Corporations Go Transnational." *Journal of South-east Asian Studies* 17 (2): 336-365.

Low, Nguan-kian. 1973. "Nepotism in Industries: A Comparative Study of Sixty Chinese Modern and Traditional Enterprise." Academic Exercise, Department of Sociology, University of Singapore.

Miyamoto, Mates. 1984. *Family Business in the Era of Industrial Growth.* Tokyo: University of Tokyo Press.

Omohundro, John T. 1981. "Social Networks and Business Success for the Philippines Chinese." *The Chinese in Southeast Asia,* eds. Linda Y.C. Lim and L.A. Peter Gosling. Singapore: Maruzen Asia.

Tan, Siew-yong. 1976. "Management Practices in Industrial Organization: A Cultural Profile." Singapore: Academic Exercise, Department of Sociology, University of Singapore.

Tan, Lian-soo. 1981. "Singapore: An Economy with a Western or Chinese Outlook?" Academic Exercise, Department of Business Administration, National University of Singapore.

Ward, Barbara. 1972. "A Small Factory in Hong Kong: Some Aspects of its Internal Organization." *Economic Organization in Chinese Society,* ed. W.E. Willmott. Stanford: Stanford University Press.

Ward, John. 1987. *Keeping the Family Business Healthy: How to Plan for Continuing Growth, Profitability, and Family Leadership.* San Francisco: Jossey-Bass.

Willmott, William E. 1960. *The Chinese in Semarang: A Changing Minority Community in Indonesia.* Ithaca: Cornell University Press.

Wong, Siu-lun. 1985. "The Chinese Family Firm: A Model." *British Journal of Sociology* 36: 58-72.

Yong, Ching-fatt. 1987. *Tan Kah-kee: The Making of an Overseas Chinese Legend.* Singapore: Oxford University Press.

Yong, Hon-loon. 1973. "Practise of Nepotism: A Study of Sixty Chinese Commercial Firms in Singapore." Singapore: Academic Exercise, Department of Sociology, University of Singapore.

State Capitalism, Multinational Corporations, and Chinese Entrepreneurship in Singapore[1]

Tan Hock

Introduction: The Retreat of Chinese Entrepreneurship in the Post Colonial Era

Since the early 1960s, the phenomenal rise of state capitalism and the multinational corporations (MNCs) in Singapore has largely upstaged the traditional role of Chinese entrepreneurship as a driving force of economic growth.

The role of Chinese entrepreneurship in Singapore can be better understood in a historical context. During the British colonial rule,[2] the authorities pursued a *laissez faire* economic policy within the general framework of a small open economy. This led to a burgeoning trade and commerce without much need for promoting manufacturing industries. The economic expansion had accorded the Chinese entrepreneurship an opportunity to widen its domain of activities from trade and commerce into banking, finance, insurance, and other services (both within Singapore and with other countries). The Chinese entrepreneurs also gained ground in real estate development and construction, but they were scarcely involved in manufacturing industries.

A small open economy with a *laissez faire* policy well in place could have been continued. In the post colonial era economic growth in Singapore could have followed the same path. In this case, Chinese entrepreneurship might have still played an important role in the process of economic growth. However, the *laissez faire* policies came to an end in the post colonial era, because they bore the hallmark of colonialism and they could not survive an age filled with anti-colonial sentiments. Moreover, the socio-economic inequalities prevailing in the colonial rule appeared to have worked against a *laissez faire* policy as well.

Although *laissez faire* policies ended with colonialism, the new government did not endorse the opposite policy, economic nationalism. Economic nationalism was the policy overwhelmingly adopted by many of the developing nations (including Taiwan and South Korea) at their initial stages of growth, and often beyond those stages. This scenario would also have given Chinese entrepreneurship a prominent role in the economy. However, the rejection of a *laissez faire* policy in Singapore did not result in an adoption of economic nationalism due to a number of interacting factors. In the first place, Singapore was poorly endowed with natural resources. Thus, the authorities in the post colonial era did not have to worry about the loss of national control over the vital economic resources, in contrast to the situation that many of the resource-rich developing nations had to face in their post colonial era. Second, in the early 1960s, there was a huge deficiency in national savings, which led to a large desire for foreign capital inflows. This need for foreign capital acted as an additional disincentive to adopt economic nationalism, because this might have worked against borrowing from foreign sources. Third, the ideas of democratic socialism, which were popular in Western Europe at that time, also found a place in Singapore's politico-economic process. Such ideas boosted numerous economic policies and state institutions designed to correct social inequalities and to meet certain growth objectives, rather than to fulfill the ideals of economic nationalism.

Meanwhile, the tendencies inherent in Chinese entrepreneurship interacted with the prevailing socio-economic environment to retard further the possibility of either a policy of *laissez faire* or a policy of economic nationalism in Singapore. Chinese commercial entrepreneurship has always been beset by a very short investment horizon and a highly opportunistic business mentality. In addition, in Singapore, Chinese entrepreneurship also embraced an "immigrant mentality." Chinese entrepreneurs tended to consider their business endeavors in Singapore as being temporary. The businesses could always be shifted back to China if the circumstances there proved conducive. Moreover, in the entire period of the 1950s and up to the mid 1960s, the socio-political unrest accompanying the decolonization of Singapore, and the subsequent uneasiness in the relations between Singapore and Malaysia tended to reinforce the "short-term" and "opportunistic" nature of the Chinese businesses. In these same years, those who would be the industrial entrepreneurs were expected to be export-oriented even without initial protection. This fact probably prevented Chinese entrepreneurs from going into manufacturing industry. Being based primarily on the familial networks, Chinese businesses were also reluctant to make the transition to modern manufacturing industry without adequate incentives or policy inducements. The combined effects of these factors delayed the transition of the Chinese commercial entrepreneurship into industrial entrepreneurship.

Thus in the early 1960s, when the Singapore authorities were anxious to reset the sectorial priority away from a dependence on trade and services (including a large share of entrepot trade) towards a greater share of manufacturing industry, they found that the Chinese commercial entrepreneurs were not ready to become industrial entrepreneurs. This is not to say that Chinese entrepreneurship was doomed, but rather that it needed a proper socio-economic environment to embark on the transition towards industrial entrepreneurship. However, the authorities had neither the patience to let the transition occur naturally nor the willingness or knowledge (and perhaps the resources) to create a proper socio-economic environment to propel the transition. In Singapore, therefore, the various socio-economic factors occurring in the process of decolonization had diluted the role of Chinese entrepreneurship and escalated the roles of state capitalism and the MNCs.

Being an important driving force of economic growth since the early 1960s, state capitalism in Singapore had chiefly been embodied in the state-sponsored enterprises (SSEs), state monopolies (under the framework of statutory boards), and government policies on wages and savings. These state institutions and policies, together with the MNCs, exerted pronounced influences on Chinese entrepreneurship through three major channels – the product market, the savings-investment process, and other input markets (especially the labor market). I shall examine the extent of these influences in the following sections.

Economic Effects of State Capitalism and MNCs on Chinese Entrepreneurship in the Product Market

The effects of state capitalism and MNCs on Chinese entrepreneurship are a complex issue. To begin with, we shall examine the extent to which the SSEs have crowded Chinese entrepreneurs from the product market. In 1986-87, there were, on the average, 34 SSEs, compared with 166 private firms identified as Chinese-linked enterprises (CLEs) listed among the 500 largest companies in Singapore. The total sales of the SSEs were about 77 percent of the total sales of the CLEs, suggesting that the average size of the SSEs was much larger than the CLEs.[3] In general, the SSEs have competed against the CLEs far more than they have competed against the MNCs. This direct competition between the SSEs and the CLEs has taken place mostly in the economic domains traditionally occupied by Chinese firms, including construction, engineering, land development, international trading, domestic retailing, printing and publication, and shipping services.[4]

So far as state monopolies (or statutory boards) are concerned, most of them have engaged in the provisions of basic economic services, including public utilities, telecommunication services, broadcasting services, and port services. These monopolies appeared to have enjoyed economies of scale and thus became natural or regulated monopolies in the market place. The fact that the operations of these monopolies have been efficient suggests that there would be little room for the Chinese enterprises to replace them on economic grounds. Thus, the state monopolies did not have a "crowding-out effect" on Chinese entrepreneurship through the market place. They also did not have any major inducement effect on Chinese entrepreneurship because there were no linkages between them and the Chinese firms in terms of the latter acting as sub-contractors or suppliers of intermediate inputs to the former.

A "crowding-out effect" in the market place has probably been present in the massive public residential housing programs implemented by a state regulated monopoly called the Housing and Development Board. The primary objective of public housing has been to provide low-cost, subsidized housing to the less-privileged households. In the past twenty years or so, there was a spectacular rise in the proportion of the total population living in the public housing from 26 percent in 1967 to 86 percent in 1987 (with an average of 60 percent for the entire period of 1967-87).[5] Does this imply that the households were getting poorer, and hence that more and more of them were made eligible for the public housing? The answer is that the real per capita GDP rose by 3.9 times in the corresponding period without a deterioration in the distribution of income;[6] there was simply an increasing proportion of the middle-upper income households which thus became eligible to stay in the subsidized public housing. This level of the public housing program went beyond considerations of equity.

As a result, the value of the public housing exceeded that of private housing by a large margin in most of the years between 1975-87, with the exception of 1983, when a private housing boom led to a temporary reversal. As noted earlier, housing development has traditionally been a major economic activity of Chinese firms. The rapid expansion of the public housing program must have dampened Chinese entrepreneurship in this sector.

What are the effects of MNCs on Chinese entrepreneurship in the product market? In Singapore, MNCs operating in manufacturing industry have largely been export-oriented. A recent study shows that in 1986, the direct exports of MNCs made up 78 percent of their total sales, compared to 35 percent for the wholly local firms in the manufacturing industry.[7] These wholly local firms were predominantly owned by the Chinese. When compared with local firms, MNCs engage in businesses having higher capital requirements and more advanced technology (e.g., chemicals, computers, electronic components, machine tools, and petroleum [Datapool 1987 and 1988]. Thus, MNCs in the manufacturing industry did not crowd out the Chinese entrepreneurship in such product markets, because they did not compete against the Chinese firms directly.

The MNCs' operations in Singapore are usually a small part of their global operations. They have used their Singapore location to assemble products using parts and components prefabricated and imported from the rest of the world. There is little evidence to indicate that the MNCs manufacture most components of a finished product in Singapore. A recent study discovers that, as of 1986, work given out by the MNCs to the local firms (which were mostly owned by the Chinese) accounted for a mere 2.4 percent of the total input value, in the manufacturing industry as a whole.[8] This evidence confirms that the MNCs do little to encourage Chinese entrepreneurship. There are simply not many opportunities for the Chinese firms to act as suppliers of auxiliary parts and components, as well as to provide other related inputs and services.

The available evidence also gives little support to the claim that local-MNC joint ventures would be an effective instrument for stimulating the local (and mostly the Chinese) entrepreneurship. A recent official data source shows that, in 1984, there were only 8 major joint-venture firms compared with 131 wholly-owned MNCs operating in electronic products manufacturing, which by that time had already become the single largest component of the manufacturing industry in Singapore.[9] In this case, only the firms with more that 10 employees are included. In the case of smaller firms (employing less that 10 persons), the incidence of joint-ventures would be much less important.

Our discussion so far suggests that the MNCs in the manufacturing industry have neither encouraged nor discouraged Chinese entrepreneurship in the product market. This conclusion would not be valid for the MNCs operating in the services sector, which has become increasingly important in recent years. MNCs' involvements in domestic retailing, general trading (including mainly wholesale imports and exports), and commercial banking, coincide with major economic activities of the Chinese firms. The MNCs have intensively invested in domestic retailing and general trading. As of 1987, 4 of the 8 largest retailers in Singapore were multinational retail establishments, these 4 had accounted for 53 percent of the combined retail sales in this group (Datapool 1988). Meanwhile, the multinational trading companies had made up 14 of the 16 largest general trading establishments, and had accounted for 93 percent of the total annual sales of the group (Datapool 1988). The foreign dominance in the commercial banking sector has become increasingly evident. In 1987, of the 36 fully licensed commercial banks operating in Singapore, 23 of them were foreign banks, and they accounted for some 62 percent of the total assets of the commercial banking sector.[10] The omnipresence of the MNCs in these areas would, therefore, have limited Chinese entrepreneurship.

Economic Effects of State Capitalism and MNCs on Chinese Entrepreneurship in the Savings Investment Process

What are the effects of state capitalism and MNCs on the ability of Chinese to save and to invest? As a first step, we should note that Singapore's savings ratio (national savings with respect to GDP) has ranged from minus 2 percent (negative savings) in both 1960 and 1961 to 42 percent in 1987. There was a rising trend in the savings ratio over the entire period between 1960-87, subject to random variations from year to year. In the current 5-year period (1983-87), the average savings ratio was 43 percent.[11] Thus it appears that the overall savings record in Singapore has already reached the upper limit in recent years.[12] As a result, the redeployment of aggregate savings among the various economic sectors (or in-

stitutions) have become essentially a "zero-sum" game. If a particular institution
gains a greater share of the savings, a lesser amount will go to other institutions.
Now if we examine the performance of the SSEs in terms of savings, it becomes
clear that as these companies have competed with the Chinese firms in the domestic markets, their increasing capability to save would undoubtedly have an overall
effect of hampering the capability of the Chinese firms to save and hence the use
of savings for investment purposes.[13]

Meanwhile, the ability of the state monopolies and statutory boards to accumulate surpluses (or profits) has largely been dependent upon state regulations
on their prices for products and services. Presumably, if the aim of pricing regulations is to minimize their effects on private savings, then the prices might be
set as the resource replacement costs. This pricing rule can provide the necessary
incentives for state monopolies to supply the outputs to the users (including, of
course, the Chinese firms) without letting them accumulate economic profits. But
in reality, the regulated prices have been set above resource replacement costs and
hence the state monopolies have frequently made positive profits. In recent years
(1977-87), the combined net surplus (profits) of the six major state monopolies
(engaging in the provisions of civil aviation management and services, industrial
facilities, port services, public utilities, public broadcasting services, and telecommunication services)[14] has ranged between 26-36 percent of their total operation
revenues, subject to random variations from year to year. It appears that these surplus ratios are rather high. Moreover, the combined net surplus has ranged between 6-11 percent of gross national savings at current prices. This situation implies that a rather sizable proportion of aggregate savings can be attributed to the
state monopolies.[15]

Another major influence of the state in the savings and investment process has
been embodied in the nation-wide compulsory savings program, the Central Provident Fund (CPF).[16] The CPF has exerted both macroeconomic as well as micro-
economic effects on national savings. The macroeconomic effects could come into play via two important channels. The first is that, to the extent the net contributions in the CPF have been used for investments in public debt instruments,
the CPF has reduced the aggregate private savings in the economy and hence has
reduced the source of funds for Chinese firms.[17] Moreover, the approved investment schemes of the CPF have essentially led to a redeployment of resources into
those activities being favored by the government (such as housing, and other landed properties), against other private economic activities not being favored.

The microeconomic effect is that the CPF contribution has served as an important part of the opportunity cost for individuals to choose between being employed
or becoming entrepreneurs. Meanwhile, the CPF contribution has made it difficult
for those would-be entrepreneurs to save the critical capital requirements to start
their business ventures. Thus, other things being equal, the higher the CPF contribution rate, the lower the supply of investment capital for Chinese entrepreneurs.

The effects of state capitalism on Chinese entrepreneurship have also been exerted through the national savings bank, called the Post Office Savings Bank (POSB). Under the legislation, the interests earned from deposits in the POSB are exempted from income tax while those earned from deposits in other financial institutions are taxable. Other things being equal, this has given the POSB a competitive edge over other financial institutions. Singapore must be one of a few cases where the national savings bank has played a dominant role in the financial system. From 1972 to 1987, the POSB savings deposit balance, compared to the combined savings and fixed deposits balance in all other financial institutions, has increased drastically from a mere 3 percent to 33 percent.[18]

The POSB has clearly become a major competitor to private financial institutions, which are predominantly linked to Chinese ownership and control. Moreover, through investing the bulk of the assets in government securities and mortgages, the POSB has created a relocation effect on the use of national savings in favor of public expenditures (public debt instruments) and housing development, against private expenditures in general and the expenditures in non-housing activities in particular. In this regard, the effect of the POSB on Chinese entrepreneurship appears to be similar to that of the CPF discussed earlier.

How have the MNCs affected the Chinese patterns of savings and investment? It should be noted that the MNCs have contributed significantly to solving the "savings gap" in Singapore in the 1960s and the 1970s.[19] However, the nature of the savings-investment process has changed fundamentally in recent years. Gross national savings and gross capital formation have maintained an overall balance between 1983-87. Moreover, in 1986 and 1987, there were "excess savings" (the excess of gross national savings over gross capital formation measured in current prices) amounting to 8 percent and 7 percent of gross capital formation, respectively.[20] Therefore, at present, the role of MNCs in the savings and investment could hardly be justified on the ground of fulfilling a "savings gap." Foreign investments from the MNCs (in terms of corresponding capital inflows) now appear to be "redundant" in a financial sense,[21] except for increasing the immediate accumulation of foreign reserves, which would have to be weighed against the future profit repatriation and the eventual de-investment, assuming that all investments are subject to a finite time-frame.

However, the investments made by MNCs have been partially financed by borrowings in the domestic market. This is possible because Singapore is a financial center in which there are few restrictions on foreign loans. Thus, other things being equal, the demand for investment funds by MNCs would push up the interest rates, thus making it difficult for Chinese firms to borrow in the domestic financial market.

Economic Effects of State Capitalism and MNCs on Chinese Entrepreneurship in the Labor Market

As noted earlier, a major argument, especially in the 1960s, in support of state capitalism and the MNCs is employment creation. Singapore's unemployment rate was 9 percent in 1960.[22] The average unemployment rate remained rather high at 7.8 percent for 1966-69. There was also a disguised unemployment in the 1960s, the magnitude of which cannot be estimated from the official sources. In the following decade of 1970-79, the average unemployment rate fell considerably to 4.4 percent.[23] In general, the unemployment rate has been falling since the early 1970s, until a state of full employment was reached in recent years.

With full employment and with mobility of labor between firms and across industries (and sectors), the continuous expansions of the SSEs and MNCs have led to a reduction of labor and to an increase in the cost of employment facing the Chinese firms. This has given rise to both wage and non-wage differentiations between the SSEs and MNCs on one hand, and the Chinese firms, on the other. The presence of the SSEs and MNCs has unequivocally hindered the Chinese entrepreneurship in the labor market due to the mobility of labor from the Chinese firms to the SSEs and MNCs in response to wage and non-wage differentiations between them. This "crowding out effect" has been greater on small- and medium-sized Chinese family firms, which have largely been operating at the lower end of the technological scale. The failures of these firms to upgrade their technology, management practices, and work environment have made it difficult for them to attract and retain workers.

Moreover, to the extent that these firms have competed with the Chinese firms in the same product market and have duplicated the similar production capacities, the presence of SSEs and MNCs in the labor market also gives rise to additional social costs. In the case of the state monopolies providing essential economic services (such as public utilities, telecommunication services, and the like), they have, of course, reduced the labor supply in the private sector. But this would not involve a social cost because the provisions of such services are non-substitutable by Chinese firms. Meanwhile, these services are essential to the economy, including of course the Chinese firms.

The effects of wages policies on Chinese entrepreneurship are also an important issue. Since the early 1970s, the authorities have regularly pursued a national wages policy to influence both the absolute wage levels of various employments, and the annual changes in wages throughout the economy. In addition, the authorities have periodically adjusted wages in the public sector, which has economy-wide effects because of the leading role of the public sector.

When the wages in general are adjusted upward by the national wages policy, there is no reason to believe that all workers (in both public and private sectors) receive similar age increases. Thus, every round of the wage increase (or decrease, which was a rare possibility) has created an opportunity of wage differentiations. As a result, financially weak firms have difficulties matching higher wages. Labor supply to the "weak" firms has fallen and the quality of labor remaining in these firms has deteriorated. In the Singapore context, the "weak" firms have largely been Chinese firms, especially the small- and medium-sized family firms. Meanwhile, when the wage level in the public sector goes up, *ceteris paribus*, it has set in motion the mobility of labor from the private sector (especially from the small- and medium-sized Chinese firms) to the public sector. Thus the combined effects of the two wages policies have been to hamper the Chinese entrepreneurship, at least in the short term.

The effects of the national wages policy and the wage adjustment policy can also be analyzed in terms of how they have shaped individuals' incentives for entrepreneurial risk; the opportunity cost of taking entrepreneurial risk moves in the same direction as changes in the wage level. The experience in Singapore has shown that the upward adjustments in both the general wage level of the economy and the wage level in the public sector have not necessarily been consistent with market forces and labor productivities. The effects of such adjustments have necessarily increased the opportunity costs (and decreased the incentives) for entrepreneurial risk taking.

Finally, as the wage adjustment policy has a specific purpose of preserving an "elitist" public sector labor force, especially at the upper divisions of the public sector employment, it also has the effect of increasing the opportunity costs for risk taking because many potential entrepreneurs are locked in public sector employment.

Concluding Remarks

Our discussion illustrates that the simultaneous rise of state capitalism and of the MNCs in Singapore occurred because of various constraints on economic growth. Part of the constraints was the failure of Chinese entrepreneurship to assume the pivotal role in propelling economic growth in the critical stage in the 1960s. Nevertheless, the continuing expansion of state capitalism and the MNCs in Singapore has hindered Chinese entrepreneurship in the product market, in the savings-investment process, and in the labor market.

To the extent that state capitalism and MNCs have outgrown their original purposes, should they be restricted? There appears to be no general answer to this question. Clearly, in a small open economy, the role of the state monopolies could not be effectively substituted by private business organizations in a number of important economic activities, such as the supplies of basic economic services that involve large capital requirements and the productions of which enjoy economies of scale. Thus, as noted, it is apparent that state monopolies did not universally crowd out Chinese entrepreneurship.

However, the "crowding-out effects" of the SSEs and MNCs on Chinese entrepreneurship have been significant. There have been social costs involved in the activities of these firms in that they have duplicated the production capacities of the Chinese enterprises. Even if the SSEs and MNCs have engaged in export-oriented activities in which they did not compete directly with the Chinese firms in the product market, they have still discouraged Chinese entrepreneurship through the savings-investment process and the labor market. As discussed above, some government policies have also exerted adverse effects on Chinese entrepreneurship in similar ways.

At this point, one may be tempted to ask whether a reversal of the *status quo* would stimulate the Chinese entrepreneurship in Singapore. Recent examples of de-emphasizing the role of state capitalism in developed countries (particularly in Britain) and the liberalization of economic policies in the socialist countries (particularly in the USSR, Hungary and Poland) have shown that a return to the private initiatives to play the catalytic roles of organizing production and of risk taking, would be a more effective means of accelerating economic growth. In Singapore, the notion of privatization has now been widely accepted as an essential approach toward industrial restructuring, and it is, potentially, an important driving force of economic growth in the future – although a complete privatization of the SSEs has not yet occurred. In the process of privatization, the financing of divestments in the SSEs would tend to adversely affect the private savings unless the compulsory CPF savings could be tapped for the purpose.

Moreover, if SSEs have provided a countervailing force to the role of MNCs, this role could now be served by invigorating Chinese entrepreneurship in Singapore. The proper role for SSEs would be to operate in those areas requiring high capital or technology requirements that Chinese firms would normally have a great deal of difficulties to get involved without initial protection. In such economic activities, the resource relocation from the Chinese firms towards the SSEs would not involve a social cost, and hence the "crowding-out" of Chinese entrepreneurship by the SSEs would not be a sensible case.

Finally, if the liberal policy toward the MNCs was originally designed to augment national economic welfare by stimulating rapid economic growth, the omnipresence of the MNCs at present must also be examined on the grounds of national economic welfare as well, including the role of MNCs in stimulating Chinese entrepreneurship into creating production linkages with the MNCs, technological trickle-down, and the like. It is questionable that a continuing liberal policy towards the MNCs has been pursued with a proper balance of the economy-wide benefits and costs. When the growth of the MNCs has become a self-fulfilling process, it would hardly be consistent with the ultimate goal of maximizing national economic welfare.

Notes

[1] Research on this paper has been supported by the Singapore Turf Club Grant and the National University of Singapore Research Grant. The author is grateful to Boey Wai Ling for her research assistance. Thanks are due to Gary Hamilton for his useful comments on an earlier draft.

[2] Singapore was completely under British colonial rule between 1819-59, with a brief period of Japanese occupation between 1942-45. Between 1959-63, Singapore had an internal self-rule government while it remained as a British colony. In 1963, Singapore joined the newly-emerged Malaysia as an autonomous state, and in 1965, it became an independent nation on separation from Malaysia.

[3] The figures are calculated from Datapool (1987 and 1988). These data do not make a distinction between SSEs and CLEs. We have identified the SSEs from two other major sources: namely, Temasek Holdings (1988) and Ministry of Finance (1987). The CLEs are identified in terms of their character of ownership and control available from various other data sources.

[4] It might be added, parenthetically, that if the SSEs were established to engage in activities with high capital requirements or with more advanced technology with the purpose of inducing the private (and mostly the Chinese) enterprises to come in at a later stage, then the inducement effects on Chinese entrepreneurship would depend on the nature of privatization. To the extent, however, that privatization has so far been confined to a partial divestment of the ownership of SSEs to the general public, while the state has retained an effective control in the presumed privatized companies, the divestment then has little effect on encouraging the Chinese entrepreneurship. This appears to be what has happened in recent years with the partial divestment exercises of some state-owned enterprises, including such major SSEs as Keppel Corporation, Sembawang Shipyard, and Jurong Shipyard (the three major ship repairing and ship-building groups), Singapore Airlines (the largest corporation in Singapore in recent years in terms of sales and profits), and Neptune Orient Lines (the national shipping company). The details are available in Datapool (1987 and 1988).

[5] Figures obtained from the Department of Statistics over a number of years (Yearbook of Statistics).

[6] The actual per capita GDP (at 1985 prices) was S$4,189.73 in 1967 compared to S$16,498.97 in 1987. The figures are calculated from Department of Statistics (Yearbook of Statistics).

[7] Figures given here are calculated from figures from the Department of Statistics (*Report on the Census of Industrial Production 1986*).

[8] This figure is calculated from the data provided by the Department of Statistics (*Report on the Census of Industrial Production 1986*).

[9] The figures are calculated from Department of Statistics (*Singapore Manufacturers and Products Directory 1984*).

[10] Calculated from Peat Marwick Management (1987).

[11] Calculated from data in Department of Statistics (*Singapore National Accounts 1987*).

[12] In recent years, Singapore's saving ratio has far exceeded the savings ratios of most other countries (both developed and developing).

[13] A comprehensive figure on the savings performance of the SSEs is not available. But we could use the combined net profits of some SSEs listed among the 500 largest com-

panies in Singapore as a rough indicator of their savings performance. In 1986-87, the combined net profits of these SSEs were 3 percent of gross national savings on the average. This figure, of course, understates the actual savings capability of the SSEs as a whole (calculated from Datapool 1987 and 1988).

[14] These six major state monopolies include the Civil Aviation Authority of Singapore, the Jurong Town Corporation, the Port of Singapore Authority, the Public Utilities Board, the Singapore Broadcasting Corporation, and the Telecommunication Authority of Singapore.

[15] Calculated from the Annual Reports of the various Statutory Boards and from Department of Statistics (Various Years).

[16] Under the CPF legislation, the mandatory contribution rates ranged from 10 percent in the early 1960s to 35 percent in 1987 of the employees' monthly income. About half of the contribution was deducted from the employees' income and the other half being "topped up" by the employers concerned. But apparently the employers' share of the CPF contribution was simply the imputed income of the employees. In 1984-85, the contributed rate was the highest at 50 percent. But this was brought down to 35 percent in 1986 by means of reducing the employers' share of the CPF contribution rate. This was undertaken as part of the fiscal measures of redressing the recession of 1985-86. The combined contribution rate has since been revised upward. The CPF program provides for early fund withdrawals by the member employees for a number of specific purposes including investments in certain quoted stocks and shares of Singapore companies, and government securities. The money can also be used for the financing of housing, other landed properties, and medical expenditures. The details are available in the Central Provident Fund Board (Various Years).

[17] The net contributions in the CPF are the differences between the gross CPF contributions minus the funds taken out for early withdrawals and for retirements. Between 1967-87, the net contributions ranged between 1-21 percent of gross national savings (at current prices), with an overall average of 13 percent for the entire period. This is calculated from figures given in the Central Provident Fund Board (Various Years).

[18] This is calculated from figures given by the Monetary Authority of Singapore (*MAS Annual Report*, Various years) and the Department of Statistics (*Yearbook of Statistics*, Various Years).

[19] Between 1960-69, gross national savings had fallen short of gross capital formation in Singapore by about 59 percent a year on a *de facto* basis. In the next ten years between 1970-79, the average "savings gap" reduced to about 32 percent per year. The "savings gap" was largely financed by the foreign investment due to the MNCs. Figures calculated from the Department of Statistics (1988c) (*Singapore National Accounts 1987*).

[20] Figures calculated from the Department of Statistics (1988c) (*Singapore National Accounts 1987*).

[21] At present, the justification for MNCs in Singapore is to meet a "technological gap" (rather than a "savings gap"). Thus it is the technological aspect of investment by the MNCs which still makes sense.

[22] The unemployment rate in 1960 is calculated from the United Nations Industrial Survey Mission (1961). Data on unemployment rates in other years of the early 1960s cannot be obtained from official sources.

[23] Figures obtained from the Department of Statistics (*Yearbook of Statistics*, Various Years).

References

Central Provident Fund Board. Various Years. *CPF Annual Report. Singapore*. Singapore: Central Provident Fund Board.

Datapool. 1986. *National Directory of the Largest Singapore Companies*. Singapore: Datapool(S) Ltd.

Datapool. 1987. *Singapore 500*. Singapore: Datapool(S) Pte. Ltd.

Datapool. 1988. *Singapore 500*. Singapore: Datapool(S) Pte. Ltd.

Department of Statistics. Various Years. *Report on the Census of Industrial Production*. Singapore: Department of Statistics.

Department of Statistics. Various Years. *Yearbook of Statistics*. Singapore: Department of Statistics.

Department of Statistics. 1983. *Economic and Social Statistics, Singapore, 1960-1982*. Singapore: Department of Statistics.

Department of Statistics. 1985. *Singapore Manufacturers and Products Directory. 1984*. Singapore: Department of Statistics.

Department of Statistics. 1986. *Report on the Survey of Wholesale Trade, Retail Trade, Restaurants and Hotels. 1985*. Singapore: Department of Statistics.

Department of Statistics. 1988a. *Report on the Survey of Services, 1985*. Singapore: Department of Statistics.

Department of Statistics. 1988b. *Report on the Survey of Wholesale Trade, Retail Trade, Restaurants and Hotels. 1986*. Singapore: Department of Statistics.

Department of Statistics. 1988c. *Singapore National Accounts. 1987*. Singapore: Department of Statistics.

Housing and Development Board. Various Years. *HDB Annual Report*. Singapore: Housing and Development Board.

Ministry of Finance. 1987. *Report of the Public Sector Divestment Committee*. Singapore: Ministry of Finance.

Ministry of Trade and Industry. Various Years. *Economic Survey of Singapore*. Singapore: Ministry of Trade and Industry.

Ministry of Trade and Industry. 1986. *The Singapore Economy: New Directions*. Singapore: Ministry of Trade and Industry.

Peat Marwick Management Consultants Pte. Various Years. *Survey of Financial Institutions in Singapore: A Statistical Profile*. Singapore: Peat Marwick Management Consultants Pte.

Temasek Holdings Pte. Ltd. 1988. *Directory of the Government-linked Companies*. Singapore: Temasek Holdings Pte. Ltd.

Stock Exchange of Singapore. Various Years. *Company Handbook*. Singapore: The Stock Exchange of Singapore.

The United Nations Industrial Survey Mission. 1961. *A Proposed Industrialization Program for the State of Singapore*. New York: United Nations.

Part Two

Business Networks in Japan and South Korea

Introduction

Writers frequently comment on the similarities between the South Korean *chaebol* of today and the *zaibatsu* in pre-World War II Japan. Both *chaebol* and *zaibatsu* are terms represented by the same Chinese characters and denote large family owned and centrally controlled business networks. However, what analytic similarities might exist between these two types of business organizations does not translate into an empirical similarity between the business networks in these two economies today. In most regards, the organization of the Japanese and South Korean economies differs significantly. For instance, Japanese business networks reach down into the small and medium-sized firm sector to create the vast sub-contracting networks upon which the "just-in-time" production system depend. Individual firms are small, relative to the networks in which they are embedded. In South Korea, by contrast, the firms are much larger and rely more heavily on assembly lines, in-house manufacture of parts, and other techniques of mass production. Besides the system of production, the organization of the economies differ dramatically in their financial institutions, the ownership and management of the business networks, and in the relation between state official and business leaders.

The chapters in Part Two concentrate on the distinctive organizational features of the inter-firm networks in the two economies. In Japan, the distinctive feature is the inter-corporate relationships within the main networks. Okumura describes the general relationships and identifies their underlying principles. Ueda empirically examines one of the manifestations of inter-corporate interlocks, interlocking directorships, and shows how they operate. Orrù theorizes the nature of these relationships and how they frame the structure of the entire economy.

In South Korea, the distinctive features of the business networks are the relations of the family-owned *chaebol* with the Korean state. Kim's chapter describes the *chaebol* and discusses their relations with the state. Zeile analyzes this relationship empirically, by showing the links between the state's industrial policy, the growth of *chaebol* diversification, and the *chaebol*'s economic performance.

A. Japanese Business Networks

Intercorporate Relations in Japan

Okumura Hiroshi

Trade Relations between Corporations

We can identify four agents of trade: (1) individual consumers or families, (2) corporations, (3) nonprofit institutions (government, state, etc.), and (4) foreign countries. When corporations are paired as a common agent with all other trade agents, there are four types of trading relationships: (1) corporation/individual consumer, (2) corporation/corporation (intercorporate), (3) corporation/nonprofit institutions, and (4) corporation/foreign countries. Among the four types of trade relations, the second type, intercorporate trade, is conspicuously present in Japan. No accurate statistics exist to support this theory, but many examples point to this conclusion. When compared with other nations, the volume of wholesale trade to retail trade is four times larger in Japan. The difference between wholesale and retail trade is 1.6 in the United States, 1.9 in the United Kingdom, 1.2 in France, and 1.7 in West Germany. Most wholesale trade is between corporations, whereas retail trade occurs mainly between corporations and individual consumers. This statistic shows the large volume of intercorporate trading in Japan.

A good example of intercorporate trading can be found in the automobile industry. Japanese auto makers buy between 60 to 70 percent of their parts from other corporations. In contrast, the top four American auto makers buy only 30 to 40 percent of their parts. Trade relations between Japanese steel makers and auto makers is another example of how intercorporate trading works in the automobile industry. Nippon Steel, for example, sells its steel only to trading companies, which in turn sell that steel to auto makers. In the United States, U.S.X. sells its steel directly to the top three auto makers. Sogo Shosha, the general trading company, is unique; because it acts as an intermediate, it accelerates intercorporate trading.

There are several reasons that intercorporate trading is so extensive in Japan. First, Japanese corporations are not as diversified as United States corporations. They tend to specialize in certain narrow areas of production within the same industry. Sales may be undertaken by sales companies, while the production process itself is subdivided with some components even being sent to subcontractors. Second, heavy industry increases the amount of intercorporate trading, because heavy industry by its very nature feeds into the subsequent manufacture of other commodities. In Japan the proportion of heavy industry to all other industries is very high. A third reason for widespread intercorporate trading is that the capital combinations between corporations are very extensive and strong.

Certain characteristics of intercorporate trading distinguish it from the trade relations between corporations and other trade agents. First, Japanese corporations generally trade with only a small number of trading agents. The trading relationship between corporations and individual consumers differs from the intercorporate relationship because individual consumers make up a larger number of clientele. Because Japanese corporations are inclined to select and restrict their trading partners, intercorporate trading differs from trading with individual consumers. The largest steel producer in the world, Nippon Steel, for example, sells its products to only a dozen trading companies. Toyota Motors buys its automobile parts from only two or three dozen parts makers. Unlike Toyota, however, Daimler Benz, a German auto maker, buys its parts from over one thousand parts makers. Therefore, in these trading relations the Japanese corporations do not trade with many, unspecified partners, but only with a few, specified partners. This has very important implications because economic theory usually presumes that market mechanisms work only between many, unspecified trading partners.

Another characteristic distinguishing intercorporate trading relations is the difference in principle from the so-called market mechanism. In classical economic theory, the trading relation in the market mechanism is free and not specified. Corporations sell to or buy from whomever can offer the best price, quality, or service. The "invisible hand" works to determine the price and trading partners. Trade between corporations and individual consumers involves few corporations and a large number of individual consumers. When large corporations dominate the market, it is called oligopoly. In intercorporate relations, however, corporations trade face to face. Trading partners are specified and fixed, and, therefore, their relationships are long term. This tendency in trade policy is especially seen in Japan.

With the market mechanism in operation, the price of goods is supposedly determined by the competition between unspecified sellers and buyers. In contrast, when goods are exchanged between corporations, prices are not set by marketplace competition. Intercorporate trade competition is different from market mechanism competition. In intercorporate trading, corporations prefer, first, to select their trading partners and then, second, to determine price. What works here is not the "invisible hand," but the "visible hand." Suppose company A buys from company B. If company C offers a lower price than B, does A change from B to C? No. In that case company A will tell company B that company C offered a lower price, thus obligating company B to offer the same low price. Their trading relationship will not change; but the price will. In intercorporate trading, the first concern is the trading partner, after that the price.

In intercorporate trading, competition between corporations is not excluded. It is, however, different from market mechanism competition. In the market, there are many, unspecified trading partners that compete with each other. The price is determined by the competition, which, in turn, determines the trading partners. Therefore, there is always a competition for new partners. The hypothetical situation mentioned above may be reexamined by applying market mechanism competition principles. There is a long term relation between company A and company B, but company C is trying to enter the trading relationship. If company C offers a very low price and company B cannot offer the same price, or if C introduces a new product and B cannot offer the same product, company A will change its partner from company B to company C. Often these changes will occur when company A is trying to diversify its products or to apply a new method.

This type of intercorporate competition is a competition for trading partners. When a company tries to get new partners it will offer extraordinary price cuts for certain partners, without considering the market. Some Japanese economists say this phenomenon is "excessive competition," but this competition for new partners is partial and short term, but heated.

In intercorporate trading, we always find reciprocity: company A buys from company B if B buys from A. This reciprocal dealing is thought to be unfair trading because it restricts trade. Such reciprocal dealing is prohibited by law in the United States, especially after the conglomerate merger movement in 1960s. However, reciprocal dealing in the United States would not be very common anyway. If company A and company B each produces a single kind of product and company A sells to B, it is unlikely that company A would need to buy the product that company B produces. It is only when companies diversify their products that reciprocal dealing is possible.

But the situation is different in Japan. The general trading companies (Sogo Shosha) serve as intermediaries for intercorporate trading. If company A sells to company B, there is only a one-way trading relation; there is no reciprocity. But if the general trading company is the intermediary, then reciprocity can occur. Company A sells a product to company T (general trading company) and company T sells that product to company B. At the same time company A buys materials or parts from company T and company B buys from T. In this example there are two reciprocal deals, one between companies A and T and the other between companies B and T. Almost all big Japanese corporations trade with general trading companies, so there is in actuality a very large web of reciprocal dealings in Japan. Reciprocal deals are also very common within the enterprise groups. For example, in the Mitsubishi group, Mitsubishi Corporation (the general trading company of the group) serves as the intermediary for trade among all Mitsubishi group companies. This creates a dense reciprocal business.

With reciprocal dealing, trading partners are fixed and new entries are very difficult. Therefore, if foreign companies try to enter into the Japanese market, they usually experience many difficulties establishing reciprocal relations with Japanese companies.

Up to this point trade relations have been discussed only in terms of goods, but there are also many trade relationships involving money, i.e., financial transactions. In this area, the main bank system is peculiar to Japan. All Japanese corporations have a main bank, which is usually the largest lender to the member corporations. This is the so-called *keiretsu yushi*. The main bank has the responsibility of caring for its member corporations. If a corporation goes bankrupt, the main bank buys back bonds issued by the corporation. How do companies select their principal bank? Is it a result of competition? No. It was determined historically. The main bank for all Mitsubishi group companies, for example, is Mitsubishi Bank. The main bank comes first, afterwards the price (interest rate) is determined. The relationship between the main bank and the corporations is face-to-face. It is not a market relation. In this relationship, there is also reciprocity. The main bank lends money to the corporation. The corporation, in turn, deposits money into the main bank. It is an obliged account. This differs somewhat from compensating accounts in the United States.

There is competition among banks to get corporations to be their main bank. This competition is not centered on interest rates, nor is it determined by market mechanisms. Other factors are more important. The same situation is found between securities companies and corporations. All listed corporations have a lead securities company that underwrites the new issue of stock and bonds. These relations are fixed and long-term.

Intercorporate relationships among manufactures, trading corporations, banks, and securities companies are based on face-to-face relations not only in Japan, but in the United States and European countries too. In these countries, however, this relationship bears the character of a "spot" or one-time only relationship, and is not long term or fixed. Only in Japan can a long term, fixed relationship be found between corporations.

Capital Relations between Corporations

All large Japanese corporations have many *keiretsu* companies. These include affiliate, subordinate, and subcontracting companies. According to the Japanese Fair Trade Commission, in 1986, the largest 100 non-financial corporations had 3,899 subsidiary companies (companies with over 50 percent of their issued stocks owned by the parent corporation) and 9,519 affiliate companies (companies with 10 to 50 percent of the issued stock owned by the parent corporation). This is an example of a vertical relationship in which the parent corporation controls its *keiretsu* companies unilaterally. The parent corporation owns its *keiretsu* company's stocks and sends directors unilaterally.

Large parent corporations also combine horizontally into "enterprise groups."
Before the Second World War the *zaibatsu* dominated the Japanese economy. Mitsui, Mitsubishi, Sumitomo and Yasuda were famous "*zaibatsu*." After the war, the
head of the American occupation forces, General Douglas MacArthur, dissolved
the "*zaibatsu*," but after the Korean War (1950-52) these *zaibatsu* groups were
reborn as the enterprise groups. Today we can find six major enterprise groups in
Japan: Mitsubishi, Mitsui, Sumitomo, Fuyo, Daiichi-Kangyo and Sanwa groups.
In these groups each member corporation owns other members' stocks and holds a
position in the presidential club, where important information involving member
corporations is discussed. These horizontal combinations are peculiar to post-war
Japan. In fact, the combined economic power of these six major enterprise groups
is stronger than that of the prewar *zaibatsu*.

These vertical (*keiretsu*) and horizontal (enterprise group) relationships are
based on capital relations, i.e., stock ownership. Corporations own much of the
stock in other corporations in Japan. Over 60 percent of all stocks listed are owned
by corporations (including manufacturing, trading corporations, banks, etc.). This
phenomenon is a conspicuous characteristic of the Japanese stock ownership. This
phenomenon could perhaps be called the "corporatization" of stock ownership to
distinguish it from the "institutionalization" of the stock ownership in the United States and the United Kingdom. In the United States and the United Kingdom
financial institutions (e.g., pension funds, investment trusts, life insurance companies, and trust departments of banks) own stocks as agents of others. But in Japan
many corporations own stocks at their own risk in order to gain and maintain control of the companies. Institutional investors, however, own stock in order to earn
profit for the principal. In Japan many corporations own a large amount of other
corporations' stocks to control them. This type of ownership makes the "corporatization" of stock ownership a phenomenon peculiar to Japan.

In the United States many big corporations own other corporation's stocks, but
the amount of the stock is much less than that owned by the Japanese corporations.
According to the Securities and Exchange Commission, only about 15 percent
of all stocks in the United States are owned by corporations. Commercial banks
do not own stocks because they are prohibited by the Bank Act from doing so.
The Clayton Act also restricts the corporate ownership of stock. Therefore, United States corporations own much less stock than do Japanese corporations. The
Japanese Anti-Monopoly Act restricts corporate stock ownership, but in reality
the restriction clause consists of only dead words and has no effect. For example,
over 50 percent of Japan Victor Company's stock is owned by Matsushita Electric. And Japan Victor Company competes in the same market with Matsushita
Electric. Can you imagine this case in the United States?

According to the Japanese Fair Trade Commission, the largest 100 non-
financial corporations own stocks valued at 7.9 trillion yen. In contrast their net
capital value is 8.7 trillion yen. This value of stock, however, is book value. If we
calculate the market value, it amounts three or four times more than book value.

Why do Japanese corporations own so much stock? They own the stock to control other corporations. This point seems self-evident in the case of vertical intercorporate relations. But many scholars do not think control is an issue in the case of horizontal ownership. For example, in the Mitsubishi group each member corporation owns only a small percentage of the other corporations' stock. They do not own enough stock to gain control. But if we look at the Mitsubishi group as a whole, they own 20-30 percent of each corporation's stocks; so as a group they can control each other. This situation can be looked at as mutual control based on mutual ownership.

In the 1960s, many Japanese corporations were afraid of being taken over by foreign corporations and tried to stabilize their own stocks. Toyota Motors, the pioneer, endeavored to stabilize its stocks by asking related banks, trading companies, steel companies, and subcontractor companies to buy Toyota Motor's stocks to defend it from a possible take-over. Toyota Motors stabilized over 50 percent of its stock in a short time. Many corporations followed Toyota's example. As a result of this practice, there are no take-overs in Japan; in contrast take-overs are an epidemic in the United States and the United Kingdom. With the movement to stabilize stockholding, the corporations asked related corporations to own their stocks. They bought stocks to control each other, and once they bought the stocks, they usually did not sell them.

Mutual stock holdings among corporations also leads to personal relationships, particularly to interlocking directorates. There are many cases of interlocking directors in Japan. But this practice is not nearly as common in Japan as it is in the United States. Besides interlocking directorships, relationships are formed among members of the president's clubs. Here the personal relationships are particularly evident.

Capital exchanges and the personal relationships based on them are long term and fixed. Some businessmen say this indicates a "blood relationship" between the corporations, but we must not confuse the interpersonal with the intercorporate relation. It is important to distinguish between the corporation and the individual person. In interpersonal relations, there is emotion; people love and hate; therefore the relationship is capable of change. But in intercorporate relations, there is no emotion; the relationship is long term and fixed. In the enterprise group, many corporations have been linked with each other for over 100 years. It is important to note that these long term, fixed relationships are always based on capital relations, i.e., stock ownership.

Principle of Intercorporate Relations

Generally speaking, economic theory presupposes the existence of market mechanisms that coordinate the actions among individual people where there are many unspecified producers and consumers. Economists think the price is determined by supply and demand in the marketplace. In this presupposition, the subjects of economic conduct are many unspecified individuals. This leaves the market free and the price mechanism is the principle of all transactions.

At the end of the nineteenth century, big corporations emerged as the main producers. Accordingly, economists advanced a theory of monopoly and oligopoly. These theories, however, presuppose that producers are monopolists or oligopolistic and that the consumers are a large number of unspecified individuals. They discuss only the number of producers, and do not take seriously the idea that corporations are different from individuals. They think that corporate conduct is identical to individual conduct. Hence, they conclude that corporations and individuals would act according to the same principles in the same market. Their main concern is only whether the number of producers are few or many.

Criticizing these theories, Oliver Williamson (1975) advocated the transaction cost theory in his book *Markets and Hierarchies*. Following this theory, Japanese professor A. Goto (1982) wrote that the principle of intercorporate relation is neither market nor hierarchy, but the intermediate area between the two. He thinks that if transaction costs increase, the corporation (hierarchy) will internalize the costs, but if administrative costs are too high, corporations will turn to the market. Japanese cost theorists, however, believe there is an intermediate area between market and hierarchy; this is the enterprise group. Their theory is interesting, but they still have not found the principles of intercorporate relationships. These relationships are not intermediate; instead there are genuine principles at work in the intercorporate relation. The intercorporate relationship is not functional, but rather structural. The corporation is an early structure that was formed historically, and did not just appear out of nowhere to fulfill functional needs. Intercorporate relations represent relations among entities. Corporations conduct themselves functionally, but they did not form to fulfill those exact functions. E. Cassirer (1953) tried to reduce substances to the functions, but could not reduce all substances to the functions. Similarly, modern economic theory has tried to reduce substances (corporations) to functions (market mechanism), and so too has failed to find the principle of intercorporate relations.

Professor Imai (1988) tried to explain the Japanese enterprise group by a theory of information. He said that the enterprise group is a kind of information club. But in my opinion the enterprise group is not an information club, in which member corporations come and go freely. Instead they formed historically, so the structure itself is important.

Professor Nakatani (1984) wrote that enterprise groups were formed to share risks. But the enterprise groups in Japan were formed after the *zaibatsu* broke up. Their member corporations combined historically from the *zaibatsu* era, and did not freely combine to share their risks. Their relationship was not formed freely or functionally in light of market mechanisms.

Professor Dore (1973) contrasts the long term relationships between corporations in Japan with short term relationships in the United Kingdom. He said that these long term bonds provide one explanation for Japanese economic strength. He said long term relationships are characteristic of Japanese people. It was said that *giri* (obligation) and *ningyo* (sympathy) is embedded in Japanese tradition. But the relationship among the individual people is different from intercorporate relationships. We can make an analogy between the marriage and the merger or between the family and the parent-subsidiary company. But the principle is different. The merger of corporations is not a marriage because there is no feeling of love or hate between the corporations. One corporation sells or buys the other corporation, but the family cannot sell or buy children. Therefore, there must be another principle in the intercorporate relation.

In the 1980s, many people attached great importance to the market mechanism not only in the United States, the United Kingdom, and Japan, but also in the Soviet Union and China. In capitalist countries deregulation and privatization have become very popular. According to the theories of Hayek (1973) and Friedman (1984), they have prevailed. Even in socialist countries, market mechanism has been regarded as important and necessary. But the Socialists do not find that intercorporate relationships are different from market mechanism. They also do not lay much emphasis on the structure of the corporation (or enterprise). Professor Dore pinpointed "obligation" or long term relationships as the reason that the Japanese economy is strong. Some economists also considered the *keiretsu* or the enterprise group in Japan. They believe that Japanese corporations put weight on quality control in order to maintain strength in long term relationships.

Perhaps the long term relationship is the reason Japanese corporations are so strong and have succeeded. It may also be the reason that trade friction exists between Japan, the United States and the European Union. The United States and the European Union say that Japanese corporations prefer to buy from the related *keiretsu* or enterprise group companies rather than from foreign companies, even when their price is lower and the quality better than Japanese counterparts. Some Americans say that it is unfair that the stabilization of stock ownership prevents takeovers of Japanese corporations, while, at the same time, Japanese corporations are taking over many American companies. With the extensive and dense relationships among Japanese corporations, foreign companies feel frustrated in trying to enter the Japanese economy. They simply do not know the reality of intercorporate relations in Japan.

Some economists say the situation is changing in Japan. It is true that the relationship between banks and corporations have undergone some changes and that the ties between them are not as strong as they once were. Also many subcontract parts makers have begun to sell their products to companies other than their parent firms. These changes, however, have not become a general phenomenon. They are only partial. Some corporations have changed main banks, but the main bank system has not changed. Some subcontractors have changed buyers, but they have not ceased to be a subcontractors.

Intercorporate relationships in Japan have not changed significantly. Changing this situation would require a second *zaibatsu* dissolution. And this would require another General MacArthur.

References

Cassirer, Ernst. 1953. *Substance and Function*. New York: Dover Publications.

Dore, Ronald. 1973. *British Factory-Japanese Factory: The Origins of National Diversity in Industrial Relations*. Berkeley: University of California Press.

Friedman, Milton. 1984. *Market or Plan?* London: Centre for Research into Communist Economies.

Goto, Akira. 1982. "Business Groups in a Market Economy." *European Economic Review* 19: 53-70.

Hayek, Friedrich. 1973. *Economic Freedom and Representative Government*. London: Institute of Economic Affairs.

Imai, Ken-ichi. 1988. "The Corporate Network of Japan." *Japanese Economic Studies* 16: 3-37.

Nakatani, Iwao. 1984. "The Economic Role of Financial Corporate Grouping." *The Economic Analysis of the Japanese Firm,* ed. Masahiko Aoki. Amsterdam: Elsevier, 227-258.

Williamson, Oliver E.1975. *Markets and Hierarchies*. New York: Free Press.

Types and Characteristics of Interlocking Directorates in Japan[1]

Yoshiaki Ueda

Introduction

The purpose of this paper is to shed some light on the characteristics of interlocking directorships in large Japanese corporations. First, the types of interlocking directorates in 1983 will be examined. Second, some features of Japanese "network specialists" will be clarified. Third, the reconstitution of broken ties in two city banks between 1983 and 1988 will be analyzed.

Interlocking directorates in Europe and North America have been studied by many political economists, sociologists and organizational theorists (Mizruchi 1982, 1987; Scott and Griff 1984; Stokman et al. 1985; Mintz and Schwartz 1985; Carroll 1986). But in Japan, the problem of interlocking directorates has attracted little attention. There are several reasons for this lack of interest. First of all, the received wisdom holds that instances of interlocking directorates are scarce in Japan. It is commonly believed that personal networks in the Japanese business world are formed by retired directors and officers of large companies. Such persons do not usually sit on two or more corporations at the same time, and hence they are considered different from multiple directors. Second, data on stockholdings were easier to obtain than on interlocking directorates. The lists of ten to twenty large stockholders of corporations listed on the stock market are available every year. By contrast, data on interlocking directorates have been only partly available. Consequently, in order to find out multiple directors, the names on every board of directors had to be identified and compared with one another. Because this is a very laborious work, researchers were reluctant to study them. Third and most importantly, many Japanese scholars prefer the analysis of interlocking stockholdings to that of interlocking directorates. For example, Futatsugi (1988) compared the networks of intercorporate shareholdings with those of interlocking directorships and concluded that the two networks were quite similar in their patterns and that personal interlocks can be regarded as partial duplicates of larger and more intense intercorporate capital ties.[2] He also maintains that the meaning of personal interlocks is ambiguous and difficult to ascertain while the nature of intercorporate stockholdings is rather transparent and uniform in quality. On the basis of these observations, Futatsugi questions the value of studying interlocking directorates in their own right.

Nevertheless, I have concentrated on the study of Japanese interlocking directorates since 1983 for the following reasons. First, the publication of *Yakuin Shikiho* (*Who's Who of Corporate Executives*), which has an index of directors, by *Toyo Keizai* (*The Oriental Economist*) every year since 1983 made it easier to obtain data on interlocking directorates. Second, my previous research (Ueda 1986) uncovered that a total of 1,082 corporations or over 60 percent of the sample of 1,795 companies – which consists of all (1,772) listed companies and 23 mutual life insurance companies – had one or more multiple directors in 1983. This finding suggests that, contrary to the popular belief, interlocking directorates are quite common in Japanese corporations. Third, the significance of studying interlocking directorates should be stressed, though Futatsugi has questioned it. As he has stated, the networks of interlocking directorates and interlocking stockholdings overlap to a large extent in Japan. However, his view that personal ties duplicate capital links comes not from an intraclass approach but rather from an interorganizational approach. According to Palmer (1983), the interorganizational approach considers organizations as entities that possess interests, while the intraclass approach regards individuals within the capitalist class or business elite as actors that possess interests. Few Japanese studies have taken the latter approach to date, but I think that the intraclass approach should not be neglected in studying interlocking directorates, because when viewed from this perspective, the pattern of interlocking directorates may provide clues to the structure of the decision-making system of the economy as a whole. The significance of studying interlocking directorates may lie in this area.

Types of Interlocking Directorates

Types of Dyadic Multiple Directors in 1983

On the basis of the intensity of the interlock between two companies, Scott and Griff (1984, pp. 24-5) classify multiple directors into the following three categories (Table 1):

1) The most intense interlock is the *tight* interlock, which exists when a person holds an executive directorship in both company A and company B. Tight interlocks, therefore, normally occur within enterprises and are typically found between a parent company and its operating subsidiaries.
2) A *primary* interlock occurs when an inside, executive director of one enterprise (company A) holds an outside, non-executive directorship in another (company B).

3) A *loose* interlock is the least intense type of interlock, and results when a person holds an outside position on two boards.

Table 1:   Intensity of Interlocking Directorates

		Position in Company A	
		Inside	Outside
Position in Company B	Inside	Tight interlock	Primary interlock
	Outside	Primary interlock	Loose interlock

Source: Scott and Griff (1984, p. 25).

This typology is based on the assumption that "interlocks involving executives are more 'intimate' and therefore stronger than those which do not" (Scott and Griff 1984, p. 26).

In my previous study (Ueda 1986), I found that there were 952 dyadic multiple directors among 28,776 directors of 1,795 corporations in 1983. Using the above typology, I classified these directors in order to discern the characteristics of interlocks in Japan. Table 2 shows the combinations of their positions. Tight interlocks accounted for 39 (4.1 percent). For example, H. Yamamoto was both managing director of Matsushita Refrigeration and president of Wakayama Precision. Both companies are affiliate companies of Matsushita Electric Industrial. The majority of interlocks, however, were primary interlocks. When auditors were included as outside positions, primary interlocks amounted to 700 (73.5 percent). More than three fourths of Japanese dyadic interlocking directorates were composed of tight and primary interlocks. Scott and Griff (1984, p. 27) point out that these interlocks "often come into being as an expression of such institutional links as capital and commercial relations between enterprises." And, Useem (1984, p. 47) regards primary interlocks as "the product of highly specific dyadic ties among pairs or small cliques of firms" and argues that such interlocks can be seen as "an instrument for reinforcing intercorporate resource exchanges." In both views, interlocking directorates are considered as a concomitant of real economic activities between enterprises. In this sense, I agree with Futatsugi's argument mentioned above that interlocking directorates correspond to intercorporate capital relationships, but such an interorganizational perspective alone is insufficient to illuminate the significance of interlocking directorates.

Table 2 also shows that there were only 52 (5.5 percent) loose interlocks. This type of interlock is "considered to be induce[d] by common institutional orientations outside the selected corporations or to be due to personal qualifications only" (Stokman et al. 1985, p. 38). For example, M.A. Jervis was vice president

Table 2:   Types of 952 Dyadic Multiple Directors in 1983

| | | Position in Company A, no. (%) | | | |
		Inside Director	Outside Director	Full-time Auditor	Part-time Auditor
	Inside Director	39 (4.1)	481 (50.5)	1 (0.1)	218 (22.9)
Position in Company B, no. (%)	Outside Director	—	52 (5.5)	7 (0.7)	39 (4.1)
	Full-time Auditor	—	—	1 (0.1)	44 (4.6)
	Part-time Auditor	—	—	—	70 (7.4)

Source: Ueda (1988, p. 110).

of Shell Oil and an outside director of Mitsubishi Petrochemical and Showa Oil. In this case, the interlock between Mitsubishi Petrochemical and Showa Oil was considered an "induced interlock." S. Muramoto was an outside director of Dai-Ichi Kangyo Bank and Nippon Light Metal. However, since he was the former president of Dai-Ichi Kangyo Bank, this loose interlock could be considered as a residue of former primary interlock. H. Tsuda was an outside director of Sumitomo Cement and Sumitomo Trust & Banking, and the former chairman of Sumitomo Corporation. He had formerly induced the interlock between Sumitomo Cement and Sumitomo Trust & Banking by virtue of the two primary interlocks between these firms and Sumitomo Corp., but when he retired as a director of Sumitomo Corp., the primary interlocks were dissolved and only the induced one remained as a loose – although no longer induced – interlock. This type of interlock might be denoted "remaining interlock" after the retirement of the director from the base company. As for the interlocks between auditors, there was a total of 115 (12.1 percent). It is noteworthy that they were formed by fifteen lawyers, one professor, two accountants and four retired officers of the Bank of Japan or the Tax Administration Agency. However, no simple explanation is advanced for these interlocks as in the case of primary interlocks.

"Network Specialists" in Japan

Stokman et al. (1985, pp. 38-9) treats multiple directors with four or more directorships but without any inside positions as "network specialists," and argues that,

"They are the opinion leaders in business and their positions in many different corporations can provide them with information from many different sources." Network specialists, therefore, form enlarged loose interlocks as mentioned above and function to integrate smaller components into a larger network. Do network specialists exist in Japan? If so, what kind of persons are they?

Table 3: Y. Okaya's Directorships in 1983

1.	Ikuma Machinery Works	Outside Director
2.	Chubu-Nippon Broadcasting	Outside Director
3.	Asahi-Seiki Manufacturing	Part-time Auditor
4.	Aichi Tokei Denki	Part-time Auditor
5.	Nagoya Railroad	Part-time Auditor
6.	Toho Gas	Part-time Auditor

Source: Ueda (1988, p. 118).

As shown in Table 3, Y. Okaya had more than four positions of outside directors and part-time auditors. He was the president of Okaya & Co., which was an unlisted company, but a time-honored trading firm with mainlines consisting of steel products and machinery. The headquarters was located in Nagoya, the third largest city of Japan, where all six companies in the table were also located. Okaya was one of the economic leaders in Nagoya and seemed to play a role in forming Nagoya's intercorporate network. He may therefore be called a local network specialist. Table 4 shows the intercorporate networks formed by T. Tanaka. He was the former chairman of Tokio Marine & Fire Insurance, which was one of the financial cores of the Mitsubishi enterprise group. Tokyu Corporation in the table was the core of the Tokyu group, a large independent enterprise group, which was not directly connected to the Mitsubishi group. Therefore, Tanaka seemed to play a role in bridging Mitsubishi group with Tokyu group through a loose interlock of Mitsubishi Oil and Tokyu Corporation. This resulted in one large network composed of 851 firms (Ueda 1986). He could thus be regarded as a network specialist on a wider scale than Okaya. In both cases, "remaining interlocks," as mentioned before, constituted many of the interlocks, and it was these loose interlocks, rather than tight interlocks within each enterprise group, that played an important role in forming this large network. The directors who form these "remaining interlocks" may be considered the Japanese type of network specialists.

Table 5 lists the companies and positions which K. Ibe, chairman of Sumitomo Bank, had in 1983. He had only one inside position at Sumitomo Bank, and the other nine positions were outside directors and part-time auditors. Primary interlocks spread like a star with Sumitomo Bank at the core. This structure represents

Table 4:   T. Tanaka's Directorships in 1983

1.	Isukyu Corp. (Railroad)	Outside Director
2.	Mitsubishi Oil	Part-time Auditor
3.	Tokyu Corp. (Railroad)	Part-time Auditor
4.	Yamatane Securities	Part-time Auditor

Source: Ueda (1988, p. 118).

a typical institutional link, and there were many multiple directors with similar structures. For example, E. Toyota, chairman of Toyota Motor Corporation, had seven outside directorships. N. Ando, honorary chairman of Odakyu Electric Railway, had six outside directorships. Such multiple directors tended to sit on the boards of banks, insurance companies, and core companies of independent enterprise groups. They played the role of reinforcing the unity of each group. However, although such network specialists as Okaya and Tanaka had looser interlocks than Ibe, they played a more significant role in creating a large network across business group boundaries.

Table 5:   K. Ibe's Directorships in 1983

1.	Sumitomo Bank	Chairman
2.	Sumitomo Cement	Advisory Director
3.	Tokyo Steel Mfg.	Advisory Director
4.	Kubota	Advisory Director
5.	NEC Corp.	Outside Director
6.	Sumitomo Realty & Development	Outside Director
7.	Matsushita Electric Industrial Co.	Outside Director
8.	Mitsui O.S.K. Lines	Outside Director
9.	Rengo	Outside Director
10.	Asahi Broadcasting Corp.	Part-time Auditor

Source: Ueda (1988, p. 117).

Reconstitution of Broken Ties

The reconstitution of accidentally broken ties has been studied by Palmer (1983), Ornstein (1982), and Stearns and Mizruchi (1986) in order to find out the significance or function of interlocking directorates. Several hypotheses were tested in their studies, but in this paper, two cases will be described so as to illustrate the characteristics of broken-tie reconstitution in Japan. Stearns and Mizruchi focused on industrial companies, and studied the continuity of their interlocks with financial institutions. My study, however, focuses on two city banks, Mitsubishi Bank and Sumitomo Bank. These are leading firms in their respective enterprise groups. I examine the changes in their interlocking directorates between 1983 and 1988, the reconstitution of broken ties in particular. I believe that such an analysis may throw light on the structure of Japanese enterprise groups and the relationships between industrial corporations and banks.

The Case of Mitsubishi Bank

Table 6 shows changes in the interlocking directorates of Mitsubishi Bank between 1983 and 1988. For example, T. Nakamura, chairman of Mitsubishi Bank, was also a part-time auditor of Mitsubishi Petrochemical in 1983, and therefore, there was a tie between Mitsubishi Bank and Mitsubishi Petrochemical. In 1988, he was still an auditor of Mitsubishi Petrochemical but had not sat on the board of Mitsubishi Bank since 1986. In this case, the tie between Mitsubishi Bank and Mitsubishi Petrochemical seemed to have been broken. This was also true for Mitsubishi Oil, Mitsubishi Estate, and Mitsubishi Warehouse & Transportation. These companies were members of the Mitsubishi group together with Mitsubishi Bank and, despite the discontinuity in personal interlocks, maintained the relationship of stockholdings or loans with Mitsubishi Bank. Why were the human ties broken? The case of Mitsubishi Heavy Industries gives us a hint. Nakamura's successor as auditor at Mitsubishi Heavy Industries was H. Yamada, the new chairman of Mitsubishi Bank, in 1987. However, because Nakamura retired as chairman of Mitsubishi Bank in 1986, this tie had been broken for a year. That is, there seems to be a time lag in the reconstitution of broken ties, hence the ties broken in 1988, such as the one with Mitsubishi Petrochemical, may be reconstituted in the future.

As for Tokio Marine & Fire Insurance and Meiji Life Insurance, their ties with Mitsubishi Bank were not broken, and the continuity of interlocks was maintained. When the chairmanship of Mitsubishi Bank was passed from Nakamura to Yamada, the interlocked positions of those companies were also changed at the same time. The chairmen or presidents of Mitsubishi Bank, Tokio Marine & Fire Insurance and Meiji Life Insurance continued to sit on each other's boards, which showed that these companies maintained tight relationships as the financial core

194   Yoshiaki Ueda

Table 6:   Reconstitution of Broken Ties at Mitsubishi Bank

Interlocked Company	Multiple Director	
	1983	1988
1. Mitsubishi Petrochemical	T. Nakamura (Chairman)	T. Nakamura (*)
2. Mitsubishi Oil	T. Nakamura (Chairman)	T. Nakamura (*)
3. Mitsubishi Estate	T. Nakamura (Chairman)	T. Nakamura (*)
4. Mitsubishi Warehouse & Transportation	T. Nakamura (Chairman)	T. Nakamura (*)
5. Mitsubishi Heavy Industries	T. Nakamura (Chairman)	H. Yamada (Chairman)
6. Tokyo Marine & Fire Insurance	T. Nakamura (Chairman)	H. Yamada (Chairman)
7. Meiji Life Insurance	T. Nakamura (Chairman)	H. Yamada (Chairman)
8. Kirin Brewery	H. Yamada (President)	H. Yamada (Chairman)
9. Mitsubishi Corporation	H. Yamada (President)	H. Yamada (Chairman)
10. Honda Motor	H. Yamada (President)	H. Yamada (Chairman)
11. Tokyo Keiki	W. Horie (Full-time Auditor)	*

The position at the bank is shown in parentheses.
* No position or no multiple director.

Source: Ueda (1989, p. 44).

of the Mitsubishi group. Such an exchange system of chairmen and/or presidents could result in more effective coordination and cooperation among the companies. Interlocks of Kirin Brewery, Mitsubishi Corporation and Honda Motor with Mitsubishi Bank were kept by Yamada, whose position changed from president to chairman. In any case, the chairman or president of Mitsubishi Bank had been sent to the boards of the companies shown in Table 6 successively to maintain and continue the constant interlocking directorates with them, though some ties of companies were broken temporarily.

The tie with Tokyo Keiki had been broken since W. Horie retired from Mitsubishi Bank in late 1983. Tokyo Keiki had another multiple director, T. Okazaki, advisory director of Taiyo Kobe Bank in 1983, but this tie was also broken. As a result, Tokyo Keiki had no interlocks with either banks in 1988. However, Taiyo Kobe Bank was the main bank of Tokyo Keiki, and the former vice president of Taiyo Kobe Bank served as the chairman of Tokyo Keiki in 1988. Although the ties with the two banks were both broken, then, in 1988 the link with Taiyo Kobe Bank seemed stronger than the relationship with Mitsubishi Bank. On the other hand, Tokyo Keiki's board in 1988 included directors from Mitsubishi Heavy Industries and Japan Unisys, both of which engaged in technological cooperation with Tokyo Keiki. All of this seems to suggest that the management of Tokyo Keiki prefers "technological" interlocks to "financial" ones. Management strategy of a firm, therefore, may be a factor in the patterns of corporate interlocks.

The Case of Sumitomo Bank

Table 7 represents the changes in interlocking directorates of Sumitomo Bank. As shown in Table 5, K. Ibe's position changed between 1983 and 1988 from chairman to advisory director of Sumitomo Bank, and during the same period the number of his directorships decreased from ten to five. The interlocks with Sumitomo Cement, Sumitomo Realty & Development, Mitsui O.S.K. Lines and Rengo were maintained, though the chairman of Sumitomo Bank changed from Ibe to I. Isoda in late 1983. S. Hotta was an advisory director of Royal Hotel, but retired as an advisor director of Sumitomo Bank in 1984. Although the ties seemed to be broken, there was a time lag between the retirement from Sumitomo Bank and the retirement from the interlocked companies as explained in the case of Mitsubishi Bank.

As president of Sumitomo Bank, Isoda in 1983 and S. Tatsumi in 1988 were not involved in interlocking directorates. However, when Isoda took the chairmanship, he started to have some interlocked positions in other companies. Interlocking directorates of Sumitomo Bank, therefore, could be regarded as an attribute not of the president but of the chairman.

The tie with Kubota was broken in 1984. Kubota was a member of the Fuyo group, but Sumitomo Bank as well as Fuji Bank, the flagship firm of the Fuyo group, was its main bank. The percentage of stockholdings the two banks had was the same. The tie by T. Matsuzawa, chairman of Fuji Bank, also was broken at the same time as Ibe. Such a case seems to indicate that Kubota had kept an equal distance from Fuji Bank and Sumitomo Bank, or conversely, these two banks influenced Kubota equally. Interlocks between Kubota and the two banks were disconnected, but other institutional links continued the same as before the ties were broken.

Table 7:   Reconstitution of Broken Ties at Sumitomo Bank

Interlocked Company	Multiple Director 1983	1988
1. NEC Corporation	K. Ibe (Chairman)	K. Ibe (Advisory Director)
2. Matsushita Electric	K. Ibe (Chairman)	K. Ibe (Advisory Director)
3. Tokyo Steel Mfg.	K. Ibe (Chairman)	K. Ibe (Advisory Director)
4. Asahi Broadcasting Corporation	K. Ibe (Chairman)	K. Ibe (Advisory Director)
5. Sumitomo Cement	K. Ibe (Chairman)	I. Isoda (Chairman)
6. Sumitomo Reality & Development	K. Ibe (Chairman)	I. Isoda (Chairman)
7. Mitsui O.S.K. Lines	K. Ibe (Chairman)	I. Isoda (Chairman)
8. Rengo	K. Ibe (Chairman)	I. Isoda (Chairman)
9. Rubota	K. Ibe (Chairman)	*
10. Royal Hotel	S. Hotta (Advisory Director)	S. Hotta (*)
11. Daishowa Paper Mfg.	S. Wada (Director)	*

The position at the bank is shown in parentheses.
* No position or no multiple director.

Source: Ueda (1989, p. 45).

In 1983, Daishowa Paper Mfg. was in financial difficulties, so S. Wada, a director of Sumitomo Bank, was sent to the board as vice president. When Daishowa Paper Mfg. rebuilt its finances the following year, Wada returned to Sumitomo Bank and the tie was broken. Sumitomo Bank was the main bank of Daishowa Paper Mfg., but it gradually decreased its share of loans during Daishowa's difficulties. As a result, the main bank was replaced by the Industrial Bank of Japan in 1986. As for stockholdings, Sumitomo Bank was the largest stockholder (5.00 percent) of Daishowa Paper Mfg. in 1983, but was the fourth largest (4.22 percent) in 1988. Stearns and Mizruchi (1986, p. 526-7) pointed out that the lending relationship creates a unique partnership between the supplier and consumer of credit. When a loan is in force, the financial firm may wish to monitor and evaluate its partner's activities. If the nonfinancial firm incurs a financial crisis, a financial firm with loans outstanding may feel the need to influence corporate policy to protect its investment. Sumitomo Bank sent a director to the board of Daishowa to take responsibility as the main bank, and after fulfilling its duty, it decided to cut its connection with Daishowa. This case seemed to show one of the typical mechanisms of interlocking directorates.

Conclusion

The purpose of this study was to shed some light on the structure, mechanism and function of interlocking directorates in Japan by examining the types of interlocking directorates and the patterns of broken-tie reconstitutions.

To recapitulate, most of the interlocks in Japan were primary interlocks and based on institutional links. Over 70 percent of dyadic multiple directors were primary interlocks, and when the careers of the directors were considered, even most of the loose interlocks were based on institutional links. However, this study suggested that directors who may be regarded as "network specialists" seemed to exist in the Japanese corporate world. These network specialists played an important role in forming a large network composed of 851 firms in 1983. These network specialists were usually retired directors of large companies who maintained "remaining interlocks." As Granovetter (1973) remarked, it is the "weak ties" – the loose interlocks in this case – that are important in forming a large network as a whole.

Next, the reconstitution of broken ties in the cases of Mitsubishi Bank and Sumitomo Bank were examined. There seemed to be a time lag in the replacement of directorships, hence the ties formed by multiple directors of enterprise groups, some of which appeared to be broken, were in fact continued and the system of interlocking directorates was maintained as a whole. As for the relationship between banks and industrial companies, the ties may have been broken because of the change in management strategy or financial condition. A larger number of cases are needed, however, to reach more general conclusions.

This study presented only a few examples of interlocking directorates observed in Japan. The next step is to adopt a more systematic approach toward larger intercorporate networks as wholes, in order to further our understanding of the Japanese interlocking directorates as a system. Studies by Japanese scholars in the past mostly took the interorganizational approach and regarded intercorporate stockholdings as a better measure of intercorporate relationships than interlocking directorates. However, the intraclass approach which stresses the interpersonal rather than interorganizational connections may be more effective in the attempt to discover the real significance of interlocking directorates in Japan.

Notes

[1] I am particularly grateful to Dr. Gary Hamilton for his suggestions and advice. Also, I thank the other participants of the conference for their comments and encouragement. The work reported here is part of a research project supported by the Japanese Ministry of Education, Grant-in-Aid for Encouragement of Young Scientists (No. 01730060) in 1989.
[2] Applying the method of Leontief's input-output analysis to the matrix of interdependent stockholdings, Futatsugi mathematically analyzed the structure of Japanese intercorporate stockholdings. For details of his study, see Futatsugi (1982, 1986).

References

Carroll, W.K. 1986. *Corporate Power and Canadian Capitalism.* Vancouver: University of British Columbia Press.
Futatsugi, Y. 1982. *Nihon no Kabushiki Shoyu Kozo* [*The Structure of Stockholdings in Japan*]. Tokyo: Dobunkan.
Futatsugi, Y. 1986. *Japanese Enterprise Groups.* Monograph no. 4. Kobe: The School of Business Administration, Kobe University.
Futatsugi, Y. 1988. "Yakuin no Kennin-haken Niyoru Kigyokankankei" ["Intercorporate Relationships of Corporate Directors"]. *Kenkyu Nenpo* 34: 1-47.
Granovetter, M. 1973. "The Strength of Weak Ties." *American Journal of Sociology* 78: 1360-80.
Mintz, B. and M. Schwartz. 1985. *The Power Structure of American Business.* Chicago: University of Chicago Press.
Mizruchi, M.S. 1982. *The American Corporate Network 1904-1974.* Beverly Hills, CA: Sage.
Mizruchi, M.S. and M. Schwartz. 1987. *Intercorporate Relations: The Structural Analysis of Business.* Cambridge, UK: Cambridge University Press.
Ornstein, M.D. 1982. "Interlocking Directorates in Canada: Evidence from Replacement Patterns." *Social Networks* 4: 3-25.
Palmer, D. 1983. "Broken Ties: Interlocking Directorates and Intercorporate Coordination." *Administrative Science Quarterly* 28: 40-55.
Scott, J. and C. Griff. 1984. *Directors of Industry: The British Corporate Network 1904-76.* Cambridge, U.K.: Polity Press.
Stearns, L.B. and M.S. Mizruchi. 1986. "Broken-tie Reconstitution and the Functions of Interorganizational Interlocks: A Reexamination." *Administrative Science Quarterly* 31: 522-38.

Stokman, F.N., R. Ziegler and J. Scott. 1985. *Networks of Corporate Power: A Comparative Analysis of Ten Countries*. Cambridge, U.K.: Polity Press.

Ueda, Y. 1986. "Intercorporate Networks in Japan: A Study of Interlocking Directorates in Modern Large Corporations." *Shoken Keizai* 157: 236-54 [Rep. in *Elite Sociology: G. Mosca, V. Pareto and Contemporary Studies*, ed. John Scott, Brookfield, Vermont: Edward Elger, 1989.]

Ueda, Y. 1988. "Nihon Kigyo ni Okeru Yakuin Kennin no Ruikei Bunseki" ["Interlocking Directorates in Japan: Types and Characteristics of Interlocks"]. *Kokumin Keizai Zasshi* 158 (4): 105-20.

Ueda, Y. 1989. "Yakuin Kennin Nettowaku no Danzetsu to Shufuku" [Reconstitution of "Broken Ties: An Analysis of Interlocking Directorates in Japan"]. *Soshiki Kagaku* 23 (1): 39-49.

Useem, M. 1984. *The Inner Circle: Large Corporations and the Rise of Business Political Activity in the U.S. and U.K.* New York: Oxford University Press.

Practical and Theoretical Aspects of Japanese Business Networks

Marco Orrù

In recent decades the study of Japanese business has gained momentum in the social sciences. Economists, students of organizations, management scholars, other social scientists and business experts are all eager to unravel the mystery of the Japanese economic miracle by investigating management practices (Clark 1979), institutional business routines (Abegglen and Stalk 1985), organizational patterns (Caves and Uekusa 1976; Vogel 1975), and cultural and religious values as they bear on the economic action of individuals, firms, and business alliances (Dore 1987). The study of large inter-market and independent industrial groups has attracted considerable attention within the current scrutiny of things Japanese; the past few years have witnessed a veritable research boom in this area (e.g., Okumura 1982a, 1982b, 1984; Shimokawa 1985; Futatsugi 1986; Ueda 1986; Nishiyama 1984; Hamilton and Biggart 1988; Gerlach 1987; Orrù, Hamilton and Suzuki 1989). Michael Gerlach's (1992) *Alliance Capitalism* is the latest, most detailed example in this line of research.

The study of organizations, especially business organizations, has also advanced significantly in recent decades, by showing that a market explanation cannot alone account for the conduct of economic affairs. Oliver Williamson's institutional economics (1975, 1981) emphasized the role of hierarchies where markets fail. Ouchi (1980) took a step beyond the markets/hierarchies dichotomy and introduced the "clan" as an additional pattern informing economic action under organizational conditions characterized by goal incongruity and high ambiguity levels. More recently, organizational theorists like Thorelli (1986), Powell (1989), and Jarillo (1988) adopted networks as yet another frame for the analysis of economic organizations. Powell (1989, p. 8) characterizes networks as "neither a market transaction nor a hierarchical governance structure, but a separate, different mode of exchange, one with its own logic."

Significantly, the advances in organizational insight have occurred in part because of the increasing attention paid to non-US and, more broadly, to non-Western economies and their organizational logic (e.g., Lorenzoni and Ornati 1988; Piore and Sabel 1984). These advances suggest that the classical market model is the historical product of specific Western cultural developments and is alien to other societies. Such a model is often proven inadequate in explaining the conduct and the organizational patterns of non-Western economies.

This study of Japanese business networks has a practical and a theoretical aim. Practically, it goes beyond current assessments of business linkages and provides a more adequate description of networking patterns in the Japanese economy by adopting the metaphor of "gravitational fields." Theoretically, it sharpens our understanding of networks as legitimate organizational patterns which inform economic conduct, by identifying the technical and institutional factors which create and sustain business networks. The paper develops through four steps. First, I describe the existing analysis of networks in the Japanese economy; second, I propose the metaphor of "gravitational fields" to better describe network patterns in the Japanese economy; third, I review the organizational literature on networks and distinguish between the technical and the institutional requirements of networks and their interaction in various cultural settings; and fourth, by incorporating the evidence obtained from Japanese and other East Asian economies, I suggest ways to improve and consolidate the notion of networks as key organizational features. Here, I argue that careful attention to culturally specific organizational forms is an indispensable step toward the development of sound theoretical insights into the working of economic organizations.

Current Assessment of Japanese Business Networks

The study of large Japanese corporations and of their networking patterns is an area of growing interest within current research on Japan. Those addressing such topics are nearly unanimous in identifying striking differences between corporate networking in Japan and in the West – particularly in the United States. Whereas in the U.S. the individual firm or corporation is the protagonist on the economic scene, in Japan, the organizational pattern of top-level capitalism has been described as a community of firms in which individual businesses are linked to each other through easily identifiable networks which vary in type and in strength. Among the various forms of business linkages, ownership networks have clear prominence; but financing, production, exchange, and distribution networks are also significant. Typically, the various types of networks overlap, and reinforce each other, according to the patterns established and sanctioned through the ownership of stocks.

Within the arena of the largest Japanese corporations, researchers have focused on the horizontal inter-market networking within and among established economic groups (*kigyo shudan*), and on the vertical production networks of major corporations within business groups and of large independent industrial firms. Tables 1 and 2 provide a list of the major groups in this area.

Table 1: Major Japanese Inter-Market Groups

Mitsubishi*	Mitsui**	Sumitomo***	Fuyo****	DKB*****	Sanwa******
MTB Bank	MUI Bank	SMT Bank	Fuji Bank	D-I K Bank	SNW Bank
MTB T & B	MUI T & B	SMT T & B	Yasuda T&B	Asahi MLI	Toyo T&B
Meiji MLI	MUI MLI	SMT Life	Yasuda MLI	Taisei M&F	Nippon LI
Tokio M&F	Taisho M&F	SMT M&F	Yasuda M&F	Fukoku MLI	Orient Ls
MTB Corporation	MUI & Co.	SMT Corporation	Marubeni Co.	Nippon K K Sec.	Nissho IC
MTB Construction	Mitsukoshi	SMT Forestry	Taisei Corp.	C. Itoh & Co.	Nichimen
Kirin Brewery	MUI Mining	SMT Coal Min.	Nisshin Flour	Kanematsu-Gosho	Iwatani
MTB Rayon	MUI Constr.	SMT Constr.	Sapporo Brew	Kawasho Corp.	Takashimawa
MTB Paper Mills	Sanki Eng.	SMT Chemical	Nichirei Corp	Shimizu Constr	Toyo Constr
MTB Chem Inds	Nippon Flour	SMT Bakelite	Nisshin Spin	Nippon Zeon	Ohbayashi C
MTB Petrochemical	Toray Inds	Nippon S.G.	Toho Rayon	Asahi Denka K	Sekisui Hou
MTB Gas Chem	Oji Paper	SMT Cement	Sanyo-Kokusaku	Shiseido Co.	Teijin Ltd
MTB Plastic Ind	MUI Toatsu Ch	SMT Metal Inds	Showa Denko	Yokohama Rubber	Unitika Ltd
MTB Monsanto Chem	MUI Petrochem	SMT Electric	Nippon Oil&Fats	Kawasaki Steel	Ube Inds
MTB Oil	Onoda Cement	SMT Light Metal	Kureha Chem Ind	Nippon Lt Metal	Tokuyama
Asahi Glass	Japan Steel	SMT Aluminum	Toa Nenryo Kogyo	Furukawa Co.	Sekisui Ch.
MTB Mining & Cement	MUI M & S	SMT Heavy Inds	Nihon Cement	Furukawa Electr	Kansai Pnt
MTB Steel Mfg	MUI Engineer.	NEC Corporation	Nippon Kokan	Niigata Engineer	Tanabe Seiy
MTB Metal	MUI Real Est	SMT Realty	Kubota Ltd.	Iseki & Co.	Fujisawa Ph
MTB Aluminum	MUI OSK Lines	SMT Warehouse	Nippon Seiko	Fuji Electric	Maruzen Oil
MTB Kakoki	MUI Warehouse		Oki Electric	Yaskawa Electric	Toyo Tire
MTB Electric			Yokogawa Electr	Fujitsu Ltd.	Osaka Cement
MTB Heavy Inds			Canon Inc.	Kawasaki Hvy Ind	Kobe Steel
MTB Motors			Tikyo Tatemono	Isuzu Motors	Nakayama SW
Nippon Kogaku			Keihin E E Rail	Asahi Optical	NTN Toyo
Nippon Yusen			Tobu Railway	Nippon Express	Iwatsu Elec
MTB Estate			Showa Line	Kawasaki Kisen	Hitachi Zos
MTB W/House & Trans				Shibusawa W/Hse	Yamashita-S
				Korakuen Co.	

* Only members of the "Mitsubishi Kinyo-Kai" are included.	**** Only Fuyo member-firms of the "Fuyo-Kai" council are included.
** Only Mitsui member-firms of the "Nimoku-Kai" council are included.	****** Only DKB member-firms of the "Sankin-Kai" council are included.
*** Only members of the "Hasukui-Kai" council are included.	******* Only Sanwa member-firms of the "Sansui-Kai" council are included.

204   Marco Orrù

Table 2: Major Independent Financial and Industrial Groups*

1. Tokai
Tokai Bank
Chuo T&B
Chiyoda MLI
Toyo Menka
Okaya & Co.
Matsuzakaya Co.
Misawa Homes
Nachi-Fujikoshi
Nippon Sharyo

2. Matsushita
M Electric I.
Kyushu M. E.
M Kotobuki
M Refrigerat.
M Seiko
M. Elect. Works
Asahi Nat Light
M Housing Prod
M Industr Equip
M Graphic Comm
M Communication
Victor Co Japan
M Electronics

3. IBJ
IBJ Bank
Wako Sec
IBJ Leasing
Konoshima Chem
Toyo Soda Mfg
Plas-Tech Co.
Taihei Chem
Shin-Daikyowa
Nippon Polyur.
Rodogaya Chem.
Daikyo Oil
Nichireki Chem
Nippon Yakin
Nippon Seisen
Ikegai Corp.
Riken Corp.
Nasu Stainless
Japan Line
Sanwa Soko

4. Toshiba-IHI
Toshiba Corpor
Shibaura E Wrk
Nishishiba Ele
Kitashiba Elec

5. Nippon Steel
Nippon Steel
Daido Steel
Nippon Stl MP
Osaka Steel
Nichia Steel
Taihei Kogyo
Nippon Tetrapod
Sanko Metal
Nippon Stl Chem
Kurosaki Refr
Harima Refract
Nippon Stl WP&E
Nittetsu Steel
Nittetsu Curtain
Nihon Teppan
Nippon Stl LP
Hirohata Kaiun
TOS Steel Tube
TOS Machine
TOS Tungaloy
I-Shibaura Mach

6. Hitachi
Hitachi Ltd
Hitachi Denshi
Yagi Antenna
Nakayo Telecom
Kokusai Electr
Hitachi Heating
Hitachi Medical
Hitachi Koki
Shin-Kobe Elect
Japan Servo
Hitachi Condenser
Hitachi Maxell
Hitachi Plant Eng
Hitachi Chemical
Nippon Muki
Hitachi Metals
Toyo Brass
Hitachi Cable
Kyosan Electric
Nippon Tool Work
Hitachi Seiko
Hitachi Cstr Mach
Hitachi K. Kogyo
Babcock-Hitachi
Toyo Machinery
Tokico Ltd

8. Nissan
Nissan Motor
Nissan Diesel
Nissan Shatai
Nihon Radiator
Atsugi Mtr Pts
Nissan Koki
Tsuchiya Mfg
Kanto Seiki
Kiriu Mach Mfr
Aichi Mach Inds
Ikeda Bussan
Fuji Tekko
Japan E C S
Hasimoto Frmg
Kinugawa Rubber
Shin Nippon
Tokyo Sokuhan
Nissan Prce MS
Niss. Diesel MS
Nissan Trading
Nissan Real Est
Yokohama Trans
Niss M Carrier
Nissan M Serv
Nissan M Sales

10. Toyota
Toyota Motor
T Machine Wrks
T A Loom Works
T Auto Body
Kanto Auto Wrks
Aisin Seiki
Aisan Inds
Takaoka Ind
Arakawa A Body
Central Motor
Taiho Kogyo
Asmo Co.
Nippondenso Co
Tokai Rika
Jeco Co.
T Spinning & W
Kyowa Leather
Toyoda Gosei
Aichi Steel Wk
Chuo Spring
Tokyo S Metal
Trinity Ind
Toyoda-Sulzer
Toyoda Tsusho
Tokyo T Motor
Tokyo Toyopet

M Elect. Comp.	T Electr Appl.	I-Construc Mach	Shin Meiwa Inds	9. Seibu Saison	Chiyoda F&M
M Battery Ind.	T Heating Appl	Star Farm Mach	Kokusan Denki		Towa Real Est
National House	Onkyo Corporat	I-Materials H E	Hitachi Sales	Seibu D Stores	Sun River
Wakayama M T	Tokyo Electric	TOS Seiki	Nissei Sangyo	Seiyu Ltd.	Toyota Ctr R&D
National Bicycle	Markon Electr.	Tokyo Optical	Hitachi Air & Ref	S D Sto Kansai	
Miyata Inds	T Components	TEC Electronics	Hitachi Auto Appl	Nagano Seiyu	11. Tokyu
Victor Musical	T Battery	TOS Elec Equipm	Hitachi Credit	Seiyu Foods	
Teichiku Rec	IHI Industries	TOS Medical Sys	Hitachi Lease	Seibu Credit	Tokyu Corpor
M Elec Trading	I Ship & Chem.	TOS Cold Chain	Hitachi Transport	Kansai Seiyu	Izukyu Corp.
Nat Securities	I MP Machinery	I-Constr Mater.	Hitachi Elevator	Family Mart	Gunma Bus
M Invest & Dev	T House & Liv.	IHI Marine	Hitachi Elec Svc	S Oil& Gas Trad	Jotetsu Corp
M Distribution	T Eng & Constr	Toshiba Credit	Nippon Bsn Cons	Hotel Seibu Or	Sotetsu Tran
M Rs Institute	T Chemical	I-Factoring		Restaur Seibu	Tokyu Land
	T Silicone	Kaisho Shipping	7. Seibu Railway	Yoshinoya Co.	Tokyu Constr
	T Glass	TOS Phys Distr		S Allstate L I	Tokyu Trading
	T Ceramics	Japan Bus. Auto.	Seibu Railway	Allstate A&F I	Tok Dep Stores
	T Monofrax		Seibu Bus	S Barclays Fin	T Store Chain
			Izuhakone Railwy	Asahi Industry	Tok Recreation
			Seibu Transport	Mikasa C-C Bot	T Hotel Chain
			Kokudo Keikaku	Seiyo Corporat	Tokyu Tourist
			Seibu Golf	Parco Corporat	T Adver Agency
			Prince Hotels		T Hotels Inter
			Seibu Construct		
			Seibu Real Estate		

* Listed Tokai firms are members of the "Satsuki-Kai" council. Firms listed in all other groups are those whose group owns 50% or more of shares held by the top ten stockholders in that firm.

Source: Dodwell (1986).

Intra-Group Networks

The existing literature has emphasized the study of a most remarkable type
of Japanese business network, where individual firms are clearly identified as
members of giant economic groups like Mitsubishi, Mitsui, and Sumitomo. Researchers have detailed the various networking systems which help sustain the
identity of business groups: sharing of a common name and logo; membership of
the leaders of the major firms in their group's "Presidents' Club"; membership in
the public relations committee of the group; mutual cross-holding of stocks among
group firms; preferential trade relations; common source of financial resources;
and interlocking directorates. All these overlapping webs reinforce a networking pattern which is most aptly described by the crossholding of shares among
a group's member firms. Table 3 provides figures on the crossholding of stocks
for firms belonging to the Sumitomo group.

Table 3:   Mutual Stocks Ownership in the Sumitomo Group Selected Firms, 1984 (in %)

Owned By	1.	2.	3.	4.	5.	6.	7.	8.	9.	10.
1. Sumitomo Bank	—	3.44	—	4.49	4.75	4.17	3.88	4.93	5.94	5.11
2. S Trust & Banking	1.91	—	—	2.89	4.27	3.75	5.46	3.90	3.80	2.50
3. S Life Insurance	6.28	4.26	—	5.04	4.52	8.37	4.47	5.18	9.17	7.22
4. S Marine & Fire	1.89	1.56	—	—	3.24	1.20	0.92	1.82	2.72	2.92
5. S Corporation	1.77	3.50	—	2.23	—	1.30	1.78	3.14	3.49	2.41
6. S Chemical	1.43	1.63	—	1.15	2.30	—	—	—	—	0.47
7. S Metal Inds	1.94	3.12	—	1.17	4.13	—	—	0.93	0.71	0.90
8. S Metal Mining	0.38	1.29	—	1.30	2.18	0.25	0.26	—	0.82	1.15
9. S Heavy Industries	0.33	1.51	—	0.88	1.62	0.17	—	—	—	0.06
10. Nihon Electric	1.21	3.05	—	2.00	4.91	0.53	0.81	3.00	—	—

Source: "Kigyo Keiretsu Soran '86," *Toyo Keizai Shinposha.*

While the shares held by each individual firm might seem minimal, the collective ownership by group firms in any individual member firm is substantial
(around 20-30 percent). When calculated as a percentage of the top ten shareholders, the group's stockholdings usually exceed 50 percent.

The business groups' internal cross-holding of shares has been interpreted as
the quintessential form of horizontal control among group firms (Okumura 1984),
a means of clearly marking off the territory of the group (Sumiya 1986), and a way
of achieving group solidarity (Kosei Torihiki Iinkai Jimukyoku 1983). Ronald

Dore (1987, p. 178) accurately described the economic logic of business group alliances:

The main *raison d'être* of these groups is as networks of preferential, stable, obligated, bilateral trading relationships, networks of relational contracting. They are not conglomerates because they have no central board or holding company. They are not cartels because they are all in diverse lines of business... To extend earlier analogies, it is a bit like an extended family grouping, where business is kept as much as possible within the family, and a certain degree of give and take is expected to modify the adversarial pursuit of market advantage.

Within the business group, general trading companies act as intermediaries between and among firms to foster internal trade (Okumura 1982a) and to spread market risks across industrial sectors (Sheard 1984); financial institutions provide preferential loans and help individual firms in times of economic crisis (Sheard 1986); industrial firms actively collaborate on matters of research and development and help each other during economic downturns (Gerlach 1987). All these factors have led Nakatani (1984, p. 244) to argue that "The relative high capacity of the Japanese economy for adjustment to changed market conditions may thus be closely related to the industrial organization in Japan as characterized by group formation."

Inter-Group Networks

Intra-group stability and cohesiveness are characteristic of large Japanese business groups, but networks extend beyond such groups. Scholars have also highlighted the existence of network linkages among large business groups. For instance, Japan's six largest inter-market groups (Mitsubishi, Mitsui, Sumitomo, Fuyo, DKB, and Sanwa) hold shares in, and cross-finance each other's firms (Okumura 1982b), join together in large national projects and in crucial R&D activities (Dodwell 1986), and are collaboratively represented in all major national business associations. Okumura identified a pattern of cross-holding of shares among the largest business groups (see Table 4) but he quickly dismissed such pattern as secondary when compared with the one that obtains within each business group.

In contrast to extensive intragroup stockholding there is very little intergroup stockholding except for unilateral ownership by financial institutions. Thus, when it comes to stock ownership the enterprise group is self-contained and deliberately avoids interchanges with other enterprise groups (Okumura 1982b, p. 71).

The relatively low level of significance attributed to inter-market relations notwithstanding, it is apparent to scholars of Japanese business that business groups are linked to each other at multiple levels. As Suzuki (1988, p. 53) remarked, "The outright rivalry that had characterized inter-group relations during the period of Japan's high economic growth waned and was supplanted by great

Table 4:   Mutual Stocks Ownership by Enterprise Groups, 1977 (in %)

Owned by	Mitsui	Mitsubishi	Sumitomo	Fuyo	DKB	Sanwa	Total
Mitsui	—	0.79	1.16	1.60	2.35	2.98	8.88
Mitsubishi	1.02	—	0.44	2.30	2.59	2.07	8.42
Sumitomo	1.06	0.17	—	1.24	0.98	1.03	4.48
Fuyo	0.96	1.02	1.00	—	2.92	8.36	14.26
DKB	1.47	1.96	0.68	2.27	—	10.21	16.59
Sanwa	0.72	0.63	1.06	1.39	2.10	—	5.90
Total	5.23	4.57	4.34	8.80	10.94	24.65	—

Source: Okumura (1982b, p. 70).

cooperation following the oil crisis of the mid-seventies. This trend is clearly reflected in the proliferation of major inter-group joint ventures."

Keiretsu Networks

A third network pattern, characterized by production ties among firms is the so-called *keiretsu* network. This web centers on a very large industrial firm (which can itself be a member of an inter-market group or an independent industrial firm), and a set of dependent subsidiaries, affiliates, and subcontracting firms located upstream and downstream in the production process. Table 5 presents two examples of *keiretsu* arrangements of large industrial corporations.

Within this context, substantial ownership of stocks (between 20 and 45 percent on average) sanctions the hierarchical control of mother firms over their subsidiaries and affiliates. Futatsugi argues that the logic of vertical alignments "implies that all the raw material needed for production can be procured within the group" (1986, p. 57). Self-sufficiency and the ability to buffer one's own firm from market upheavals emerge as key factors in *keiretsu* alignments, just as they have been shown to be key factors in *kigyo shudan* alliances. The difference between the two types of networks is one of degree rather than a qualitative difference. Dore (1983) discussed in detail the philosophy underlying "relational contracting" in Japan and emphasized that the same logic of mutual benevolence applies to both horizontal and vertical alignments. Orrù, Hamilton and Suzuki (1989) argued that all firms, no matter how large or how powerful, are bound by duties according to their role position – a crucial characteristic of both vertical and horizontal inter-firm relations in Japan.

Table 5:   *Keiretsu* Affiliations of Mitsubishi Chemical and Matsushita Electric (Percentage Shares Owned and Number of Directors Dispatched; 1985 Data)

Mitsubishi Chemical Industries			Mitsubishi Electric Industrial		
Affiliated Firm	% Owned	#Dirs	Affiliated Firm	% Owned	#Dirs
Nippon Kasei Chemical	37.4	6	Matsushita Communication	61.3	4
Taiyo Sanso	36.3	3	Kyushu Matsushita Electric	50.1	4
Teikoku Kako	25.0	3	Matsushita Kotobuki	56.9	3
Mitsubishi Plastics	48.1	13	Victor Company of Japan	50.9	2
Kawasaki Kasei Chemicals	36.2	6	Matsushita Refrigeration	50.5	5
Nippon Synthetic Chemical	49.1	4	Matsushita Seiko	50.4	4
Kodama Chemical Industry	9.2	3	Matsushita Electric Works	28.3	2
Nitto Kako	44.6	3	Asahi National Lighting	21.9	0
Toyo Carbon	47.2	6	National House Industrial	26.5	2
			Wakayama Machine Tools	47.0	0
			Miyata Industry	42.9	4
			Matsushita Electric Trading	50.3	12
Average	37.0	5.2	Average	44.7	3.5

Source: Dodwell (1986).

Strategic Groups

The final network pattern researchers have highlighted is episodic alliances (*kinoh-teki shudan*) which are formed around the development and utilization of resources and of technologies. General trading firms (*sogo shosha*) are instrumental in the emergence of strategic groups which collaborated in the development of nuclear energy sources in the 1950s. "During the 1960s and '70s the six major industrial groups successfully established joint ventures in the fields of leasing, computers and development, etc." (Dodwell 1986, p. 12). Large industrial groups (like Toshiba, Hitachi, and Nissan Motors) have more recently entered the arena of strategic group formation. Currently, all major groups in Japan are involved in the construction of Osaka's international airport, and in the area of satellite communications and the communication field more broadly, as they seek to compete with Nippon Telegraph & Telephone.

An illustration of strategic alliances is provided by the recently approved U.S.-Japan joint production of the FSX fighter plane. The "Japan Economic Journal" detailed how such a project has already provided a platform for strategic networking among large Japanese corporations. Kawasaki Heavy Industries is building a three-billion yen plant for the development of flight control software; Mitsubishi Electric Co. and Mitsubishi Heavy Industries will also develop computer software for use in the defense sector; Mitsubishi Space Software (an affiliate of Mitsubishi Electric) will participate in WESTPAC (a research project for the development of SDI for the Western Pacific region); Ishikawajima-Harima Heavy Industries' president expressed the desire of Japan's aerospace industry to move speedily with the FSX project; and the Japanese Defense Agency has already set up a three-year test program with Mitsubishi Electric and Fujitsu Ltd., to develop an experimental forward-looking infrared (FLIR) scanner for adoption in the FSX fighter.

While the areas of joint multi-group activities shift over time as national economic priorities emerge, the collaboration among groups has been a constant feature of the Japanese economy for the past several decades, and it has greatly intensified during the 1980s. Strategic alliances are not a prerogative of Japanese firms alone but they are unmatched in their density by any other nation.

Japanese Business Networks as Gravitational Fields

The current assessment of Japanese business networks greatly enhanced our understanding of organizational patterns in Japan as it identified the wealth of networking linkages spanning up and down, and across Japan's business scene. But such assessment seems to suffer from excessive rigidity in its identification of mutually exclusive network typologies, and in its uncritical acceptance of Japanese businesses' own definition of their location within networks. Periodic publications appear regularly, which seek to neatly classify each of the major Japanese corporations according to their inter-market group affiliation, but no mention is made of the multiplicity of webs across the *kigyo shudan* landscape. The internal cohesiveness of groups is emphasized at the expense of broader network patterns. Moreover, even within each business group, there is little sense of the varying strength of membership ties for different member firms.

I propose a different approach to network patterns in Japanese business – one which is less guided by officially assigned labels, and more responsive to actual network linkages as shown by ownership and financial ties among firms. To this end I introduce the notion of "gravitational fields" to correct the excessively rigid, univocal notion of group membership which has been emphasized in the existing literature on business groups. Here I will adopt Larson's (1964, p. 115) use of gravitational field "to describe the region in which the gravitational effect makes its appearance, and to call the magnitude of this effect at any specific location the 'strength of the field' at that point." The advantage of conceptualizing business networks as gravitational fields is that they can be simultaneously assigned to a strong network field, while they are also acknowledged to be related, with varying gravitational strengths, to other network fields. Ultimately, we should obtain a gravitational field which encompasses, directly and/or through other fields, all actors (business groups, independent industrial firms, strategic alliances) in the Japanese economy.

The *Kigyo Shudan's* Gravitational Field

The apparently homogeneous, cohesive arena of intra-group networks is shown, under close scrutiny, to consist of dense ties which differ in strength. In its compilation of relevant data, Dodwell (1986, p. 34) identified four levels of group inclination of firms, according to stock ownership figures: nucleus (i.e., Presidents' Club firms), strong (50 percent and above), medium (30-49 percent), and weak (less than 30 percent). To this classification we can add one higher level for the leaders of the group (usually the main bank, the general trading company, and the leading industrial firm). Applying this five-level classification we obtain a gravitational field like the one illustrated in Figure 1 for the firms belonging to the Mitsui business group.

The metaphor of networks as gravitational fields allows us to interpret the organizational pattern of *kigyo shudan* as a concentric web of firms subjected to gravitational pulls which vary in strength and intensity; the firms at the core of the group are subjected to (and themselves produce) the strongest gravitational field through multiple, saturated network ties. As we move toward the periphery of the field, the linkages become more tenuous and less systematic.

A paradox emerges in the gravitational arrangement of *kigyo shudan*. Because of the weaker gravitational pull we would expect peripheral firms in the group to be subject to the influence of other surrounding gravitational fields; in fact, it is not the peripheral firms, but the core firms of the group which are subject to multiple pulls through cross-cutting and overlapping linkages. As we will see below, the gravitational field of inter-group networks shows at its core the same firms which constitute the core of each group's gravitational field.

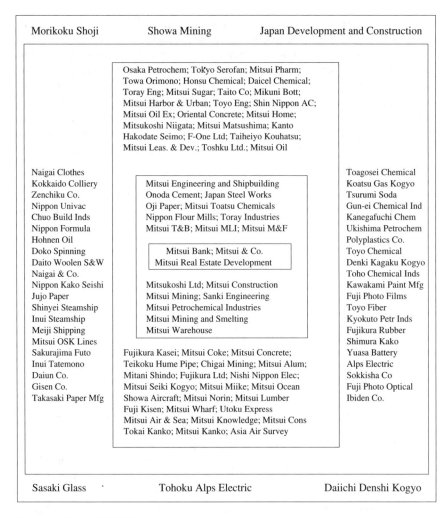

Morikoku Shoji   Showa Mining   Japan Development and Construction

Osaka Petrochem; Tokyo Serofan; Mitsui Pharm;
Towa Orimono; Honsu Chemical; Daicel Chemical;
Toray Eng; Mitsui Sugar; Taito Co; Mikuni Bott;
Mitsui Harbor & Urban; Toyo Eng; Shin Nippon AC;
Mitsui Oil Ex; Oriental Concrete; Mitsui Home;
Mitsukoshi Niigata; Mitsui Matsushima; Kanto
Hakodate Seimo; F-One Ltd; Taiheiyo Kouhatsu;
Mitsui Leas. & Dev.; Toshku Ltd.; Mitsui Oil

Naigai Clothes   Toagosei Chemical
Kokkaido Colliery   Mitsui Engineering and Shipbuilding   Koatsu Gas Kogyo
Zenchiku Co.   Onoda Cement; Japan Steel Works   Tsurumi Soda
Nippon Univac   Oji Paper; Mitsui Toatsu Chemicals   Gun-ei Chemical Ind
Chuo Build Inds   Nippon Flour Mills; Toray Industries   Kanegafuchi Chem
Nippon Formula   Mitsui T&B; Mitsui MLI; Mitsui M&F   Ukishima Petrochem
Hohnen Oil   Polyplastics Co.
Doko Spinning   Mitsui Bank; Mitsui & Co.   Toyo Chemical
Daito Woolen S&W   Mitsui Real Estate Development   Denki Kagaku Kogyo
Naigai & Co.   Toho Chemical Inds
Nippon Kako Seishi   Mitsukoshi Ltd; Mitsui Construction   Kawakami Paint Mfg
Jujo Paper   Mitsui Mining; Sanki Engineering   Fuji Photo Films
Shinyei Steamship   Mitsui Petrochemical Industries   Toyo Fiber
Inui Steamship   Mitsui Mining and Smelting   Kyokuto Petr Inds
Meiji Shipping   Mitsui Warehouse   Fujikura Rubber
Mitsui OSK Lines   Shimura Kako
Sakurajima Futo   Fujikura Kasei; Mitsui Coke; Mitsui Concrete;   Yuasa Battery
Inui Tatemono   Teikoku Hume Pipe; Chigai Mining; Mitsui Alum; Alps Electric
Daiun Co.   Mitani Shindo; Fujikura Ltd; Nishi Nippon Elec; Sokkisha Co
Gisen Co.   Mitsui Seiki Kogyo; Mitsui Miike; Mitsui Ocean   Fuji Photo Optical
Takasaki Paper Mfg   Showa Aircraft; Mitsui Norin; Mitsui Lumber   Ibiden Co.
                        Fuji Kisen; Mitsui Wharf; Utoku Express
                        Mitsui Air & Sea; Mitsui Knowledge; Mitsui Cons
                        Tokai Kanko; Mitsui Kanko; Asia Air Survey

Sasaki Glass   Tohoku Alps Electric   Daiichi Denshi Kogyo

Source: Dodwell (1986).

Figure 1:   Gravitational Field of Mitsui's Business Group (1985 Data)

The Field of Inter-Group Networks

Inter-group networks have received scant attention in the current literature, and their significance is downplayed with the argument that these linkages are a symbolic tribute to Japanese norms of reciprocity (the *giri* constraint) rather than expression of organizationally meaningful network patterns (Futatsugi 1986; Okumura 1982a). But pitting the strong ties of intra-group relations against the weak ties of inter-group relations disregards their partaking of similar network patterns. A better view of these two types of business networks is to locate them on a continuum in which both strong and weak ties are comprehensively taken into account.

The data on inter-group stockholdings presented in Table 4 above and the pattern identified in Figure 1 for intra-group networks allow us to identify the gravitational field of inter-group networks as presented in Figure 2.

		Mitsui & Co		
		Mitsui Real Estate Devel.		
		Toray Inds.		
		Mitsui Eng. & Shipbuilding		
Mitsubishi Corporation	Mitsubishi Bank	Mitsui Bank	Sumitomo Bank	Sumitomo Chemical
Mitsubishi Heavy Inds	MTB Trust & Banking	MUI Trust & Banking	Sumitomo Trust & Banking	Sumitomo Metal Inds
Asahi Glass	Tokyo Marine & Fire Insurance	Taisho Marine & Fire Ins.	Sumitomo Marine & Fire Insur.	Sumitomo Metal Mining
Mitsubishi Chemical Inds	Meiji Mutual Life Insurance	Mitsui Mutual Life Insurance	Sumitomo Life	NEC Corporation
Marubeni Corporation	Yasuda Mutual Life Insurance	Asahi Mutual Life Insurance	Nippon Life Insur	Nissho Iwai Corporation
Taisei Corporation	Fuji Bank	Dai-Ichi Kangyo Bank	Sanwa Bank	Nichimen Corporation
Nippon Kokan	Yasuda Trust & Banking	Taisei Marine & Fire Insur	Toyo Trust & Banking	Teijin Ltd
Kubota Ltd.	Yasuda Marine & Fire Ins.	Fukoku Marine & Fire Ins.	Daido Mutual Life Insur.	Kobe Steel
		Nippon KK Sec.	Orient Leasing	
		C. Itoh & Co		
		Kawasaki Steel		
		Furukawa Co		
		Furukawa Electr		

Source: Dodwell (1986).

Figure 2:   Gravitational Field of the Six Largest Inter-Market Groups (1985 Data)

The characteristics of the inter-group gravitational field are as follows: (1) the life insurance companies of the six inter-market groups are at the core of the network, (2) city banks and other financial institutions are one step removed from such core, (3) general trading companies and leading industrial corporations are located in the third sector. (Solid lines indicate concentric gravitational spheres, while dotted lines mark the boundaries of each of the six inter-market groups.)

Previous research (Orrù, Hamilton, and Suzuki 1989) shows that the six inter-market groups do not display a uniform involvement in inter-group networks: the ex-*zaibatsu* groups (Mitsubishi, Mitsui, and Sumitomo) show higher levels of internal cohesion and lower levels of inter-group involvement. The city-bank groups (Fuyo, Sanwa, and DKB), instead, have weaker internal control, but stronger inter-group ties. The historical pattern can be described as a transition from relatively self-sufficient, autonomous groups before World War II, to more flexible, interdependent and overlapping arrangements since the post-War era, for both inter-market and independent industrial groups. Networking activities have accordingly intensified in recent decades, both within the Japanese economy and in the international arena.

The Field of Independent Industrial Groups

Independent industrial groups have received much less scrutiny than inter-market groups by scholars of Japanese business. The rationale is, perhaps, that independent groups are a secondary feature of Japan's economy; and yet, many crucial, and often fastest growing industrial sectors of Japan's economy (iron and steel production, transportation machinery, electrical and electronics) are led by independent industrial groups like Nippon Steel, Toyota Motors, and Hitachi Ltd. There is nothing secondary about these giant groups; in fact, between 1983 and 1985 most independent groups outperformed inter-market groups in their growth rate for annual sales, net income, and number of employees. Independent groups display not only industrial strength, but financial strength as well – on average, they rely on loans much less than the industrial firms who belong to business groups. Some independent groups, like Toyota and Matsushita, have no external loans whatsoever – a fact which earned Toyota the nickname of Toyota Bank. But the label of "independent" groups would mislead us if we thought they were organizational islands in the Japanese economy.

Independent groups are organized as *keiretsu*; that is, they are characterized by a very large, highly successful leading firm, and a vertical alignment of subsidiaries and affiliates which are closely tied to the mother-firm through significant ownership of stocks. However, if we examine the ownership pattern of the leading industrial firms, we will realize that control over the leading firm is not internal to the group (as in the *kigyo shudan*), but rather it is dispersed across other independent and inter-market financial institutions. Table 6 shows the ownership linkages for the leading firms of independent groups, and for the main banks of inter-market groups, and allows us to envision yet another network pattern.

In earlier writings (Orrù, Hamilton, and Suzuki 1989) the notion of "maxi-business group" was proposed to describe the pattern of relations among the largest independent industrial firms and the major Japanese financial institutions. Such notion seemed revolutionary when first advanced, but it appears much more plausible when couched in the context of Japan's networks as gravitational fields. The maxi-business group is yet another instance of the expansive networks of Japanese business which, at this level, includes not only the six inter-market groups, but also the largest independent financial and industrial groups.

The networking of independent groups with inter-market groups does not rest on unilateral dependence of the former on the latter; rather, it is truly a multilateral network for the reciprocal advantage of the parties involved. A graphic depiction of this additional field is provided in Figure 3.

The gravitational field of inter-market and independent firms shows the following features: (1) the core of the field comprises not only the life insurance companies of major inter-market groups, but also independent insurance companies; (2) at the second gravitational level are not only the major financial institutions of the six inter-market groups, but also independent financial groups (like the Tokai Bank, the Industrial Bank of Japan, and the Long Term Credit Bank of Japan) and the largest independent industrial corporations (Nippon Steel, Itachi Ltd, Nissan Motor, Toyota Motor, Matsushita Electric, Toshiba Corporation, etc); (3) at the third level we have, beside the leading industrial firms which belong to inter-market groups, other large industrial firms aligned in the *keiretsu* of independent groups (e.g., Matsushita Electric Works, Toyoda Automatic Loom Works, Nissan Real Estate). Overall, the pattern obtained shows a systematic linkage among firms which belong to inter-market groups and to independent industrial groups – they are all shown to partake of one large gravitational field. Such network provides the financial and industrial giants of the Japanese economy with additional stability – both through the substantive investments each party makes in other businesses, and through the symbolic gesture of expressing approval, and confidence in the conduct of other economic actors (individual firms and groups) in the Japanese economy.

Japanese Business as a Unified Field

Many other kinds of networks could be added to the ones presented above. Directorship interlocks (Ueda 1986), trade linkages (Young 1982), and loan distribution patterns (Sheard 1986) can be described according to the principle of gravitational fields that was adopted. But the networks presented above should suffice to make the case for a web of business linkages in Japanese business which is much broader and more encompassing than it has hitherto been claimed.

Table 6: Inter-Group Stock Ownership in Japan's Leading Firms (in %; 1985 Data)*

Owner Group / Owned Firm	MTB	MUI	SMT	FUY	DKB	SNW	TOK	IBJ	NIP	HIT	NIS	TOY	MAT	TOS	TYU	SEI	DML
MTB BANK	19.5					3.4			1.8								4.0
MUI BANK		12.1				4.1						4.5		2.5			4.0
SMT BANK			15.8			4.6			2.0				3.6				1.9
FUY BANK				15.3		2.9			2.4		2.0						3.1
DK BANK	2.0			1.3	7.8	4.0								1.2			3.1
SNW BANK	3.5					11.5			2.1	1.6		2.4					2.9
TOKAI BANK	2.3				2.3	2.8	3.8		1.1			5.4					2.3
IBJ	6.2				1.7	4.4		1.0	2.6	1.5	2.3		1.0				2.9
NIPPON STEEL	3.6	1.6	1.7	3.6		4.6		3.4									1.8
HITACHI	2.3			2.2	2.2	6.3		2.6									2.8
NISSAN			3.0	9.7		4.4		5.9			2.3						5.8
TOYOTA		9.6				8.7	5.0					4.4					2.3
MATSUSHITA	1.5		11.0			4.1							3.7				
TOSHIBA	7.4					6.2	1.8										
TOKYU	4.3		2.2			7.9		2.2							2.8		4.8
SEIBU	0.8	1.2		1.2	0.8	0.8		1.1								50.4	7.9

* The ownership matrix only includes figures for the top ten shareholders (i.e., an empty cell does not mean the total absence of ownership of shares.

Key to abbreviations: MTB=Mitsubishi; MUI=Mitsui; SMT=Sumitomo; FUY=FUYO; DKB=Dai-Ichi Kangyo Bank; SNW=Sanwa; TOK=Tokai Bank; IBJ=Industrial Bank of Japan; NIP=Nippon Steel; HIT=Hitachi Ltd.; NIS=Nissan Motor; TOY=Toyota Motor; MAT=Matsushita; TOS=Toshiba Ltd.; TYU=Tokyu; SEI=Seibu; DML=Dai-Ichi Mutual Life.

Source: Compiled from Dodwell (1986).

Mitsui & Co.	Mitsui Real Estate Devel	Mitsui Eng. & Shipbuilding	Toray Inds	Towa Real Estate
Chuo Shoji			Toyoda Automatic Loom Works	Toyoda Tsusho
Nissei Sangyo	Nissan Real Estate	Fuji Heavy Industries		Konosuke Matsushita
Mitsubishi Corporation	Mitsubishi Bank	Mitsui Bank	Sumitomo Bank	Sumitomo Chemical
Mitsubishi Heavy Inds	MTB Trust & Banking	MUI Trust & Banking	Sumitomo Trust & Banking	Sumitomo Metal Inds
Asahi Glass	Tokyo Marine & Fire Insurance	Taisho Marine & Fire Ins.	Sumitomo Marine & Fire Insur.	Sumitomo
	Long Term Credit Bank of Japan	Tokai Bank	Industrial Bank of Japan	Matsushita Electric Works
	Nippon Steel	Hitachi Ltd	Nissan Motor	Sumitomo Metal Mining
Mitsubishi Chemical Inds	Meiji Mutual Life Insurance	Mitsui Mutual Life Insurance	Sumitomo Life	NEC Corporation
	Dai-Ichi Mutual Life Insurance			Tokyo Electric
Marubeni Corporation	Yasuda Mutual Life Insurance	Asahi Mutual Life Insurance	Nippon Life Insur	Nissho Iwai Corporation
Seibu Constr	Toyota Motor	Matsushita Electric	Toshiba Corp.	Tokyu Land
Seiyu Ltd	Tokyu Corpor	Seibu Railway	Seibu De Stores	Tokyu Construction
Taisei Corporation	Fuji Bank	Dai-Ichi Kangyo Bank	Sanwa Bank	Nichimen Corporation
	Yasuda Trust & Banking	Taisei Marine & Fire Insur	Toyo Trust & Banking	
Nippon Kokan				Teijin Ltd
	Yasuda Marine & Fire Ins.	Fukoku Marine & Fire Ins.	Daido Mutual Life Insur.	Kobe Steel
Kubota Ltd.	I-H-I	Nippon KK Sec.	Orient Leasing	New Japan Securities
Japan Securities Clearing	Okuma Machinery Works	C. Itoh & Co.	Furukawa Corpor	Nisshin Steel
Toyo Soda Mfg	Chiyoda MLI	Kawasaki Steel	Furukawa Electr	Topy Industries

Source: Dodwell (1986).

Figure 3:   Gravitational Field of Inter-Market and Independent Groups' Firms (1985 Data)

To conclude this description of Japanese networks, I submit that the various types of gravitational fields described above can all be subsumed under a unified pattern. The label "community of firms" is most appropriate for describing the sense of shared economic responsibilities and duties which characterizes Japan's business world; but the specific dynamic features of this community can only be brought out if we understand such community to be not an amorphous amalgam of equal firms with interchangeable responsibilities. Instead, we must appreciate the different roles played by Japan's leading life insurance companies, the major city banks and lesser financial institutions, independent and inter-market industrial firms, and general trade corporations within the larger picture of business organizations. Next, we must turn to the significance of networking patterns in Japanese business for an improved theory of organizational networks.

Current Theories of Business Networks

In the 1970s, after decades of unchallenged market models of explanations of economic phenomena, transaction-cost economics (TCE) corrected the existing models by emphasizing the role of firm hierarchies within markets, and by showing how hierarchies provided solutions to market imperfections. TCE submits that under the environmental conditions of uncertainty and of small numbers, and the human conditions of bounded rationality and opportunism, it is more advantageous for firms to organize in a vertical hierarchy, rather than rely on market mechanisms, to keep the costs of inter-firm transactions at a minimum. TCE has become a legitimate theory in the area of institutional economics, but it has been criticized for not going far enough in embedding economic action within a social context. Granovetter (1985) provided a compelling critique of TCE in his "Economic Action and Social Structure," by arguing that economic action is couched in interpersonal social relations, and that therefore pure market conditions and pure bureaucratic hierarchies are equally unlikely to be observed in the economic arena.

Students of organizations have sought to capture the middle ground that characterizes economic action, between one extreme of free-floating interactions of isolated firms, and the other extreme of tightly controlled and hierarchically structured sets of firms. The middle ground between markets and hierarchies has been variously labelled as "relational contracting" (Dore 1983), "planned co-ordination" (Richardson 1972), "clans" (Ouchi 1980), "relational exchange" (Goldberg 1980), and "networks" (Thorelli 1986; Jarillo 1988; Johanson and Mattson 1987; Powell 1989). While there is variation in the emphasis each label provides for this middle ground, the consensus is that what goes on between markets and hierarchies is a crucial component in the conduct of economic affairs. For ease of reference, I will refer to this as the literature on economic networks.

The literature on economic networks projects itself in two directions by addressing the causes and the functions of networks. On the one hand, researchers are interested in the origins of networks, in what brings networks into existence. On the other hand, researchers ask what networks accomplish – organizationally – that markets and hierarchies cannot. That is, what is the privileged realm of economic networks. Let's look at the functions of networks first.

Concerning the advantages of economic networks, the general consensus is that they provide inter-firm coordination coupled with flexibility; they supply access to valuable technological information with little investment of time and resources from each member of the network; they guarantee the effective and reliable exchange of strategic information within the network; they minimize the risks associated with the development of avant-garde, resource intensive technologies; and they allow for the pooling of human resources in high demand, high skill areas. Powell (1989, p. 13) provides this description:

Networks are lighter on their feet than hierarchies. In network modes of resource allocation, transactions occur neither through discrete exchanges nor by administrative fiat, but through networks of individuals engaged in reciprocal, preferential, mutually supportive actions. Networks can be complex: they involve neither the explicit criteria of the market, nor the familiar paternalism of the hierarchy. A basic assumption of network relationships is that one party is dependent upon resources controlled by another, and that there are gains to be had by the pooling of resources. In essence, the parties to a network agree to forego the right to pursue their own interests at the expense of others.

Network formations are observed in a variety of economic areas (Powell 1989) – in the construction industry (Eccles 1981), publishing (Coser, Kadushin, and Powell 1982), film and recording industry (Peterson and White 1981), German textiles industry (Sabel et al. 1987), Northern Italian small industrial firms (Lazerson 1988) and, of course, Japanese business alliances (Gerlach 1992). Powell (1989) argues that the common denominator of most empirical cases of network formation is that they are found in "highly competitive and/or resurgent industries" where the old market mechanisms prove inadequate in dealing with new economic needs.

The question of what brings networks into being and where do networks come from has also been extensively addressed in the existing literature. Two classes of factors emerge from the literature which seeks to account for network formations: institutional factors and technical factors. The former refer to socially constructed routines of interaction which favor networking arrangements, while the latter point to environmental pressures of economic survival which demand network-type solutions. Of course, in most empirical cases, institutional and technical factors coexist. So, for instance, Ouchi's clans theory (1980) specifies that clans obtain under the unfavorable technical condition of high performance ambiguity and the favorable institutional condition of low opportunism – a situation which is the obverse of market conditions. But even acknowledging that institutional and technical requirements intermingle, we can distinguish them analytically according to the emphasis placed on them by various students of economic networks. Let's look, in turn, at the institutional side and at the technical side of the arguments.

Institutional Requirements of Networks

Ouchi's notion of clan refers to a kin-type network which is not necessarily based on blood relations. Ouchi (1980, p. 132) remarks that "industrial organizations can, in some instances, rely to a great extent on socialization as the principal mechanism of mediation or control" – the clan network provides such socialization. Beyond the reciprocity of market interactions and the legitimate authority of bureaucracies, the explicit normative requirement of clans is that they must share common values and beliefs. "Common values and beliefs provide the harmony of interests that erase the possibility of opportunistic behavior" (Ouchi 1980, p. 138). The way for clans to share values and beliefs is to conduct themselves according to mostly implicit, traditionally accepted kinds of behavior. "The set of traditions in a formal organization may produce a unified, although implicit philosophy or point of view" (Ouchi 1980, p. 139). Ouchi claims that Japanese firms possess the clan-like qualities which make it possible to minimize problems of mediation and control.

Dore (1987) is much more forthcoming in his support of an institutional explanation of "relational contracting" in Japanese business networks. As he puts it, Japanese relational contracting rests on the goodwill and benevolence of the parties involved. For the Japanese, "It is not just that benevolence is the best policy… Benevolence is a duty… Most Japanese feel more comfortable in high-trust relations of friendly give-and-take in which each side recognizes that he also has some stake in the satisfaction of the other" (Dore 1987, pp. 181-183). In a network-type arrangement, the stability and the trustworthiness of business relations is crucial, and such qualities can be provided by the implicit, mutual normative expectations of Japan's economic actors.

Powell's discussion of rationales for network formations leads him to emphasize trust as a key ingredient of networks. "Certain social contexts encourage cooperation and solidarity, or a sense of generalized reciprocity… The more homogeneous the group, the greater the trust, hence the easier it is to sustain network-like arrangements" (Powell 1989, pp. 49-50). Similar aspects are emphasized by Whitley (1989, p. 9) who calls attention to the "homogeneity of human and material resources" in East Asian societies, and by Lincoln (1989, p. 5) who describes Japan's business scene as characterized by "an extraordinary reliance on diffuse, personalistic network relations of commitment, trust, and obligation in conducting administrative and economic affairs."

In his research on inter-firm networks among Chinese businesses in Hong Kong, Wong (in this volume) has suggested that the emergence of business networks requires not only the inter-personal trust based on familial ties, but also a system-level trust which sees the external economic order as reliable and legitimate. As Wong (in this volume) puts it, "Trust among family members facilitates quick decisions and secrecy, making the family unit adaptable to rapidly changing and uncertain situations. But will this engender distrust outside the family?" He goes on to argue that "To complement personal trust, system trust is required. System trust includes confidence in the legal framework, the political structure, and the financial set-up". While Wong points out that in Hong Kong a basis for system trust is provided by the island's British colonial infrastructure, Kao (in this volume) observed that Taiwan's legal framework for supporting networks based on system trust is much more problematic. Accordingly, business networks beyond the inter-personal level are often episodic and short-lived.

From an historical approach, Hamilton's (in this volume) chapter on the organizational foundations of modern Chinese commerce highlighted the historical development, in Chinese society, of an affinity for network-like economic arrangements. On the one hand, Hamilton identified regional associations as a gravitational center for the creation of networks: whether it was a matter of towns or provinces, "belongingness was always a function of actual social relationships among people. The actual networks defined the group." On the other hand, family-centered economic activities in China can also be classified as networks which can expand or contract according to specific needs. "Families in China represent networks of people joined together by specific sets of familial relationships... In China, no one person controls the family, but all are obligated within its networks" (Hamilton in this volume).

The literature presented above (and more evidence could be provided from other cultural contexts) makes a strong case for the institutional embeddedness of networks – business or otherwise. Networks cannot exist in a social vacuum; they cannot operate effectively or sustain themselves over time unless the non-contractual normative elements available through values, traditions, and norms of conduct are clearly recognized and widely upheld by all parties involved. But this is obviously only one piece of the networks' puzzle; next, we must turn to the environmental conditions which call network types of organizations into being.

Technical Requirements of Networks

The available literature on business networks, and on organizations in general, has identified a variety of technically-based requirements which characterize the emergence of networks. Population ecologists (Hannan and Freeman 1977; Aldrich 1979) provide a basic explanations for the rise and spread of particular organizational forms by emphasizing ecological fitness as crucial for the selection and retention of specific organizational forms.

Investigating the general characteristics of business networks, Powell (1989) identified two technical factors which demand network forms of organizations: know-how and speed. Economic activities which require intensive knowledge skills demand, at the same time, the unfettered, rapid dissemination and exchange of such knowledge. The crucial resource in this context is human capital which cannot be monopolized by any individual organization. In his study of Japanese corporate groups, Imai (1988, p. 34) comes to a similar conclusion by identifying Japan's industrial networks as "formed basically with the human network as its axis." Powell's second requirement, speed, refers to the need for easy and quick access to information – a network is, at its core, a communication network. The faster communication is exchanged, the more easily network members can adapt to rapidly changing technical environments.

Technological requirements of networks are addressed by contingency theory and convergence theory. From both perspectives, "technology operates to shape organization... Common shifts in the type and complexity of technology will give rise to common outcomes in organizational designs and management practices" (Lincoln 1989, p. 9). But the evidence to back the hypotheses of contingency and convergence theories in the Japanese economy is contradictory at best (cf. Marsh and Mannari 1977; Lincoln, McBride, and Hanada 1986). Lincoln (1989, p. 9) writes:

A mounting body of evidence on the technology-organization relation in diverse societal settings, including Japan, suggest that technology interacts in complex ways with local cultures in determining how organization, management, and industrial relations systems respond.

At a macroeconomic level, conditions in world markets have been identified as factors prompting new types of organizational forms in Japan (Cole 1971, 1979). Tracing the development of different types of business alliances, from the early *zaibatsu* to the post-World War II corporate groups to the recent industrial networks, Imai identified structural economic conditions demanding the emergence of new types of business patterns. Regarding industrial networks, Imai (1988, p. 22) argues:

In facing the oil crisis, Japanese business had to concentrate on energy saving through a comprehensive effort at utilizing all applicable technologies... As a consequence, there was a drastic growth of the specializations linked with each other within the industrial system... Such growth of specialization... is characterized by what can be termed a network phenomenon in that it happened in a way that transcended corporate boundaries and industrial borders and linked the technologies horizontally while at the same time causing technology transfers.

Imai characterized (1988, p. 25) Japanese industrial networks as having distinctive characteristics which separate them from the *zaibatsu* and from more recent corporate groups; in practice, his tri-partite typology appears to be largely overdrawn. The commonalities among the three types of organizations overwhelm any difference they might exhibit; most definitely, these three organization types are not at odds with each other, but rather converge together in the larger picture. So, for instance, while it is clear that former *zaibatsu* groups are much more stable than more recent industrial networks, it would be a mistake to consider networks an inherently unstable, or to assume that network instability is a weakness. Thinking of it as network flexibility would already emphasize the strength of such an arrangement. It is still far from evident, anyway, that Japanese industrial networks are, in fact, unstable. Beyond his specific analysis of networks, Imai (1988, p. 25) is correct, however, in identifying "unceasing innovation [as] the fundamental strength of the network industrial system." At this point, we must ask, What do various explanations of networks add up to? And how does the Japanese business network system outlined in this paper help us improve our knowledge of the topic and the theory of networks in general?

Japanese Practice and Network Theory

The evidence on Japanese business organizations is most relevant to network theory since networking arrangements in Japan's economy appear to be so pervasive. Thus far, I have amply illustrated the multiple overlapping and expansive linkages that obtain among the major corporations in Japan's economy, and I have presented an overview of existing theories of economic networks. The last step, now, is to ask what can we learn about business networks and about network theory from studying the Japanese case. In this concluding section I will argue that four key insights emerge from Japanese networking practices.

First, network theories have identified technical and institutional requirements of business networks. Perhaps implicit in the theories but in need of clarification is the notion that the technical and institutional requirements of networks cannot work at odds with each other, but rather they must converge to achieve feasible networking practices. The relative weight of each component and the degree of convergence between them is a matter of empirical investigation. The available evidence seems to suggest that within Anglo-Saxon societies, technical requirements are more prominent factors in the rise of business networks. Networks arise in particular industrial sectors (e.g., construction, computers and software development) which demand such arrangements for reasons of technical efficiency. In East Asian, Latin American, and Continental European societies, instead, the institutional traits appear comparatively more prominent, in various ways, in the formation of network systems (e.g., Japan's group centered decision processes, Taiwan's family centered business activities, Italy's and France's political determination of economic viabilities). But obviously, in both instances, one component alone cannot provide networking without the other component also being present. The degree of convergence between institutional and technical requirements of networks is also amenable to empirical specification. Here, the Japanese case seems to provide an extreme example of optimal "elective affinity" between technical and institutional requirements of networks – that is, the solution to problems of high-tech, intensive research and development activities is couched in a networking scenario in which structural ties of all sorts among major corporations and down the economic hierarchy are institutionally strong, and are either already in place or sought very vigorously.

A second related insight is that networks, more than other organizational arrangements rest and capitalize on linkages among people. If commodities are the key component of markets and rules are the main characteristic of hierarchies, people and their exchange of available knowledge are distinctive features of networks. In the information age, networks are at the organizational forefront. The shift in emphasis from commodities, to rules, to people can help understand, perhaps, the shift in the performance abilities and fitness of different economies around the world. Comparatively speaking, networks show more affinity for group-centered institutional arrangements than markets or hierarchies; as networks become crucial in answering the technical requirements of the economic environment, one would expect certain societies to be in a better position to maximize their economic networking potentials. The identification of socially generalized inter-personal trust relations and of system trust structures, for instance, makes it possible to predict the type and level of stability of business networks favored by different societies. Which economic networks are successful, and to what extent, is of course an issue for empirical verification.

The third insight provided by Japanese business networks is that networks themselves are not an island in the open seas of the world markets; rather, as my presentation of Japan's gravitational fields demonstrates, networks intersect with each other to obtain, so to speak, a network of networks. Imai's (1988) tripartite distinction of *zaibatsu* groups, city-bank groups, and industrial networks is helpful for understanding the change in emphasis of Japan's networking practices, but it would be misleading to disregard the most important, constant feature of these practices: all business groups and independent corporations, regardless of their historical roots, are active participants in the networking which characterizes Japan's economic system today. Being faithful to the empirical phenomenon of Japan's business networks requires us to abandon the notion that we have to draw a boundary line somewhere, that there must be an either or, an in or out which will clearly discriminate network members from non-members. The evidence shows that drawing artificial lines between networks might hinder, rather than help our understanding of Japan's networking patterns. The evidence also provides a warning sign against network theories that try to achieve premature closure on definitional problems of what does or does not count as a network. The very notion of networks which build on flexible, expansive links among its members should provide us with an open-ended view of network configurations.

Fourth and last, like markets and hierarchies, networks do not exist in a cultural vacuum but feed from and themselves reflect the traits of specific social contexts. The identification of ideal traits of networks should be used as a heuristic device for sensitizing our research hypotheses, but they should not be mistaken for the real thing – the real world of networks. A theory of networks would do little to advance our knowledge of organizations if it substituted a universalistic, a-historical theory of markets with a similarly a-historical, universalistic theory of networks. Unless we keep cultural specificities and variations in mind when studying networks, we will have defeated our own aim of bridging economic action and social structure.

References

Abegglen, James C. and George Stalk. 1985. *Kaisha, The Japanese Corporation.* New York: Basic Books.

Aldrich, Howard. 1979. *Organizations and Environments.* Englewood Cliffs, NJ: Prentice Hall.

Caves, Richard E. and Masu Uekusa. 1976. *Industrial Organization in Japan.* Washington, DC: The Brookings Institute.

Clark, Rodney. 1979. *The Japanese Company.* New Haven, CT: Yale University Press.

Cole, Robert E. 1971. *Japanese Blue Collar.* Berkeley, CA: University of California Press.

Cole, Robert E. 1979. *Work, Mobility, and Participation.* Berkeley, CA: University of California Press.

Coser, Lewis, Charles Kadushin, and Walter W. Powell. 1982. *Books: The Culture and Commerce of Publishing.* New York: Basic Books.

Dodwell Marketing Consultants. 1986. *Industrial Groupings in Japan.* Revised Edition. Tokyo: Dodwell.

Dore, Ronald P. 1983. "Goodwill and the Spirit of Capitalism." *British Journal of Sociology* 34: 459-82.

Dore, Ronald P. 1987. *Taking Japan Seriously.* Stanford, CA: Stanford University Press.

Eccles, Robert. 1981. "The Quasifirm in the Construction Industry." *Journal of Economic Behavior and Organization* 2: 335-57.

Futatsugi, Yusaku. 1986. *Japanese Enterprise Groups.* Kobe: School of Business, Kobe University.

Gerlach, Michael. 1987. "Business Alliances and the Strategy of the Japanese Firm." *California Management Review* 30 (1): 126-42.

Gerlach, Michael. 1992. *Alliance Capitalism.* Berkeley, CA: University of California Press.

Goldberg, Victor P. 1980. "Relational Exchange." *American Behavioral Scientist* 23 (3): 337-52.

Granovetter, Mark. 1985. "Economic Action and Social Structure." *American Journal of Sociology* 91: 481-510.

Hamilton, Gary G. and Nicole Woolsey Biggart. 1988. "Market, Culture, and Authority." *American Journal of Sociology* 94 (Supplement): 52-94.

Hannan, Michael T. and John Freeman. 1977. "The Population Ecology of Organizations." *American Journal of Sociology* 85 (5): 929-64.

Imai, Ken-ichi. 1988. "The Corporate Network of Japan." *Japanese Economic Studies* 16: 3-37.

Jarillo, Jose-Carlos. 1988. "On Strategic Networks." *Strategic Management Journal* 9: 31-41.

Johanson, Jan and Lars-Gunnar Mattson. 1987. "Interorganizational Relations in Industrial Systems." *International Studies of Management and Organizations* 17 (1): 34-48.

Kosei Torihiki Iinkai Jimukyoku (Fair Trade Commission). 1983. *Kigyo Shudan no Jittai ni Tsuite* (On the State of Affairs of Business Groups). Tokyo: Kosei Torihiki Iinkai Jimukyoku.

Larson, Dewey B. 1964. *Beyond Newton*. Portland, OR: North Pacific Publishers.

Lazerson, Mark. 1988. "Organizational Growth of Small Firms." *American Sociological Review* 53 (3): 330-42.

Lincoln, James R. 1989. "Japanese Organization and Organization Theory." *Research in Organization Behavior,* eds. B.M. Staw and L.L. Cummings. Greenwich, CT: JAI Press, Vol. 12.

Lincoln, James R., Kerry McBride, and Mitsuyo Hanada. 1986. "Organizational Structures in Japanese and US Manufacturing." *Administrative Science Quarterly* 31: 338-64.

Lorenzoni, Gianni and Oscar A. Ornati. 1988. "Constellations of Firms and New Ventures." *Journal of Business Venturing* 3: 41-57.

Marsh, Robert M. and Hiroshi Mannari. 1977. *Modernization and the Japanese Factory.* Princeton,NJ: Princeton University Press.

Nakatani, Iwao. 1984. "The Economic Role of Financial Corporate Grouping." *The Economic Analysis of the Japanese Firm,* ed. M. Aoki. Amsterdam: Elsevier.

Nishiyama, Tadonori. 1984. "The Structure of Managerial Control: Who Owns and Controls Japanese Business?" *The Anatomy of Japanese Business,* eds. Kazuo Sato and Yasuo Hoshino. New York: Sharpe.

Okumura, Hiroshi. 1982a. "Interfirm Relations in an Enterprise Group." *Japanese Economic Studies* 10: 53-82.

Okumura, Hiroshi. 1982b. *Mitsubishi: Nihon o Ugokasu Shudan* [Mitsubishi: A Business Group that Moves Japan]. Tokyo: Daiyamondo.

Okumura, Hiroshi. 1984. "Enterprise Groups in Japan." *Shoken Keizai* 147: 169-189.

Orrù, Marco, Gary G. Hamilton, and Mariko Suzuki. 1989. "Patterns of Inter-firm Control in Japanese Business." *Organization Studies* 10 (4): 549-574.

Ouchi, William G. 1980. "Markets, Bureaucracies, and Clans." *Administrative Science Quarterly* 25: 129-141.

Piore, Michael J. and Charles F. Sabel. 1984. *The Second Industrial Divide: Possibilities for Prosperity*. New York: Basic Books.

Peterson, Richard A. and Howard White. 1981. "Elements of Simple Structures." *Urban Life* 10 (1): 3-24.

Powell, Walter W. 1989. "Neither Market nor Hierarchy: Network Forms of Organization." *Research in Organizational Behavior,* eds. Barry M. Staw and Larry L. Cummings. Greenwich, CT: JAI Press, Vol. 12.

Richardson, George B. 1972. "The Organization of Industry." *Economic Journal* 82: 883-96.

Sabel, Charles F., Gary Herrigel, Richard Kazis, and Richard Deeg. 1987. "How to Keep Mature Industries Innovative." *Technology Review* 90 (3): 36-45.

Sheard, Paul. 1984. "Financial Corporate Grouping." Discussion Paper No. 44. Canberra: Research School of Pacific Studies, Australian National University.

Sheard, Paul. 1986. "Main Banks and Internal Capital Markets in Japan." *Shoken Keizai* 157: 255-85.

Shimokawa, Koichi. 1985. "Japan's Keiretsu System." *Japanese Economic Studies* 12: 3-31.

Sumiya, Toshio. 1986. *Gendai Nihon Shihon Shugi no Shihai Kozo* [The Structure of Domination in Modern Japanese Capitalism]. Tokyo: Shimpyoron.

Suzuki, Mariko. 1988. "A Sociological Approach to the Understanding of Japanese Business Groups." Unpublished manuscript. Davis: University of California.

Thorelli, Hans B. 1986. Networks: Between Markets and Hierarchies." *Strategic Management Journal* 7: 37-51.

Ueda, Yoshiaki. 1986. "Intercorporate Networks in Japan." *Shoken Keizai* 157: 236-254.

Vogel, Ezra. 1975. *Modern Japanese Organization and Decision Making*. Berkeley, CA: University of California Press.

Williamson, Oliver E. 1975. *Markets and Hierarchies*. New York: Free Press.

Williamson, Oliver E. 1981. The Economics of Organization." *American Journal of Sociology* 87: 548-77.

Withley, Richard D. 1989. "Enterprise Structures in their Societal Contexts." Unpublished Manuscript. Manchester: Business School.

Young, Alexander K. 1982. *The Sogo Shosha*. Tokyo: Tuttle.

B. South Korean Business Networks

The Industrial Organization and Growth of the Korean Chaebol: Integrating Development and Organizational Theories[1]

Eun Mee Kim

Introduction

The *chaebol* (business conglomerates) have played a critical role in the recent history of the South Korean economy and its development.[2] They have been the agent of development, spearheading Korea's rise in the world economy. The *chaebol*, which grew at a phenomenal rate during the Park Chung Hee regime (1961-1979), represent the dominant form of industrial organization in Korean development. The Hyundai *chaebol*, for example, grew at an average rate of 32.1 percent every year between 1971 and 1983 (Kim, E.M. 1987), and the five largest *chaebol* were responsible for 17.4 percent of value added in the manufacturing sector in 1982 (Lee and Lee 1985).

There are two purposes of this research. The first is to suggest a theoretical framework for better analyzing industrial organizations in the Third World by incorporating both the very broad, macro perspectives offered by theories of development and the micro orientation of the institutional approach to organization. Second, the research is intended to provide a better understanding of the emergence and growth of the industrial organization that was integral to the miraculous economic development in South Korea. The historical origin of the Korean *chaebol* is examined, with emphasis on the question of how it became the central actor in Korea's developmental drama.

A framework that concentrates on patterns of industrial authority, offered by Hamilton and Biggart (1988), provides a useful point of departure. In their analysis of the distinct types of industrial organization that emerged in Japan, Korea, and Taiwan, these researchers challenge economic and cultural explanations, arguing instead that "enterprise structure represents situational adaptations of preexisting organizational forms to specific political and economic conditions" (Hamilton and Biggart 1988, p. 87). Their study marked a significant development in the fields of both economic development and formal organization.

Although the *chaebol* show unique characteristics as industrial organizations, they have been largely neglected by organizational scholars. The details of their emergence, their co-optation by national-development planning, and their extraordinary growth provide interesting material with which to examine various organizational theories.

Theories of Economic Development and Organization

Studies on Korean development that have utilized various conventional theories of development (i.e., modernization, dependency, world system, or neoclassical economics) have not been able to provide a full and correct analysis of the role of the *chaebol* in Korean development. While development scholars have focused on the similarities found in the Northeast Asian or East Asian models of development, they have overlooked the qualitative differences among these nations in the industrial organizations and state-society relations that emerged (Cumings 1987; Evans 1987).

Many of the so-called strong-state development studies in the tradition of Gerschenkron (1962) or of dependent development (Cardoso and Faletto 1979; Evans 1979) argued that the state is the most important actor in bringing about economic growth in the latecomers. Such studies thus attributed Korea's miraculous economic development solely to the state, with only a passing mention of the *chaebol* (Amsden 1989; Lim 1983; Koo 1984). The *chaebol* was portrayed as being entirely *created*, *maintained*, and *managed* by the Korean state, and was, therefore, treated as an enterprise that is not very different from a public one, an enterprise with limited autonomy.

Although such state-centered approaches do correctly portray the significance of the Korean state and its tight control of the *chaebol*, they often fail to analyze the *chaebol* as separate entities that are ultimately private enterprises taking risks and making decisions. Recent changes in the state-business relationship in Korea suggest that the *chaebol* are gaining even more autonomy (Kim, E.M. 1988). Therefore, it is important that they be studied apart from state policies.

The studies that utilized the neoclassical economics approach concluded that Korea's economic development was made possible by the vigorous private sector, with some state guidance. However, these studies neglect the fact that the state was not only market-enhancing and market-protecting, but often market-distorting and market-creating. In the West, industrial organizations are treated like private enterprises, relatively free from state control and working in a relatively competitive market. Such studies of Korea, thus, did not take seriously the real constraints and control of the state and how these affect the daily activities and long-term plans of industrial organizations.

A better approach to understanding of the Korean *chaebol* lies somewhere between the strong-state and the neoclassical economic approaches. A revisionist perspective is needed to explain the industrial organization in those Third World countries having strong, autonomous states. The industrial organization of the *chaebol* should be analyzed as a private enterprise, but one with significant state-constraints.

According to Kiggundu, Jorgensen, and Hafsi (1983), a critical shortcoming of the study of organization in less developed countries (LDCs) is that organizational theories – which have mostly been developed in industrialized nations – are unable to fully incorporate the environment that LDCs face. These researchers found that studies that focused on the technical core (i.e., organizational tasks and technology) had very few problems in the use of conventional theories. However, serious difficulties were found when conventional theories were used to study the relationship between the *organization* and its *environment*. Clearly, the conventional theories need to be modified if they are to be used to analyze the organization and its environment in the setting of an LDC.

The study done by DiMaggio and Powell (1983) provides a very useful operationalization of the emergence of different types of industrial organizations as responses to the external environment. Their definition of the external environment shows promise for the analysis of the organization and its environment in an LDC. Their key thesis is that internal efficiency is not the only goal of organizations and that institutional legitimacy, political power, and social fitness are objectives of modern organizations. It is, therefore, critical to examine the organization and its environment instead of focusing solely on its internal structure.

In the process of attaining legitimacy, political power, and social fitness, organizations undergo three mechanisms of institutional isomorphic change (DiMaggio and Powell 1983). The first is the process of *coercive isomorphism*, in which organizations are influenced by direct-authority relationships. The expansion of the central state and the centralization of capital are examples of institutions of influence. The second mechanism is *mimetic isomorphism*, which results from the organization's attempts to respond to uncertainties in its environment by mimicking existing organizational structures that have weathered the uncertainties. The last mechanism is *normative isomorphism*, which results from the professionalization of managers, either through widespread business and management education in universities or through the growth and elaboration of professional networks.

Although the above study provides a useful way to explain the environment and the responses of industrial organizations to it, it has two critical shortcomings. First, their study does not explain "why" and "how" certain organizations become models of isomorphic change. The theory explains that weaker organizations are influenced by stronger organizations, but fails to address the key issue of why certain organizations come to power. Without a better understanding of this critical process, it is impossible to identify which organizational forms are likely to flourish in the future. It does not tell us, for example, why the Japanese *zaibatsu* served as the initial setup for Korean businesses. And it does not explain why and how the state had become more powerful and resourceful relative to the business groups in the beginning of the 1960s.

Second, it does not capture the tremendous internationalization that has occurred in businesses and their activities at the end of the twentieth century. The conditions surrounding organizations in LDCs in the latter half of the twentieth century are qualitatively different from those that existed when the industrialized countries were developing. The world is now far more tightly knit, with better communications and transportation technology than ever before. The export-led industrialization strategies that many LDCs have adopted also put enterprises in these countries in direct contact with their counterparts in industrialized countries. Much has been researched about the role of MNCs and the consequences of their investment in LDCs, in particular on short- and long-term growth and on inequality. But, very little has been studied about their influence on industrial organizations in the Third World. The rapid increase of foreign direct investment and the technology transfers of MNCs in many LDCs since World War II have caused enterprises in LDCs to come into direct contact with those in industrialized countries. The colonial experiences of many LDCs are also important sources of influence. The legacies of the colonial state and the dominant forms of industrial organizations of the colonizers will continue to have significant impacts on the now-independent LDCs.

A better understanding of the *chaebol* in Korean development can be attained by incorporating the organizational theory offered by DiMaggio and Powell (1983) – which can explain how *chaebol* as an industrial organization flourished in Korea – and the more macro analyses provided by development studies and the political economy perspective. The latter will provide historical insights into the process of how certain institutions and organizations gain power and resources to become the origin of isomorphic change (rather than to become the receptor of such change). The macro understanding offered by the political economy perspective also enables us to capture the internationalization of industrial organizations in LDC.

The Industrial Organization of the *Chaebol*

The *chaebol* is similar to the Japanese *zaibatsu* of pre-World War II years, with some differences. The *chaebol* is a group of companies that often has a trading company at the center. Its strength comes from (1) its *large size*, based on the combined assets of the companies; (2) *flexibility*, based on the ease of mobilizing and exchanging capital, technology, and personnel among the companies; and (3) *self-sufficiency*, based on the wide range of businesses the *chaebol* owns (diversification).

The *chaebol* is vertically integrated. This integration is maintained by family ownership of companies (unlike the *zaibatsu* which are increasingly run by professional corporate managers) and is strengthened by traditional Confucian values of filial piety and loyalty toward the family. The boards of directors are dominated by sons, brothers, and sons-in-law. A recent study by Shin and Chin (1989) shows that among the members of the boards of directors there are still strong ties based on family, region of birth, and high-school alumnae. Family ties among top executives are strong and form the basis of the *chaebol*. While the share of professional managers in the *chaebol* has increased in recent years, the more important trend is the professionalization of family members. The sons and sons-in-law of the *chaebol* owners are educated as professional managers; often they are sent to the United States to earn MBAs from prominent business schools, such as Stanford, MIT, Harvard, and Columbia.

Another important aspect of the *chaebol* is its wide range of businesses. Such diversification appears to have grown stronger over time, and it is a critical characteristic in the determination of whether a group of companies are a *chaebol*.[3] Diversity gives the *chaebol* self-sufficiency and prevents it from becoming excessively dependent on the state. For example, owning an insurance or other financial-services company gives the *chaebol* much-needed flexibility in cash flow, since they are not permitted to own banks.

In fact, an important distinction between the Korean *chaebol* and the pre-World War II Japanese *zaibatsu* lies in access to credit. Unlike the *chaebol*, *zaibatsu* were allowed ownership of banks. The banks were nationalized by President Park in 1961 so that the state could gain power in the economy and control the *chaebol*. Foreign loan capital and foreign direct investment are also approved and carefully monitored by the state. In the earlier period of foreign direct investment, and in cases of public and commercial loans, the state has acted as the acquirer and distributor of foreign capital (Kim, E.M. 1989). Therefore, the *chaebol* rely heavily on the state for credit, and the state uses this to attract *chaebol* into certain sectors and to reward them. Although the Korean state has privatized many banks since 1981, it has effectively blocked ownership by the *chaebol* and their family members (Park et al. 1986, pp. 34-37).

In comparison to the earlier zaibatsu, the *chaebol* engage in less outside contracting and rely mostly on their own companies for parts and assembly. In other words, there is no wide and systematic integration between the *chaebol* and other middle and small firms, as in Japan.

The *chaebol*, like any other private firm, is prevented by law from employing current government officials. However, it often recruits retired officials with whom it has close contact during the officials' tenure in government, offering them honorary positions as well as such active duties as lobbying with the government. Like government officials, military officers are not allowed to be employed in the private sector until after retirement. They are then particularly sought after by *chaebol* with investments in the defense industries to help lobby the military and the government.

An important source of *chaebol* strength comes from its ease of mobilization and exchange of capital, technology, and personnel among the companies within it. It is not unusual for top executives to be transferred from one company to another; those known for their management skills may be transferred to companies that are in trouble or that are rapidly expanding. Research and development are often coordinated between companies, and expenses and even laboratory space may be shared. Although the ownership of companies is maintained separately, immediate cash funds are often arranged through financial-service and insurance companies, and loans can be arranged between companies without the complicated bureaucracy involved in acquiring bank loans.

The *chaebol*'s large size and the variety of its businesses give it great flexibility and self-sufficiency, which help it to gain leverage in its dealings with the state. The less the *chaebol* is forced to rely on the state for resources – whether those resources are capital, technology, or marketing information and expertise – the more independent and stronger it will become.

The Emergence of the *Chaebol*

The history of the *chaebol* in Korea is rather short. As of 1983, forty of the fifty largest *chaebol* had been founded after the end of the Japanese colonial period (1910-1945), and nineteen had been established between 1951 and 1960 (Kim, E.M. 1987). The history is even shorter when one considers that the foundation dates are usually those of the mother firm, and not those of their *chaebol* establishment. The most rapid growth into "*chaebol*-dom" has occurred in the 1960s and 1970s.

The history of entrepreneurship in Korea is also short. It was only after signing the Kangwha Treaty with Japan in 1876 that Korea first saw enterprises within its borders. Jones and Sakong (1980) note that prior to 1876, Korea had no industrial entrepreneurship and only a very weak mercantile class. After the signing of the treaty, Korea saw the establishment of foreign firms, most of them from Japan (Jones and Sakong 1980). There was an influx of Japanese enterprises during the Japanese colonial period (1910-1945), which filled the vacuum resulting from the absence of indigenous industrial entrepreneurship.

Such industrial organization could not develop during the Japanese colonial period, due to the strength of the Japanese colonial government and its policy of assimilation. The only type of industrial organization allowed was one that was owned and managed by the Japanese. It was direct importation in the strictest sense, without much effort being made to adapt to the Korean business environment. There was, in fact, nothing much to speak of as a "Korean" business environment; what little had existed was wiped out by the Japanese policy of assimilation.

Many of the Japanese enterprises that established businesses in Korea were subsidiaries or branches of Japanese *zaibatsu,* and Japanese managers and workers migrated to Korea to work in these enterprises (Jones and Sakong 1980; Mason et al. 1980). The Korean economy during this period was thus largely run by the Japanese, and it is crucial to note that the *zaibatsu* were the first and most dominant form of industrial organization encountered by the Koreans.

The process of mimetic isomorphism (DiMaggio and Powell 1983) can help to explain the adoption of the *chaebol* as the major industrial organization following both the Japanese colonial period and during the 1960s, when rapid economic development was pursued.

The first major point is the lack of indigenous industrial organization and the position of the Japanese *zaibatsu* as the only dominant industrial organization with which Koreans have had any experience. Although there were three years of U.S. military occupation (1945-1948) following the Japanese defeat in World War II, no American firms established subsidiaries in Korea during that time. And there was simply not enough time between the end of the colonial period (1945) and the beginning of the Park regime (1961) for any major development of indigenous industrial organization, especially because of the interruption of the Korean War (1950-1953).

The businesses that formed after the colonial period ended took what the Japanese had left behind in their hasty retreat from Korea in the summer of 1945. The organizational structure of the Japanese firms thus formed the initial setting for Korean enterprises.

The mimetic isomorphism speaks to the uncertainties in the environment and to how those influence organizations adopt an existing industrial organization in order to minimize the risks (DiMaggio and Powell 1983). In any time period since Korea's liberation from colonial power, the uncertainties of the Korean economy have far outweighed the stability and certainties; in 1945, when Korea had its first opportunity to develop its own industrial organizations, the economic outlook was very bleak. It was inevitable that Korean businesses would adopt many features of the *zaibatsu* in their industrial organization.

Another critical time in the development of the *chaebol* came in 1961, when President Park Chung Hee announced economic development plans. The First Five-Year Economic Development Plan, begun in January 1962, called for drastic and fundamental changes in the Korean economy, with "rapid" economic development to be based on exports of light manufactured goods. Before 1961, the Korean economy had been basically agrarian, with relatively few manufacturing firms and a small number of mercantile businesses. Three drastic changes were ordered by the state: (1) a transition from agriculture to industry; (2) a transition from commercial activities to industrial manufacturing; and (3) export.

Export was a major risk factor for Korean businesses, since there were virtually no exports of manufactured products prior to the 1960s. Local firms lacked not only the expertise to produce goods targeted for Western markets, but also the marketing technology to export goods. Under such conditions of uncertainty, it was a given that Korean businesses would continue to develop the *chaebol* as the dominant industrial organization, rather than invent or adopt some other type of industrial organization (which would result in increased risks and uncertainties).

The Park regime's commitment to economic development illustrates the process of coercive isomorphism. When Park Chung Hee came into power in 1961, it was through a military coup. Park had two major tasks in front of him: one was to gain legitimacy and the support of the people, and the other was to bring about economic development. The previous regime, headed by Rhee Syngman, had been marred with incompetence and corruption and had been accused of showing favoritism toward certain *chaebol*, resulting in the excessive accumulation of wealth by several of the *chaebol*. The Park regime demonstrated a clean break from the Rhee regime by charging these *chaebol* with the illicit accumulation of wealth and prosecuting them. And in order to show that he had come into power not for personal interests but for the interests of the public, Park pursued a strategy of rapid economic growth to improve the living conditions of the Koreans.

The preference for large, existing firms over small and medium sized firms was intended as a way to attain development in the most rapid way by achieving the economies of scale necessary for exports. However, there is little evidence that the Park regime actually preferred the *chaebol* in its earlier years over other types of industrial organization. This situation changed, of course, and by the early 1970s the state-*chaebol* relationship had become interdependent and symbiotic (Kim, E.M. 1988).

The Park regime nationalized the banks in 1961. This move placed credit under state control, effectively making *chaebol* and private firms dependent on state officials. Moreover, foreign loan capital and foreign direct investment were also tightly controlled and closely monitored by the state. Distribution of both domestic and foreign capital thus rested in the hands of the state, which could then easily implement its economic-development plans and control the private sector.

The state used the nationalized banks to reward companies that conformed to state policies, and to attract firms into sectors in which they otherwise saw too little profit and too much risk. An example of the former policy was the low-interest-rate, no-strings-attached export loan given to firms that were successful in exports. This policy was prevalent in the 1960s, while the next decade was dominated by the second policy. An example of that policy, begun in the early 1970s, was the loan provided to firms to invest in state-targeted, heavy manufacturing industries. These were automobiles, shipbuilding, chemicals, iron and steel, nonferrous metal, and electronics and electrical appliances.

Such centralization of resources is an important mechanism of *coercive isomorphism*. As the state becomes the sole source of capital, the industrial organizations become more alike. Even when the state does not deliberately prescribe a certain type of industrial organization, the organizations will assume similar structures, because they all rely heavily on one source for capital.

As will be documented later, in the section on growth, the adaptability of the industrial organization to the changes in state policy appears to have been crucial to the growth of the *chaebol*. The *chaebol* that followed the state's push for heavy manufacturing in the 1970s are the ones that grew most rapidly in the 1970s and early 1980s. All of this evidence points to the enormous power that the state wields over the *chaebol*.

The *chaebol* responding to such controls developed the vertically integrated and diversified huge conglomerates that could better withstand changes in state policies and that could one day become self-sufficient in both capital and technology. A fully diversified *chaebol* – with such broad-ranging companies as, for example, sugar, flour, textiles, toys, department stores, automobiles, shipbuilding, construction, insurance, and computers – would be fine no matter which way state policy turned. The industrial organization of the *chaebol* is thus a unique combination of the remnants of the pre-World War II *zaibatsu* and of the responses of Korean businesses to the constraints and challenges of the Korean state and the international context.

The Growth of the *Chaebol*

The fifty largest *chaebol* were studied in a preliminary analysis. Among these, there were two natural breaks in terms of total assets in 1983. The first break was at the four largest *chaebol*, and the next was at the ten largest (including, of course, the four largest). Since the growth of *chaebol* as a whole has been due mainly to the growth of the larger ones, I have limited my analysis to the top ten *chaebol*.[4]

Firm level data for the ten largest *chaebol* have been collected through various primary sources.[5] This data set contains information on the ten largest *chaebol* (with each *chaebol* consisting between nine and thirty-two firms) for the period between 1970 and 1983. The foundation date, total assets, sales, debt, capital, exports and major products (e.g., light or heavy manufacturing,[6] construction, finances, trade, and other services) for each firm were coded and put into the computer for analysis by means of SPSSX.

One of the most astonishing features of the *chaebol* has been their extraordinary growth in a short period of time. The growth rates of the *chaebol* are presented in Table 1.[7] In the twelve-year period from 1971 to 1983, Hyundai, Daewoo, and Sun Kyong grew most rapidly. Hyundai's average annual growth rate of assets was 32.1 percent, Daewoo's was 46.3 percent, and Sun Kyong's was 35.1 percent. The figures for the early 1970s alone are even more impressive. Between 1971 and 1975, the average annual growth rate of Hyundai was 57.9 percent; of Daewoo, 105 percent; and of Sun Kyong, 67.7 percent. These are phenomenal growth rates, and they are five to nine times higher than the rate at which the Korean economy as a whole grew during the same years.[8]

A major characteristic shared by these three *chaebol* today is a high concentration in heavy manufacturing. In 1970, Hyundai had 85 percent of its total assets in

Table 1:   Basic Indicators of the Ten Largest Chaebol, 1971–1983

Rank*	Chaebol	Foun- dation Year**	Total Assets***		Average Annual Growth Rates of Assets (%)****		
			1971	1983	1971–80	1981–83	1971–83
1.	Hyundai	1947	158,261	4,469,342	38.0	19.2	32.1
2.	Samsung	1951	415,978	3,371,603	18.4	35.4	19.1
3.	Daewoo	1967	34,679	3,340,367	53.7	11.6	46.3
4.	Lucky/ Goldstar	1947	437,060	2,714,511	17.2	16.4	16.4
5.	Ssangyong	1954	310,424	1,711,715	16.8	13.3	15.3
6.	Sun Kyong	1953	40,049	1,477,873	36.7	0.6	35.1
7.	Han Jin	1945	83,734	1,340,120	32.9	7.5	26.0
8.	Korea Explosives	1952	256,424	1,173,064	11.7	37.0	13.5
9.	Dae Lim	1939	64,522	943,307	31.8	5.7	25.1
10.	Kukje	1949	153,489	896,205	19.3	8.8	15.8

   * Ranking based on total assets in 1983.
  ** Foundation year of the mother firm.
 *** Total Assets in 1980 constant Korean million Won.
**** Average annual growth rate was calculated using 1980 constant prices.

heavy manufacturing; and Daewoo and Sun Kyong had none. By 1983, however, Hyundai, Daewoo, and Sun Kyong had 52 percent, 46 percent, and 49 percent of their total assets in heavy manufacturing, respectively. Although Lucky-Gold Star also had 76 percent of its total assets in heavy manufacturing, it did not grow as much as the others, possibly because this *chaebol* was mainly in electrical appliances and electronics. Although the electrical appliances and electronics industry was designated as a state-targeted industry in the 1970s, it did not receive financial support because the government had determined that it already met international standards.

The growth rates of heavy-manufacturing assets have been much higher for Hyundai and Daewoo than for other *chaebol*, especially in the early 1970s (see Table 2).[9] These two *chaebol* invested heavily in state targeted industries. Hyundai was involved in automobiles and shipbuilding; the Hyundai Motor Company has been a major producer of automobiles in Korea, and since 1982 it has been working with Mitsubishi Automobiles and the Mitsubishi Corporation of Japan. It has been very successful in exporting automobiles to Canada and the United States since 1986.

Table 2: Average Annual Growth Rate of Assets in Heavy Manufacturing of the Ten Largest Chaebol (%), 1970–1983*

Rank**	Chaebol	Foundation Year***	1971–1975	1976–1980	1981–1983
1.	Hyundai	1967	81.0	57.7	15.5
2.	Samsung	1969	16.2	48.6	23.6
3.	Daewoo	1974	—	31.6	17.7
4.	Lucky/Goldstar	1970	8.9	23.2	15.0
5.	Ssangyong	1970	−4.0	49.4	6.8
6.	Sun Kyong	1972	—	—	−6.0
7.	Han Jin	None	—	—	—
8.	Korea Explosives	1970	9.4	9.5	35.7
9.	Dae Lim	1970	−42.8	218.2	12.0
10.	Kukje	1970	13.5	7.4	2.9

  * Average annual growth rate was calculated using 1980 constant prices.
 ** Ranking based on total assets in 1983.
*** Foundation year of the first heavy manufacturing firm.

Daewoo, the youngest of the ten, grew precisely because of its investment in heavy manufacturing. For example, in 1974, its first heavy manufacturing company was founded with total assets of 2.1 million won. In 1975, total assets in heavy manufacturing increased to over 237 million won – a drastic increase of one hundred-twelve times compared to the previous year. Most of Daewoo's twenty-four firms are involved in heavy manufacturing (e.g., automobiles, heavy machinery, shipbuilding, and electronics) and construction. Daewoo was able to amass a huge amount of capital from exporting textiles to the United States at the end of 1960s and the beginning of the 1970s, before the U.S. adopted a quota system for textile imports. Because Daewoo was so successful in exports, it became a major recipient of the state's export loans (which had interest rates that were roughly one-third of those for loans from private banks). With the capital it had earned from the lucrative export business, together with the low-interest state loans, Daewoo was able to become a major heavy manufacturing *chaebol* by the mid-1970s.

The rapid growth rate of heavy manufacturing in Hyundai and Daewoo coincided with the shifting emphasis in state policy from light to heavy manufacturing in the early 1970s, with the beginning of the Third Five-Year Economic Development Plan and the 1973 Pronouncement for the Development of the Heavy and Chemical Industries.

Those *chaebol* that did not adapt to the state's policy shift did not grow as fast. Lucky-Gold Star, already mentioned, is one example. Another example is Samsung. While this *chaebol* did decrease its light manufacturing share somewhat over the years, it is still largely invested in this area and in other consumer durables, such as electrical appliances. As a result, Samsung did not grow as fast as Hyundai or Daewoo during the twelve-year period.

A more extreme case is that of Kukje, which took a direction totally opposite to that suggested by the state and moved from heavy to light manufacturing. Kukje had been a shoe-manufacturing firm for more than two decades and could not be defined as a *chaebol* until the mid-1970s, when it rapidly expanded its business. Its share in light manufacturing increased sharply, from 0 percent in 1975 to 11 percent in 1980. This move contributed to Kukje's high debt rate and thus to its bankruptcy in 1985.[10]

Along with heavy manufacturing, the construction industry also experienced rapid growth (see Table 3). Construction companies in Korea played an essential role not only in meeting the increased demands in the domestic market due to rapid economic growth, but also in serving as an important source of foreign capital earnings. By the early 1970s, a few *chaebol* realized that Korea's relative advantage in exporting of light manufactured goods would not last forever. To increase and prolong their growth, the *chaebol* would have to turn to heavy manufacturing. Construction was a way to acquire foreign capital and, at the same time, to develop heavy manufacturing firms. It provided opportunities to develop backward linkages with heavy machinery, construction material, and engineering firms, among others.

Hyundai was the first Korean construction company to go the Middle East in the mid-1970s. Although Japan had already gone to the Middle East a few years earlier, Hyundai still managed to obtain large construction contracts there, including the $931 million Jubail Industrial Harbor Project in Saudi Arabia in 1979. With its tremendous success in the Middle East, by 1978, Hyundai had become the largest *chaebol* in Korea, a position it still holds in terms of total assets.[11]

Hyundai's success led other large *chaebol* to quickly establish construction companies and send them off to the Middle East. With the exceptions of Hyundai, Daewoo, and Dae Lim which had construction companies before the construction boom in the Middle East, all other large *chaebol* established theirs in the 1970s. By 1980, all ten *chaebol* had construction companies. However, due to the saturation of the construction market in the Middle East, increased unrest in that region, and the lack of experience of some of the construction companies, those *chaebol*

Table 3:   Average Annual Growth Rate of Assets in Construction of the Ten Largest Chaebol (%), 1970-1983*

Rank**	Chaebol	Foundation Year***	1971–1975	1976–1980	1981–1983
1.	Hyundai	1947	12.5	26.0	13.0
2.	Samsung	1974	—	—	1.8
3.	Daewoo	1968	75.8	27.2	−0.9
4.	Lucky/Goldstar	1975	—	—	9.3
5.	Ssangyong	1972	—	23.2	30.0
6.	Sun Kyong	1977	—	—	46.8
7.	Han Jin	1972	—	5.6	33.8
8.	Korea Explosives	1975	—	71.4	30.3
9.	Dae Lim	1939	−0.3	59.3	2.0
10.	Kukje	1977	—	—	—

* Ranking based on total assets in 1983.
** Average annual growth rate was calculated using 1980 constant prices.

that went into construction in the late 1970s specifically to enter that market either left with little profit or, in some cases, went bankrupt.

Samsung, which had been the largest *chaebol* for over two decades, lost its position to Hyundai. There were several contributing factors, including the fact that Samsung had remained a largely light manufacturing *chaebol* and did not have a construction company until later, and on a much smaller scale. Samsung's business strategy was to protect its current business and enjoy the status quo, avoiding unnecessary risks. However, this strategy also ensured that the company would have no major breakthroughs, as Hyundai did with construction.

Another important feature of *chaebol* growth is the increase in the diversification of businesses during the thirteen-year period being analyzed, with the largest *chaebol* experiencing the greatest increase in diversity. Table 4 gives figures for the four largest *chaebol*. With the exception of Samsung, in 1970, all *chaebol* were involved in either light or heavy manufacturing exclusively (Samsung was the only *chaebol* involved in both). By 1983, however, all but two of the large *chaebol* were in both light and heavy manufacturing.[12]

The *chaebol*'s diversity is crucial to their position within the Korean economy, since their influence is derived from their ability to be more or less self-sufficient through ownership of a wide variety of firms, among them the often lucrative retail- and service-oriented businesses. Their flexibility in mobilizing and utiliz-

Table 4:   Share of Assets in Business in the Four Largest Chaebol (%), 1970–1983

Rank*	Chaebol	Year	Light Manufac- turing	Heavy Manufac- turing	Construc- tion	Finances	Trade	Other Services
1.	Hyundai	1970	0	85	15	0	0	0
		1975	0	86	12	2	0	0
		1980	1	51	37	3	6	2
		1983	3	52	34	1	2	8
2.	Samsung	1970	66	8	0	22	1	3
		1975	51	13	0	18	14	4
		1980	29	28	7	21	10	5
		1983	17	33	5	32	8	5
3.	Daewoo	1970	21	0	79	0	0	0
		1975	1	39	43	11	2	4
		1980	2	38	51	7	1	1
		1983	1	46	35	14	1	3
4.	Lucky/ Goldstar	1970	0	84	0	0	16	0
		1975	0	93	2	2	3	0
		1980	1	85	3	5	5	1
		1983	1	76	5	12	5	1

* Ranking based on total assets in 1983.

ing personnel, capital, and technology within their member firms greatly enhances their power.

For example, investment in the financial services is an effort by the *chaebol* to become less reliant on the state-owned banks for immediate cash flow. By 1983, the four largest *chaebol* had some investments in this sector. Hyundai is an exception with only one percent of its assets in this sector, but others have over ten percent, with Samsung leading with nearly one-third of its assets in financial services.

The debt/equity ratio is another indicator of *chaebol* health and vitality, as well as of its financial stability. Table 5 presents the debt/equity ratios of *chaebol* over time. Between 1970 and 1980, the four largest *chaebol* had the lowest ratios, which indicates that their financial structures were healthier and that these *chaebol* were thus better able to withstand hard times.

Table 5:   Debt/Equity Ratio of the Ten Largest Chaebol, 1970–1983

Rank*	Chaebol	1970	1975	1980	1983
1.	Hyundai	2.9	6.1	3.7	3.0
2.	Samsung	3.2	2.5	7.4	8.0
3.	Daewoo	7.0	4.9	3.7	6.1
4.	Lucky/Goldstar	1.6	3.9	5.5	4.7
5.	Ssangyong	2.4	2.8	7.2	5.5
6.	Sun Kyong	—	6.1	11.5	5.4
7.	Han Jin	3.8	17.5	10.5	5.1
8.	Korea Explosives	3.2	7.1	7.7	3.2
9.	Dae Lim	1.8	1.6	2.2	3.2
10.	Kukje	4.7	3.7	5.5	9.5

* Ranking based on total assets in 1983.

During the severe recession of 1980, debt/equity ratios increased dramatically for Korean manufacturing firms as a whole. Similarly, the debt/equity ratios of the smaller *chaebol* (Ssangyong, Sun Kyong, and Korea Explosives) showed a sudden rise. The declining world economy in 1979 and the social and political unrest in Korea resulting from the assassination of President Park in that same year contributed significantly to that country's unstable economic conditions.

While the other large *chaebol* were in relatively good positions to deal with this crisis, Samsung's debt/equity ratio had been rising since 1980, possibly due to its rapid expansion in the heavy industries since 1975. Among the ten largest *chaebol*, Samsung experienced one of the fastest rates of accumulation of assets in heavy manufacturing between 1976 and 1980 (Table 2). This sudden, large investment, which was poorly timed (occurring right before the great recession of 1980), appears to have contributed to Samsung's high debt/equity ratio. This investment resulted in shifting Samsung's industrial orientation quite drastically. Samsung, which had only eight percent of its total assets in heavy manufacturing in 1970, suddenly found itself with 28 percent of its assets in this area in 1980. This was accompanied by a drastic reduction in the light manufacturing sector, which had been a very lucrative business for Samsung: in 1980, assets in the area were less than one-third, down from two-thirds of its total assets in 1970. Hyundai, which was already largely invested in the heavy manufacturing sector, slightly decreased its growth in this area in the latter half of the 1970s. This continued investment without major re-shuffling may explain its relatively low debt/equity ratio in 1980. The smaller *chaebol* were not large enough to successfully manage the economic crisis, and as a result they had high debt/equity ratios in 1980.

By 1983, nearly all of the ten *chaebol* in this study seemed to have overcome the crisis and brought their debt/equity ratios to pre-crisis levels or even lower (as in the case of Han Jin). Kukje's ratio, however, was still very high. This high debt finally resulted in Kukje's bankruptcy in February of 1985.

To sum up this section, it was in the 1970s that the *chaebol* experienced their most rapid growth, with the careful guidance of the Korean state at the beginning of the decade. Those that shifted or continued their investment in heavy manufacturing grew most rapidly in contrast to other *chaebol*. Hyundai and Daewoo were becoming more important not only in the domestic economy, but also in the international economy.

The largest *chaebol* were also increasing in diversity. This greatly strengthened their power in the economy, since their sheer size made it harder for the state to ignore them when making important economic policy decisions.

The 1970s were thus a crucial period for the growth of the *chaebol*, with regard both to their significance in the economy and to their bargaining power against the Korean state.

Conclusion

The emergence and growth of the *chaebol* are critical issues in the understanding of Korea's economic development, because it is not just the state, but the *chaebol* that made Korea's miraculous development possible in such a short time. This paper is an effort to understand the *chaebol* as an industrial organization in the process of rapid economic development, pursued by a strong and autonomous state.

DiMaggio and Powell's (1983) theory of isomorphism helps us explain some key features of the proliferation of the *chaebol* during Korea's economic development. The processes of coercive, mimetic, and normative isomorphism help us understand that the unique industrial organization of the *chaebol* is a result of both political and economic processes. The goal of the *chaebol* is to survive and maintain itself in the face of a constraining and constantly re-orienting state, and an expanding world economy.

Three major factors contributed to the emergence of the *chaebol* as the dominant form of industrial organization in the 1960s: (1) the relatively short history of entrepreneurship in Korea; (2) the Japanese colonial period, with its legacy of the *zaibatsu;* and (3) the Park Chung Hee regime's commitment to economic development. The uncertainties and risks involved in the rapid transition of the economy to industrialization and exports, suggested by the Park regime at the beginning of the 1960s, illustrated mimetic isomorphism at work. Instead of devising a new industrial organization, which would have multiplied the risks they would be taking, Korean enterprises adopted the *zaibatsu* type of organization and nourished the *chaebol*. The Park regime's decision to support large firms and to nationalize the banks also helps to explain the coercive isomorphism of this period.

The subsequent growth of the *chaebol* is tied directly to state intervention in the economy. The evidence suggests that the most rapidly growing *chaebol* were the ones that followed the state's decision to invest in heavy and chemical industries at the beginning of the 1970s.

However, DiMaggio and Powell's theory does not help us understand why the state and the Japanese *zaibatsu* came to play such dominant roles over the formation and development of the *chaebol*. Their study provides us with no explanations as to why certain organizations – i.e., the *zaibatsu* and the state – become empowered and are able to influence others, while other organizations are subject to such influence. Without an understanding of how certain organizations become influential, we cannot fully understand the process of isomorphic change in industrial organizations.

Here, the political economy perspective and development studies provide an explanation as to why the *zaibatsu* during the Japanese colonial period, and the state in the 1960s and 1970s came to play such influential roles in the formation of the *chaebol*.

The strong and autonomous colonial government of Japan, and its policy of assimilation in the business sector enabled the Japanese *zaibatsu* to be the dominant businesses in Korea and left lasting impacts on future Korean businesses. This historical explanation helps us understand why the Korean *chaebol* share some similarities with the pre-World War II *zaibatsu*.

The Park regime was able to pursue economic development plans forcefully in the 1960s, because it had no ties to the business groups or to the landed class, and had access to foreign military and economic aid and loans. In its pursuit of rapid economic growth, the state recognized the advantages of working with the existing businesses, and the *chaebol* also realized that they really did not have any other choice than to cooperate with the state in order to survive. The *chaebol* learned how to cope with the strong, intervening state, and tried to minimize the risks associated with the drastic and frequently shifting of economic policies. As a result, the *chaebol* have invested very broadly over all industrial sectors and service industries, and developed a flexible management style in utilizing capital and personnel among their firms.

There are three important conclusions of this study. First, the process of capitalist economic development in late developing countries can best be understood with a comprehensive analysis of the state and the industrial organizations. Although activities of the businesses in such late-comers are severely circumscribed by strong state intervention, these businesses are ultimately private, making their own decisions and taking their own risks. They need to be treated as critical actors in the developmental drama, and not as mere puppets of the state.

Second, the industrial organizations in the Third World in the latter part of the twentieth century cannot be understood with only conventional organizational theories. Historical and political economic analyses can provide crucial insights into which organization will become resourceful and powerful to be able to influence others through isomorphic change. Such analyses allow us to predict which organizations are likely to become dominant, and be the origin of isomorphic change.

Third, the tremendous internationalization of business activity since the 1960s needs to be better incorporated in the study of industrial organizations in the Third World. The industrial organizations of the First World can influence their counterparts in the Third World through routine contacts of trade, direct investment, and technology transfers. Such routine encounters with foreign industrial organizations are happening with greater frequency and intensity than ever before. Whether these influential organizations in other nations can exert the same degree and nature of pressures for isomorphic change as those within the nation is an important issue that needs to be examined further. If the process of isomorphic change can be found across national boundaries, it will be a significant finding that will affect future studies of industrial organizations.

Notes

[1] I would like to thank Gary Hamilton, William Zeile, Hagen Koo, Jon Miller, and Herman Turk for their valuable suggestions and comments on earlier versions of this paper. However, I am fully responsible for this paper.

[2] This paper deals exclusively with South Korea; I will use the terms *Korea* and *South Korea* interchangeably.

[3] By 1983, eight of the ten largest *chaebol* had businesses in light manufacturing, heavy manufacturing, and services. Even the Hyundai *chaebol*, on the one hand, known for its investment in heavy industries, had begun to invest in light industries by 1980. On the other hand, the Samsung *chaebol*, famous for its nondurable and durable consumer products, had also shifted its investment emphasis from light manufacturing in 1970 (66 percent of total assets) to gradually increase heavy manufacturing. By 1983, Samsung's assets in heavy industries (33 percent of total assets) exceeded those in light industries (17 percent of total assets) for the first time in its history.

[4] In 1973, the twenty largest *chaebol* contributed one-fifth of Korea's Gross Domestic Product (GDP) in manufacturing; by 1978, they were contributing roughly one-third. The figures for the five largest *chaebol* are even more impressive: they were responsible for 8.8 percent of the GDP in manufacturing in 1973, and for 18.4 percent by 1978. These figures show the magnitude of these *chaebol* and demonstrate the fact that the increasing capital concentration over time was due mainly to the growth of the largest *chaebol* (E.M. Kim 1987; Koo 1984).

[5] The information was compiled from the *Korean Company Handbook* (Korea Productivity Center 1973-82) and from *Maekyung: Annual Corporation Reports* (Maeil Kyungje Shinmun 1984, 1986).

[6] The classification of light versus heavy manufacturing is based on the Industrial Classification Index of the Korean Census Bureau. Light manufacturing includes the following three product categories: food, beverages, and tobacco; textiles, wearing apparel, and leather; and wood and wood products, including furniture. Heavy manufacturing firms include those producing chemicals, petroleum, coal, rubber, and plastic products; nonmetallic products, except products of petroleum and coal; basic metal; and fabricated metal products, machinery, and equipment. This differentiation is quite close to the distinction made between traditional and modern industries. It is important to note that electronics and electrical appliances are included in heavy rather than light manufacturing.

[7] The average annual growth rates of the *chaebol* are calculated using 1980 constant prices.

[8] The GNP of Korea grew at an average annual rate of 11.26 percent from 1971 to 1983, based on 1980 constant prices (Economic Planning Board 1989). The GNP per capita between 1965 and and 1986 grew at an average annual rate of 6.7 percent, which was the second fastest in the world (World Bank 1988).

[9] The relatively large assets in the heavy manufacturing sector are partially due to the capital-intensive nature of this sector in comparison to the light manufacturing sector. The sales figures would be a better indicator of the growth of the heavy versus the light manufacturing sectors. However, as sales figures were incomplete, I used the second-best measure, the assets.

[10] There have been many rumors and speculation about the "real" cause of Kukje's bankruptcy. Some argue that it was Kukje president Yang Jeong Mo's unwillingness to cooperate with the Chun Doo Hwan regime that was the real cause of its forced bankruptcy by the state. There are, however, two important issues. The first is that Kukje's investment decisions since the mid-1970s represented rapid expansion efforts, resulting in high debt. The second is that all *chaebol* in Korea have relatively high debt/equity ratios compared to businesses in other nations. Since the banks were owned by the state until the recent partial privatization in 1981, the *chaebol* were at the mercy of the state. The state had the resources and capability to prevent a bankruptcy if it deemed this necessary. However, the important issue is that the state remained passive and "allowed" Kukje to go bankrupt. Therefore, although Kukje's financial problems may not have been caused by the state as some argue, it is plausible to argue that the bankruptcy could have been prevented by active efforts of the state, but that the state chose not to exert such efforts.

[11] Recent sales figures show Samsung as the largest *chaebol*. In 1987, its sales were $22,484 million; and sales for Hyundai, the largest *chaebol* in terms of assets, were $19,045 million (Management Efficiency Research Institute 1988).

[12] The Han Jin *chaebol* operates exclusively in passenger transportation, including Korean Airlines, while Dae Lim is involved exclusively in construction.

References

Amsden, Alice.1989. *Asia's Next Giant*. Oxford: University of Oxford Press.

Cardoso, Fernando H. and Enzo Faletto. 1979. *Dependency and Development in Latin America*. Berkeley: University of California Press.

Cumings, Bruce. 1987. "The Origins and Development of the Northeast Asian Political Economy: Industrial Sectors, Product Cycles, and Political Consequences." *The Political Economy of the New Asian Industrialism,* ed. Frederic C. Deyo. Ithaca: Cornell University Press.

Deyo, Frederic C., ed. 1987. *The Political Economy of the New Asian Industrialism*. Ithaca: Cornell University Press.

DiMaggio, Paul and Walter Powell. 1983. "The Iron Cage Revisited: Institutional Isomorphism and Collective Rationality in Organizational Fields." *American Sociological Review* 48 (April): 147-160.

Economic Planning Board. 1989. *Major Statistics of Korean Economy*. Seoul: Economic Planning Board.

Evans, Peter B. 1979. *Dependent Development: The Alliance of Multinational, State, and Local Capital in Brazil*. Princeton: Princeton University Press.

Evans, Peter B. 1987. "Class, State, and Dependence in East Asia: Lessons for Latin Americanists." *The Political Economy of the New Asian Industrialism,* ed. Frederic C. Deyo. Ithaca: Cornell University Press.

Gerschenkron, Alexander. 1962. *Economic Backwardness in Historical Perspective*. Cambridge, MA: Harvard University Press.

Hamilton, Gary G. and Nicole Woolsey Biggart. 1988. "Market, Culture, and Authority: A Comparative Analysis of Management and Organization in the Far East." *American Journal of Sociology* 94 (Supplement): 52-94.

Jones, Leroy P. and Il Sakong. 1980. *Government, Business, and Entrepreneurship in Economic Development: The Korean Case*. Cambridge, MA: Harvard University Press.

Kiggundu, Moses N., Jan J. Jorgensen, and Taieb Hafsi. 1983. "Administrative Theory and Practice in Developing Countries: A Synthesis." *Administrative Science Quarterly* 28: 66-84.

Kim, Eun Mee. 1987. "From Dominance to Symbiosis: State and *Chaebol* in the Korean Economy, 1960-1985." Ph. D. Dissertation. Providence: Brown University.

Kim, Eun Mee. 1988. "From Dominance to Symbiosis: State and *Chaebol* in Korea." *Pacific Focus* 3 (2): 105-121.

Kim, Eun Mee. 1989. "Foreign Capital in Korea's Economic Development: 1960-1985." *Studies in Comparative International Development* 24 (4): 24-45.

Koo, Bohn-Young. 1984. "The Role of the Government in Korea's Industrial Development." *KDI Working Paper* 8407.

Korea Productivity Center. 1973-82. *Korean Company Handbook*. Seoul: Korea Productivity Center.

Lee, Gyoo-Eog and Seong-Soon Lee. 1985. *Gieop Gyeolhabgwa Gyeongjeryeog Jipjoong* [Corporate Mergers and Concentration of Economic Power]. Seoul: Korea Development Institute.

Lim, Myo Min. 1983. "Jeongyeongryeon eui Naemag – *Chaebol* eui Amtu" [The Inside Stories of the Federation of Korean Industries – Struggle between *Chaebol*]. *Shindonga* (3).

Maeil Kyungje Shinmun. 1984. *Maekyung: Annual Corporation Reports.* Seoul: Maeil Kyungje Shinmun.

Maeil Kyungje Shinmun. 1986. *Maekyung: Annual Corporation Reports.* Seoul: Maeil Kyungje Shinmun.

Management Efficiency Research Institute. 1988. *Analysis of Financial Statements – Fifty Major Business Groups in Korea.* Seoul: Management Efficiency Research Institute.

Mason, Edward S., et al. 1980. *The Economic and Social Modernization of the Republic of Korea.* Cambridge, MA: Harvard University Press.

Park, Yeong Cheol, et al. 1986. *Geumyoong Saneop Baljeone Gwanhan Yeongoo 1985-2000* [Research on the Development of the Financial Industry 1985-2000]. Seoul: Korea Development Institute.

Shin, Eui Hang and Seung Kwon Chin. 1989. "Social Affinity Among Top Managerial Executives of Large Corporations in Korea." *Sociological Forum* 4 (l): 3-26.

World Bank. 1988. *World Development Report.* New York: Oxford University Press.

Industrial Policy and Organizational Efficiency: The Korean *Chaebol* Examined

William Zeile

Introduction

A number of recent studies in industrial organization have been concerned with explaining the institutional phenomenon of business groups. In many countries, a large share of industrial activity is organized through networks of legally-independent firms, affiliated with one another under a common group name. The group form of organization is particularly salient in the Republic of Korea, where "financial cliques," or *chaebol*, reach into all sectors of the economy.[1] Character-ized by the central control of member-firms through mutual shareholding or direct family ownership, the *chaebol* have grown rapidly in the last three decades, both in size and in number. Today they occupy a dominant position in the Korean econ-omy and are beginning to make their presence known in world markets.

In his chapter in the recently-issued *Handbook of Industrial Organization*, Richard Caves writes that the widespread presence of business groups calls into question an assumption that has been standard in economic theory, namely "that a clean boundary separates the purely administrative allocations made within the firm from purely market transactions that the firm undertakes with other agents" (Caves 1989, p. 1228). A number of theories, mostly based on transactions costs and missing markets, have recently been advanced to explain the existence of this seemingly deviant institution. Encaoua and Jacquemin (1982) argue that the en-terprise groups observed in Europe are basically organized along the same lines as the multidivisional corporation in the United States, with the independent compa-nies of the European group corresponding to the divisions of the M-form corpo-ration. Their presence is thus essentially explained by the arguments Williamson (1975) and Chandler (1977) have advanced for the superiority of the multidivi-sional corporate structure over earlier functional structures. Goto (1982), on the other hand, views business groups as a distinct institution for resource allocation situated between the firm and the market, arguing that they possess the advantages of reducing transactions costs which arise in the market, while avoiding the scale diseconomies or loss of control which can result from expanding firm size (even with a multidivisional organizational structure). Both interpretations emphasize the advantages of combining a decentralization of decision-making at the operating level with the centralized allocation of capital between operating units.

The presence of business groups in a number of developing countries has been noted by Leff (1978), who argues that they are an efficient organizational response to conditions of market failure. Specifically, the group form of organization makes it possible to overcome deficiencies in the markets for primary factors (such as capital, information, managerial honesty, and competence), intermediate products, and risk. The failure of markets for intermediate products (resulting from the transactions costs associated with a small number of buyers and sellers) explains the vertical integration of groups, while the absence of markets for risk and uncertainty explains group diversification into unrelated product lines. In developing countries, the group form of organization also has the important advantage of facilitating economies in the use of scarce entrepreneurial resources. In fact, Leff argues, by substituting for missing markets, "the group constitutes a pattern of industrial organization which permits structure rather than gifted individuals to perform the key interactivity function of entrepreneurship" (Leff 1978, p. 668).

Amsden (1989), in a similar vein, views the business group as an institution characteristic of late-industrializing countries. The reasons for the existence of this organizational form, however, are traced not to conditions of market failure, but to the very exigencies of late industrialization:

The diversified business group is a variant of the modern industrial enterprise that is found in every industrialized country and that is multidivisional, comprised of large-scale production units, and managed hierarchically. Yet the diversified business group in late-industrializing countries is unique in that it is more diversified in unrelated products than the modern industrial enterprise on the one hand, and more centrally coordinated than the conglomerate on the other (in terms of intra-group flows of both human and financial capital). Its broad diversification and central coordination are explained as functions of lateness (Amsden 1989, p. 151).

Amsden argues that learning (as opposed to invention or innovation) is central to the process of late industrialization. Insofar as business groups in late-industrializing countries lack the technical or marketing expertise of advanced industrial enterprises, they cannot grow by developing new related product lines or by moving into higher quality niches in their existing markets; thus, to diffuse risk or utilize slack resources, they diversify widely, producing at the bottom end and middle level of many unrelated markets. The high degree of central coordination observed for business groups (involving the transfer of personnel and resources between member firms engaged in different activities) is also explained by their status as learners: problems encountered in the process of learning in a newly-entered industry can be quickly overcome by temporarily mobilizing the managerial and engineering talent of more-established enterprises. Experience accumulated by the group's salaried managers in the areas of feasibility studies, task force formation, purchase of foreign technical assistance, training, equipment purchase, new plant design and construction, and operation start-up give the group a major advantage in entering industries characterized by large learning requirements. The organizational structure of the large diversified business group, exemplified by the Korean *chaebol*, is thus seen to be an important factor contributing to the rapid industrial transformation experienced in the Republic of Korea.

A complete discussion of the reasons for the prominence of business groups in the Korean economy, however, cannot ignore the important role of government. Jones and Sakong (1980) examine how the selective dispensation of government favors to well-connected businessmen during the Rhee regime of the 1950s permitted a number of *chaebol* to be created from a virtually nonexistent equity base. Such favors included the sale of former Japanese assets at bargain prices; the selective allocation of aid funds and materials, and of import quotas and licenses, in the context of rapid inflation and an overvalued currency; privileged access to cheap bank loans; and the non-competitive award of government and U.S. military contracts for reconstruction activities. Jones and Sakong further state that while the opportunities for "zero-sum" accumulation through government favoritism were much-reduced during the Park regime, the government continued to promote the expansion of the *chaebol* indirectly "through its single-minded devotion to growth and its credit policy" (Jones and Sakong 1980, p. 279). Koo (1984) points to the credit policies of the Park government as major factor contributing to the rise of the *chaebol*, contending that such policies have resulted in a worsening distribution of income. Lee, Urata, and Choi (1986) also take the position that government policies designed to promote rapid economic growth contributed to the expansion of the *chaebol*, maintaining that it "is not an overstatement to say that advantages of the protection and incentive policy involving tax, banking, and commercial policy measures, were almost exclusively enjoyed by the business groups" (Lee, Urata, and Choi 1986, p. 7).

In this paper, attention is focused on the respective roles of organizational efficiency and government credit-rationing policies in accounting for the dominance of Korean industries by business groups. To quantify the dimensions of business group activity in the Korean economy, this study draws heavily on a database of member firms of the top fifty *chaebol* in 1983, constructed from Korean language sources at the Institute of Governmental Affairs, University of California, Davis.[2] We begin, in the following section, with an examination of Korean business group diversification across industries. The third section describes the magnitude of business group concentration in Korea's economy, both at the aggregate level and at the level of individual industries. A formal test for organizational efficiency in the pattern of industry dominance by business groups is presented then, while the section "The *Chaebol* and Government Credit-Rationing Policies" investigates the relationship between Korean business group activity across industries and government credit-rationing policies in the 1970s.

Chaebol Diversification

The most conspicuous feature of Korea's business groups is the very pervasiveness of their activities across all sectors of industry. Korea's leading *chaebol* tend to be highly diversified, with operations ranging from shipbuilding to the manufacture of musical instruments, from petroleum refining to the processing of dairy products, and from building construction to air transport services. Table 1 summarizes the major industrial activities of the leading ten *chaebol* in 1983.[3] Altogether the top ten *chaebol* control over two hundred legally-independent firms. Within manufacturing, most of these groups include at least two or three large-scale enterprises (generally in the heavy industries) and a number of smaller firms with diverse product lines. For the leading ten *chaebol*, there is an average of eleven manufacturing firms per group, while the average for the top fifty *chaebol* is six manufacturing firms per group. As for non-manufacturing activities, virtually all of the leading *chaebol* have member firms specializing in construction or commerce, and many have firms specializing in transport services or insurance. Among the top fifty *chaebol* in 1983, there were thirty groups active in the construction industry, and thirty-one groups with firms specializing in commerce and trade. In addition, there were twenty-four *chaebol* active in finance and insurance, twenty-one groups with activities in transport and storage, and seventeen groups with firms specializing in business services.

Each manufacturing firm listed in our *chaebol* database for 1983 has been classified according to its major manufacturing activity at the four-digit level of the Korean Standard Industrial Classification (revised, 1984).[4] On the basis of this classification, measures of manufacturing diversification have been calculated for each business group. These measures are reported in Table 2, which also presents a simple count of *chaebol* manufacturing activities. Given the assumption that each manufacturing firm completely specializes in its major manufacturing activity, the measures indicate the degree of diversification between the activities of the different member firms of a *chaebol*, but not the diversification (if any) within individual member firms.

Four different indices (defined in Table 2) have been employed to measure diversification. Each index takes on a numerical value between zero and one, with higher values indicating greater diversification. The first two measures, H* and S*, are based on manufacturing industry sales. The index H* is Berry's (1971) complement to the Herfindahl index applied to the distribution of a group's manufacturing activities. It reflects both the number of industries in which a *chaebol* is active and the degree of equality between the sales shares of the different activities. The index S* is the complement to the group's specialization ratio, indicating the degree to which a *chaebol* is active in industries distinct from its major manufacturing activity. Whereas H* captures the entire distribution of a group's manufacturing activities, S* focuses exclusively on the upper tail of this distribution.

Table 1: Major Activities of Top 10 *Chaebol*, Ranked by Sales, 1983

Sales Rank	Name	Number of Member Firms			Major Manufacturing Activities	Major Non-Manufacturing Activities
		Total	Manu-facturing	Non-manu-facturing		
1.	Hyundai	32	18	14	Shipbuilding and repair, motor vehicles, steel, machinery	Construction, commerce and trade, transport and storage, insurance
2.	Samsung	29	14	15	Electronics, sugar refining, textile weaving, shipbuilding and repair	Commerce and trade, insurance, construction, broadcasting
3.	Lucky/Goldstar	24	15	9	Petroleum refining, electronics, chemicals, non-ferrous metals	Commerce and trade, construction finance, insurance
4.	Sunkyung	14	7	7	Petroleum refining, textile fibers, office equipment	Commerce and trade, construction, transport and storage
5.	Daewoo	24	15	9	Shipbuilding and repair, motor vehicles, industrial machinery, electrical appliances	Commerce and trade, finance, transport and storage
6.	Ssangyong	14	7	7	Petroleum refining, cement, paper	Commerce and Trade, construction, transport and storage, insurance
7.	Kukje	18	8	10	Steel, agricultural machinery, chemicals, paper	Commerce and trade, construction, insurance, transport and storage
8.	Hanguk Hwayak	18	9	9	Petroleum refining, chemicals, dairy products	Commerce and trade, construction, insurance
9.	Hanjin	12	1	11	Cement	Transport and storage, construction, finance, insurance
10.	Hyosung	20	16	4	Textile fibers, rubber tires and tubes, electrical machinery, leather	Commerce and trade, construction

Table 2:   Indices of Manufacturing Diversification for Korean *Chaebol*, 1983 (4-digit level of Korean Standard Industrial Classification)

Rank Name	Number of Manufacturing Activities	H*	S*	S_w*	V*
1. Hyundai	13	0.772	0.601	0.541	0.405
2. Samsung	9	0.757	0.582	0.466	0.378
3. Lucky/Goldstar	10	0.644	0.457	0.446	0.284
4. Sunkyung	6	0.161	0.086	0.701	0.701
5. Daewoo	12	0.817	0.710	0.639	0.633
6. Ssangyong	7	0.567	0.467	0.523	0.523
7. Kukje	7	0.619	0.416	0.733	0.591
8. Hanguk Huayak	7	0.654	0.541	0.780	0.370
9 Hanjin	1	0	0	0	0
10. Hyosung	14	0.817	0.670	0.770	0.662
Average for Top 10 *Chaebol*	8.6	0.581	0.453	0.560	0.455
(Standard Deviation in Parentheses)	(3.86)	(0.280)	(0.236)	(0.232)	(0.213)
Average for Top 20 *Chaebol*	6.6	0.472	0.351	0.437	0.321
(Standard Deviation in Parentheses)	(3.81)	(0.283)	(0.244)	(0.271)	(0.238)
Average for Top 50 *Chaebol*	4.7	0.384	0.277	0.320	0.243
(Standard Deviation in Parentheses)	(3.16)	(0.254)	(0.216)	(0.251)	(0.220)

Diversification indices defined:

$$H^* = 1 - \frac{h - ai^2}{i = 1}$$

where $a_i = \dfrac{\text{Sales by Group in Manufacturing Sector i}}{\text{Total Manufacturing Sales by Group}}$

$$S^* = 1 - S$$

where $S = \dfrac{\text{Sales in Group's Leading Manufacturing Sector}}{\text{Total Manufacturing Sales by Group}}$

$$S_w^* = 1 - S_w$$

where $S_w = \dfrac{\text{Number of Employees in Group's Leading Manufacturing Sector}}{\text{Total Number of Employees in Group's Manufacturing Activities}}$

$$V^* = 1 - V$$

where $V = \dfrac{\text{Number of Group Employees in all Sectors Vertically Related to Group's Major Manufacturing Sector}}{\text{Total Number of Manufacturing Employees in Group}}$

Our third measure of diversification, S_w*, is the complement to the group's specialization ratio based on manufacturing industry employment. To the extent that a group's manufacturing activities differ in factor intensity, this measure may present a distorted picture of group diversification, since it gives undue weight to industries which are labor-intensive. The measure based on sales data ($S*$) may also be somewhat biased, however, since manufacturing activities downstream in the production process are given more weight than the group's contribution to value added warrants. Thus both measures are presented for comparison.

Finally, a measure of diversification has been constructed which lumps together industries which are vertically integrated or otherwise very closely related. The index $V*$ is defined as one minus the ratio V, where V is the total number of workers employed by a *chaebol* in all manufacturing sectors vertically (or very closely) related to its major manufacturing activity divided by the group's total manufacturing employment. Employment rather than sales figures are used in this measure so as to avoid double-counting. Following the approach used by Gort (1962), I have identified the activities vertically related to the group's major activity on the basis of qualitative information. The index $V*$ indicates the degree to which a *chaebol* diversifies into manufacturing lines completely unrelated to its primary manufacturing activity. It thus serves as a lower bound for our measures of group diversification in manufacturing.

Taken together, the measures show a considerable amount of diversification in manufacturing activities for most of Korea's top fifty *chaebol*. Examining the figures reported in Table 2, we see that the average *chaebol* has firms operating in five different manufacturing industries, with secondary activities accounting for 28 percent of its total manufacturing sales and 32 percent of its total manufacturing workforce. Even when we consider vertical linkages between manufacturing activities, a full quarter of the average chaebol's manufacturing workforce is employed in industries altogether unrelated to its primary manufacturing activity.

As one might expect, manufacturing diversification tends to increase with business group size. For the top ten *chaebol*, the average diversification indices are one and a half to two times as large as the averages for the top fifty *chaebol*. Four of the most diversified groups, however, do not rank among the top twenty-five *chaebol* in terms of sales. The coefficient of correlation between $H*$ and *chaebol* manufacturing sales is 0.367, while that between $S*$ and manufacturing sales is 0.355.

Examining diversification measures for individual *chaebol*, there are five groups out of the top fifty for which the value of $H*$ exceeds 0.75: Daewoo, Hyosung, Lotte, Hyundai, and Samsung. For nine groups (including the five just listed), $H*$ and $S*$ assume values greater than 0.65 and 0.50, respectively. The index S_w* takes on a value greater than 0.50 for twelve groups, while the value of $V*$ exceeds 0.50 for eight groups.[5]

At the four-digit level of industry classification, only ten chaebol have activities in fewer than two manufacturing sectors. A number of *chaebol*, however, have manufacturing firms operating almost exclusively in industries which are vertical-ly (or otherwise very closely) related. For example, Kolon, whose major manufac-turing activity is textile fiber spinning, also has firms producing made-up textile goods and ready-to-wear apparel, and a firm engaged in the bleaching, dyeing, finishing of textiles. Similarly, Doosan, whose major firm is a brewery, has mem-ber firms involved in the manufacture of glass bottles, metal cans, non-alcoholic beverages, and machinery used in the beverage industries. Vertical integration of this kind is reflected in a low value for the index V^*. Altogether there are twenty-four groups (out of the forty-nine active in manufacturing) for which the value of V^* is less than 0.20. Only six of these groups, however, rank among the top twenty *chaebol* in terms of total sales. Amsden's statement that business groups in late-industrializing countries diversify widely into unrelated product lines thus appears to hold true for Korea's top twenty *chaebol*, but cannot be accepted as a blanket characterization of all Korean business groups.

Business Group Concentration in the Korean Economy

The overall importance of business groups in South Korea's economy is indicat-ed in Table 3, which presents measures of aggregate concentration for the top fifty *chaebol*.[6] The table shows a general increase in the *chaebol* share of economic ac-tivity in the 1970s and early 1980s, with a concurrent rise in the number of group-member firms. As of the mid-1980s, the top fifty *chaebol* accounted for nearly a fifth of South Korea's gross domestic product. Within mining and manufacturing, the *chaebol* share of employment was 22 percent and the share of sales some 45 percent. Aggregate concentration appears to have leveled off since 1983, perhaps reflecting recent changes in government credit and tax policies.[7]

Comparative figures for aggregate concentration in the United States are avail-able for manufacturing. In 1976 the largest fifty U.S. manufacturing firms ac-counted for 24 percent of total U.S. manufacturing value added, while the share for the largest one hundred firms was 34 percent. The manufacturing employment share for the largest fifty firms was 18 percent, and that for the largest one hundred firms 24 percent.[8] For Korea's top fifty *chaebol*, the 1986 shares in manufacturing value added and employment were 28.3 percent and 22.9 percent, respectively. Thus, the degree of aggregate concentration in manufacturing for Korea's busi-ness groups falls somewhere between that of the largest fifty and the largest one hundred manufacturing firms in the United States. In making this comparison, one should keep in mind that the top fifty *chaebol* do not include among their member firms all of South Korea's largest fifty manufacturers. Some of the largest manu-facturing firms in South Korea are government or quasi-government enterprises, unaffiliated with the privately-owned *chaebol*.[9]

Table 3: Aggregate Concentration Figures for Top Fifty Chaebol (Shares in Percent)

	1975*	1980**	1983***	1986***
Number of Member Firms	398	—	552	547
Value Added Share of GDP	13.4	15.6	19.1	18.8
Value Added Share of Non-Agricultural GDP	18.6	18.2	22.1	21.4
Employment Share in Mining and Manufacturing	—	28.5	22.5	22.1
Sales Share in Mining and Manufacturing	—	40.6	45.3	44.3

* Figures for 1975 are for the top 46 chaebol, and are taken from Jones and Sakong (1980). The authors estimate the value added figures indirectly, using company data on profits and sales together with the coefficients from Korea's input-output tables.
** The 1980 figures for employment and sales shares in Mining and Manufacturing are taken from Chong-Hwan Chu (1985). Value added shares for 1980 were calculated from data in *Korea's Fifty Major Groups for 1983 and 1984* (MERI, 1985) and *Economic Statistics Yearbook,* 1986 (Bank of Korea, 1986).
*** Figures for 1983 and 1986 calculated from data in *Korea's Fifty Major Groups for 1983 and 1984* (MERI, 1985), Financial Analysis of *Korea's 50 Major Groups for 1986* (MERI, 1987), Firm Directory of Korea for 1985 (*Daily Economic News,* 1986), *Firm Directory of Korea for 1986* (Korea Productivity Center, 1987), *Report on Industrial Census,* 1983 (Economic Planning Board, 1985), and *Economic Statistics Yearbook,* 1987 (Bank of Korea, 1987).

Korea's *chaebol* also figure prominently in a number of non-manufacturing sectors. In 1986, the top fifty *chaebol* accounted for 32 percent of the country's total value added in construction, 20 percent of value added in transport and storage, and 17 percent of value added in commerce and trade. In foreign trade, almost half of South Korea's exports are handled by seven general trading companies, all of which are member firms of the top ten *chaebol*.[10] Since the early 1980s, when the Korean government began to privatize the major national banks, the *chaebol* have come to assume an increasingly dominant role in finance. Although government regulations restrict single shareholders to 8 percent of total ownership, the top ten *chaebol* are reported to now collectively control from 22 percent to 57 percent of the ownership of South Korea's five nationwide commercial banks.[11] Since there are no limitations on the ownership of Korea's local banks, each is practically owned by single *chaebol*. As for non-bank financial institutions, Chong-hwan Chu (1985) reports that the leading *chaebol* in 1984 controlled ten of Korea's twenty-five securities companies, five of its six life insurance companies, and eight of its thirteen casualty insurance companies (Chung-hwan Chu 1985, p. 24).

Table 4 gives some indication of the variation in business group dominance across manufacturing sectors. At this level of aggregation, there are five industries (out of the twenty total) where the top fifty *chaebol* account for more than 50 percent of total industry sales, and another eight industries where the *chaebol* sales share exceeds 25 percent. For some of these industries, the large *chaebol* sales share corresponds to a large number of groups active in the industry.

At the level of individual manufacturing industries, the pattern of *chaebol* concentration appears to be oligopolistic, with groups competing against each other in similar markets. Examining the manufacturing activities of group-member firms at the four-digit level of the Korean Standard Industrial Classification, we find that, for the 78 manufacturing industries in which *chaebol* are active, there are an average of 3 groups and 3.8 group-member firms operating in each industry. For each of these industries, I have calculated the ratio of sales by the top fifty *chaebol* to total industry shipments for the year 1983.[12] Among the 17 industries where the total *chaebol* sales share exceeds 50 percent, there are an average of 5.4 *chaebol* and 7.1 *chaebol*-member firms per industry; in only 4 of these industries are there fewer than 3 groups active.

The 1983 *chaebol* industry sales share was also calculated for the 72 manufacturing sectors employed in the statistical analysis reported in the next section. At this level of aggregation, the relationship between group concentration and standard measures of market concentration was investigated. Published measures of the Herfindahl index of concentration are available for 1981 at the five-digit level of the Korean Standard Industrial Classification.[13] These measures were aggregated to the level of the 72 manufacturing sectors, using industry sales as weights. For these 72 industries, the coefficient of correlation between the sales share of the top fifty *chaebol* and the weighted-average Herfindahl concentration index is only 0.051. In contrast, the correlation between the total *chaebol* sales share and the number of *chaebol*-member firms in the sector is 0.678. Thus, *chaebol* dominance of Korean industries is not associated with higher market concentration, but is related to the number of group-member firms competing with each other. In general, individual *chaebol*-member firms do not enjoy the status of exclusive monopolists in the industries in which they operate; rather, they compete with other firms in oligopolistic fashion.

This conclusion is supported also by commodity market data at a much more disaggregated level. In 1982, there were 2,260 commodity markets in Korea, 533 of which were monopolistic (the leading firm accounting for more than 80 percent of market sales), 251 of which were duopolistic (the sales share of the leading two firms together exceeding 80 percent), and another 1,071 of which were oligopolistic (the sales share of the leading three firms exceeding 60 percent).[14] Lee Kyu-uck (1986) presents data on the 1982 market shares of the top thirty *chaebol* for the 1,125 commodity markets in which they participate. According to his

Table 4:   Chaebol Activity by Broad Manufacturing Sector (Shares in percent)

	Sales Share of Top 50 Chaebol*	Number of Chaebol Active in Sector	Number of Chaebol Member Firms	Total Number of Korean Establishments
Food Products	33.7	15	25	3,424
Beverage & Tobacco	27.6	6	9	1,041
Textiles	38.4	15	29	5,598
Garments & Apparel	12.6	7	10	3,468
Leather Products	15.2	3	6	1,194
Lumber & Wood Products	31.5	7	10	2,579
Pulp & Paper Products; Printing & Publishing	6.7	5	6	3,045
Chemical Materials	54.3	15	22	747
Chemical Products	24.0	8	12	683
Petroleum & Coal Products	91.9	8	8	312
Rubber Products	76.8	4	10	599
Plastic Products	0.1	1	1	1,507
Non-Metallic Mineral Products	44.6	17	20	2,809
Basic Metal	28.0	13	22	1,055
Metal Products	26.7	7	9	2,975
Machinery	34.9	21	26	2,532
Electrical & Electronic Products	50.9	19	34	2,292
Transportation Equipment	79.0	13	28	1,193
Precision Machinery	14.0	1	2	481
Miscellaneous Industrial Products	5.2	2	2	1,709

*   Calculated from 1983 sales data for each chaebol-member firm and 1983 industrial census data. [Firm Directory of Korea for 1985 (*Daily Economic News* 1986), *Korea's Fifty Major Groups for 1983 and 1984* (MERI 1985), and *Report on Industrial Census for* 1983 (EPB 1985).]

figures, a single *chaebol* commands a market share greater than 80 percent in only 78 of these markets, and a share greater than 60 percent in 136 markets. Examining rankings of market shares, however, there are 846 markets where a *chaebol*-member firm ranks third or higher, again suggesting inter-group competition of an oligopolistic nature.[15]

Test for Organizational Efficiency

Can the pattern of Korean industry dominance by business groups be explained on the basis of organizational efficiency? A statistical test of such an explanation is presented by Encaoua and Jacquemin (1982) in their study of French industrial groups. Encaoua and Jacquemin advance the hypothesis that the predominance of business groups in certain industries represents "an efficient organizational adaptation to given industry characteristics" (Encaoua and Jacquemin 1982, p. 32). Citing arguments by Chandler (1977), Spence (1975), and others, they identify such industry characteristics as scale economies, research and development activities, large capital requirements, and extensive international operations as favoring the internal coordination of resources within large, diversified organizations over external transactions through the market. On the basis of organizational efficiency, business groups should be active mainly in industries possessing some or all of these characteristics.

Encaoua and Jacquemin test this proposition against French industry data for 1974, regressing the industry employment share of French industrial groups against five explanatory variables: industry economies of scale, multiplant economies, research activity, capital requirements, and level of export. Their results for the French case support the hypothesis that the distribution of groups among industries responds to efficiency considerations.[16]

A similar test for efficiency in the pattern of relative industry dominance by groups can be constructed for the Korean case. For this purpose, we adopt the econometric model used by Encaoua and Jacquemin, with some minor modifications. The basic regression equation is:

$$CHAESS = a_0 + a_1 KR + a_2 RES + a_3 MLTP + a_4 ES + a_5 EXP + e$$
where
CHAESS = the share of industry sales by the top fifty *chaebol*;
KR = capital requirements, measured by the ratio of industry total fixed capital (i.e., the value of total tangible fixed assets minus land) to the number of establishments in the industry;
RES = research activity, measured by the ratio of research and development expenditures to total industry sales;

MLTP = multiplant economies, measured by the ratio of the number of plants in the industry to the number of firms in the industry;

ES = plant economies of scale, measured by the average plant size of plants of minimum efficient scale. Following the methodology used by Comanor and Wilson, this measure is taken to be the average employment size of the largest establishments accounting for 50 percent of total industry employment, divided by total employment in the industry;

EXP = level of export, measured by the ratio of industry exports to total industry output.

In accordance with the arguments presented by Encaoua and Jacquemin, the expected signs of the explanatory variables are all positive. Business groups are expected to predominate in industries characterized by large capital requirements because of the large transactions costs involved in obtaining finance: the internal capital markets of business groups make it possible to economize on these transactions costs, thus reducing the cost of capital. Furthermore, the existence of large fixed costs in capital-intensive industries is a source of market failure, favoring centralized management through large organizations. Extensive research and development requirements in an industry favor the group form of organization over market transactions between independent firms for two reasons: first, the interdependence of research and development with production and marketing favors the integration of these activities within a common organization; and, second, the public-goods nature of technological knowledge creates transactions costs in interfirm trading which can be avoided through internal transfers between the member firms of a group. The coordination of resources within business groups also makes possible the realization of scale economies, both at the level of the plant and in the multi-plant operations of firms. Finally, in industries where exports are important, the high degree of uncertainty and the high cost of information in marketing products internationally should favor internal coordination through organizations with extensive domestic and international operations.[17]

The regression sample consists of 1983 data for seventy-two manufacturing sectors selected to match the categories of the Korean Standard Industrial Classification (Revised, 1984) with the categories of the 1983 input-output tables.[18] Sales data for individual *chaebol*-member firms (classified by industrial sector) were taken from the *chaebol* database and totaled for each manufacturing sector; the total *chaebol* sales figures for each industry were then divided by the industry shipments data in the Report on Industrial Census, 1983 to determine the *chaebol* sales share, the dependent variable in the regression equation. Data used to calculate industry capital requirements (KR), research activity (RES), and economies of scale (ES) are from the Report on Industrial Census, 1983. The data for industry level of export (EXP) come from the 1983 Input-Output Tables, and the industry values for multiplant economies (MLTP) were calculated from data in the Report on Establishment Census, 1981.[19]

The regression results, reported in Table 5, provide weak to moderate support for the hypothesis of organizational efficiency based on industry characteristics. In the basic regression equation (Equation 1), the capital requirements and research activity variables are statistically significant (at the 1 percent and 5 percent levels, respectively), but industry exports is not; moreover, the estimated parameters for the economies of scale and multiplant economies variables display the wrong sign. The incremental contribution of industry exports and plant economies of scale to the model is negative, as can be seen (in Equation 2) by the increase in the adjusted R-square when these variables are deleted; the multiplant economies variable appears to contribute to the model's explanatory power, but in a manner opposite to that predicted by theory. Most of the variation in *chaebol* sales share explained by the model is accounted for by just one variable, industry capital requirements.[20]

Some further insight on the relation between the industry sales shares of business groups and the explanatory variables of the model can be obtained by dividing the sample into subsets. Table 6 shows the mean values and standard deviations for four subsets of industries defined by *chaebol* sales share. We see that, for all five explanatory variables, the mean values for the sample subset with a *chaebol* sales share greater than 50 percent exceed the mean values for the sample as a whole. This is marginally the case for four of the variables (ES, MLTP, RES, and EXP), but for capital requirements the mean for this subset is almost three times as large as that for the whole sample.

Note, however, the absence of a monotonic increase (with *chaebol* sales share) in sample subset mean values for any of the explanatory variables. Indeed, for two of the variables (ES and MLTP), the sample subset displaying the largest mean is that for which the *chaebol* share of sales is zero. This explains why the estimated parameters for these two variables are negative in sign. When the twelve observations in this subset are excluded from the sample, we get the regression results reported in Equation 4 of Table 6, where the signs for ES and MLTP are positive.[21] This finding suggests that the Korean *chaebol* are excluded (perhaps by government monopoly) form certain industries characterized by large scale economies. Examining the individual industries in this sample subset, we do indeed find some industries with large scale economies (tobacco, edible oils, fertilizers, and pesticides) where government enterprises are dominant. Thus, the relative degree of dominance of Korean industries by business groups appears to be consistent with expectations based on industry characteristics, if one controls for the presence of government enterprises.

The regression results definitely confirm one prediction of the organizational efficiency model: business groups tend to predominate in industries characterized by large capital requirements. It may be that reductions in transactions costs, made possible by the group form of organization, give the *chaebol* a major advantage in entering such industries. Amsden (1989), however, argues in reverse fashion that it was the involvement of Korean companies in capital-intensive in-

Table 5: Regression Equations Relating Chaebol Sales Share to Structural Variables
(t-Statistics in parentheses)

Eq.	Observations	Intercept	KR	RES	MLTP	ES	EXP	Adj.-R**	F
(1)	72	50.8969* (2.55)	0.0043* (4.93)	5.0672** (1.72)	−28.9989 (−1.68)	−0.3485 (−0.81)	0.0337 (0.26)	0.25	5.79
(2)	72	52.5616* (2.84)	0.0040* (5.12)	4.7590*** (1.65)	−30.8730 (−1.86)			0.27	9.54
(3)	72	22.9286* (7.47)	0.0031* (4.61)					0.22	21.27
(4)	60	−18.0257 (−0.53)	0.0018** (1.81)	3.5052 (1.24)	34.1379 (1.12)	1.0149*** (1.45)	0.1696*** (1.30)	0.33	6.73

 * Positive sign significant at 1% level.
 ** Positive sign significant at 5% level.
 *** Positive sign significant at 10% level.

Table 6: Mean Values and Standard Deviations (in parentheses) of Structural Variables in Subsets of Industries Defined by Sales Share of Top 50 Chaebol

Variables	CHAESS = 0	0 < CHAESS ≤ 20%	20% < CHAESS ≤ 50%	CHAESS _ 50%	Sample
CHAESS (%)	0	11.4	30.5	72.1	28.3
	(0)	(6.1)	(6.4)	(16.7)	(27.3)
ES (%)	11.0	1.5	5.1	7.3	5.4
	(12.1)	(1.3)	(5.2)	(8.9)	(7.6)
MLTP	1.24	1.07	1.10	1.19	1.14
	(0.40)	(0.06)	(0.08)	(0.21)	(0.20)
RES (%)	0.69	0.72	0.89	0.85	0.79
	(0.65)	(1.28)	(0.78)	(0.93)	(0.97)
KR (Million Won)	1461	324	1334	4640	1754
	(3043)	(246)	(2450)	(7836)	(4320)
EXP (%)	20.9	23.5	14.8	22.2	20.4
	(19.6)	(24.5)	(15.0)	(29.1)	(22.5)
Number of Industries	12	24	20	16	72

dustries which gave rise to diversified business groups. According to Amsden, capital-intensive industries are distinguished by extensive learning requirements, and require a large cadre of salaried managers and engineers. Through early involvement in such capital-intensive industries as sugar refining and cement production, Korea's leading *chaebol* developed a technological and managerial capacity which later enabled them to establish new firms in ever-more-complex industries. This contrasts with the experience of firms which started out in the light industries (such as Korea's major textile companies), which were never able to diversify and expand into large business groups. Applying this argument with an eye to our regression results, we might say that, in a late-industrializing country such as Korea, the learning requirements of new capital-intensive industries constitute a barrier to entry which Korea's business groups are well-equipped to overcome, by virtue of their previous involvement in capital-intensive industries. In adopting this interpretation, however, one should keep in mind the fact that many of Korea's major capital-intensive industries were actively promoted by a government which exercised firm control over the allocation of financial resources.

The *Chaebol* and Government Credit-Rationing Policies

The finding that the *chaebol* share of industry sales is significantly correlated with industry capital requirements suggests an alternative explanation of business group dominance based on favorable access to scarce credit. Throughout the period of the Park regime (1961-1979), the Korean government exercised substantial control over all formal sources of credit, both domestic and foreign. Government industrial policy dictated the credit decisions of Korea's major city banks, which had been nationalized in 1961 as part of the Park government's campaign against "illicit wealth accumulation" during the Rhee regime. The government also operated a number of special banks, and provided long-term loans for fixed capital investment through the Korea Development Bank. Foreign loans to Korean firms were subject to government control under a system whereby the Korea Exchange Bank issued guarantees to foreign lenders.

Government intervention in the allocation of credit increased considerably in the 1970s, subsequent to the major reductions in interest rates mandated by the August 3 Presidential Emergency Decree of 1972. With interest rate ceilings (at negative real rates) in effect, the government used credit-rationing as a major policy instrument to promote the development of a number of infant industries, broadly referred to as the "heavy and chemical industries." The only real alternative to government-rationed credit was the informal financial sector (curb market), where nominal interest rates were two to three times as high as the rates charged for general bank loans. Given the heavy dependence of Korean firms on debt finance (see

Table 7), access to government-controlled credit was critical to a company's successful growth, particularly in the more capital-intensive industries.[22]

Table 7:   Debt/Equity Ratios for 1983, Comparative Figures by Broad Industrial Sector (Figures in Percent)

	Manufacturing	Construction	Wholesale Trade
South Korea			
Top 5 Chaebol	353.5	608.6	559.6
Top 10 Chaebol	360.9	678.6	599.5
Top 20 Chaebol	378.5	609.0	615.2
Top 50 Chaebol	370.7	552.0	655.2
All Enterprises	360.3	481.1	489.1
International Comparisons			
United States	104.3	—	—
Japan	323.7	—	—
Taiwan	158.5	519.9	—
West Germany	217.6	820.8	—

Source: *Firm Directory of Korea for 1985* (Daily Economic News, 1986), *Korea's Fifty Major Groups for 1983 and 1984* (Management Efficiency Research Institute, 1985), and *Financial Statements Analysis* (Bank of Korea 1984 and 1987).

In general, the system of credit-rationing in the 1970s favored large firms at the expense of small- and medium-sized firms. Since, under the system of interest-rate ceilings, banks were not permitted to charge differential interest rates on the basis of risk assessment, they generally attempted to reduce transactions costs and potential losses from default by giving preferential treatment to large, well established firms. Smaller firms thus tended to be more dependent on the curb market for securing needed loans.[23] Large enterprises also received favorable treatment in the form of special policy loans (with interest rates even lower than the rates for general bank loans), which were largely directed to firms producing for export and firms in targeted heavy industries.

The relative ease with which large-scale enterprises could secure access to low-cost loans is shown in Table 8, which presents figures on the overall cost of loans for manufacturing firms grouped by employment size.[24] Insofar as most of the manufacturing firms affiliated with the *chaebol* can be classified as large, the *chae-*

bol would have enjoyed preferred treatment in terms of the cost of finance. In 1983, over 70 percent of the manufacturing firms associated with the top fifty *chaebol* were firms employing more than 300 workers. For Korean enterprise as a whole, however, firms employing more than 300 workers accounted for less than 3 percent of the total number of manufacturing firms.[25]

Table 8:   Overall Cost of Loans for Manufacturing Enterprises Grouped by Employment Size (Figures in Percent)

Year	Large Enterprises	Small and Medium Enterprises	Difference
1972	11.97	13.53	1.56
1973	8.37	11.17	2.80
1974	8.77	9.94	1.17
1975	9.74	12.62	2.88
1976	10.55	12.65	2.10
1977	10.38	12.14	1.76
1978	10.56	13.47	2.91
1979	12.86	15.27	2.41
1980	15.71	19.84	4.13
1981	17.94	18.65	0.71
1982	15.78	15.17	−0.61
1983	13.73	12.90	−0.83

Source: Bank of Korea, *Financial Statements Analysis* (Annual). Overall borrowing costs were calculated for each sector as the ratio of interest expenses and discount paid to total loans. For the years prior to 1976, the Bank of Korea defines large enterprises as enterprises employing 200 or more workers, while small and medium enterprises are those employing 5 to 199 workers. Since 1976, large enterprises have been defined as enterprises employing 300 or more workers, and small and medium enterprises as enterprises employing 5 to 299 workers.

Group membership in itself may also have given firms an advantage in securing loans from banks and development finance institutions. Such an advantage would have enabled the *chaebol* to benefit enormously from the government's credit subsidies by establishing new firms in industries targeted for development.

To determine the responsiveness of the *chaebol* to government credit incentives in the 1970s, two measures of industry credit preference have been constructed for fifty-five manufacturing industries from annual data reported in the Bank of Korea's Financial Statements Analysis. The first measure is the overall cost of loans for the industry (calculated as the ratio of interest expenses and discount paid to total industry loans), averaged over the years 1973-1979. This measure reflects differential access to different types of loans, including low-cost bank loans, foreign loans, and general loans by banks, non-bank financial institutions, and others. Since Korean banks were not permitted to charge a risk premium on loans, and since government guarantees of foreign loans would have eliminated the need for foreign lenders to charge differential risk premiums, this measure should approximate the true relative cost of loans for different industries. The second measure is the share of foreign loans in total industry loans, again averaged over the years 1973-1979. For most years in the 1970s, effective interest rates for foreign loans were much lower than the rates charged for domestic bank loans. Foreign loans were strictly controlled by the government, and were largely used to finance imports of machinery and equipment for targeted industries.[26]

In the absence of longitudinal data on firm production or sales, I have used data on the date of establishment of *chaebol*-member firms (classified by industrial sector) to gauge the relative increase over time in business group activity across manufacturing industries. Altogether, over a third of the 296 manufacturing firms affiliated with the top fifty *chaebol* in 1983 were established during the period 1973-1979. The number of *chaebol*-member firms established in 1973-1979 was totaled for each of the fifty-five manufacturing sectors for which we have measures of industry credit preference.

Table 9 reports the coefficients of correlation between the industry number of *chaebol*-member firms established in 1973-1979 and the two measures of industry credit preference. Both correlations are significant at the 2 percent level, and both display the expected sign: the industry number of group-member firms established in 1973-1979 increases both with lower industry loan costs and with a higher industry proportion of foreign loans to total loans. Although the correlations are not very high, it appears safe to conclude that the *chaebol* responded positively to government credit incentives in the 1970s by establishing new firms in targeted industries. This responsiveness to the Park government's industry promotion measures may partly account for the wide degree of diversification (examined before) which today characterizes many of Korea's business groups.

The legacy of credit-rationing policies in the 1970s is reflected in the 1983 distribution of *chaebol*-member firms among industries. As shown in Table 9, the industry number of *chaebol*-member firms in 1983 is significantly correlated with the two measures of industry credit preference for the period 1973-1979. This may explain our earlier finding that the *chaebol* appear to be competing with each other in the same manufacturing industries. Responding to government credit incentives, the *chaebol* in the 1970s established new firms in the same targeted industries; as a result, the market structure of these industries in the 1980s tends to be oligopolistic rather than monopolistic.

While it appears that Korean business groups have been responsive to industry credit incentives, a question remains as to the degree to which *chaebol* dominance

Table 9:   Correlations Between Measures of *Chaebol* Activity and Loan Preference Across 55 Manufacturing Sectors

	CHAESS	GNF3E9	GNF83	CST3A9	FLT3A9	CST83
CHAESS	1.000					
GNF3E9	0.362*	1.000				
GNF83	0.503*	0.833*	1.000			
CST3A9	−0.164	−0.332*	−0.341*	1.000		
FLT3A9	0.338*	0.316*	0.337*	−0.375*	1.000	
CST83	0.421*	−0.133	0.076	0.080	−0.028	1.000

*   Significant at the 2% level.

Definition of variables:

CHAESS = Sector sales share of top 50 *chaebol* in 1983.
GNF3E9 = Number of member firms of top 50 *chaebol* established in sector during the period 1973-1979.
GNF83   = Total number of group-member firms (top 50 *chaebol*) in sector in 1983.
CST3A9 = Average annual cost of loans for the period 1973-1979.
FLT3A9 = Foreign loans as a proportion of total loans for sector (aveage for 1973-1979).
CST83   = Sector cost of loans for the year 1983.

of industries can be attributed to favorable treatment by the government. Since we lack individual company data on loans and the cost of finance, this question cannot be answered in a satisfactory manner. Table 9, however, does indicate the possibility of preferential treatment: there exists a significant relationship between *chaebol* dominance of industries (measured by sales share) and one measure of credit preference, the share of foreign loans in total industry borrowing for the period 1973-1979.[27] Since foreign loans in the 1970s were generally used to finance imports of capital goods, this is consistent with our previous finding that business group dominance of Korean industries is significantly correlated with industry capital requirements. It remains an open question whether the *chaebol* were able to assume a dominant role in capital-intensive industries because of privileged access to foreign loans, or whether there is something about the organizational structure or technological capacity of business groups which pre-determined their dominance of such industries independent of any government favoritism. Either way, one is led to the conclusion that the Park government's promotion of capital-intensive industries in the 1970s did much to contribute to business group dominance of the Korean economy at the aggregate level.

Conclusion

Business groups play a major role in the Korean economy, accounting for nearly a fifth of gross domestic product and close to thirty percent of manufacturing value added. Korea's groups tend to be highly diversified, with member firms spread across a wide range of manufacturing and non-manufacturing industries. In a developing country like Korea, the broad diversification of business groups can perhaps be explained as an institutional device for diffusing risk in the context of rapid structural change and the absence of well-functioning markets for insurance or capital. It may also reflect a superior ability on the part of experienced groups to establish operations in industries characterized by large learning requirements. For the Korean case, however, there is evidence that group diversification in part represents a response to credit incentives created by a strongly-interventionist government to promote the development of favored industries.

A major focus of this paper has been the pattern of business group dominance across Korean manufacturing industries. It has been proposed by some economists that the dominant presence of business groups in certain industries can be explained as an efficient organizational adaptation to given industry characteristics. A formal test of this hypothesis for Korean groups shows that the degree of industry dominance by business groups is significantly related to industry capital requirements, with the contribution of other explanatory variables being at best marginal.

Korean group dominance of industries requiring large amounts of capital may be related to government credit-rationing policies in the 1970s. The evidence suggests that large firms enjoyed an advantage in securing loans at favorable interest rates, and that foreign loans were approved mainly for industries now dominated by the *chaebol*. In a rapidly developing economy like Korea's, it is possible that large business groups possess a natural advantage in entering certain capital-intensive industries, through accumulated experience and superior endowments of managerial and engineering resources. It may be that the Park government, in allocating credit at subsidized rates for the development of heavy industries, favored the *chaebol* because it was convinced of their superior ability to get the job done. It is also possible that the *chaebol* would have established a dominant presence in capital-intensive industries even in the absence of credit distortions. Even so, we can say with considerable confidence that the government-led channeling of resources into the development of heavy industries greatly accelerated the growth of business groups, increasing their aggregate dominance of the Korean economy.

Notes

[1] In Chinese characters the term *chaebol* is a combination of the character expressing "wealth" or "finance" with the character "clique." The Japanese pronunciation of
these two characters is *zaibatsu*, which is the term used to describe the giant industrial
groups in pre-war Japan. Throughout this paper, any reference to Korea refers to the
Republic of Korea.

[2] The database was constructed by Wan-Jin Kim (currently with the Economics Department at Seoul National University) during his residence in 1987-1988 as a researcher at the Institute of Governmental Affairs. The database includes firm-level
data on sales, assets, debts, profits, employment, and year of establishment, for the
550 member firms of the top 50 *chaebol* in 1983. Each listed firm in the database has
been classified by its major industrial activity at the four-digit level of the Korean
Standard Industrial Classification (revised, 1984). The major sources for the database
are Korea's Fifty Major Groups for 1983 and 1984 (Management Efficiency Research
Institute 1985) and Firm Directory of Korea for 1985 (Daily Economic News 1986).

[3] The figures presented in Table 1, and in the accompanying discussion in the text, are
taken from the database described in Footnote 2. With the exception of Kukje, which
was forced into bankruptcy in 1985, all of the groups listed in Table 1 also ranked
among the top ten *chaebol* in 1986.

[4] Altogether there are 105 manufacturing sectors at the four-digit level of the Korean
Standard Industrial Classification (revised, 1984), most firms produce more than one
product at the five-digit level of disaggregation, which includes over 500 manufacturing sectors.

[5] Our four measures of diversification are highly correlated with each other across the
sample of forty-nine groups active in manufacturing. The two measures most closely correlated with one another are H* and S*, with a correlation coefficient equal to
0.983. The measures least correlated with one another, H* and V*, have a correlation
coefficient equal to 0.708. Table 2 shows that the indices S* and Sw* (calculated on
the basis of sales and employment data, respectively) assume radically different values for the *chaebol* Sunkyung. This is because the leading manufacturing sector for
Sunkyung in terms of sales and petroleum refining employs very few workers.

[6] Unless otherwise indicated, all figures on *chaebol* sales or value added shares presented in this paper are for South Korea's top fifty *chaebol* ranked by total sales. Chong-
hwan Chu (1985) identifies a total of 155 *chaebol* in South Korea for the year 1980,
and presents data on *chaebol* sales and employment in mining and manufacturing.
Based on his data, the top fifty *chaebol* in 1980 accounted for 79 percent of total *chaebol* employment and 81 percent of total *chaebol* sales in mining and manufacturing.
Thus, the figures presented here for the top fifty *chaebol* can be taken as representative
of total *chaebol* activity in South Korea's economy.

[7] There is an unfortunate tendency among some scholars to draw erroneous inferences
from comparisons of *chaebol* total sales with South Korea's GNP. Amsden (1989),
for example, on the basis of a table reproduced from Kim (1987) showing the ratio
of *chaebol* sales to Korean GNP, concludes that in 1984 "the three largest *chaebol*
alone accounted for a staggering 36 percent of national product in Korea" (p. 116)
and that "the top ten *chaebol* accounted for almost 70 percent of GNP" (p. 136). Such
a statement presupposes an incorrect definition of gross national product. If one is to

make any inference about the contribution of the leading *chaebol* to Korean GNP, the only meaningful comparison is the ratio of *chaebol* value added to GNP. As Table 3 shows, in 1986 the top fifty *chaebol* in reality accounted for a little less than 20 percent of South Korea's GNP.

[8]   The figures on aggregate concentration in the United States are from U.S. Census Bureau data presented in White (1981).

[9]   In 1977, 53 of the largest 100 Korean firms were member firms of the top thirty *chaebol* (see Chu 1985, p. 31). Leroy Jones (1975) reports that Korean public enterprises in 1972 accounted for 31 percent of Korean value added in mining and 15 percent of value added in manufacturing. In that year twenty of South Korea's largest fifty enterprises were public enterprises. Since then, some large public enterprises have been taken over by individual *chaebol*. South Korea's largest steel producer, the Pohang Iron and Steel Company, remains a quasi-government enterprise, with 30 percent of its ownership held directly by the government, and 45 percent held by the Korea Development Bank (see Amsden 1989, p. 315).

[10] As of June 1987, there are a total of eight general trading companies operating in Korea, the smallest of which is a public corporation. The seven largest general trading companies are owned by Hyundai, Samsung, Daewoo, Lucky Goldstar, Sunkyong, Ssangyong, and Hyosung. For a complete discussion, see Lee Sung-soo (1987).

[11] Figures from *Business Korea*, reported in Leipziger et al. (1987), Volume 1, Table 4.10. According to these figures, the 8 percent limit on individual ownership is exceeded by some of the *chaebol*.

[12] The figures on total *chaebol* sales by manufacturing industry were calculated from the 1983 database. The data on total industry shipments is from the Economic Planning Board's Report on Industrial Census, 1983.

[13] These measures are reported in Appendix 2 of Lee, Lee, and Kim (1984).

[14] See Lee, Urata, and Choi (1986), Table 3.

[15] Lee Kyu-uck (1986), Table 3. Leroy Jones (1975) reports that, as of 1972, many of the most concentrated industries in Korean mining and manufacturing were dominated by government enterprises.

[16] The adjusted R-square for the different variants of their general econometric model ranges from 0.4188 to 0.5171. All of the variables are significant at the 1 percent level, with the exception of the level of export variable, which is significant at the 10-percent level. The sample used by Encaoua and Jacquemin consists of 270 industries at the four-digit level of the French industrial classification. The data on industrial groups is from a 1980 study by the Center for Mathematical Economics of the University of Paris I and the French National Institute of Statistics. This study identifies a total of 319 French industrial groups for the year 1974.

[17] Inclusion of the export share variable in the efficiency model is probably a misspecification for the Korean case. The rationale given by Encaoua and Jacquemin for its inclusion is the high degree of uncertainty and the high cost of information in marketing products internationally, which should favor internal coordination through large-scale organizations. To represent this by the share of industry product exported, however, presupposes that the enterprises manufacturing for export are necessarily involved in the marketing of their products overseas. This definitely is not the case in Korea, where some seven general trading companies (all *chaebol*-affiliated) are responsible for marketing nearly half of the country's exports.

[18] Most of the sectors in the sample correspond to the categories of the Korean Standard Industrial Classification at the four-digit level, but in some cases KSIC sectors were aggregated to match the sectors in the input-output tables.

[19] This census is taken every five years. I make the necessary assumption that the data for the number of firms and plants in each industry has not changed much in two years.

[20] The two variables capturing scale economies are somewhat collinear with industry capital requirements: the simple coefficient of correlation between KR and ES is 0.483, and that between KR and MLTP is 0.555. Encaoua and Jacquemin report that the highest correlation coefficient between independent variables for their sample (that between KR and ES) is 0.34.

[21] There is, however, a noticeable problem of multicollinearity in Equation 4: although the adjusted R-square increases to 0.33, the marginal contribution of the capital requirements variable is significant only at the 5-percent level. For the reduced sample of 60 industries, the simple coefficient of correlation between KR and ES is 0.714, while the correlation between KR and MLTP is 0.633. The correlation between MLTP and ES is 0.536.

[22] Throughout the 1970s, loans from banks, non-bank financial institutions, foreign sources, and others accounted for between 42 and 58 percent of the total financing requirements (internal and external) of Korean corporations. The debt:equity ratio of Korean manufacturing firms gradually increased from 313 percent in 1972 to 377 percent in 1979, and then jumped to over 450 percent during the severe recession of 1980-1981. In the early 1980s, the Korean government acted to increase real interest rates for bank loans, thus narrowing the interest rate gap between formal and informal credit. Preferential lending rates for policy loans were abolished in June 1982. An analysis of of Korea's credit-rationing policies in the 1970s is presented in Zeile (1991).

[23] Lim (1981), Table 12, presents figures for 1977 showing a decrease in the ratio of curb market debt to total liabilities with firm size.

[24] As Table 8 indicates, in recent years the government has begun to favor small and medium enterprises, in an effort to correct for past discrimination. In the early 1980s the government implemented a requirement that 55 percent of the increase of any local bank's credit and 35 percent of the increase of any nationwide city bank's credit be directed to small- and medium-sized firms. In 1984, the government froze the share of total bank credit going to the top thirty *chaebol* at the 1983 levels; however, these restrictions were later lifted in 1985.

[25] Chang and Choi (1988), in a multivariate regression explaining the variance of interest costs (averaged for the years 1975-1984) across a sample of 182 listed Korean manufacturing companies, show a strong negative correlation between company size (measured by total assets) and interest costs. The focus of their discussion of the regression results, however, is on the signs of their dummy variables for group membership, which (controlling for company size) they find to be significantly positive. For firms listed on the stockmarket, its seems that the cost of credit for group-affiliated firms is higher than that for non-group firms of identical size. This could be due to the fact that many of the large non-*chaebol* firms listed on the stockmarket are government-invested enterprises (which would have received preferential treatment over private firms in the government's credit-rationing policies). One would expect that the signs of the *chaebol* dummy variables would be negative if the variable controlling for firm size were removed from the regression equation. One might also

question whether their sample of listed firms (which includes only 63 of the total 421 member firms of the top 30 *chaebol* they examine) is representative of all manufacturing firms in terms of the relative cost of finance for group-affiliated and non-group-affiliated firms. Finally, one should note that in averaging over the period 1975-1984 they include observations for years (in the 1980s) when the government made an effort to reverse earlier policies favoring the *chaebol*.

[26] A more complete discussion of these measures is present in Zeile (1991). The level of industry aggregation employed was dictated by the level of detail in the industry aggregate balance sheets reported in Financial Statements Analysis. Most of the fifty-five manufacturing sectors correspond to the three- and four-digit levels of the Korean Standard Industrial Classification.

[27] It is interesting to note that there is a significant positive correlation between the *chaebol* share of industry sales and the industry cost of loans for 1983. This is consistent with the observation that the Korean government has in recent years attempted to limit the amount of credit made available to the leading *chaebol*.

References

Amsden, Alice. 1989. *Asia's Next Giant: South Korea and Late Industrialization.* New York: Oxford University Press.

Bank of Korea. Various years. *Economic Statistics Yearbook.* Seoul: Bank of Korea.

Bank of Korea. Various years. *Financial Statements Analysis.* Seoul: Bank of Korea.

Berry, Charles H. 1971. "Corporate Growth and Diversification." *Journal of Law and Economics* 14 (October): 371-383.

Caves, Richard E. 1989. "International Differences in Industrial Organization." *Handbook of Industrial Organization,* eds. Richard Schmalensee and Robert D. Willig. Amsterdam: North Holland.

Caves, Richard E. and Masu Uekusa. 1976. *Industrial Organization in Japan.* Washington, D.C.: The Brookings Institution.

Chandler, Alfred D., Jr. 1977. *The Visible Hand: The Managerial Revolution in American Business.* Cambridge, Mass.: Belknap Press.

Chang, Sea Jin and Unghwan Choi. 1988. "Strategy, Structure and Performance of Korean Business Groups: A Transactions Cost Approach." *Journal of Industrial Economics* 37 (December): 141-158.

Chu, Chong-hwan. 1985. *Chaebol Kyugjeron* [Economics of the *Chaebol*]. Seoul: Cheonghum Munhwasa.

Cole, David C. and Yung Chul Park. 1983. *Financial Development in Korea, 1945-1978.* Cambridge, Mass.: Harvard University Press.

Comanor, William S. and Thomas A. Wilson. 1967. "Advertising, Market Structure and Performance." *Review of Economics and Statistics* 49 (November): 423-440.

Daily Economic News. 1985. *Firm Directory of Korea for 1985.* (In Korean.)

Daily Economic News. 1986. *Firm Directory of Korea for 1986.* (In Korean.)

Economic Planning Board. 1983. *Report on Establishment Census, 1981.* Seoul: Economic Planning Board, Republic of Korea.

Economic Planning Board. 1985. *Report on Industrial Census, 1983.* Seoul: Economic Planning Board, Republic of Korea.

Encaoua, David and Alexis Jacquemin. 1982. "Organizational Efficiency and Monopoly Power: The Case of French Industrial Groups." *European Economic Review* 19: 25-51.

Gort, Michael. 1962. *Diversification and Integration in American Industry.* Princeton: Princeton University Press.

Goto, Arika. 1981. "Statistical Evidence on the Diversification of Japanese Large Firms." *Journal of Industrial Economics* 29 (March): 271-278.

Goto, Arika. 1982. "Business Groups in a Market Economy." *European Economic Review* 19: 53-70.

Hamilton, Gary, William Zeile, and Kim Wan-Jin. 1989. "The Network Structures of East Asian economies." *Capitalism in Contrasting Cultures,* eds. Steward Clegg and S.Gordon Redding. Berlin: de Gruyter.

Hong, Wontack and Yung Chul Park. 1986. "The Financing of Export-Oriented Growth in Korea." *Pacific Growth and Financial Interdependenece,* eds. Augustine H.H. Tan and Basant Kapur. Sydney: Allen and Unwin.

Kim, S.K. 1987. "Business Concentration and Government Policy: A Study of the Phenomenon of Business Groups in Korea, 1945-1985." Unpublished D.B.A. dissertation. Cambridge, Mass.: Harvard University.

Koo, Hagen. 1984. "The Political Economy of Income Distribution in South Korea: The Impact of the State's Industrialization Policies." *World Development* 12 (10): 1029-1037.

Jones, Leroy P. 1975. *Public Enterprise and Economic Development: The Korean Case.* Seoul: Korea Development Institute.

Jones, Leroy P. and Sakong, Il. 1980. *Government, Business, and Entrepreneurship in Economic Development: The Korean Case.* Cambridge, Mass.: Harvard University Press.

Lee, Kyu-uck. 1986. "The Concentration of Economic Power in Korea: Causes, Consequences, and Policy." *Industrial Development Policies and Issues,* ed. Kyu-uck Lee. Seoul: Korea Development Institute.

Lee, Kyu-uck, Ja-hyung Lee, and Chu-hun Kim. 1984. *Shichang kwa Shichang Kujo* [Markets and Market Structure]. Seoul: Korea Development Institute.

Lee, Kyu-uck and Sung-sun Lee. 1985. *Kiup Kyolhap kwa Kyongjeryuk Chichung* [Firm Integration and Concentration of Economic Power]. Seoul: Korea Development Institute.

Lee, Kyu-uck, Shujiro Urata, and Inbom Choi. 1986. "Recent Development in Industrial Organizational Issues in Korea." Seoul: Korea Development InstituteWorking Paper 8609.

Lee, Song-soo. 1987. "Korea's General Trading Companies." *Monthly Review* (Korea Exchange Bank) 21 (July): 3-19.

Lee, Young-ki. 1985. "Conglomeration and Business Concentration – The Korean Case." *Industrial Policies of the Republic of Korea and the Republic of China.* Seoul: Korea Development Institute.

Leff, Nathaniel H. 1978. "Industrial Organization and Entrepreneurship in the Developing Countries: The Economic Groups." *Economic Development and Cultural Change* 26 (July): 661-675.

Leipziger, Danny M. 1988. "Industrial Restructuring in Korea." *World Development* 16 (January): 121-135.

Leipziger, Danny et al. 1987. *Korea: Managing the Industrial Transition.* Washington, D.C.: The World Bank.

Lim, Youngil. 1981. *Government Policy and Private Enterprise: Korean Experience in Industrialization.* Berkeley: Institute of East Asian Studies.

Management Efficiency Research Institute. 1985. *Korea's Fifty Major Groups for 1983 and 1984.* Seoul: Management Efficiency Research Institute. (In Korean.)

Management Efficiency Research Institute. 1987. *Financial Analysis of Korea's Fifty Major Groups for 1986.* Seoul: Management Efficiency Research Institute. (In Korean.)

Scherer, Frederic M. 1980. *Industrial Market Structure and Market Performance.* Chicago: Rand McNally.

Shin, Joon-Sang. 1988. "Recent Changes of Corporate Financing in Korea." *Monthly Review* (Korea Exchange Bank) 22 (February): 3-17.

Song, Dae-hee. 1985. "The Role of Public Enterprises in the Korean Economy." *The Industrial Policies of the Republic of Korea and the Republic of China.* Seoul: Korea Development Institute.

Spence, Michael. 1975. "The Economics of Internal Organization." *Bell Journal of Economics* (Spring): 163-172.

White, Lawrence J. 1981. "What Has Been Happening to Aggregate Concentration in the United States?" *Journal of Industrial Economics* 29 (March): 223-230.

Williamson, Oliver E. 1975. *Markets and Hierarchies: Analysis and Antitrust Implications* New York: Macmillan Publishing Company.

Zeile, William. 1991. "Industrial Targeting Through Government Credit Rationing: The Korean Experience in the 1970s." East Asian Business and Development Working Paper No. 41. Davis: Institute of Governmental Affairs, University of California.

Part Three

Conclusion

The Theoretical Significance of Asian Business Networks

Gary G. Hamilton

This chapter expands theoretically what the other chapters in this book ground empirically. When the first edition of this book was published in 1991, the topics of Asian business groups and business networks, especially outside Japan, were largely unstudied. But in the last few years, a number of additional studies have appeared, or soon will appear, that further document the dynamics of business networks (e.g., Aoki 1990; Fruin 1992; Gerlach 1992; Gereffi and Korzeniewicz 1994; Granovetter 1994; Kim Forthcoming; Numazaki 1993; Orrù, Biggart, and Hamilton 1991; Shieh 1992; Zeile 1993). Taken together, these studies raise questions about the rather simplistic descriptions of the Asian business organizations that accompanied the early interpretations of Asia's economic development. Many of these interpretations made Asian business organizations the explicit outcomes of state policy or the timeless manifestation of Confucian culture. However, by placing Asian business networks in a comparative perspective and by showing the differences among these networks in Asia, the chapters in this book reveal that the story of Asian economic development is much more complex than these early accounts would suggest. These chapters imply, in fact, that a full understanding of Asian business networks might substantially challenge Western economic and sociological theory.

This concluding chapter will delineate two of the most obvious challenges. The first challenge concerns the origins of economic organization. Do the types of economic organizations found in an economy at any one point in time arise as consequences of market dynamics, state policies, or enduring cultural formations? The authors represented in this book do not advocate any of these positions, but rather argue more broadly that Asian relational networks are the institutionalized medium for all types of activities – political and social, as well as economic. Asian business networks are, therefore, social constructions that reflect institutionalized and normative prescriptions for the formation of cohesive groups. That network configurations differ systematically among Asian societies can be traced, in part, to the distinctive and institutionally rooted ways in which Chinese, Korean, and Japanese put together their social groups. Second, most of the chapters in this book suggest that, as the main vehicle for organizing economic activity, business networks also significantly help shape what economists call "industrial structure."

Put into the terminology developed by transaction cost theorists, the hierarchies of Asian economies are built from these business networks. Specific strategies to fashion network configurations precede and condition the establishment of capitalist markets. Implicitly, then, efficiency in economic performance and competitiveness in global markets grow out of attempts to systematize existing network configurations. In other words, the trajectories of Asian economic development are "path dependent," with the initial conditions being shaped by the organizational strategies that are institutionally and normatively available in each society.

I will discuss each of these theoretical implications in turn.

Networks as an Institutional Medium of Economic Activity

The capitalist economies of East and Southeast Asia are organized through business networks. Trained in Western economics to conceptualize economic activity in terms of markets and individual firms, many analysts of Asian capitalism have been slow to acknowledge the presence, not to mention the importance, of these business networks. For example, in such an important book as Robert Wade's *Governing the Market: Economic Theory and the Role of Government in East Asian Industrialization*, the author (1990, p. 70) observes,

Taiwan's dualistic industrial structure is densely interconnected, and the export success of the smaller firms cannot be understood independently of the productive performance of the big firms. This being said, I should stress that the organization of firms – their size, the way they grow, their methods of doing business, and the relationships between them – is a major gap in the argument of this book. Any discussion of an economy's development should give a central place to the organization of firms and industries. But since little evidence is available on this subject for Taiwan, and since my primary interest is the uses of public power, I say little more about it.

Although Wade says little about how Asian firms are interconnected, the researchers in this book have a lot to say about these linkages and about implications of these linkage for doing business in Asia.

Moreover, by showing that networks are the main organizational units of Asian capitalist economies, the researchers represented in this book are not merely filling a gap in Wade's argument, but rather are substantially changing the nature of the argument itself. Indeed, in the final analysis, how Asian economies actually develop and perform depends on the dynamics and effectiveness of the inter-firms networks themselves, rather than on the encouraging actions of governments or on the entrepreneurial efforts of acquisitive individuals, even though both of these levels of actions are certainly important and contribute to growth. The perspective developed in this book suggests that an adequate interpretation of capitalism in Asia, including the trajectories of development, must emphasize the organizational characteristics and institutional foundations of Asian economies. The most important organizational features of these economies are the business networks, and, therefore, an adequate understanding of Asian capitalism must be built on an analysis of how business networks organize the economy and how they, in turn, influence economic performance.[1]

The role of business networks in Asian economies, however, must be carefully specified, because it is easy to misunderstand their importance. It is incorrect to argue, for instance, that Asian economies have industrialized strictly because of these business networks. Such networks can be found in many societies, some economically well developed and others exceedingly poor (e.g., Strachan 1976). The presence or absence of business networks does not define the crucial difference about whether societies become capitalistic or not. After all, one of the most extensively capitalist countries in the world, the United States, has fewer and relatively more unstable business networks than do countries in Asia, but this fact does not make the United States any less capitalistic (Biggart and Hamilton 1992). Instead, the correct way to view Asian business networks is to see them as an *institutional medium of economic activity*.

By using the term "institutional medium," I want conceptually to emphasize the "means of action," rather than the "goals of actors." Unlike the goals of actors, which may be individual, idiosyncratic, and opportunistic, the "means of action" are interpersonal and shared. They consist of a "set of material practices and symbolic constructions… which constitutes [a society's] organizing principles and which is available to organizations and individuals to elaborate" (Friedland and Alford 1991, p. 248).

Such organizing principles are to a society what syntax and grammar are to a language. The medium of expression among people is a mutually intelligible language, and the rules of that language provide a shared linguistic structure by which individuals are able to convey their personal thoughts and intentions to others. Similarly, an institutionalized medium of action among people is a mutually intelligible set of established social rules that people use to achieve their personal goals. Like linguistic structure in a language, social rules are mutually recognized conventions, a sort of social grammar that is available for utilization and that, when used, structures the action itself.

Mark Granovetter (1985) has argued that people use such rules to organize groups in all spheres of activity, including the economy. Economic action is always social action, in that it always involves people interacting in ways that they deeply and intuitively understand and that they employ to gain economic, social, and political advantages. That people use social conventions to organize groups does not lessen their rationality. Rather, people rationally pursue what they socially understand and desire. An institutional medium shapes but does not determine the goals and strategies of individual pursuit.

In applying this idea to Asia, the authors represented in this book show that key players in East and Southeast Asian economies follow widely accepted and well

established procedures for organizing social groups. The groups that they organize are purposefully engaged in economic activity. By constructing groups according to established procedures, these business people create specific kinds of
social networks, composed of such people as family members, friends, and trusted
colleagues. When viewed in light of their economic characteristics, these social
networks consist of clusters of interconnected firms. In this book, we call these
interfirm clusters "business networks." The significant point to be made in this
chapter is that business networks in East and Southeast Asia differ sociologically,
organizationally, and economically from inter-firm networks found in the United
States.

Gordon Redding's formulation of this phenomenon, which is found in this volume, is the correct one: Throughout Asia, business networks are more significant –
that is, stronger, more resilient – than the individual firms that make up the networks. Firms are relatively weak; they come and go; they are ephemeral, produced
as spinoffs from other firms or shut down as easily as an office is emptied and a
door is closed. The inter-firm networks are relatively strong; they last over the long
term and represent, symbolically and often in reality, the continuity of collective
interests – the perduration of families, communities, and sets of friends and relatives. By contrast, business networks in the United States are relatively weak and
generally represent short-term economic interests of interconnected firms (Bearden and Mintz 1987). The institutional medium of the American economy is *not*
the network, but rather the firm. Legally delineated corporations organizationally
define the contours of the American economy, and, accordingly, inter-firms networks in this economy are situational and opportunistic.

The Sociological Characteristics of Asian Networks

In an institutional sense, then, Asian economies are network-based, whereas the
United States economy is firm-based.[2] Underlying this difference in the institutional character of economies is a more fundamental sociological difference in the
makeup of Western and Asian societies.[3] To clarify this contrast, I should note that
in recent years a network approach to social analysis has emerged in Western social science, which has spawned a large literature on network structures in Western
societies (e.g., Alba 1982; Paulson 1985; Wellman and Berkowitz 1988; Powell
1990; Nohria and Eccles 1992). In an effort to describe Asian business networks,
it is important, as a first step, to make a clear distinction between the formal properties of networks and their embedded and substantive character. The distinction
is important because most of the new network theory is largely methodological
and formal and is not particularly relevant to the study Asian business networks.[4]
Western network theory is based on voluntarist assumptions inherent in Western
individualism: Autonomous individuals or firms are interlinked; the basis of the

linkage between actors rests on rational calculation and voluntary action; and the precise formal pattern of involvement, whether a configuration of friends or firms, has empirical effects. Like other forms of Western theory, Western network theory is "self-centered." By contrast, Asian networks are based on neither practices nor theories of voluntarism and individualism. Asian networks are normative, relational, hierarchical, and substantive.

To describe these characteristics, it is useful to draw on Fei Xiaotong's classic study, *Xiangtu Zhongguo* (published 1947), in which he explains the organizational differences between Chinese and Western societies.[5] In a recently translated version published under the title *From the Soil: The Foundations of Chinese Society*, Fei (1992) argues that Chinese society is built up from very different organizing principles than is found in Western societies. Western societies rest on what he calls an "organizational mode of association" (*tuantigeju*), whereas Chinese society rests on what he terms a "differential mode of association" (*chaxugeju*). He illustrates the difference between the two modes of association with two metaphors.

Western society resembles the way rice straws are collected in China. Each haystack is build up from individual straws: Straws are collected into bundles; bundles are made into larger bundles; and then these bundles are collected and made into haystacks. In Western society, he says (1992, pp. 61-62), "individuals form organizations. Each organization has its own boundaries, which clearly define those people who are members and those who are not." These organizations are then part of larger organizations (e.g., a department in a university, a division in a corporation), which in turn make up yet larger organizational units (e.g., counties made up the state and states made up the country). These organizational entities serve as devices for framing the individualism that is such a prominent feature of Western society. Chinese society, he argues, is not based on individualism and is not built up from this sort of organizational logic. Chinese society consists neither of organizational frames for individuals nor of hierarchies of discrete organizations. Instead, it is based on overlapping networks of people linked together through differentially categorized social relationships. Fei says Chinese society metaphorically resembles the concentric rings that are formed when a stone is thrown into a pond. "Everyone stands at the center of the circles produced by his or her own social influence. Everyone's circles are interrelated. One touches different circles at different times and places" (1992, pp. 62-63).

The key point of Fei's description of Chinese society is the concept of *chaxugeju*, the differential mode of association. *Chaxugeju* refers to a social structure made up of institutionalized networks of normative social relationships. For instance, the family in the West is a discrete organization composed of distinct individuals, but in China the family or household (*jia*) is part of a potentially vast institutionalized web of relationships. In Chinese society, *chaxugeju* means that people think of themselves as being linked to other people through normatively defined sets of social relationships, from which they obtain a sense of themselves, not as autonomous individuals, but as personal embodiments of morally defined roles. From the participants' points of view, Chinese society consists of institutionalized webs of social relationships that identify people to whom participants in those networks are personally obligated. By contrast, in Western society, people think of themselves as freely choosing among which organizational entities to affiliate (e.g., one's workplace, clubs, one's residential location, schools, even households), from which they, in turn, obtain a sense of themselves as autonomous individuals with rights and duties.

Insofar as both form the building blocks of their respective societies, the institutionalized networks of relationships in China are roughly equivalent to institutionalized organizations in the West. Given this fact, then, what networks theorists refer to as networks in their study of Western societies differ qualitatively from the networks that prevail in Asia. By and large, networks in the West consist of empirically and situationally defined interactional patterns that exist among individuals and explicit organizations, such as might be represented in a sociogram of interaction among children in a classroom or in an interlock chart of relationships among corporate boards of directors. In Chinese society, however, networks specify sets of people normatively linked together in pre-defined relationships; these networks exist whether or not the linked individuals interact at all or interact according to the rules of their specific relationships.

The only Asian society that Fei describes is Chinese society. Still, from the logic of his analysis, it is clear that the general contrast, as opposed to the specific details, also applies to other Asian societies. The reason for its broader application is because Fei is making a civilizational argument. Western society obtains its particular institutional features from a unique developmental foundation resting on transcendental monotheism, as personified by Christianity in particular (Hamilton 1994). By contrast, East Asian civilization does not rest on monotheism or even on a belief in a transcendental realm of reality. Asian cosmology was and continues to be rooted in hierarchical relational patterns interlinking a naturally functioning universe, a naturally functioning earth, and a naturally functioning human order. The "naturalness" inherent in the human order is fixed to essential human roles. Asian societies differ somewhat in how they characterize these roles and in which roles are emphasized more than others, but they do not differ in how they conceptualize humans in relation to social order. Humanness derives from embodying roles. To realize oneself and one's human potential is, therefore, to fulfill obligations inherent in one's relations with others. Asian societies are necessarily and coercively relational.

Based on this brief characterization, which is more fully developed elsewhere (Fei 1992; Hamilton 1994), one can identify five features of social networks in East Asian societies.[6] First, networks are discontinuous. For instance, the networks linking kinsmen are not equivalent to *tongxiang* (fellow-regional) networks: moreover, as Fei makes clear, each person's embeddedness in a set of networks differs from that of every other person in the same networks. How a male

head of household normatively relates to others in a kinship network is not equivalent to the prescriptions for how his daughter should act. Networks are substantive, prescriptive, and differentiating. Therefore, they do not link people together
in a single, uniform way.

Second, each link in a person's network is defined in terms of a dyadic, hierarchical social tie.[7] Each tie is normatively defined and connotes sets of prescribed
behavior (*li*). People in a dyadic relationship interact on a personal level based upon personal obligation as defined by the substantive content of the specific relationship and upon the norms of reciprocity that govern interpersonal interactions.
In this sense, dyadic relationships represent structures of authority. I use the term
authority here in a purposeful way, in that the authority represented in a dyadic tie,
say between a father and son or between an older and younger sibling, rests upon
what Weber terms the "legitimate" exercise of power. In this context, legitimacy
refers to the priority, appropriateness, and inescapability of human relationships
as defined by the Confucian civilizational areas of East Asia.[8]

Third, networks are preset and normative, but whether a person lives up to the
demands of the relationships is a matter for active achievement. In this sense, a
person has to achieve a reputation for "uprightness" (*zheng*), a characteristically
Asian word meaning, in this context, "true to form." The ability to act morally
and obediently within a role set – that is, to act true to form – is regarded as a
prized personal characteristic, much as honesty is in the West. The significance
of uprightness and filiality (*xiao*) is to see that it is an attribute that attaches to the
person regardless of the actions of the other person in the dyad. The upright person, for instance, the filial son, is obedient to his parents even if his parents are
wrong or abusive. It is the reputation for being upright, for always being obedient
to role demands, that allows others to trust and predict how one will act. The reputation for achieved morality especially applies to those relationships that demand
the most obedience, specially relationships within a kinship network. Obedience
in most demanding relationships will lend creditability to one's claims to uprightness in less demanding relationships (Fei 1992; Hwang 1987).

Fourth, the moral content of behavior in such a network-based society is
relation-specific and situationally defined. There is no assumption, as there is in
the West, of abstract standards, such as justice and honesty, equally applying to
all participants regardless of their situation. Embedded in a world of differentially
categorized social relationships, Asians define what is appropriate moral behavior by reading the situation and by knowing the social categories of, and sets of
relationships between, the actors involved.

Fifth, networks have no explicit boundaries. Asians do not join networks in
the way that Westerners join organizations. Categories of networks are largely
pre-defined as sets of binding relationships. But actual networks are socially constructed by people who, for whatever reasons, want to conform to the demands of
the relationships. Such networks can be quite flexible, and can expand or contract
depending upon the circumstances. To illustrate the flexibility of networks, Fei

(1992) gives the example of the family from "The Dream of the Red Chamber," whose network of kinsmen expands with the family's expanding wealth and contracts to a small core as the family loses its riches and political connections. Similarly, a prosperous, well-connected businessman may attract many people willing to do business with him, but will likely lose them if his business goes bad.

This absence of clear boundaries allows a person to extend his or her network ties to another person with whom they have no pre-set relationship. As Kao describes in his contribution, this type of linkage is accomplished by finding the appropriate person who has ties to a network in which the other person is located and obligated. This "appropriate person," this middleman, serves not only as bridge between networks, but also as a guarantor of trustworthiness and uprightness of the person who is trying to make the linkage. After the two parties are linked, their subsequent relationship will depend upon their own evaluations; the relationship may become an intimate one and be reinterpreted as belonging to a category of close relationships.[9]

Because networks are so flexible, a society based upon networks contains no sharp boundary lines, but only ambiguous zones of more or less dense and more or less institutionalized network configurations. This flexibility, however, should not be misconstrued. Networks are, at once, both highly utilitarian vehicles of self-interest and highly ritualistic and personally restrictive. The ability to manipulate and maneuver within networks depends on many things, including one's reputation for uprightness, that is, upon one's moral behavior. The pursuit of self interest and the reification of cultural formats are, therefore, inexorably linked.

As Fei (1992) suggests, these organizing principles apply equally to actions within political, economic, and social arenas. Political institutions are based on factional networks, and, in the private sector, economic institutions are based, symbolically at least, on community and family centered networks, several types of which are described in the chapters of this book.

Fei's theory of *chaxugeju* clarifies what it means to say that networks are the medium of Asian economic development. Systems of normative networks are the medium for all organized activity in Asian societies. Economic activity is no exception. Therefore, a major part of the task of analyzing Asian economies is to understand how these normative network structures shape economic activities and influence the trajectories of economic development.

Relational Norms and the Reproduction of Network Structures

Even though East Asian economies are network-based, the networks differ substantially among economies in East and Southeast Asia. These differences emerge at many levels – within firms, in the banking sector, in the organization of the macro-economy, and with the development of state policies. To explain these dif-

ferences in terms of only a few factors is to confuse the issue. These societies differ on many dimensions; therefore, it should not be surprising that they differ on
the economic dimension as well. That they differ, however, does not mean that we
cannot contrast them and understand them comparatively, each in its own terms.

One place to cut into this Gordian knot is the family. Understanding how households extend into kinship and community networks and how they define and control their assets gives a vantage point from which one can examine an economic
landscape that consists largely of family owned firms. In the private sector, Chinese firms of all sizes in Taiwan, Hong Kong, and Southeast Asia are overwhelmingly family owned and controlled. The same is true in South Korea. In Japan,
however, family ownership is the rule only in small and medium-sized firms. As
described by Okumura and Orrù, in the networks of large firms, shared corporate
ownership and managerial control is much more common than family ownership.
Even in the corporate context, however, family metaphors are still used to define
relationships among firms.

Although dominated by family ownership and control, Chinese and Korean
business networks differ dramatically, and both differ just as dramatically from
the situation in Japan. As Kim's chapter shows, Korean *chaebol* are very large,
diversified, and vertically integrated networks of independent firms. The *chaebol*
account for a very large proportion of the total output of the economy, especially the export-oriented sector. The *chaebol* are owned and centrally controlled by
heads of households, the *jaejang*, who function as patriarchs. The *chaebol,* however, are much larger than what can be owned and controlled by a single household. The family owners, therefore, extend their patriarchal scope beyond the immediate family to incorporate others whose loyalty and expertise they require for
management and control. They draw in affinal relatives, classmates, people from
their home towns, and others whose connections heighten their loyalty. They also rely on the state for controlling the labor force and on connections with state
officials to stabilize the economic and fiscal environment.

The *chaebols'* use of patriarchal authority as an organizing principle that extends beyond the family creates a patrimonial dynamic in both the economy and
the society. As outlined by Weber (1978) and others following him, a patrimonial dynamic feeds competition among contending elite families and pits the power and prerogatives of these elite families against state officials, who continually
find their power challenged by such imperious elites. The elite families and the
state are, simultaneously, both fully dependent on and in conflict with each other. Nicole Biggart (1991) shows that such a dynamic is characteristic of capitalist
organization in contemporary South Korea.

Unlike in South Korea, in the Chinese-dominated economies of Hong Kong and
Taiwan, small and medium-sized firms dominate the export sector. These small
and medium-sized firms are linked together horizontally in production networks
(Shieh 1992; Redding and Tam 1986). In all the Chinese-dominated economies,
including Singapore, large private, Chinese-owned business groups normally do

not develop in the final goods manufacturing sector, but rather dominate in the production of intermediate goods and in the service and non-state owned financial and property sectors. These large firms are not vertically integrated, but are rather highly diversified and are organizationally segmented into separately managed units. As Tong's chapter shows, despite segmentation, family ownership and asset control remains very important, but the system of control is not patrimonial in order to create a large internally cohesive network. Rather the mode of family control is to maximize their potential gain by closely monitoring business opportunities through networks of friends and relatives, by centrally controlling the utilization of assets, and by decentralizing day to day management (Numazaki 1993; Hamilton and Kao 1990; Redding 1990).

In Japan, as Okumura's and Orrù's chapters describe, large firms in business networks mutually own one another. These large "corporate networks," as Imai (1992) calls them, spread horizontally across the economy, so that each business group has substantial stakes in diverse sectors, and vertically, so that the economic activity in each sector is linked and coordinated even beyond the mutually owned firms that make up the group. At the tail end of these vertical networks are the tertiary links in the subcontracting and distribution chains that are composed largely of family-owned small and medium-sized firms. In this location, family ownership and household management is important, as are personal networks that extend beyond the family. But outside of this tertiary portion of the economy, family ownership is much less common, in large part because larger firms require increasing and long-term integration in an community of firms. Public offerings of shares, mutual shareholding, the acceptance of outside direction and possibly directors, and the coordination of many spheres of economic decision-making with those of the wider network of firms – these inevitably reduce the salience and legitimacy of patriarchal forms of enterprise management.

These distinct configurations of business networks can, in part, be interpreted in light of the institutionalized inheritance practices. In Chinese areas, partible inheritance is the normative practice. Although many variations are possible, the principle is that at the father's death, the household divides (*fen jia*), with each son establishing his own household. Each son is to receive an equal share of his father's estate. In the dynastic period, the effects of partible inheritance was clearly seen in landowning. Large contiguous landholdings were extremely rare. Even the very wealthiest landowners owned scattered plots, which were acquired piecemeal over a period of time. Centralized coordination and efficient cultivation of these scattered plots were difficult, and therefore, as a consequence, the land was rented to tenants, on a sharecropping basis. As a family's holdings increased, land management became a form of portfolio management. Then, at the father's death, the scattered plots could be divided equitably, and the process of accumulation would begin again.

Modern Chinese capitalism has reproduced some of the structural elements of the agrarian landowning system. The diverse capitalist holdings of many wealthy

Chinese businessmen resemble the scattered plots of earlier times. Knowing that family assets will be divided at the time of their deaths, Chinese entrepreneurs often do not elect to enlarge, through vertical or horizontal integration, the size of their successful firms. Rather they elect to diversify their assets by starting new, separately managed firms in other geographical areas or other economic sectors. The pattern of diversification is usually opportunistic, the result of business deals done with overlapping sets of partners (Numazaki 1993; Hamilton and Kao 1990). This investment strategy leads to diverse holdings scattered across the economic landscape. The entrepreneur's form of control over these holdings is portfolio management, as opposed to "work process" management. Even before his death, the entrepreneur often divides his holdings into distinct groups of firms and places a different son in charge of each group. In these positions the sons can begin the process of building their own networks of connections that will be important to their success as entrepreneurs after their father dies. As this description shows, partible inheritance is an aspect of an organizational dynamic that leads to the reproduction of economic structures under very different economic conditions.

The same reproductive patterns hold for South Korea. By the middle of the Yi dynasty, elite Korean households had begun to practice a form of primogeniture. Unlike in late imperial China, the political structure of Korea encouraged the formation of powerful lineage groups, conventionally called clans or great families *(ta jia)* These privileged elites controlled the countryside, fought primarily with each other for wealth and prestige, and had exclusive access to official positions in the imperial bureaucracy. In order to preserve the hegemony of a single line of inheritance within the lineage, the eldest son would inherit the largest portion (usually two thirds of the total) of the father's estate and, in addition, would assume control of the corporate lands of the clan. The practice permitted the ownership of large contiguous blocks of land that could be managed centrally. Unlike the free, economically engaged peasantry that developed in China, the South Korea system encouraged the formation of a more servile peasantry, many of whom were formally classified as slaves.

The concentration of the economy in the hands of a few elite families and the holdings those families centralized in large contiguous blocks are elements of the traditional economy that has been reproduced in modern South Korean capitalism. The post-Korean war sponsorship of key individuals resulted in the formation of a new elite. The foreknowledge that they have the ability to pass on their estates organizationally more or less intact meant that Korean entrepreneurs could pursue strategies of building and centrally managing very large, densely interconnected business networks. The knowledge that if they did not enlarge their holdings in this way they could be at the mercy of – and perhaps forced out business by – those who were expanding, encouraged the aggressive construction of huge, hotly competitive networks. The control of these networks emphasized work-process management, in the sense that the economic activities of each firm are coordinated with and, often, the result of, the economic activities of other firms in the group. In

terms of concentration and family ownership, the structure of the capitalist economy has reproduced some of the key elements of the traditional economy.

Japan has also reproduced key elements of its traditional structure. In traditional Japan, the family, in principle, was always secondary to the community. The
household pattern reinforced this principle. The Japanese normative practice is
the three generation stem family (*ie*), which consists of only one married couple
of each generation and their unmarried children (Long 1987). Other married sons
and daughters leave the stem family to start new households. The married son or
daughter who remains with the parents inherits all the household property. These
property-holding stem families are, in turn, integrated in and held to be responsible to a community (*mura*) that consists of unrelated families. Primogeniture in
this context is practiced, but patriarchal authority is truncated and contextualized
in the community in which the household is embedded. Elite households are able
to pass on property and privilege, but also the responsibilities of the community.

The structure of Tokugawa Japan reflected these patterns of households embedded in the hierarchical levels of the agrarian society: communities of peasants,
merchants, and aristocratic lords. Modern Japan also reproduces, in a totally different economic, social, and political context, many of the structural elements of
the traditional system, namely the interplay, as Aoki (1992) shows, between the
ie and *mura* principles of Japanese society. Perhaps better than anyone has done
to date, Orrù in an earlier chapter describes the relational hierarchies in corporate
communities in modern Japan.

In all three cases, the organization of society emphasizes the priority of relationships, and the elites in all three societies structure their authority by identifying and ranking these relationships. Despite similarities at a cultural level, at the
institutional level, the similarities developed into very different structural patterns
and laid the foundations in modern times for very different developmental trajectories.

Conclusion

How do these embedded networks, these networks of interpersonal relationships
that develop within these institutionalized environments, influence economic organization and economic performance? The implicit answer given by the chapters
in this book is that embedded networks set up affinities for certain types of organizational configurations. When participants reproduce these affinities in a context of economic action in order to achieve specific goals, economic and otherwise, the resulting economic organizations take on systemic qualities that relate
to their performances in larger economic arenas. In other words, Asian business
networks, although rooted in traditional structural patterns, represent dynamic industrial structures that reflect their ongoing economic integration in local, nation-

al, regional, or global markets. In other words, it is the economic performance of networks, rather than the networks themselves, that creates the economic dynamic.

If this conceptualization is correct, therefore, these economies should be conceptualized as being "path dependent." Where these economic structures start organizationally influences the direction they go and how they change. The affinity of organizational segmentation in Chinese economies pushes entrepreneurs to take a different route to achieve economic competitiveness than the routes that South Korean or Japanese entrepreneurs favor. The selection of these different organizational strategies means that efficiency and effectiveness is relative, is socially constructed in each organizational context. In the context of globalizing economies, organizational innovations follow from the path-dependent search for economic power. As these economies developed, they began to specialize in very different spheres of economic activity, and this economic differentiation has continued and grown over the past decade (Feenstra, Yang, and Hamilton 1993).

The momentum of development and the direction of economic change continues to depend on trends in the globalizing economy. That domestic enterprises are integrated in the global economy does not mean that there will be a convergence in the industrial structures of these economies. Quite the reserve is true. The creation of specialized niches in the global economy that relate directly to embedded networks in local economies means that the conditions of entrepreneurial success will further be preserved and enhanced. In this sense, globalization creates the conditions for localization, for the continuation of path-dependent trajectories of economic development. Asian business networks are the building blocks of these trajectories.

Notes

[1] Mark Granovetter (1985, p. 501) has made this point in more general terms when he argues, "that social relations between firms are more important, and authority within firms less so, in bringing order to economic life than is supposed in the markets and hierarchies line of thought."

[2] Nicole Woolsey Biggart and I (1992) have contrasted firm-based economies in the West with network-based economies in Asia at much greater length.

[3] I have developed this point at much greater length in a discussion of civilizational effects on economic organization (Hamilton 1994).

[4] As many proponents of network theory readily admit, this new perspective is largely a methodological approach to the study of social patterns (Mufune 1991). Reminiscent of Georg Simmel's ideas on dyads and triads in social life, the new network theorists have not only developed techniques to analyze the network configurations, but have also argued that particular formal properties (e.g., density, centrality) adhere to specific types of configurations. Accordingly, such network theorists would argue that the

properties of Asian business networks would derive from the formal qualities of the network structures, such that the same formal structure located in one society would have identical properties in another society.

To be sure, some characteristics of interaction in Asian networks derive from the formal patterning of participants. But even those quite sympathetic to the new network approach are still dissatisfied with the gap between network theory and network substance. For instance, in a 1982 review of network analysis, Richard Alba (1982, p. 68) concluded, "A theory formulated at the level of networks qua networks is unlikely to be able to produce all the powerful results that network analysis stands in need of. In my opinion, network analysis needs to descend from the heavens of formal abstractions to the muck of substantive research and to become acclimated to the conditions prevailing in different substantive fields."

[5] For a translation of Fei's book and a description of his contribution, see Fei (1992).
[6] The following discussion is drawn from Hamilton and Wang (1992).
[7] These interpersonal ties are colloquially known in Chinese as *guanxi*. For an excellent description of *guanxi*, see King (1991).
[8] For some discussion of the nature of Confucian orthodoxy in late imperial times, see Liu Kwang-Ching (1990).
[9] Besides Kao's chapter in this volume, also see Hwang (1987), King (1991), and Yang (1989).

References

Alba, Richard D. 1982. "Taking Stock of Network Analysis: A Decade's Results." *Research in the Sociology of Organizations* 1: 39-74.

Aoki, Masahiko. 1990. "Toward an Economic Model of the Japanese Firm." *Journal of Economic Literature* 28 (March): 1-27.

Aoki, Masahiko. 1992. "Decentralization-Centralization in Japanese Organization: A Duality Principle." *The Political Economy of Japan. Volume Three: Cultural and Social Dynamics,* eds. Shumpei Kumon and Henry Rosovsky. Stanford: Stanford University Press.

Bearden, James and Beth Mintz. 1987. "The Structure of Class Cohesion: The Corporate Network and its Dual." *Intercorporate Relations: The Structural Analysis of Business,* eds. Mark S. Mizruchi and Michael Schwartz. Cambridge, UK: Cambridge University Press.

Biggart, Nicole Woolsey. 1990. "Institutionalized Patrimonialism in Korean Business." *Comparative Social Research* 12: 113-133.

Biggart, Nicole Woolsey and Gary G. Hamilton. 1992. "On the Limits of a Firm-based Theory to Explain Business Networks: The Western Bias of Neoclassical Economics." *Networks and Organizations: Structure, Form, and Action,* eds. Nitin Nohria and Robert G. Eccles. Boston: Harvard Business School Press.

Feenstra, Robert C., Tzu-han Yang, and Gary G. Hamilton, 1993. "Market Structure and International Trade: Business Groups in East Asia." Working Paper no. 46. Davis, California: Research Program in East Asian Business and Development Working Paper Series, University of California, Davis.

Fei, Xiaotong. 1992. *From the Soil: The Foundation of Chinese Society.* Berkeley: University of California Press.

Friedland, Roger and Robert R. Alford. 1991. "Bringing Society Back in: Symbols, Practices, and Institutional Contradictions." *The New Institutionalism in Organizational Analysis,* eds. Walter W. Powell and Paul J. DiMaggio. Chicago: University of Chicago Press.

Fruin, W. Mark. 1992. *The Japanese Enterprise System: Competitive Strategies and Cooperative Structures.* Oxford: Clarendon Press.

Gereffi, Gary and Miguel Korzeniewicz. 1994. *Commodity Chains and Global Capitalism.* Westport: Praeger.

Gerlach, Michael. 1992. *Alliance Capitalism: The Strategic Organization of Japanese Business.* Berkeley: University of California Press.

Granovetter, Mark. 1985. "Economic Action and Social Structure: The Problem of Embeddedness." *American Journal of Sociology* 91 (November): 481-510.

Granovetter, Mark. 1990. "The Myth of Social Network Analysis as a Separate Method in the Social Sciences." *Connections* 13 (1-2): 89-112.

Granovetter, Mark. 1994. "Business Groups." Forthcoming in *Handbook of Economic Sociology,* eds. Neil Smelser and Richard Swedberg. Princeton: Princeton University Press.

Hamilton, Gary G. 1994. "Civilizations and the Organization of Economies." Forthcoming in *Handbook of Economic Sociology,* eds. Neil Smelser and Richard Swedberg. Princeton: Princeton University Press.

Hamilton, Gary G., Nicole Woolsey Biggart, and Marco Orrù. 1993. *Network Capitalism: Economic Organization in Industrial East Asia.* Unpublished manuscript.

Hamilton, Gary G. and Cheng-shu Kao. 1990. "The Institutional Foundations of Chinese Business: The Family Firm in Taiwan." *Comparative Social Research* 12: 95-112.

Hamilton, Gary G. and Wang Zheng. 1992. "Introduction." *From the Soil: The Foundations of Chinese Society.* Fei Xiaotong. Berkeley: University of California Press.

Hwang, Kwang-kuo. 1987. "Face and Favor: The Chinese Power Game." *American Journal of Sociology* 92 (4): 944-74.

Imai, Ken-ichi. 1992. "Japan's Corporate Networks." *The Political Economy of Japan. Volume Three: Cultural and Social Dynamics,* eds. Shumpei Kumon and Henry Rosovsky. Stanford: Stanford University Press.

Kim, Eun Mee. Forthcoming. *Big Business, Strong State: Collusion and Conflict in Korean Development.* Berkeley: University of California Press.

King, Ambrose Yeo-chi. 1991. "Kuan-hsi and Network Building: A Sociological Interpretation." *Daedalus* 120 (2): 63-84.

Liu, Kwang-Ching, ed. 1990. *Orthodoxy in Late Imperial China.* Berkeley: University of California Press.

Long, Susan Orpet. 1987. "Family Change and the Life Course in Japan." Ithaca: China-Japan Program, Cornell University.

Mufune, Pempelani. 1991. "Some Problems in the Use of Network Analysis for Comparative Enquiry." *International Sociology* 6 (1): 97-110.

Nohria, Nitin and Robert G. Eccles. 1992. *Networks and Organizations: Structure, Form, and Action.* Cambridge, Mass.: Harvard Business School Press.

Numazaki, Ichiro. 1993. "The Tainanbang: The Rise and Growth of a Banana-Bunch-Shaped Business Group in Taiwan." *The Developing Economies* 31 (4): 485-510.

Orrù, Marco, Nicole Biggart, and Gary G. Hamilton. 1991. "Organizational Isomorphism in East Asia: Broadening the New Institutionalism." *The New Institutionalism in Organizational Analysis,* eds. Walter W. Powell and Paul J. DiMaggio. Chicago: University of Chicago Press.

Paulson, Steven K. 1985. "A Paradigm for the Analysis of Interorganizational Networks." *Social Networks* 7: 105-126.

Powell, Walter W. 1990. "Neither Market Nor Hierarchy: Network Forms of Organization." *Research in Organizational Behavior* 12: 295-336.

Redding, S. Gordon 1990. *The Spirit of Chinese Capitalism.* Berlin: Walter de Gruyter.

Redding, S. Gordon and Simon Tam. 1986. "Network and Molecular Organizations: An Exploratory View of Chinese Firms in Hong Kong." *Proceedings of the Inaugural Meeting of the Southeast Asia Region Academy of International Business,* eds. K.C. Mun and T.S. Chan. Hong Kong: The Chinese University of Hong Kong Press.

Shieh, G.S. 1992. *"Boss" Island: The Subcontracting Network and Micro-Entrepreneurship in Taiwan's Development.* New York: Peter Lang.

Strachan, Harry. 1976. *Family and Other Business Groups in Economic Development: The Case of Nicaragua.* New York: Praeger.

Wade, Robert. 1990. *Governing the Market: Economic Theory and the Role of Government in East Asian Industrialization.* Princeton: Princeton Universtiy Press.

Wellman, Barry and S.D. Berkowitz. 1988. *Social Structures: A Network Approach.* Cambridge, UK: Cambridge University Press.

Yang, Mayfair Mei-hui. 1989. "The Gift Economy and State Power in China." *Comparative Studies in Society and History* 31 (1): 40-41.

Zeile, William J. 1993. *Industrial Targeting, Business Organization, and Industry Productivity Growth in the Republic of Korea, 1972-1985.* Unpublished Dissertation. Davis: Department of Economics, University of California.

Glossary of Chinese Terms

baishen	拜神	worship
bang	幫	clique
baochia (baojia)	保甲	decimal system fo registration and surveillance. Ten households a *jia* and ten *jia* a *bao*
chan (chen in Mandarin)	橙	orange
ganqing	感情	emotional feelings
guanxi	關係	relationship; personal connection; network
gum (gan in Mandarin)	柑	mandarin orange
hang	行	trading house; merchant association (in *Song* dynasty)
hegu	合股	combined shares; pooled capital to form a partnership
hong (hang in Mandarin)	行	trading house
huiguan	會館	regional commercial association or guild
jia	家	family
jigou	機構	organization; institution
ku jin gan lai	苦盡甘來	bitterness ends and sweetness begins; sweet are the fruits of labor
la guanxi	拉關係	to pull *guanxi*; to draw upon personal connection for help
laoban	老板（闆）	boss
li	禮	ritual; propriety

lichia (lijia)	里甲	decimal system of registration and surveillance. A region of hundred and ten households is a *li*
sangang	三綱	the three closest relationships. The relationships between emperor and officials, father and son, and husband and wife
sun yung (xinyong in Mandarin)	信用	a gentlemen's agreement, trustworthiness
Tainanbang	台南幫	the *Tainan* clique
tianxia	天下	land under heaven; China or the world
tongnian	同年	the same age
tongxiang	同鄉	the same place of origin
tongxiang guanxi	同鄉關係	a form of regional relationship, from the same place of origin
tongxiang hui	同鄉會	native-place association
tongzong	同宗	common ancestry; common surname
wulun	五倫	Confucian five relationships
xiao	孝	filial piety
xingyong	信用	a gentlemen's agreement, trustworthiness
yuan	元	the Chinese currency
zhongguo	中國	middle kingdom; China

List of Contributors

Edward Chen is Professor of Economics and Director of the Centre of Asian Studies at the University of Hong Kong. He is the author of numerous books and articles on the economic development in East and Southeast Asia. His most recent book is *Foreign Direct Investment in Asia*, published by Asian Productivity Organization in Japan.

Gary G. Hamilton is Professor of Sociology at the University of Washington, Seattle. He is the author of many articles on historical and comparative perspectives on Chinese society and economy. His most recent book is an introduction and translation (with Wang Zheng) of Fei Xiaotong's *Xiangtu Zhongguo,* entitled *From the Soil: The Foundation of Chinese Society as Viewed by Fei Xiaotong*, published by the University of California Press.

Kao Cheng-shu is Dean of Social Sciences and Professor of Sociology at Tunghai University in Taiwan. With research funded by the National Science Council and the Chiang Ching-kuo Foundation, he organized a team of graduate student researchers to investigate the social foundations of Taiwan's economic development. He is the author of several books and numerous articles on sociological theory. Several additional books reporting on the current research project will be published soon.

Eun Mee Kim is an Associate Professor of Sociology at the University of Southern California. She is the author of numerous articles analyzing the relationship between the South Korean state and the *chaebol*, South Korea's industrial conglomerates. She has just produced a book on this topic entitled *Big Business, Strong State: Collusion and Conflict in Korean Development, 1960-1990*, which has been published by the University of California Press.

Eddie C.Y. Kuo is Professor and Dean of the School of Communications Studies, Nanyang Technological University. He is the author of many books and articles on Singapore society. His most recent book is *Information Technology and Singapore Society: Trends, Policies, and Applications*, published by Singapore University Press.

Numazaki Ichiro is a Lecturer in the Research Institute for Japanese Culture at Tohoku University in Sendai Japan. After completing three years of field research in Taiwan from 1986 through 1989, he received his Ph.D. in Anthropology from Michigan State University in 1991. The author of several articles on Taiwan business groups, he is currently preparing his dissertation on the same topic for publication as a book.

Okumura Hiroshi is Professor of Economics at Ryukoku University in Kyoto, Japan. One of the world's leading experts on Japanese business groups, he is the author of numerous books in Japanese on Japanese business structure. A number of his articles also appear in English. His most recent book, *Corporation Capitalism*, has been translated into English and published by MacMillan.

Marco Orrù, at the time of his death in 1995, was an Associate Professor of Sociology at University of South Florida in Tampa. His research on Japanese and other East Asian and Western European business organizations appeared in numerous journals and in the book *The New Institutional in Organizational Analysis*, edited by Paul DiMaggio and Walter Powell, published by University of Chicago Press.

S. Gordon Redding is Professor and Dean of the Hong Kong Business School at the University of Hong Kong. He is the author of many articles on Chinese business organization. His most recent book is *The Spirit of Chinese Capitalism*, published by Walter de Gruyter.

Tan Hock is Lecturer in the Department of Economics at the National University of Singapore. A Ph.D. from Southern Illinois, he was formerly an Assistant Professor at the University of East Asia in Macau. He has research interests in economic development, international economics, and monetary economics.

Tong Chee Kiong is Senior Lecturer in the Department of Sociology at the National University of Singapore. He received his undergraduate training at the University of Singapore and his M.A. and Ph.D. degrees from Cornell University in the United States. His research interest centers on the study of ethnicity and business organization in Southeast Asia. His publications include *Rethinking Assimilation and Ethnicity: The Chinese in Thailand, Between Worlds: Sacred Elites in Southeast Asia*, and *Economic and Ethnicity: The Chinese in Southeast Asia*.

Ueda Yoshiaki is an Associate Professor in the Faculty of Business Management at the University of Marketing and Distribution in Kobe, Japan. He has written a number of articles and is currently writing a book on interlocking directorates in Japanese business groups.

Gilbert Wong is Lecturer in the Department of Management Studies at the University of Hong Kong. His research emphasizes the corporate and financial structure of Hong Kong businesses. A statement of his research interests has been published in *Administrative Science Quarterly*.

Wong Siu-lun is Professor of the Department of Sociology at the University of Hong Kong. He has published numerous articles and book chapters on Chinese economic sociology and is the author for *Emigrant Entrepreneurs: Shanghai Industrialists in Hong Kong* (Oxford University Press, 1988).

William Zeile wrote the paper presented in this volume while working as a graduate student researcher at the Institute of Government Affairs, University of California, Davis. He is currently a staff economist with the Bureau of Economic Analysis, United States Department of Commerce.